The Death and Return of the Author

The Death and Return of the Author

Criticism and Subjectivity in Barthes, Foucault and Derrida

Third Edition

SEÁN BURKE

EDINBURGH UNIVERSITY PRESS

© Seán Burke, 1992, 1998, 2008

First published 1992
Reprinted 1993
Second Edition 1998
Reprinted 1999, 2004, 2007
Third Edition 2008

Reprinted 2010, 2011

Edinburgh University Press
22 George Square, Edinburgh

Set in Linotron Bembo by
Koinonia Ltd, Bury and
printed and bound in Great Britain
by CPI Antony Rowe, Chippenham, Wiltshire

A CIP record for this book is
available from the British Library

ISBN 978 0 7486 3711 9 (paperback)

For James Killian Burke

He who lives more lives than one
More deaths than one must die
Oscar Wilde, *The Ballad of Reading Gaol*

You will remember how Plato, in his project for a Republic, deals with writers. In the interests of the community, he denies them the right to dwell therein ... Since Plato the question of the writer's right to exist has not often been raised with the same emphasis ...

Walter Benjamin, *Understanding Brecht*

Imagine the inartistic natures, and those only weakly endowed, armoured and armed by a monumental history of the artists: against whom will they now turn their weapons? Against their arch-enemies, the strong artistic spirits ... whether they are aware of it or not, they act as though their motto were: let the dead bury the living.

Friedrich Nietzsche, 'On the uses and
disadvantages of history for life'

Contents

Preface to Second Edition

Akaky Akakievich, the little clerk made immortal by Gogol, returns from the dead to haunt the government department by which he has been humiliated. Akaky had no sooner invested his life's savings in a new overcoat than he was robbed of it by a gang of thieves. Subjected to further scorn within his department, and treated with contempt by an Important Person in his efforts to recover the stolen overcoat, Akaky succumbed to a fever and died. Seeming to undo the institutional death to which his living body had been condemned, the clerk's literal death allows him to assert the significance of a unique existence. The last act of Akaky's ghostly life is to tear the Important Person's overcoat from his back: chastened, the latter learns to respect people in their rightful singularity.

Reduced to parable, this story indicates the mixture of comedy, pathos and high seriousness with which the death of the author has needed to be treated. It also points to the ever-jagged intersections between institutional and existential mortality. In ending the first edition of this book with the image of a haunting, I suggested that the return criticism invariably makes to the author must also be acknowledged in principle. Easy to recognise, though, the duty of formulating such a return is quite another charge. It has rightly been commented of this book that, while a good case is made against the death of the author, positive alternatives are absent. If a return to the author was to be made, it was first necessary to show that such a return was justified. This task took an entire book. A positive programme – a theory of authorship perhaps – could only be distilled from many books by many authors or theorists. That said, I will briefly sketch the main issues that any such programme would confront.

Immensely valuable work is current in the areas of copyright, intellectual ownership, changing historical conceptions of authorship, the politics of authorship in relation to particular eras, cultures and social configurations. As a centre of controversy, authorship is indeed becoming an indexed item in the literary and cultural encyclopedia rather than the shortfall of theoretical, political or historicist programmes. Further work might also be attempted on the ethics of authorship, the question of legacy and the contractual nature of the signature. Comparative studies of theological, philosophical, scientific and literary authorship could be conducted with considerable gains to our understanding of the relation between human agency and knowledge. Research of this cast would clarify the field of authorship in terms of the author-function, but an area of considerable philosophical and interpretative difficulty would remain to be addressed. This issue – which I touch upon in the section 'Subjectivities' and at the close of the 'Epilogue' – is the need to arrive at a model of situated subjectivity. We are a long way off any such model, but the spectre of the inconceivable should not deter us from its adventure.

The main argument of this book remains unaltered. I have added a section on Derrida's reading of Plato ('The Myth of Writing') and an epilogue which reviews recent technological arguments whilst advocating an embodied sense of authorship. A second edition also seemed a good opportunity to speak more candidly about the growing breach between academic literary criticism and broad intellectual culture. This breach is marked by a 'politics' of theory which seems to have very little to do with politics in anything like a 'real world'. The death of the author marks a significant point in this melancholy retreat. Looking back, it seems that an institutional affair of self-regulation (impersonalist reading) was all along masquerading as a dark truth of textual ontology (the death of the author). When one also takes into account the sheer incomprehensibility of 'the death of the author' to even the finest minds outside the institution, it is clear that the concept functioned to keep the non-academic at bay: thereby, one more obstacle to the re-emergence of a culture of letters was put in place. It was from an impatience with this insularity that *The Death and Return of the Author* emerged. Attentive readers of the subtext of this work will also notice that this impatience is not turned toward the three subjects of this book – strong poets of the age as they are – but against an Anglo-American critical institution which has needed arguments from authority in the deconstruction of authority along with generous spirits through whom to dignify ordinary insecurities.

A reviewer has noted that this is an impersonal work. Perhaps there is *some* inconsistency here, but a personal defence of authorship would not be taken seriously – particularly coming from one who is not an author. In the realm of acknowledgements, where the personal is permissible, if not the political, I would like to record the history of my debts in writing this work.

The first edition was conceived, researched and written between 1986 and 1989, with certain rewritings and additions in 1991. For two years, I was the recipient of a British Academy State Studentship for which I remain very grateful.

Circumstances dictated that I wrote this work in almost complete academic isolation, and so I count myself very lucky to have been in regular contact with Cairns Craig. The insight and intelligence which he showed in supervising this work continue to surprise me today. Also, I should like to thank Randall Stevenson, Faith Pullin, Alistair Fowler and Sandra Kemp. From my home town, it gives me pleasure to acknowledge Tim Petersen, my brother Kevin, my sister Tracey and friends at the Gower Hotel, Cardiff. I would also like to thank Tríona Carey, Aisling Roche, John Carter, Patrick Maguire and Timothy Parry. Most of all, I want to acknowledge the unstinting support I received from my parents, John and June Burke.

With regard to this second edition, I would like to thank Robin Dix, Michael O'Neill, Bert Nutter, Charles Martindale, C. J. Rowe and – in what feels like an act of second nature – Patricia Waugh whose grace and intelligence also brighten worlds far beyond the Academy.

Preface to Third Edition:
The 'Life Death' of the Author

Upon completion of the main body of this work in 1989, of its 'subjects', both Roland Barthes and Michel Foucault had passed through the metaphorical to the literal sense of 'the death of the author'. The death of Barthes is woven into the close of Chapter 1; upon the death of Michel Foucault this work was silent, even given a second edition when the details of his fatal illness were abroad. Between this interleaving and this silence is the discrimination between responsible, ethical use of biographical information and the unethical lapse from the pertinent to the impertinent, the critical to the sensational. The decision as to what aspects of the life can with justice be brought to bear upon the work is both essential and impossible to formalise. It depends, amongst many other things, upon the authorisation the work gives us to trespass this borderline between the textual and the personal, the corpus and the corpse.[1]

The deaths of Barthes, Foucault and Paul de Man affected Jacques Derrida profoundly, and a good amount of his later work was given over to reflections on the passing of contemporary philosopher-theorists. In their intellectual depth, their emotional sincerity, their grace, the fourteen obituaries collected in *The Work of Mourning* amount to an strenuous reflection on the death of the other, of the others who are also authors.[2] Intellectual historians down the generations may well turn expeditiously to this collection, it doing for the late-twentieth century what, in 3 AD, Diogenes Laertius's *Lives* did for ancient philosophy. These 'responses', read alongside Derrida's other thanatographical work of the 1990s (for example, *Memoirs of the Blind*, *Aporias: Dying* and *The Gift of Death*), could also be taken as a preparation for his own death in the long tradition anteceding the *Phaedo* in which Montaigne's *Essays*, Kierkegaard's *Fear and Trembling*, Freud's *Mourning and Melancholia* and Heideggerian 'being-towards-death' are only moments which come most readily to mind.[3]

Death, Wittgenstein famously reminded us, is not an event in life because it cannot be lived through.[4] 'Life' and 'death' are *pre-conceived* as opposites by all self-conscious beings, yet one cannot begin to construct, a binarism in which one side can neither be experienced or defined. *Life death (la vie la mort)* is Derrida's creative response to this impasse. Placed side-by-side – unpunctuated, beyond conjunction or separation – *la vie la mort* represents an affirmative attempt to think 'life and death as one'.[5] It lies beyond or fails to satisfy philosophical intelligibility, can only be articulated in the realm of the (rationally) inarticulable. Mystical if not religious, poetic in essence, if not in form, *life death* belongs in the boundless Wittgensteinian 'whereof'. Contemporaneous with Derrida's exploration of 'hauntology', it reflects his hesitant definition of 'deconstruction' as 'the experience of the impossible'. It also marks the culmination of an ever more explicit turn to authorship as the 'promise of return' (55) in the textual traces or inheritance left behind by the proper name.

LIVING ON: LEGACY, CANONISATION

Beginning in 1981 with 'The Deaths of Roland Barthes', Derrida's dedicated works of mourning place their emphasis less on the death of the body than the 'originary' death which is marked with the bestowal of the proper name.[6] 'The name races towards death even more quickly than we do', he writes. 'It is in advance the name of a dead person' (130). Its ominous essence is pronounced 'especially when we speak, write, publish' (179). The name and death of an author is thus a particular concentration of the *fort/ da* played out universally in bereavement. Death is drawn baptismally into life so as to allow for the textual return of that which had lived. In this unconditional work of mourning, death alone from death can save.

A preoccupation with the proper name as both the original mark of death and the promise of return allows for a transference, so very common amongst a certain canonical class of elegiac writers, for whom the written provides both a bulwark against encroaching darkness and a self-consciously evanescent sense of circumventing the uncircumventable. Great writers, we are taught time and again, seek to transcend impermanence through art whilst acknowledging that death shall indeed have dominion. 'Will there even be any heirs?', Derrida asks in a question hovering between the self-doubt of one who wonders whether his work will stand the test of time and the confidence of a Nietzsche whose concern is not with if but *when* the worthy will rise from the as-yet unborn to rightly inherit and promulgate the teaching:

> I have simultaneously ... *the double feeling* that ... one has not yet begun to read me, that even though there are ... many very good

readers (a few dozen in the world, perhaps, people who are also writer-thinkers, poets), in the end it is later on that all this has a chance of appearing; but also, on the other hand, and thus simultane-ously, I have the feeling that two weeks or a month after my death, *there will be nothing left*.[7]

The anxiety is ancestral; that of legacy, self-assessment. The desire is for posthumous canonisation, to return in one's work, to achieve *revenance*. To cultivate, propitiate, to conjure such *revenance* has been the ethical obliga-tion of pedagogy from the memorised oral traditions of antiquity to the modern university. It has, no less, been the posthumous demand made by the great author to intellectual culture at large. Such is not the building of monuments which, for Hegel, marked the end of philosophy. The secular miracle of *revenance* depends not on *stasis* but *kinesis*, on the proven ability of works from Homer to Hölderlin, Aristotle to Averroës, Virgil to Virginia Woolf, to remain in dialogue across centuries, climes and cultures. It is the other-bound, generous refusal of any 'return to the same' that allows poets such as Yeats and Keats, philosophers such as Hegel and Husserl, to communicate across a century as if from mountaintops while history unfolds below their intertextual, interpsychic encounters. The *revenant* is the author whose works are not tombs, pyramids, or sepulchres, but indefi-nitely iterable: 'a work might or might not survive, based upon its own *qualities*, for one, two, or perhaps, like Plato, for twenty five centuries.'[8]

That two such seemingly incompatible concepts as canonicity and iterability should be interanimative testifies to the critical homage the Derridean work pays to tradition in unsettling its foundations.[9] Those who celebrated and those who denounced Derrida as an opponent of the autho-rial canon could only have done so from a conflation of the canonical and the immutable. It is through *ekphrasis*, the endless reopening and request-ioning of canonical philosophical works (works like Plato's *Phaedrus* that themselves refuse to settle or be settled) that Derrida revivified the philo-sophical canon just as the Yale school reopened the great works of romantic poetry. In an era given to conflate excellence with elitism, Derrida (whose subtle inversion of the priorities of centre and margins was reduced to the bludgeoning tool of militant cultural studies) himself became a canonical author whilst bringing others, most notably Emmanuel Levinas, into a tradition that has rephrased itself for each succeeding era.

ADIEU LEVINAS, *ADIEU* DERRIDA:
'THE OTHER RETURNING, TRULY GHOSTLY'

'Who will read at his grave ...?', Sean Gaston found himself wondering on 12 October 2004, the day before Jacques Derrida's funeral. 'Will it be Jean-Luc Nancy or Hélène Cixous? Philosophy *or* literature?'[10] Just under a decade earlier, all knew that it fell to Derrida to speak of what Emmanuel Levinas had been and might become. Obituary itself attains its purest form when the orator is of a stature and sensibility comparable to the departed, and when the latter is known not just through his writings, his lectures and seminars, but also through his personality, his deeds, his friendship in the immediacy of the 'face to face' obligation. With Derrida's 'Adieu' to Levinas in 1995, all these requisites were in place for a commemoration which was also a profound regeneration of the philosophical impulse. Upon Derrida's passing, though, a line seemed to have come to an end within philosophical and theoretical culture. The 'experience of the impossible' could not extend to Derrida speaking over his own deceased body. As upon the death of parents, nothing any longer stood between the bereaved and the bleak promontory. To shift Pericles out of season, it felt as though the autumn had been taken out of the year.

'Adieu' is the most affirmative of Derrida's 'posthumous gifts of literature'. Derrida does not hesitate to canonise Levinas, nor to call upon the highest authorial categories. He does so through the stately eulogisation of an oeuvre which will be examined down the generations, and will remain open to diverse reconfigurations as succeeding centuries seek a voice in the hour of ethico-religious crisis. Levinas spoke 'in a way that was ... at once clear, confident, calm, and modest, like that of a prophet' (208). In 'unadorned, naked words, words as childlike and disarmed as [his] sorrow' (200), Derrida bade farewell in prose of an elegiac beauty and pathos far beyond the compass of his 'humanist' detractors. Levinas's oeuvre 'is so large that one can no longer glimpse its edges':

> One can predict with confidence that centuries of reading will set this as their task. We already see innumerable signs, well beyond France and Europe, in so many works and so many languages, in all the translations, courses, seminars, conferences, and so on, that the reverberations of this thought will have changed the course of philosophical reflection in our time, and of our reflection *on* philosophy, on what orders it according to ethics, another thought of ethics, responsibility, justice, the State ... according to another thought of the other ... (202)

'Adieu' is scupulously concerned to put Levinas 'before us, in us right before us – in calling us, in recalling to us: à Dieu' (209). Yet the address cannot but remain simultaneously as the most concise, poised account of Derrida's own legacy. That Derrida would himself recoil from such a formulation and reversal, that he was at infinite pains 'to traverse speech at the very point where words fail us, since all language that would return to the self, to us, would seem indecent' (200) cannot halt this recursion and iterability.[11] In the tellingly entitled *Adieu Derrida*, Costas Douzinas says of the Birkbeck lectures upon which his commendable collection was based: 'for all of us, for the thousands of people who attended the lectures Derrida was present not as if he was dead but as if he was alive. His (ghostly) presence haunts this volume as it will haunt many volumes, texts and generations to come.'[12] As Derrida had said of Roland Barthes, a quarter of a century earlier: 'the other returning, truly ghostly' (64).

In *The Death and Return of the Author* (henceforth *DRA*), death and return are worked worked through within the argument as a rational, timeless simultaneity. The concluding sentence of the first edition, however, looked to the future for its validation. The concept of the author, it is argued at the close of 'Conclusion: Critic and Author', presents contemporary criticism with its greatest challenge, one which if not confronted as *the* question will ever disrupt any system 'in the manner of an interminable haunting, as that unquiet presence theory can neither explain nor exorcise'. Given the metaphors of 'presence' and 'haunting' so prevalent, generally, in reflections on Derrida's demise, the promise of this book's last sentence would seem to have been fulfilled. The guiding premise of *DRA* – that, as a logical necessity, the concept of the author is never more alive than when pronounced dead – was borne out in the literal context of the global responses provoked by the death of the unique, irreplaceable author that 'remains' Jacques Derrida. The dominant categories of author-criticism came into play: the homage, the assessment, the acknowledgement of debt to the master, the safekeeping and subsequent development of the legacy, the inter-relationship of work and life in a corpus calling to generations of exegesis. Theoretical culture, the world over, though it fought shy of the words, exalted, in loss, a 'genius', a 'master'. In their innumerable and heterogenous gestures of farewell, theorists could pretend to be doing nothing other than commemorating a great author. With literal death came full conceptual return. No longer dismissive of the category of authorship, criticism would today seem most unlikely to re-enact its radical exclusion in the curious manner that the banishment of poets has sporadically recurred since Plato. With regard to the 'unquiet presence' (of Derrida, or the author generally), theory need not overcompensate through 'hauntology' or hyperbolic *revenance*. To the author(s), it owes the humility of the face that has turned itself away from the Other(s) and would now see its gaze returned.

ATTEMPT AT A SELF-CRITICISM

The idea of the death of the author dominated the secondary and pedagogic theoretical productions of the 1980s. It had also become one of the few theoretical 'initiatives' to cross the line between cultures – the academy and the Press, the international colloquium and the proto-poetics of the artistic avant-garde. This polemical book, accordingly, had its origins in an incredulity that distinguished university lecturers, writers of acclaimed theoretical works, could be persuaded by an absurd non-argument so far as to propagate the annihilation of the author as a 'truth' of textual episte-mology. The tranquil assurance of impersonality imploded into a rhetoric of death and literary regicide; the objectivising tendency through modernist poetics, formalism, New Criticism, structuralist poetics and narratology (to abuse science in the metaphor) reached a state of critical mass.[13] In despair of a science of cosmology, the once dispassionate atheist began to desecrate the church. The poststructural 'death' rather than formalist 'irrelevance' of the author signalled a return – albeit negative – of critical attention to authorship. Having peaked in Anglo-American theory in the 1980s, 'the death of the author' was rarely ventured in the succeeding decade, but the return *to* – rather than the return *of* the author (which is irrepressible and especially powerful when under erasure) – was tentative at most and attended by formulaic qualifications. The return *of* the author, fittingly enough, was to find its fullest efflorescence in the site of the repression itself, in the work of the theorists from whom (sometimes erroneously) it drew its justification.

Ironically, of course, the return to and of an author who had never gone away in the first place was well underway in France many years before the notion of '*la mort de l'auteur*' had, even as hearsay, carried across to Anglo-American criticism.[14] This return was marked by Barthes's work in the 1970s, by Foucault's 1969 essay 'What is an Author?', by Derrida's 'Signature, Event, Context' of 1971. It was carried forward in Derrida's autobiographical writing, his philosophical investigation of legacy and by a sustained confrontation with mortality which centred upon textual inheritance. In legitimately uncovering a figure of death and return in Barthes and Foucault – two parricides of the mid-to-late 1960s which were soon retracted in favour of re-situating the authorial subject – this book, however, somewhat overextended its remit in implicitly superimposing the same dynamic (part structural, part psychotropic, part historical) upon Derrida's earlier work.

Derrida had nothing whatsoever to do with such metonymic or hypostasised 'deaths', 'ends' or 'disappearances'. His work, from 'Signature, Event, Context' onwards, provides the most radical, challenging openings and prospects for the emergence of an authorial theory. There is an uncharacteristic *element* of anti-authorialism in *Of Grammatology*; exemplarity is problematic, particularly given the pathological singularity of Jean-Jacques Rousseau; the interleaving of the supplement between the *Essay on the Origin of Languages* and the *Confessions* is quite brilliant, but the denial of its psychobiographical cast is unconvincing. My argument should have clearly stated, from the outset, that, aside from the 'The Exorbitant; Question of Method', authorship was in the works of 1967 the unexamined category in Derrida's thought; necessarily unexamined, because the revision of phenomenology and the overturning of structuralism had both to proceed through the most exacting meditation on the suppressed questions of language and representation. Furthermore, my treatment of the problem of exemplarity in Derrida – the fact that *Of Grammatology* uses Rousseau to stand between Plato and Hegel as the sole philosophical exponent of an era purportedly dominated by the superiority of the spoken over the written word – should have looked beyond the conventional philosophical canon. If the epoch to which Derrida (cryptically) refers is that of the Graeco-Christian logos, as inscribed from the New Testatment through patristics to Aquinas and beyond, then a significant and egregious history of the repression of the written outside full speech does indeed emerge as a central operation not of philosophy but, no less influentially, of Christian theology. What is retained (unaltered) below, then, holds, but does so only within the confines of a philosophical canon as taught traditionally, in its separation from the theological, by British and American universities.[15]

I sought for consistency between the three readings in terms of their trajectory, thereby elevating the aesthetic value of coherence over the ethical value of interruption. The failure is one of emphasis; the result a 'somewhat exorbitant' reading which provides a relatatively insightful critique of Derrida's working model of intention along the way, but should have sought to distance the Derridean oeuvre from the anti-authorialism in which both supporters and detractors found it convenient to implicate an altogether more demanding series of philosophical operations.[16] Rather than aspire to faultless commentary and thus run the fault of the reproduction or profitless return to the same, *DRA* tried to remain true to the spirit of positive ingratitude, but in so doing gave an unbalanced account of

Derrida's reflections on authorship. My research has since taken up Derrida's positive reflections on authorship, in particular the specifying function of the signature.

This book did not propose, but rather sought the opening for, a theory of authorship. Its aims were to uncover the pseudo-arguments by which 'the death of the author' promoted itself, and to disentangle the question of the biographical author from the altogether antipodean questions of philosophical subjectivity.[17] Its method of affirmation through negation of the negation (that was the death of the author) does not constitute affirmation in the sense of the positivity of presence. Such an 'achievement' is not the groundwork of authorial theory but the removal of obstacles to its development through a specifically focused reassertion of the *doctra ignoratio* from which – with Socrates – the critical spirit first took breath. A return to the author has taken place in numerous fields of knowledge, but this book remains as close as ever to its original impulse, which was that of the prolegomena, of clearing the way for path-making rather than that of forging the path itself. The ultimate aim of any corrective endeavour is its own erasure. Marxism sought a just society which would have no further need of the theory of its evolution through class struggle; psychoanalysis would see its mission as fulfilled when universal harmony between instinctual health and the social order renders analysis superfluous. The work of the judicial and policing systems strives toward a perennially crime-free society in which its institutions would retain only an antiquarian interest. Such teleological realisation-in-redundancy is perhaps impossible in these spheres. Within literary theory, though, the elimination of error is attainable and potentially constructive. An era of anti-authorialism has made the thought of the author possible – audacious even.

The two appendices are complementary, albeit in an asymmetrical manner. From distinct vantages, both seek to bring into focus the enigmatic and fragile borderline that supposedly separates a life from a work. 'The Biographical Imperative' evaluates the simultaneous recognition that events in the authorial life have shaped the work, but that reading the authorial life back into the work risks redundancy or circularity. 'The Author as Reader' reconsiders how the writer incorporates life experiences whilst writing him or herself out of the work. The work/life axis, the borderline and its *dynamis* are thus seen, respectively, from the 'critical' or 'receptive' position of the reader and a 'creative' or 'inceptive' point of view of the impersonalising literary author. 'The Biographical Imperative' is more secure in its theoretical cast, as it does not offer solutions but rather seeks more advanced ways of framing the biographical question. 'The Author as Reader' is speculative, and offers itself as a template for returning to the autobiographical (as distinct from autobiography as genre) rather than constituting a 're-turn' in itself.[18]

THE INSTITUTE OF ADVANCED AUTHORIAL THEORY

It would be satisfying to think that a third edition has moved closer toward a comprehensive coverage of the major authorial issues, but with every revisiting the space of authorship enlarges. The question of technology – a question apart – was essayed briefly in the 'Epilogue' to the Second Edition. In the ensuing decade everything (innovatively) and little (theoretically) has changed. Given that technologies incalculably outpace theorisations – between the tool and the manual arose the Egyptian Pyramids – and that their advances press upon without emanating from theory, it may be the case that mutating authorial placements can at best be registered belatedly by thought. Nor can one construct compelling theoretical subsets. Intention or legacy are no more subordinate to authorship than is the latter to the former. With one word –'legacy' – we open a structural and historical space truly without edges or circumference. Again, the relationship between the authorial and the proprietary, between these adjacent but heterogeneous rights, calls for a conceptualisation that cannot be made independently of institutional histories from Plato's Academy or Aristotle's Lyceum to the Institute of Psychoanalysis. The 'essence' of the proprietary seal differs radically under the dominance of the ecclesiastical, during the era of patronage and under the reign of the so-called 'romantic' conception of unitary artistic ownership. The current shift away from ownership by the artist/creator opens onto the very history of cultural production whilst resisting conceptualisation in its ever-changing contemporary manifestations.[19]

Similarly, the idea of a (literary) canon is taken as a subset of the 'author function' or vice versa without their inter-relationship being submitted to analysis. Indeed, many forms of anti-authorialism, when interrogated, reveal themselves to be hospitable to the idea of a situated biographical subject or the principle of the unique individual but viscerally hostile to the elitism implicit in the construction of a literary canon. The misguided assumption that canonicity and authorship are isomorphic thereby leads to incoherent assumptions of a politicised 'position' on the author. Certainly, the ethical, the political, the ethnic and sexual questions surrounding the formation of a literary canon – in radical distinction from a scientific body of knowledge – must be respected in their specificity when refracted through the theory and practice of authorship. St Jerome's construction of the biblical canon reflected prejudices that it did not uphold in principle; the more organic process which crystallised in Arnold's notion of a clerisy preserving 'the best that has been thought or known' was unwittingly based upon all order of hegemonic values that it took a century to expose. However, opposition is rarely to the principle of the canon but to its constituency. The strongest arguments for the prejudicial nature of the extant canon actually proceed from a restoration of the disinterested principles of canonicity: demonstrating the aesthetic or cultural value of a work is indispensible preparation for contending that its exclusion is ideologically motivated. That all judgements of 'objective aesthetic value' remain open to question indispensably characterises rather than compromises the principle of canonicity when properly conceived as processual rather than monumentalising. In sport or science, the issue of 'value' (and hence the charge of a prejudicially motivated process of election) requires little elucidation. No more elitism is expressed in the award of a Nobel Prize to Albert Einstein than in the selection of Edson Arantes do Nascimento to represent his nation in successive World Cup competitions: attempts at exclusion, in these cases, would be forced from the outset to declare their racial motivation.

Canon-formation in the humanities needs to be analysed by way of comparison and contradistinction from the laws of scientific incorporation of a set of proven theories into the axiomatic reserve of the discipline. Should physics divide 'Sir Isaac Newton' into a scientific marker and authorial name (denoting a biography, the unverifiable alchemical treatises and *Observations on the Prophesies of Daniel and the Apocalypse of St John*)? Or should it acknowledge an authorial field altogether more singular for the rediscovery of hermetic research which illuminates the *res gestae* – whilst remaining entirely independent of the validation – of the laws of light and gravity?[20] What is the status of those whose scientific theories have been thoroughly discredited and who have, in departing science proper, nevertheless passed into culture as authors whose work retains considerable value to the history of ideas? Or of those who, like Tycho Brahe, made possible scientific revolutions without themselves having theorised their findings, thereby remaining signficant figures in science without having impressed an innovative psyche upon the world? Scientists whose grand theories collapse into mythology would needs be placed beside the work of self-conscious mythologisers from Plato to Blake. Even a seemingly homogenous category such as anonymity itself would need to be sub-divided into distinct classes. 'Folklore proofs' in mathematics belong to a very different discursive category than does the anonymity of, say, 'Second Isaiah' or 'Homer'.

Authorship most assuredly is *more than one*.[21] It might be the case that, given the irreducible singularity of every authorial act, more theories of the author are required than have existed major authors themselves. The Baconian theory of Shakespearean authorship was not without merit: it demonstrated that our conception of the capacities of the human imagination can be changed utterly by a shift in the proper name. A full understanding of authorship will doubtless remain forever beyond the grasp of the finite mind. We can but seek more sensitive, more challenging ways of framing the question in concert with the ethical obligation to otherness in which postmodernity has discovered its distinctive intonation of the categorical imperative. Authorial theory is 'still to come'. It is the delicate, exhausting work of others, of coming decades, of many cultures and disciplines. Indeed, so very many are the modalities of the author-function that it is not overly fanciful to envisage a centre which identifies areas to be co-researched across disciplines and cultural sites of innovation. Such an 'Institute for Advanced Authorial Theory' need not take concrete form for its aims to be met quite spontaneously by fine minds drawn from their specialised subject areas to ask 'what is an author?', 'what is an artist, a composer, an inventor?, 'what is a scientist?'. Quite the opposite of the famous 'museum without walls', it would realise itself as an ongoing activity whose only centre resided in constantly reinflecting the question 'what does it mean to create a body of work that outlives its creator?'.[22] The quest of an answer, as thought has taught us, often finds its reward in uncovering some malformation in the question itself: perhaps, as when Sartre asked 'what is literature?', closer examination will reveal that Foucault's 'what is an author?' misleads from the outset in its implicit predication of an essence proper to that strange activity we call authorship.

One can regard authorship as a minor adjunct of literary studies or as a concept central to our understanding of the great achievements of the human mind. Taken in the latter spirit, it requires a full confrontation of the very bold nouns with which Derrida entitled one of his last books – *Geneses, Genealogies, Genres, & Genius: The Secrets of the Archive*.[23] As realm of *life death*, Library of Babel, canon or virtual crypt, the archive is the illimitable repository of inconceivably variegated acts of cultural impression. Medieval theologians affirmed the Books of Nature and Scripture. We, today, affirm two forms of living inscription: the miracle of genetic encoding and the mystery of persistence in one's works. If authorship is a key to but one secret of the archive, then it is indeed 'as though there were here a new departure in [critical thought] and a leap that it, and we ourselves, were urged to accomplish'.[24]

Acknowledgements

This edition represents a return to the author for its writer also, and one which can be directly retraced to the interest shown in Scandinavia for the issue of authorship. The turn to the biographical question owes itself to the enthusiasm and dedication of the Danish theorist of 'biographical performatity', Jon Helt Haarder, who invited me to speak on the themes of authorship and biography at Syddansk Universitet in 2000 (and who has also made valiant and far-sighted 'real world' efforts to establish a Centre for Biographical Studies and Authorial Theory). These lectures and ensuing discussions led me to produce the essay comprising the first Appendix whose finished form, in turn, owes much to the expert close editing of Stephen Wall. 'The Biographical Imperative' was published in *Essays in Criticism*, vol. LII, no. 3 (July 2002), pp. 191–208.

The second Appendix is based on a lecture given at the Conference on the Roles of Author and Reader in Modernist Prose at the Department of Literature and Semiotics, University of Southern Denmark, Odense, in 2000. Somewhat extended here, 'The Author as Reader' is the unpublished English verison of 'Forfatteren som læser: Selvbiographiens splittede subjekt hos Eliot, Proust og Beckett', in Gorm Larsen and John Thobo-Carlsen (eds), *Modernismens Betydende Former* (Denmark: Akademisk forlag, 2003), pp. 158–78. As if to complete this 'return', Kaisa Kurrika and Lea Rojola invited me to lead a colloquium, 'The Resurrection of the Literary Author', at the University of Turku, Finland in 2002.

An AHRC Award in 2003, supplemented by the Department of English Studies at Durham, provided the time in which the idea for a third edition took shape. Jackie Jones, who suggested a second edition in 1998, has again been an inspiration. It has also been a privilege, this time around, to benefit from her talent and experience as a close literary editor. The staff at Edinburgh University Press have, as ever, been most helpful and I would like to thank Sarah Burnett for scrupulous and intelligent copy-editing of the new material. I wish, of course, to reaffirm my gratitude to all acknowledged in the previous editions and to extend thanks to David Perrins for help with this and other projects. Christopher Norris, Nick Browne, Brian Vickers, Cairns Craig and John Drakakis have encouraged my work on authorship and Michael O'Neill has done much to maintain my confidence in academic writing generally. I would also like to extend wholehearted thanks to Mark Jenkins, John Williams, Charlotte Greig, Anthony Reynolds, Niall Griffiths, Peter Finch, and the Vulcan circle for making me feel a sense of belonging in Wales as a writer amongst writers. The extended Burke family is, as ever, the foundation upon which any writing of mine is based: an immeasurable gratitude is never beyond mention.

Nor, sadly, is a profound loss. The memory of Robin Dix, truly 'a scholar and a gentleman', abides here as it does in so many other places.

Sean Burke
Cardiff, April 2008

Prologue: The Deaths of Paul de Man

I am not given to retrospective self-examination and mercifully forget what I
have written with the same alacrity I forget bad movies – although as with bad
movies, certain scenes or phrases return at times to embarrass and haunt me
like a guilty conscience. When one imagines to have felt the exhilaration of
renewal one is certainly the last to know whether such a change actually took
place or whether one is just restating, in a slightly different mode, earlier and
unresolved obsessions... Thus seeing a distant segment of one's past resurrected
gives one a slightly uncanny feeling of repetition.

Paul de Man, New Haven, 1983[1]

Late in 1987, a short article run by the New York Times under the title
'Yale Scholar's Articles Found in Nazi Paper', set in motion a process
of reevaluation not only of Paul de Man's career as a theorist but of the
deconstructive movement in whose name he worked, and of the ethics of
detaching the text from its writer. At a time when critical theory thought
to have dispensed with the idea of authorship, the posthumous revelation
of de Man's wartime writings brought the author back to centre stage.
For critical theorists themselves, all of whom owe a debt of influence to
de Man and some the debt of friendship, the entire affair has unfolded
like a nightmare. And the nightmare in this case, as so often, is history, a
history in which, between 1940 and 1942, a young intellectual published
170 articles in the collaborationist Belgian newspaper *Le Soir*, a certain
number of which articles express anti-Semitic and pro-Nazi sentiments.[2]
It is also the history of the most appalling events, events in which Paul de
Man himself played no active role beyond his journalistic collaborationism,
and of a radical movement in literary studies to which the breadth of his
bequeathment has yet to be assessed.

De Man's life has now been scrutinised, and the picture that emerges
is of an extraordinarily complex and contradictory individual.[3] A man of
great modesty and kindness who was also capable of considerable duplicity

in both his private and public lives, de Man could at the same time show sincere sympathy to the plight of individual Jews in occupied Belgium, and pen articles condemning Jewish literature as a decadence the West could well do without. De Man's post-war reconstruction of himself also unfolds according to similar patterns of moral ambivalence. On the one hand, he was an unimpeachable teacher and academic colleague, on the other, a *de facto* bigamist who maintained fundamentally dishonest dealings with his wartime and post-wartime families. Like most figures who have led a double life, Paul de Man's biography opens to sharply contrasting interpretations.

These enigmas are deepened still further by the theoretical positions he took up on authorship. Perhaps ironically, perhaps deliberately, de Man had always denied that the writer's life in any way bore upon the interpretation of his or her work. In the first phase of his career as a literary theorist, de Man had adopted a rigorous phenomenological picture of authorship whereby the self was entirely emptied of any biographical content in the constitution of a transcendental subjectivity with no personal history or empirical concerns. Latterly, as a deconstructionist, he had rejected author-centred criticism in a different mode, affirming that there is no stable subject of writing in any guise, be it transcendental or empirical. In both phases of his career, the biographical subject is entirely eliminated: an author's personality and life history disappear irretrievably in the textual machine.

Not surprisingly, since his *Le Soir* articles have come to light, many commentators have seen factors beyond those of textual epistemology urging this flight from the self. De Man's denial of biography, his ideas of autobiography as de-facement, have come to be seen not as disinterested theoretical statements, but as sinister and meticulous acts of self-protection, by which he sought to (a)void his historical self. The attempt to efface and deface the writer in his theoretical prose is seen as a way of detaching the Paul de Man of Yale who wrote *Blindness and Insight* and *Allegories of Misreading* from the Paul de Man of occupied Belgium who also put his name to a number of collaborationist articles. Such an interpretation allies itself with de Man's textualisation of history in general, with the always rash and now infamous opinions he issued in the essay 'Literary History and Literary Modernity': 'the bases for historical knowledge are not empirical facts but written texts, even if these texts masquerade in the guise of wars or revolutions.'[4]

The *Le Soir* articles have now put into play their own history, and the 'retrospective self-examination' de Man professes foreign to his nature has been practised on his behalf. What de Man might 'mercifully forget', his legacy will ceaselessly and mercilessly recall in order to make sense of this early moment in his career, to argue its pertinence to his work as a whole, and to determine whether his subsequent career as a literary theorist is to be read in patterns of independence, further culpability or expiation. For some, the wartime writings are to be interpreted as virtually complicitous with the deconstruction he and others have practised. A movement, so the argument runs, which avoids the subjective and the ethical has no defences against lapsing into totalitarian habits of thought, and at least one commentator has gone so far as to argue that the complex work of deconstruction serves to veil an implicitly National Socialist ethos.[5] For others – mainly, but by no means exclusively, luminaries of the deconstructive movement – the wartime writings are seen as a lamentable aberration in de Man's thought, one which his subsequent work did its best, on an implicit level, to retract and rectify. Others still offer no mitigation for the wartime writings but stop short of extending their judgement to cover de Man's work as conceptual theoretician and philosopher of language.[6]

In the epigraph which opens this prologue (in many ways also an epitaph, lines written in the year of his death – 1983 – and possibly in the knowledge of cancer) de Man anticipates all the terms by which this debate has been conducted. Ostensibly he is reflecting on the volume of essays dating from the mid-1950s which have been collected as Blindness and Insight. If we read this passage against its biographical background, however, and take these statements as a secreted reflection on his Le Soir articles, de Man cuts a sinister figure indeed – a puppeteer putting in place all the strings of his legacy, an executor to his own dark codicil. The 'certain scenes' by which he is haunted may well be the harrowing footage we have of the holocaust, or they may be textual scenes, 'phrases' such as: 'one sees that a solution of the Jewish problem that would aim at the creation of a Jewish colony isolated from Europe would not entail, for the literary life of the West, deplorable consequences. The latter would lose, in all, a few personalities of mediocre value and would continue, as in the past, to develop according to its great evolutive laws.'[7]

The full extent of his *embarrassment*, his *hauntedness*, his '*guilty conscience*' will ever be unknown to us, though the majority of commentators discern a fundamental unease in his later work, the question being whether this unease results from a genuine trial of conscience, or an anxiety lest his historical secret betray itself. The '*exhilaration of renewal*' is amply evident in the princely meditations he produced on language and literature from the 1950s up to his death in 1984. Whether, though, '*such a change actually took place*', or whether he is '*just restating, in a slightly different mode, earlier and unresolved obsessions'* is the central question that has been debated with such urgency throughout the literary establishment in its journalistic and academic media.

Without wishing to add to, to neutralise or to exploit the ethical and moral questions raised by the texts of this early Paul de Man, we might note how the response to his wartime writings, both in their prosecutory and mitigatory manifestations, disinter many of the loci of traditional author-centred criticism. Six cardinal intersections of author and text appear and reappear throughout this debate.

1. *Intention*. Did the young de Man mean what he said? Did he say what he meant? Are the intentions expressed in his early articles carried through to join the intentions of his later work? Broadly speaking, those who take the view that de Man is culpable in the extreme would answer 'yes' to these questions, those who defend would say 'no', that it was the work of a young man borne along by a historical tide whose savage shores he could never have foreseen. On both sides – that of a largely anti-intentionalist deconstruction on the one hand, and a pro-intentionalist contextualism on the other – it is assumed that what he meant matters, that what he meant means something to us, and that his later work is governed by good or bad intentions in respect of these collaborationist articles.

2. *Author-ity*. As far as this debate is concerned, the fact that de Man became an authority within literary theory and a certain philosophy of language means that it matters what he said, wherever and whatever, at whatever stage of adult development, and in whatever circumstances. It is this authority that commends these texts so urgently to our attention over and above the countless other, more relentless and rabid collaborationist journalism of the time. Also the fact that de Man, like Heidegger, was a philosopher-author inclines many commentators to view his association with National Socialist ideology as having more pernicious ramifications than that of other non-discursive cultural figures such as musicians, chess grandmasters and so on.

3. *Biography*. The importance of biographical contexts to this debate goes without saying. That he was young (in his early twenties) when he wrote for *Le Soir*, that he had a child and its mother to support, that he was nephew and intellectual ward to Henri de Man (a socialist minister in the Belgian government and thereafter a collaborator), that Paul de Man was *not* a member of the Nazi party (and, for the prosecution, that he was *not* a member of any resistance organisation),

that de Man was hitherto in politics, in conversation, in society, a man in whom not the slightest traces of anti-Semitism or totalitarian politics could be discerned – countless biographical factors such as these are privileged whether offered up in exonerative or incriminatory contexts.

4. *Accountability.* That de Man must be held to account for what he had written is accepted by all parties to this controversy. On this issue, theory seems to abandon or suspend the idea that the author is a mere fiction or trace of language, for if authorship were indeed a textual illusion, there would be no charge to answer beyond that of reminding the world that in the reality of text 'Paul de Man' signs and signifies nothing. The fact is that his fellow theorists have defended de Man as a *person* and often with considerable dignity and passion. So much in itself confirms that, firstly, the signature 'Paul de Man' is something greatly in excess of a textual effect and secondly, his signature ties de Man ethically and existentially to the texts he has written.

5. *Oeuvre.* The existence of a de Manian corpus is not for a minute called into question within this debate. The three main categories of response to the wartime writings are: the interpretation of the entire oeuvre as some form of continuation of the sentiments expressed in this early work, a reading that sees the *Le Soir* articles as the expression of the mature de Manian philosophy in *statu nascendi*; the interpretation of the post-war de Manian work as an attempt to redress and retract the ideology reflected in his wartime journalism and the dissociation of the wartime writings from the de Manian oeuvre.[8] The first two positions accept the interrelationship between de Man's wartime and post-war writing, the former interpreting it as some form of continuous figure, the latter according to a corrective pattern. The third position also accepts the concept of the oeuvre, but separates an inessential juvenilia from an essential and mature canon. The debate thus differs only in the gravity of its themes from those we have witnessed concerning the relationship of an author's fledgling texts to those of his or her mature canon.

6. *Autobiography.* The debate postulates at its centre a concept of de Man's theoretical prose which sees it not as direct autobiographical expression but as, on the one hand, autobiographical suppression, and, on the other, as an elliptical and indirect form of confession. De Man's post-war texts are read either as the work – autobiographical in spite of itself – of a man who is attempting on a theoretical level to obliterate his own history; or, for his defenders, as a disguised

confessional narrative, the attempt by de Man to construct a method of rigorous textual critique that would guard against the ideological mystification to which he had succumbed in his youth. In both modes, the de Manian text is seen to be autobiographical in essence, a text which generated an entire philosophy of language and of the absence of subjectivity in order to keep its secret or to atone for its previous errors.

The de Manian legacy draws together so many of the points with which we will be concerned here.[9] Most significantly, it shows how the principle of the author most powerfully reasserts itself when it is thought absent. This reassertion takes place not only within the debate in literary studies that the affair of de Man has provoked, but also in the context of de Man's biographical relationship to his own theoretical work. In the latter case, de Man's life and work fuse in the very figure that supposedly sets them apart. Whilst he theorised about the disengagement of an author from his work in the constitution of an anonymous literary selfhood that leaves the personal self in its wake, his own life unfolded according to similar patterns. Theoretical articulations of the void of personality find a constant analogue in de Man's voiding of his personal history. Autobiography as de-facement becomes de-facement as autobiography, a cancellation of the self that is self-willed and mirrored in the life of the self-cancelling subject; text and author are united under the signs of their disunion.[10]

In an essay entitled 'The Sublimation of the Self', de Man wrote: 'Because it implies a forgetting of the personal self for a transcendental type of self that speaks in the work, the act of criticism can acquire exemplary value.'[11] By way of an irony to which he himself contributed (perhaps even anticipated), it was only when his personal existence had run its course that his personal self returned to haunt the austere and anonymous subject he left behind in his work. In his deaths, the putting-to-death of a past self, his own biological death, and the death of the writer he announced in his writing, Paul de Man has come to life as a biographical figure with a chilling and tragic intensity. As Derrida himself says:

> He, *himself, he is dead*, and yet, through the specters of memory and of the text, he lives *among us* and, as one says in French, *il nous regarde* – he looks at us, but also he is our concern, we have concerns regarding him more than ever without his being here. He speaks (to) us among us. He makes us or allows us to speak of us, *to speak to us. He speaks (to) us* [*Il nous parle*].[12]

A disembodied voice, a voice that speaks strangely to us now through the fissures of seemingly impersonal and imperturbable theoretical prose. A voice that cannot be kept silent in death. And a voice that, we shall argue, can still less be quieted by literary theory.

This voice, the voice of Paul de Man, is also the voice of authorship itself as we shall trace its disappearances and returns in modern theories of the text.[13] Henceforth I will make only occasional recourse to Paul de Man and, there, to arguably the most gifted literary theorist of his generation; and as often as not to contest his ideas on authorship which, as for all the theorists discussed here, is an area of blindness within his work. For with Barthes, Foucault and Derrida, albeit less dramatically, the authorial subject returns, the (auto)biographical disrupts, enhances and displaces aspects of their work, a return which I shall argue takes place almost instantaneously with the declaration of authorial departure.

As befits the cyclical nature of this project we have begun, so to speak, at the end; with a return of/to the author in critical theory. Both sides of this return will concern us here: the return *of* the author is as it inevitably and implicitly occurs in the practice of anti-authorial criticism; and the return *to* the author that poststructuralism in general has yet to make at the level of theory despite its failure to circumvent subjectivity at the level of its readings. What follows then, under the rubric of the death of the author, is at one and the same time a statement of the return of the author, a return that takes place in accordance with the guiding principle of this analysis – that the concept of the author is never more alive than when pronounced dead.

Introduction:
A Prehistory of the Death of the Author

When looking at the history of modern thought it is all too easy to be seduced by linear patterns of development constructed after the event. One such path is cleared by Roland Barthes when he describes the origins of modern anti-authorialism as stretching from Mallarmé, through Valéry, Proust and the Surrealists.[1] Beguiling and fastidious as it may be, this lineage is palpably false. Of the examples cited, Proust, though he opposed conventional biographicist criticism, never declared anything remotely resembling the death of the author, Valéry as often as not militated in favour of authorial control over and against the romantic notion of inspiration, and Surrealism, whilst it may have persuaded a few writers to experiment with automatic writing, has never had a clear and unmediated impact upon critical theory.[2] Every writer, as Jorge Luis Borges says, creates his own precursors (an elegant way of saying, amongst other things, that all intellectual history is post factum), and in this case Barthes is quite simply covering over a history of more humble predecessors with an august line of Gallic influences.[3] Indeed, of the predecessors cited, only Mallarmé has any place as a harbinger of authorial demise.

Not only Barthes, but Foucault and Derrida have also shown themselves eager to accept Mallarmé as a precursor, and if we look at the poet's most famous remarks on compositional aesthetics, it is easy to see how he prefigures some of the central themes evoked by anti-authorial discourses:

> The pure work implies the disappearance of the poet-speaker who yields the initiative to words animated by the inequality revealed in their collision with one another; they illuminate one another and pass like a trail of fire over precious stones, replacing the audible breathing of earlier lyrical verse or the exalted personality which directed the phrase.
>
> The structure of a book of verse must arise throughout from internal necessity – in this way both chance and the author will be

> excluded ... some symmetry, which will arise from the relation of lines within the poem and poems within the volume, will reach out beyond the volume to other poets who will themselves inscribe on spiritual space the expanding paraph of genius, anonymous and perfect like a work of art.[4]

The disappearance of the writer, the autonomy of writing, the beginning of *écriture* in an act of textual dispossession, the power of language to organise and orchestrate itself without any subjective intervention whatsoever, the notion of the intertextualising of all literature – all these proto-theoretical themes are laid out in the sparest form by this passage. With Mallarmé, the sublime origin of literature which the romantics sought alternately in imagination, or in the Muse, is now discovered within language itself. The doctrine of inspiration departs from the sublimity of divine origin and adopts its counter-sublime: the anonymous unravelling of words on the purity of a page, words written in the absence of Gods, Muses and mortals. Little wonder, then, that Barthes should establish Mallarmé as chief among the heresiarchs, or that Foucault should say:

> To the Nietzschean question: 'Who is speaking?', Mallarmé replies ... by saying that what is speaking is, in its solitude, in its fragile vibration, in its nothingness, the word itself ... Mallarmé was constantly effacing himself from his own language, to the point of not wishing to figure in it except as an executant in a pure ceremony of the Book in which the discourse would compose itself. It is quite possible that all the questions now confronting our curiosity ... are presented today in the distance that was never crossed between Nietzsche's question and Mallarmé's reply.[5]

As Foucault himself knows as well as anyone, however, no historical problematic can be contained within such delicate frames. Beyond the obvious contradiction of establishing Mallarmé as the *author*, as it were, of the author's disappearance – a founding father of the death of the father – historicising of this kind is at best mythopoeic, and at worst, perverse. For eloquent and concise as such a picture is, it is also mystificatory in that the theoretical bases of the movement against the subject of writing are obscured and displaced. Mallarmé's discourse does not situate itself at the opening of literary theory as we know it, but represents a tenebrous culmination of the romantic doctrine of inspiration. Furthermore, Mallarmé is not tendering a theoretical or even eidetic statement about writing. Rather he is evoking, on the one hand, a certain compositional mood whereby the poet attempts to empty himself of personal concerns before the poetic act and, on the other, the aesthetic will-to-impersonality such as was to re-emerge with T.S. Eliot and others early in this century.[6] An ideal of literature is adumbrated in Mallarmé, but not its theory.

Recourse to Mallarmé in this context is of course quite convenient in that his distance from theory, and his distance in time from Barthes, Foucault and Derrida ensures that their work will not be seen in derivative colours: in much the same way, Freud preferred to look to the Greek poets rather than to the nearer and more threatening figures of Schopenhauer and Nietzsche as the forebears of psychoanalytic theory. What the French poststructuralist appeal to Mallarmé shields is a more difficult and serpentine history of influences which culminated in the modern attempt to destroy the authorial subject.

One of the easier and more hospitable theoretical paths leading to the announcement of the death of the author travels along the familiar circuit by which the work of the Russian Formalists passes through Czech and French structuralism to culminate in the poststructuralism practised by Barthes, Foucault and Derrida in the 1960s. Along this route, the Formalists' reduction of the author in the interests of establishing a science of literature and language is seen to flow virtually undisturbed into the modern theory of literature. Such a history of developments, though, entirely bypasses the enormous influence of phenomenology on French thought up to the mid-1950s, an influence in which Barthes, Foucault and Derrida were immersed in the early stages of their intellectual careers.

Husserl's reformulation of the conscious subject as the ground of knowledge exerted greatest influence not in his native Germany but in a French philosophical tradition which for three centuries had lived in the shadow of Cartesianism. Faced with the development of a modern cogito, France's new generation of philosophers – most notably Jean-Paul Sartre and Maurice Merleau-Ponty – threw themselves into the Husserlian texts and the phenomenological revisions of Martin Heidegger. For this and a number of other reasons, the classic texts of structuralism – though they were all written in French – passed by with little or no recognition from an intellectual culture whose horizons were bound by the study of consciousness and the transcendental phenomenological subject.

Naturally, the phenomenological movement in France was by no means homogeneous and its various scions attest to different points of departure. Sartre's existential reading of phenomenology took its bearings from Heidegger, whilst Merleau-Ponty's work looked to the classical Husserlian formulation for its revisionary impetus. Yet all the versions of phenomenology that developed during this period shared a common focus in the question of subjectivity. Sartre's contribution – widely considered today as retrogressive and distorted – consisted largely in returning Heidegger's revision of Husserl to a more substantial grounding in the Husserlian subject, a revision in which is added a great emphasis on the ideal of individual freedom.

Though now largely out of favour, it was this existential reading of phenomenology which gained most currency during the 1940s largely as a result of Sartre's cultural and intellectual ascendancy over this period, an ascendancy comparable only to that of Voltaire some two centuries earlier. As philosopher, playwright, novelist, journalist and political activist, Sartre extended the notion of a free subjectivity beyond philosophy to literature and politics, and provided his generation with the model of the engaged author, a politically-committed writer whose work and whose activities maintained the ideals of personal and political freedom in all aspects of day-to-day existence. Such a model left a deep and lasting impression on Barthes, Foucault and Derrida. Indeed, as Derrida has said, it is 'a model that I have since judged to be ill-fated and catastrophic, but one I still love.'[7] Furthermore, the figure of Sartre constituted the initial inspiration for all three theorists to explore the phenomenological method.

Barthes, Foucault and Derrida, thus all developed as intellectuals in an environment within which the idea of the subject held the same ascendancy as language has occupied for the last quarter of a century. Phenomenological consciousness rather than linguistic structures formed the basis of their early researches. In Barthes this took the form of championing the *nouveau roman*, a loosely phenomenological genre which privileged narratorial consciousness. A statement made by Barthes in an essay of 1954 on Robbe-Grillet shows just how far he was at this time from posing the question of language. Robbe-Grillet's work, he writes, 'imposes a unique order of perception … It teaches us to look at the world no longer with the eyes of a confessor, a physician, or of God … but with the eyes of a man walking in a city with no other horizon but the spectacle before him, no other power than that of his own eyes.'[8]

Derrida, for his part, had read voraciously in the phenomenological tradition, tracing the movement back to Husserl and from there to its roots in the Hegelian phenomenology. During the mid-1950s, he was preparing a doctoral thesis entitled 'The Ideality of the Literary Object in Husserl' which likewise took no account of how language might displace or even thoroughly invalidate the concept of literary perception. Foucault, too, found his first philosophical directions in phenomenology, and these three founding figures of poststructuralism might well have developed into the most exciting phenomenological revisionists of their time were it not for the surfacing of structural linguistics in French thought during the mid-1950s. Upon the advent of what has been called the linguistic revolution, Barthes, Foucault and Derrida were all forced to radically re-question their orientation. Derrida, in a gesture of precocious intellectual sincerity, abandoned his dissertation on Husserl to review phenomenology from the perspective of language and literary interpretation (a project that was to re-emerge a decade later as *Speech and Phenomena*[9]); Foucault recast his studies of madness in terms of language; Barthes began reading avidly in the work of Lévi-Strauss and applied linguistic structures to numerous cultural sites, achieving particular notoriety amongst French scholars for his structural reading of Racinian tragedy.

What brought language to the forefront of thought at this particular time were the landmark publications of Lévi-Strauss's *Tristes Tropiques* (1955) and Jacques Lacan's 'The Agency of the Letter in the Unconscious, Or Reason Since Freud' (1957).[10] As the result of a series of historical accidents and an embedded French resistance to language analysis, structural linguistics was forced to travel the most circuitous routes in order to be readmitted to the French-speaking world in which it had originated, just as it had also to travel by way of many disciplines (anthropology, psychoanalysis, philosophy and, to a lesser extent, political theory) to discover what would seem the natural home of its applications – literary studies. The Swiss linguist, Ferdinand de Saussure's *Course in General Linguistics* had been published in France as early as 1915, but only found a receptive audience in Russia during the closing stages of the Formalist movement;[11] and it was not until the 1940s that French thought began to catch its first glimpse of the resources offered by linguistics for reappraising man's relationship with the world.[12]

Saussure's now famous insistence on the arbitrariness of the sign – that the relation between signifier and signified was based on a conventional/differential rather than a natural correspondence – opened up to Lévi-Strauss and Lacan seemingly inexhaustible possibilities for applying linguistic structures to what were hitherto considered 'natural' phenomena. In Lévi-Strauss, this took the form of analysing patterns of social relationships according to a linguistic model. Kinship structures in particular struck Lévi-Strauss as a challenging area of enquiry for linguistic anthropology, and he detected that family members were differentiated from one another in much the same way as language differentiates and categorises objects, an insight which led to his famous declaration that incest is 'bad grammar'.[13]

For Lacan, linguistic research led him to Jakobson's now famous distinction between metaphor and metonymy (the substitution of the part for the whole, i.e. the turf for horse racing) which he adapted, respectively, to Freud's characterisation of the dream process as condensation and displacement. This insight then allowed Lacan to begin his rereading of Freud from a linguistic perspective on the understanding that 'the unconscious is structured like a language.'[14]

Though working in very different areas, Lacan and Lévi-Strauss had thus come to very similar conclusions concerning the effects of the linguistic revaluation on the status of the subject in relation to knowledge. Lévi-Strauss urged that philosophical and anthropological investigation move from their concerns with conscious phenomena to the study of their 'unconscious infrastructure',[15] just as Lacan stressed that it is not man as conscious subject who thinks, acts or speaks, but the linguistic unconscious that determines his every thought, action and utterance. This 'Copernican revolution' set in motion by the foregrounding of linguistic structures threw down a direct challenge to the central and founding role of consciousness, whether registered in terms of Cartesian certainty, Husserlian phenomenology, or the doctrine of individual freedom outlined in Sartrian existentialism. In what was to become the 'slogan of the decade' for the France of the 1960s, Lévi-Strauss could thus declare: 'the goal of the human sciences is not to constitute man, but to dissolve him.'[16]

The situation of Barthes, Foucault and Derrida at this juncture in French intellectual history is decisive. A strong case could be made that poststructuralism itself could only have been born at this crossover, in the form of a movement which wishes to push the structuralist renewal of language toward the eventual dissolution of both the notions of subjectivity and those of universal structural categories.[17] In terms of the development of the idea of the death of the author, the effects of this particular historical situation are beyond doubt. Earlier movements against the author had taken the form of reactions against biographical positivism. The author was simply to be removed or sidelined in order to focus in New Criticism on 'the words on the page', in Russian Formalism on 'the literariness of literature', but these exclusions remained essentially provisional and did not take the form of a prescriptive or eidetic statement about discourse.

The intersection between phenomenology and structuralism, however, produced an iconoclastic and far-ranging form of antisubjectivism. Having been schooled in phenomenological method, and having seen two of the great sciences of the human subject – anthropology and psychoanalysis –

dispense with the subject under a structuralist sign, Barthes, Foucault and Derrida were not content with simply sidelining the authorial subject as in earlier formalisms. A phenomenological training had taught them that the subject was too powerful, too sophisticated a concept to be simply bracketed; rather subjectivity was something to be annihilated. Nor either could they be content to see the death of the subject as something applying merely to the area of literary studies. The death of the author must connect with a general death of man. At the limit, therefore, between phenomenology and structuralism the discourse of the death of the author as we know it comes into its being. An era of theory is underway in which language is 'the destroyer of all subject'[18] – the author of literary studies, the transcendental subject of philosophies of consciousness, the subject of political theory, psychoanalysis, anthropology.

For Barthes, Foucault and Derrida, the expulsion of the subject from the space of language is thus seen to extend right across the field of the human sciences, and to call into question the idea that man can properly possess any degree of knowledge or consciousness. For should it be that all thought proceeds necessarily by way and by virtue of language, then the absence of the subject from language translates into the absence of the subject or consciousness from knowledge. If knowledge itself, or what we take to be knowledge, is entirely intradiscursive, and if, as it is claimed, the subject has no an*chorage* within discourse, then man as the subject of knowledge is thoroughly displaced and dislodged. Cognition and consciousness arise as intralinguistic effects or metaphors, by-products, as it were, of a linguistic order that has evolved for thousands of years before any subject comes to speak. Man can no longer be conceived as the subject of his works, for to be the subject of a text, or of knowledge, is to assume a post ideally exterior to language. There can thus be no such thing as subjectivity whilst the subject or author – as has classically been the case – is conceived as prior to a language which exists as an entirely transparent vehicle or medium for his uses, his designs. As Foucault predicts, man as the subject and object of his own knowledge 'is in the process of perishing as the being of language continues to shine ever brighter upon our horizon'.[19] The idea of authorial absence thereby connects with the epistemological upheaval in Western thought which the theorists of the 1960s believed to be underway in the linguistic decomposition of subject-centred philosophies. Where philosophy and the human sciences had registered man, or the subject as the necessary beginning and end of knowledge, knowledge and the subject are seen to be fictive emanations of a language and a writing which endlessly subvert all attempts by the human agent to assert any degree of mastery or control over their workings.

This movement is more than a simple extension or development of earlier literary-critical opposition to the author. Whilst the New Critical and Russian Formalist projects sought to remove the author in the interests of exclusively literary concerns, the refusal amongst structuralists and poststructuralists to strictly demarcate modes of writing, their antiformalist insistence on a broad field of intertextuality which the discourses of literature, philosophy, and science traverse on an equal footing, means that the removal of the authorial subject is no longer to be retained simply as a point of intradisciplinary methodology. Furthermore, as enounced by Barthes, Foucault and Derrida, the removal of the author is not to be seen as a strategy, a means toward an end, but as a primary claim in itself. Within Russian Formalism and the New Criticism, anti-authorialism appeared as a reaction to biographical positivism. In order to establish a coherent field of critical study, it was necessary to extricate the literary object from the mass of biographical and psychological speculation within which it had been submerged in the homespun eclecticism of nineteenth-century criticism. Consequently, the question of the author – along with that of the extratextual referent in general (history, society, the world) – was sidelined or bracketed as the preliminary step toward evolving a formal, internal and rhetorical approach to the text.[20] The exclusion of the author functioned quite simply as a methodological gambit within a system which did not pose the questions of the origins and determinants of the text. The *death* or *disappearance* of the author was not at issue but rather the incompatibility of authorial categories with immanent analyses.

Within the discourse of the death of the author, however, it is not enough to exclude the author but to recognise that the author has always been absent, that there never could be an author in the first place. Barthes, Foucault and Derrida thus take anti-authorialism to the extreme of promoting authorial exclusion from a methodological prescription to an ontological statement about the very essence of discourse itself. The appearance of writing is a priori identifiable with the disappearance of the author:

> As soon as a fact is *narrated* no longer with a view to acting directly on reality but intransitively, that is to say, finally outside of any function other than that of the very practice of the symbol itself, this disconnection occurs, the voice loses its origin, the author enters into his own death, writing begins.[21]

Likewise, Foucault claims that in fabricating a text an individual can do no more and no less than create a space into which the writing subject continually disappears. The 'mark of the writer', he contends, 'is reduced to nothing more than the singularity of his absence; he must assume the role of the dead man in the game of writing'.[22] Such contentions mark a considerable advance on formalist positions which generally sought only to remove the author in order to develop formularies for addressing the text on an internal plane. Within modern French theory, however, so far from functioning as a working methodological hypothesis, the absence or demise of the author is seen as 'indubitably the *proof* of writing'[23] in all its manifestations:

> Leaving aside literature itself (such distinctions really becoming invalid) … the whole of the enunciation is an empty process, functioning perfectly without there being any need for it to be filled with the persons of the interlocutors. Linguistically, the author is never more than the instance writing, just as *I* is nothing other than the instance saying *I*: language knows a 'subject' not a 'person', and this subject, empty outside of the very enunciation which defines it, suffices to make language 'hold together', suffices, that is to say, to exhaust it.[24]

Statements of this cast − characteristically of modern anti-authorialism − are not made in a conventionally expository or discursive framework. What is presented is not offered as though it were open to question. The reader is asked to either accept the truth of what is being said as no less than a fact of writing, or to turn back nostalgically upon a humanism no longer tenable within this age of theory. And such indeed has been the general pattern of responses to the annunciation of the author's death.

On the one hand, authorial disappearance has been accepted by structuralist and poststructuralist critics almost as an article of faith. Barthes, Foucault and Derrida are invoked as though − individually or concertedly − they have indeed 'proved' that the author is absent from and irrelevant to the text. As a result of French theory, it is claimed: 'The notion of the "self" − so intrinsic to Anglo-American thought − becomes absurd. It is not something called the self that speaks, but language, the unconscious, the textuality of the text.'[25] Recourse to the author is deemed palaeocritical, the sanctuary of an establishment hankering back to an illusory innocence of criticism before contemporary theorists uncovered the absence of human and expressive qualities in the literary text. On the other hand, such defences as have been made of the author commonly rest upon a fundamentally unargued humanist opposition to the reduction of literature to an impersonal play of signification. In sometimes moralistic, sometimes commonsensical tones, the idea of the death of the author is dismissed as having no serious claim upon our attention, being best accounted for as yet another conceit of a continental avant-gardism which delights in mystificatory paradox.[26]

Naturally, there are a number of more temperate responses to balance these extremes, but even within the most composed pro- and anti-authorial discourses, there is little or no compromise or cogent debate, neither side showing itself willing to argue and justify its root presuppositions. The problem of the author is thus sustained as a source of deep controversy, but does not surface as the site of common discussion, and the chimerical body of texts which constitutes the discourse of the death of the author is not rigorously analysed or interrogated either by its partisans or detractors. The result of which is that the author-question has been largely lost in the perpetuation of this divide.

In recent times, resistance to French theory has taken on a more sophisticated and less humanist character with the emergence of the New Pragmatism. Even here, however, the broader issues raised by authorship have not been debated and the problem of intention has been pursued to the exclusion of other authorial categories.[27] Certainly it is still too early to gauge the force (or lack of it) with which the pragmatists will return (to) the author, but in so far as they have generally presented themselves as against theory, their work has tended to consolidate rather than loosen the deadlock between French theory and Anglo-American criticism.[28] Thus when hard-line pragmatists declare that the theoretical enterprise should simply come to a close they are saying no more of theory than theory often said of tradition – that it is misguided, mystificatory, and that the whole era of textual speculation it has generated should be forthwith erased (or erase itself) in the interests of reshaping literary studies. The attempt to put an end to theory thus reproduces the same impetuous and ahistorical rationale that sought to put an end to the author. No common discursive site is acknowledged, even provisionally, the articulations of theory are dismissed without so much as being touched upon,[29] and once more the texts of the death of the author remain closed to investigation, revision or critique.

The aim of this particular project and, I would argue, of literary studies in general, is not to replace the death of the author by any 'end' or 'death' of theory (if indeed any such thing is possible), for it is precisely the ideas of 'deaths', 'ends', 'closures', 'epistemological breaks', 'final ruptures', etc., that have so often barred the way to meaningful and constructive debate in recent critical history. What is proposed here, by contrast, is a close reading of anti-authorial discourses, an inquiry into how authorial absence is elaborated as a point of theory, and how it is put into practice as a guiding principle of interpretation and critical histories.[30] On the basis of what conceptual structures, then, is the idea of textual anonymity articulated? What reasons are given such that we might be led to see the disappearance of the writer as the precondition of discourse? How does the theme of the death of the author connect with the death of subjectivity in general? In what manner is the concept of the author determined within current debates about intention and representation? What implications does authorial disappearance have for the discourses within which it is promulgated? Who or what speaks in the discourse of the Dead Author? How can there be readers without there being writers? These are the questions which will concern us here, questions whose import cannot be circumvented for the fate of the author prescribes not only the ways in which we theorise, but the ways in which we read, and in which we do or do not write. We shall therefore open the texts in which anti-authorialism receives its definitive formulations, beginning with the work of Roland Barthes whose essay 'The Death of the Author' has been the single most influential meditation on the question of authorship in modern times.

1

The Birth of the Reader

Why, man, he doth bestride the narrow world
Like a Colossus; and we petty men
Walk under his huge legs, and peep about
To find ourselves dishonourable graves.

William Shakespeare[1]

Movements without manifestos are rare, and in 'The Death of the Author', Roland Barthes provided literary theory with its clearest, most uncompromising statement of intent. Written in 1967 – and not, as is often supposed, in mind of the student uprising – 'The Death of the Author' was first published in France in 1968.[2] The year of *les événements*, however, was to suit the dramatic and revolutionary nature of Barthes's essay admirably. A little like Hegel's *Phenomenology of Mind*, which was composed within earshot of gunfire from the Battle of Jena, 'The Death of the Author' has found a perfect setting against the background of May-time Paris in intellectual revolt.

For at least five years beforehand, Barthes had expressed strong reservations about the institution of authorship, and in particular the practices of auteurist criticism, that is, criticism exclusively fixed upon the the author or auteur. Working under a structuralist imprimatur, he had recommended in *On Racine* (1963) that criticism move beyond the restrictions of man-and-the-work analyses to focus on the nature of the text in and for itself. As a rejoinder to the hostile response this text met with amongst French scholars, Barthes reiterated his desire for a more systematic approach to literature in *Criticism and Truth* (1966), declaring that a science of discourse could only be established if literary analysis took language rather than authors as the starting-point of its enquiry.[3] As such, Barthes's opposition to the author remained within an inductionist itinerary: the author-question is placed within parentheses so as to facilitate the emergence of an experimental methodology. With 'The Death of the Author', however, revolutionary impulses entirely overwhelm any scientific aims. The removal of the author is no longer a means to an end, a strategy, but a property of discourse itself:

> The removal of the author ... is not merely an historical fact or an act of writing; it utterly transforms the modern text (or – which is the same thing – the text is henceforth made and read in such a way that at all levels its author is absent). (145)

The working context in which Barthes wrote this essay is also significant. At the time, he was preparing to write a microscopic analysis of Balzac's short story 'Sarrasine' – a project that was to emerge in 1970 as *S/Z* – in which the authorial perspective would be replaced by that of the reader as producer of the text.[4] 'The Death of the Author' thus forms a theoretical outline of this undertaking and opens by offering a quote from Balzac's tale as an example of the anomie proper to all writing. Immediately, Barthes establishes the lapidary cadences that are to characterise the entire essay:

> In his story 'Sarrasine' Balzac, describing a castrato disguised as a woman, writes the following sentence: '*This was woman herself, with her sudden fears, her irrational whims, her instinctive worries, her impetuous boldness, her fussings, and her delicious sensibility.*' Who is speaking thus? Is it the hero of the story bent on remaining ignorant of the castrato hidden beneath the woman? Is it Balzac the individual, furnished by his personal experience with a philosophy of Woman? Is it Balzac the author professing 'literary' ideas on femininity? Is it Universal Wisdom? Romantic psychology? We shall never know, for the good reason that writing is the destruction of every voice, of every point of origin. Writing is that neutral, composite, oblique space where our subject slips away, the negative where all identity is lost, starting with the very identity of the body writing. (142)

Such radical and vatic statements have resulted in 'The Death of the Author' becoming the centre of a controversy. What it has not become, though, is the centre of a debate or discussion. On the one hand, its dictates have been accepted unreflectively, and recourse to Barthes will be used to 'argue' the death of the author without the arguments proposed in the seven pages of his essay being themselves held up to any critical scrutiny.[5] On the other hand, and just as unfortunately, 'The Death of the Author' has seldom provoked more than derisory dismissal from its opponents. Critics who have passionately contested its thesis have rarely so much as disturbed its smooth surface. Many, many readers have been convinced that – even taken on the level of its own premises – 'The Death of the Author' is quite *wrong* and yet have been stymied by their inability to say quite why. Little is gained, for instance, when a critic writes: 'As Barthes makes explicit, his attack on the author is an attack on reason itself; and it is at least consistent that his attack is irrational.'[6] And still less is to be achieved by the *argumentum ad hominem* which is doubly self-defeating in a discussion of authorship since it implicates itself in the second fallacy of begging the question. Nevertheless, so it is said. A review of Malcolm Bradbury's *Mensonge* puts the case thus:

> The comedy has its basis in one of the loonier tenets of Deconstruction – that we do not control language: language (that impersonal, endless play of signifiers) controls us. It (rather than writers) writes books. But, though Deconstructionists may confidently proclaim the Death of the Author, they have never evinced much difficulty in reconciling this view with the scooping up of advances and royalty cheques made out to them personally, not (as you might logically suppose) to the English or French language. When it suits them, it seems, the Author turns out not to be an absolute goner, but just someone on the critical list.[7]

Even William Gass is not above taking such a passing pot-shot:

> Popular wisdom warns us that we frequently substitute the wish for the deed, and when, in 1968, Roland Barthes announced the death of the author, he was actually calling for it. Nor did Roland Barthes himself sign up for suicide, but wrote his way into the College of France where he performed *volte-faces* for an admiring audience.[8]

The essay of Gass's that commences thus (likewise called 'The Death of the Author') is a most considered and articulate redress to 'The Death of the Author', and, as a meditation on the question of authorship in general, more than has its weight against Barthes's text. Yet, as with other, more exiguous rejoinders, it leaves us not a whit the wiser as to the extraordinarily persuasive power of the essay that carries the thesis. Something of the answer to this may lie not in the manner of the author's death but in the nature of the author who apparently dies.

AUTHORSHIP AND APOTHEOSIS

The death of the author might be said to fulfil much the same function in our day as did the the death of God for late nineteenth-century thought. Both deaths attest to a departure of belief in authority, presence, intention, omniscience and creativity. For a culture which thinks itself to have come too late for the Gods or for their extermination, the figures of the author and the human subject are said to fill the theological void, to take up the role of ensuring meaning in the absence of metaphysical certainties. The author has thus become the object of a residual antitheology, as though the Satan of *Paradise Lost* had suddenly redirected his rebellion against the unsuspecting figure of Milton himself.

Barthes points up this deicidal analogy immediately. Like many other works, 'The Death of the Author' establishes a preface in its title. The reference is quite clearly to 'The Death of God' as heralded by The Madman in Nietzsche's *The Joyful Wisdom*.[9] Barthes will also reinforce this pretext: referring to the 'Author-God' and claiming that the death of the author 'liberates what may be called an anti-theological activity, an activity that is truly revolutionary since to refuse to fix meaning is, in the end, to refuse God and his hypostases – reason, science, law'. (147) It is in this dramatic and iconoclastic light that 'The Death of the Author' demands to be read: figures of usurpation, conspiracy, and assassination assist its swift momentum. Its tone, its format and ethos all suggest that a gesture of radical significance is being undertaken, that we are witness to an important moment in the transvaluation of Western values. But the deicidal analogue is not stressed merely to heighten the impact of this pronouncement, to charge the act with a significance it might not have assumed in more modest presentation. Far from it, a definite homology informs this co-implication of the writer and divinity, one which tacitly expatiates and enlivens Barthes's essay.

The author is to his text as God, the *auctor vitae*, is to his world: the unitary cause, source and master to whom the chain of textual effects must be traced, and in whom they find their genesis, meaning, goal and justification. The author thus becomes, in Derrida's words, the 'transcendental signified' and attains the supernal privilege of being at once the beginning and end of his text.[10] Accordingly, criticism accepts the role of passive exegete to the author's intentions. The text is read as natural theologians read nature for marks of design, signs of purpose. Where there is design there must be a designer, where there is the appearance of meaning there must be intention. *Post hoc, ergo propter hoc*; the old fallacy is enshrined as the universal law of literary causality. As Barthes has said elsewhere: '*Nothing is created out of nothing*; this law of organic nature is shifted without the shadow of a doubt to literary creation ...'.[11] The author also acquires the further divine attribute of omnipresence within this scheme since at every stage of textual meaning it is assumed that his designs are incarnate. Not only does the author become the cosmological and teleological principle of the text, he is made its *eschaton* also, its end understood as both goal and cessation. The text is related to a pre-established conception of the author which is both discovered and recovered within the text itself, and, by a circular determinism, the more authoritative reading is that which consorts most harmoniously with the prior model:

> Once the author is removed, the claim to decipher a text becomes quite futile. To give a text an author is to impose a limit on that text, to furnish it with a final signified, to close the writing. Such a conception suits criticism very well, the latter then allotting to itself the important task of discovering the Author (or its hypostases: society, history, psyche, liberty) beneath the work: when the Author has been found, the text is 'explained' – victory to the critic. (147)

With the author all differences and conflicts are neutralised; polysemia is cancelled. Like the God of Christianity, the author does not equivocate or beguile: man, as Milton and the Bible tell us, only fell from grace with the advent of ambiguity. The 'Author-God' of criticism is thus the univocal, absolute subject of his work: he who precedes, directs and exceeds the writing that bears his name. Correspondingly, then, the liberation of the text from its author is to reiterate the liberation of the world from God. In *The Joyful Wisdom*, Nietzsche writes:

> In fact, we philosophers and 'free spirits' feel ourselves irradiated as by a new dawn by the report that the 'old God is dead'; our hearts overflow with gratitude, astonishment, presentiment and expectation. At last the horizon seems open once more, granting even that it is not bright; our ships can at last put out to sea in face of every danger; every hazard is again permitted to the discerner; the sea, *our* sea, again lies open before us; perhaps never before did such an 'open sea' exist.[12]

Freed from the author, the text too becomes an 'open sea', a space of 'manifestly relative significations, no longer tricked out in the colors of an eternal nature'.[13] The death of the author is the first and sufficient step towards 'refusing to assign a "secret", an ultimate meaning, to the text (and to the world as text)'. (147) In this deliverance – which Barthes later characterises as the passage from a Newtonian to an Einsteinian universe[14] – the text becomes a *jouissant* affirmation of indeterminacy, a dance of the pen, a Dionysian threshing floor. To impose an author on a text is to impose an archaic monism on a brave new pluralistic world; it is to seal over the ceaseless play of differences that the death of God has opened in its wake: 'We know now that a text is not a line of words releasing a single "theological" meaning (the "message" of the Author-God) but a multi-dimensional space in which a variety of writings, none of them original, blend and clash.' (146) Not for nothing does Barthes invoke the Nietzschean deicide: the analogy informs both the author-representation that Barthes wishes to evacuate and the liberating consequences of abandoning an authocentric apprehension of the text.

This analogy – resonant and illuminating as it is in many respects – is askew in one very broad sense. The attributes of omnipotence, omnipresence, of being the first uncaused cause, purpose and end of the world are all affirmed a priori of the Christian God: they inhere in his definition, without them He is not God. Not so for the author though: we can, without contradiction, conceive of authors who do not issue 'single theological messages', who do not hold a univocal mastery over their texts. There are indeed even conceptions of authorship that are determinately anti-theological. Mikhail Bakhtin's concept of the dialogic author, for example, is constructed precisely in opposition to the univocity of epic monologism.[15] But Barthes does not seem to be concerned with particular instances of author-representations in this essay, but rather with the general attitude of criticism to the author question. As 'The Death of the Author' repeatedly implies, critical approaches to the text have been in essence theocentric, the history of literary criticism has for the most part been the history of the glorification of the author.

However, taking this claim at face value, it is not easy to see how the theologising of the author can be affirmed as a characteristic of twentieth-century literary-critical discourse. Certainly, it would be difficult to characterise Anglo-American criticism after this fashion. For a tradition suffused with notions such as the intentional fallacy, the unreliable narrator, the implied author, Barthes's essay might well seem aimed at a target that had long since retreated out of range. Whilst the work of Eliot, Crowe Ransom, Wimsatt and others, certainly left fissures by which the author might re-enter New Critical discourse, there is no question that injunctions such as the intentional fallacy, and the edict that criticism should limit itself to the 'words on the page' sufficed to thoroughly distance their activities from any form of theocentric auteurism, however tepid such an approach might seem by comparison with the work of French structuralists and poststructuralists.

Similarly, within twentieth-century Russian literary criticism, the hegemony of the author had been enduringly undermined by the Formalist movement. As early as 1916, Osip Brik and *Opoyaz* had stressed: 'The social role of the poet cannot be understood by an analysis of his individual qualities and habits. It is essential to study on a mass scale the devices of poetic craft, what distinguishes them from adjacent domains of human labour, and to study the laws of their historical development.'[16] A similar disregard for authorial subjectivity also characterised the work of the Prague Structuralists who sought to continue the Formalists' programme for establishing a science of literature. Indeed, even in terms of the French man-and-the-work criticism institutionalised by Lanson, it still difficult to see how the author is sacralised. Certainly, positivist researches of this kind are rigidly centred upon the author, but in accordance with principles of factuality rather than those of a theology of authorship. Even if this movement is traced back to the nineteenth-century positivism of Hippolyte Taine, the author is neither the original nor the final term of analysis, but the opening to the race, the milieu, the moment – a process in which the role of the author is largely that of bridging (rather than creating) text and history.

For sure, critics can be found to fit any description, and an extensive foray might reveal any number of texts in which the author is deified.[17] But what is absent is the all-pervasiveness of *theo-auteurist* criticism from which 'The Death of the Author' takes its directions. Rather, the *auteurist* position which Barthes takes arms against is itself largely hypostasised. The large body of critics who work with a more modest conception of authorship are not considered, nor the ameliorative influence such critics bring to bear upon the role of the author in literary studies. All author-positions are subsumed under an essentially nineteenth-century theocentrism, a tactic which naturally lends to the death of the author a greater urgency, a more direful necessity.

In appraising an essentially iconoclastic work, the most telling questions are often not to be addressed to the operations performed on the object, nor to the conclusions thereby reached, but rather to the manner of the representation of the object to be destroyed. How much, we should ask, of the joyous work of destruction consists in badly constructing the house? How much more suasive, more joyous, how much more effortless and apocalyptic is the demolition of an edifice built on the shakiest of foundations? Roland Barthes in 'The Death of the Author' does not so much destroy the 'Author-God', but participates in its construction. He must create a king worthy of the killing. Not only is the author to be compared with a tyrannical deity, but also with bourgeois man himself: it is, Barthes writes, 'the epitome and culmination of capitalist ideology... which has attached the greatest importance to the "person" of the author'. (143) Hence, too, the comparisons with the capitalist; and the capitalisations ('sway of the Author', 'Author diminishing', 'reign of the Author') prime for decapitation. Hence, again, the characterisation of the author as the Father to whom the book is the child.[18]

What is happening in this procedure is that Barthes himself, in seeking to dethrone the author, is led to an apotheosis of authorship that vastly outpaces anything to be found in the critical history he takes arms against. Furthermore, and in collusion with this misrepresentation, Barthes's entire polemic is grounded in the false assumption that if a magisterial status is denied the author, then the very concept of the author itself becomes otiose. In an identical spirit, Gayatri Chakravorty Spivak pronounces that 'The text belongs to language, and not to the sovereign and generating author'[19] but provides no vindication for proceeding (as she does) from this calm insight to the claim that the author has no part to play in the processes of text formation and reception. It would make little more sense to dismiss Brendel's interpretation of the *Hammerklavier Sonata* on the grounds that he neither owned the score nor the Steinway on which it was performed. That an entity is not the *causa sine qua non* does not proscribe against its being the *causa causans*. Observing light passing through a prism (though 'we know' that the prism is not the absolute origin of the resplendent spectacle before us) we do not deny its effect upon the light, still less call for the death of the prism. That the author can only be conceived as a manifestation of the Absolute Subject, this is the root message of every authocide. One must, at base, be deeply *auteurist* to call for the Death of the Author.

The Author in 'The Death of the Author' only seems ready for death precisely because he never existed in the first place. Like the reader whom Barthes would instate in his stead – 'the reader is without history, biography, psychology; he is simply that *someone* who holds together in a single field all the traces by which the written text is constituted' (148) – Barthes's Author is a metaphysical abstaction, a Platonic type, a fiction of the absolute. This 'monster of totality' is to haunt Barthes's subsequent writing.[20]

FROM WORK TO LIFE

Lowry could not invent at the level of language, only at the level of life, so that having lied life into a condition suitable for fiction, he would then faithfully and truthfully record it. No wonder he felt enmeshed. No wonder, too, that he had to revisit in order to revise; repeat the same difficult passage of existence in order to plunge further into it, make the necessary changes, get it right; and this meant only too often that he had to drink himself back into madness again, to resee what was to be rewritten; to fall down in a ditch, to find vultures perched on the washbasin, fold fearfully up in a corner like a pair of discarded trousers, or bruise his head between toilet and sink in some dirty anonymous john.

William Gass[21]

Barthes is anxious to point out that the death of the author did not occur prior to the writing of his eponymous essay, but he is also keen to establish a number of remote antecedents for this idea: namely Mallarmé, Valéry, the Surrealists and Proust.[22] For those of us who might be puzzled by the inclusion of Proust in this context, 'The Death of the Author' elaborates: 'By a radical reversal, instead of putting his life into his novel, as is so often maintained, he made of his very life a work for which his own book was the model: it is clear to us that Charlus does not imitate Montesquiou but that Montesquiou – in his anecdotal, historical reality – is no more than a secondary fragment, derived from Charlus.' (144) Barthes neglects, however, to explain why this reversal of customary literary causality should imply – or even tend toward – the diminution of the author. No less intimacy and engagement with the author is effected by reversing his place on the causal chain, nor indeed any curtailment of authorial control since this is, we are told, Proust's conscious intention. In subsequent texts Barthes will reiterate this insight, though it will be put to a very different end.

'The Death of the Author', as stated above, grew out of the early stages of Barthes's struggle with Balzac in *S/Z*. Commentators on Barthes's career are united in seeing a decisive change in direction as occurring in the late 1960s, and are all but united in seeing that change as occurring decisively in *S/Z*. This text also constitutes a certain crossroads for Barthes in terms of his attitude to authorship in that it at once puts into practice the principles of 'The Death of the Author', and at the same time willingly relinquishes some of the ground that the essay hoped to gain. This process is dramatically registered in one Janiform passage. Just as the author seems well and truly buried under the weight of this monumental reading, the critic recalls the author with the hauteur kings reserve for their vanquished:

> The Author himself – that somewhat decrepit deity of the old criticism – can or could someday become a text like any other: he has only to avoid making his person the subject, the impulse, the origin, the authority, the Father, whence his work would proceed, by a channel of expression; he has only to see himself as a being on paper and his life as a bio-graphy (in the etymological sense of the word), a writing without referent, substance of a *connection* and not of a *filiation*: the critical undertaking ... will then consist in *returning* the documentary figure of the author into a novelistic, irretrievable, irresponsible figure, caught up in the plural of its own text: a task whose adventure has already been recounted, not by critics, but by authors themselves, a Proust, a Jean Genet.[23]

This passage – unrequired by anything in his analysis, and ushered in via the most casual of pretexts [24] – would seem to presuppose a prior reading of 'The Death of the Author'. As we have stressed, Barthes is careful to point out that 'The Death of the Author' is a call to arms and not a funeral oration, that 'the sway of the Author remains powerful'. (143) Yet here, in extending a certain conditional clemency to the author – and in extending this clemency somewhat in his next work *Sade Fourier Loyola* (1971), to talk of 'the return of the author' – it is implied that the death of the author is in some sense a thing achieved; there is, after all, no return without a departure. Later again, in *The Pleasure of the Text* (1974), Barthes will say: 'As institution, the author is dead: his civic status, his biographical person have disappeared.'[25] Needless to say, as institution the author is not dead, nor was then, neither have his civic status and biographical person disappeared – agreement on this matter would not seem difficult. But the interest of this statement is more performative than constative. Again a disclaimer is the necessary prelude to the call for the author's renewal – 'but in the text, in a way, *I desire* the author: I need his figure … as he needs mine.'[26] – and again it is assumed that the death of the author has in some sense, and at some time, been realised. Yet 'The Death of the Author', at its own testament, is not the description of an 'event' prior to itself, and only the most spellbound of readers could conclude that it 'occurs' in the course of the seven pages that Barthes devotes to the subject.

The revision of an event that has not occurred is of course an oddity, but this is what seems to be happening here. A sympathetic critic might see this as an instance of Barthes's charming contrariety, a more suspicious mind would view it as the recognition of a gross exaggeration that refuses to confess itself. In all events, the course to be steered is the same. Now that the author is dead, now that the lesson has been learnt, let us return the author to our circle as a guest whose past transgressions have been forgiven but not entirely forgotten. This is the rhetorical format of the above passage, as it is, too, of other similar statements of the return of the author issued by Barthes during this period (1969–74). Two balls must be constantly kept up in the air: the author will return, but the death of the author must stand. The ingenious manner in which Barthes negotiates this problem is through recasting the relationship between author and critic in such a way that authorial return does not impinge upon the idea of the birth of the reader. Thus the author will reappear as a desire of the reader's, a spectre spirited back into existence by the critic himself. *Sade Fourier Loyola* balances these exigencies adroitly:

> The Pleasure of the Text also includes the amicable return of the author. Of course, the author who returns is not the one identified by our institutions (history and courses in literature, philosophy, church discourse); he is not even the biographical hero. The author who leaves his text and comes into our life has no unity; he is a mere plural of 'charms', the site of a few tenuous details, yet the source

of vivid novelistic glimmerings, a discontinuous chant of amiabilities, in which we nevertheless read death more certainly than in the
epic of a fate; he is not a (civil, moral) person, he is a body ... For
if, through a twisted dialectic, the Text, destroyer of all subject,
contains a subject to love, that subject is dispersed, somewhat like
the ashes we strew into the wind after death ...[27]

The death of the Father precedes the birth of a lover; and, indeed, the
pleasure of the text is itself evident in the felicity of such a presentation.
Yet this wonderful simile – 'somewhat like the ashes we strew into the
wind after death' – has its place in the *arrière pensée* of which we have been
talking. A little like Dionysus, or Christ, the author must be dead before
he can return. In a sense too, he must continue to be dead though he has
returned. The text remains the 'destroyer of all subject' yet, through the
twists of a silent dialectic, it also might contain a 'subject to love'. What
'twists' motivate this dialectic which, on the face of it, makes no sense at
all? If the text is 'destroyer of all subject' – and this is asserted uncondition-
ally – then it can contain *no* subject, much less one to love. If this dialectic
is twisted it is because it is no dialectic at all: the statements remain flatly
contradictory, they are party to no synthesis whatsoever. What is called
a 'twisted dialectic' is in its operation far from dialectic, being rather a
piece of logodaedaly, a legerdemain that seeks to screen the kind of double
postulate that Barthes is usually so quick (and so right) to deprecate. These
manoeuvres, though, are to lead Barthes into areas that a simple palinode
might have bypassed.

The author returns on condition that his life is discontinuous, fictive;
that he 'puts the work into the life'. As Barthes stipulates in an essay of
1971:

It is not that the Author may not 'come back' in the Text, in his text,
but he then does so as a 'guest'... his life is no longer the origin of his
fictions but a fiction contributing to his work; there is a reversion of
the work on to the life (and no longer the contrary); it is the work of
Proust, of Genet which allows their lives to be read as text.[28]

Biographical discourse has taken note of this life-work reversal intermit-
tently, not only in the case of Proust but those of Byron, Wilde and others,
describing the processes of persona construction, of how authors come to
identify obsessively with their characters, how an author can spend decades
living through the fictional dream he is attempting to write, how the mask
comes to wear the man, and so on. Theorists too, the Russian Formalists,
Boris Tomaschevsky and Boris Eikenbaum and, more recently, Foucault
and Paul de Man, have accepted that the fictional project can of occasion

outpace the life-work. Tomaschevsky argues that Pushkin 'poetically fostered certain facts of his life', that he invented the story of a doomed love as a background against which his Southern poems would be read, and that this biographeme played an essential role in structural juxtaposition with the poems themselves.[29] Foucault, in *I, Pierre Rivière*, examines the case history of a nineteenth century Norman peasant who wrote a forty-page confession entitled '*I, Pierre Rivière*, having slaughtered my mother, my sister and my brother…' and *then* determined to commit the deed: 'author of it all in a dual sense', Foucault says, 'author of the crime and author of the text '.[30]

Barthes, however, is not content to see the reversion of the work onto the life in its particularity; rather he makes it the universal law of literary causality and the *sine qua non* of the reintroduction of the author. For Barthes, far from being an aestheticist conceit, or merely a means of adding a dash of *ostranenie* to 'man and the work' criticism, the chiasmic movement from life-into-work to work-into-life is addressed to the question of priority. Structuralist thought had defended language against reduction to a technicist epistemology by excluding the author: this exclusion accepted, the labour of validating the irreducibility of language to experience, subjectivity, psychobiographical factors, or any pretextual drive, became effortless, tautological. Thus Tzvetan Todorov could blithely declare:

> Art therefore is not the reproduction of a given 'reality', nor is it created through the imitation of such a reality. It demands quite different qualities; to be 'real' can even … be harmful. In the realms of art there is nothing preliminary to the work, nothing which constitutes its origin. It is the work of art itself that is original; the secondary becomes primary.[31]

Barthes, perhaps more than any other theorist, is aware of the threat that the author poses to the immediacy of language. Thus if the author is to return he can only do so as the progeny of his text for, in this way, the anteriority of *écriture* remains vouchsafed. And, assuredly, Barthes would seem to have negotiated an ingenious route around this problem. The possibility of a transversal movement from work to life is not one which admits of easy refutation. The problem is that Barthes demands too much of it. Paul de Man asks:

> We assume that life *produces* the autobiography as an act produces its consequences, but can we not suggest, with equal justice, that the autobiographical project may itself produce and determine the life and that whatever the writer *does* is in fact governed by the technical demands of self-portraiture and thus determined, in all its aspects, by the resources of his medium?[32]

And de Man is right to ask the question. We can suggest this, perhaps even assert it, but 'with *equal* justice'.

What the insinuation of the *graphē* into the *bios* discloses is that work and life commute through a channel which can be traversed in both directions and not, as has been traditionally supposed, only in the direction author-to-text. The idea of fictional imperatives dictating the course of a life is therefore more than a simple *hysteron proteron*, but it does not, by any means, amount to an argument for the priority of the writing scene. Once the route has been opened, once communication has been established between an author's writing, on the one hand, and his biography, on the other, then any power of legislation against the life also influencing the work has been abdicated. At most, the notion of putting-the-work-into-the-life unsettles or tropes the mimetic tradition, but without at all departing from the essential interconnectedness of life and work. The reversal is always open to reversal, and so on, *ad infinitum*. As implied in the above epigraph we have drawn from William Gass, the relationship between work and life is one of a ceaseless and reactive interplay in which neither life *nor work* has any claim to necessary priority.

This notion of work-into-life does not figure greatly in *Sade Fourier Loyola* nor elsewhere in Barthes's corpus, and it is most certainly nowhere argued in the manner by which Derrida has attempted to trace a primal scene of writing. What it does *do*, though, at this particular juncture in Barthes's career, is to provide a point of return for the author, one which allows the reader to take biographical issues on board whilst maintaining that 'life never does more than imitate the book, and the book itself is only a tissue of signs, an imitation that is lost, infinitely deferred.' (147) The return of the author thus does not reopen the closed-casket case of his death. The author can be at once both dead and alive. The task here accomplished is that of returning the author to the house without shaking its foundations, quietly, inconspicuously, an author who can leave by the front door only if he enters from the back: the uncanniest of guests.[33] Nevertheless, once the guest is within his walls the host can have what he wishes of him. And this is what *Sade Fourier Loyola* will do.

THE 'FOUNDERS OF LANGUAGES'

Sade Fourier Loyola sets a riddle in its title. What links the Satanic Marquis, a utopian socialist and the founder of the Society of Jesus? All three, Barthes tells us, are obsessive classifiers, subdivisionists, their true passions are not the body, man and God respectively, but the inventory. Thus Sade will set the *120 Days of Sodom* the task of discovering, naming and describing the

600 perversions proper to mankind, Fourier the 1,680 passions, Loyola the minute subdivisions to which the spritual exercitant's first week of devotion is subject. They are constructors of vast programmes, systematisers, combinatory analysts *par excellence*. As such they would seem manifestations of the scriptor: 'operators' of the writing machine, assemblers and rearrangers of codes, lexicologists like the young de Quincey invoked in 'The Death of the Author'.[34] Sade, Fourier and Loyola might then seem to be writers who have worked through the principles of a deauthorised *écriture*, subjects who have fully surrendered themselves to language and have allowed it to unravel anonymously in their texts.

Yet, from the outset, Barthes declares that they are not *merely* writers, nor *merely* authors or philosophers, savants or thinkers. Sade, Fourier and Loyola are 'logothetes', 'founders of languages' and *Sade Fourier Loyola* is 'the book of Logothetes'.[35] They are initiators of writing, artificers of closed languages, subjects engaged in 'the enormous and yet uncertain task of a constructor of language, of a logo-technician'. (44) Charles Fourier is not just an inventive writer, he is an inventor of writing;[36] the *Spiritual Exercises* of Loyola have as their object 'the invention of a language'; (48) 'Sade's greatness lies not in having celebrated crime, perversion, nor in having employed in this celebration a radical language; it is in having invented a vast discourse founded in its own repetitions (and not those of others).' (126)

This idea of the 'founder of language' will give considerable pause to anyone familiar with Barthes's earlier work. The conviction that language, any language, however idiosyncratic it might appear in particular hands, invariably precedes and indeed determines the subjects of its writing is a constant premise of Barthes's work during the 1960s, and one which finds its most direct expression in 'The Death of the Author'. But with the concept of the 'founder of language' he would seem to entirely subvert this thesis. At every point at which 'The Death of the Author' attempts to justify itself, it has immediate recourse to the priority of writing: 'The text is a place where…a variety of writings, none of them original, blend and clash'; 'the writer can only imitate a gesture that is always anterior, never original'.[37] Yet *Sade Fourier Loyola* states, in full confidence: 'The language they found is obviously not linguistic, a language of communication. It is a new language.' (3)

Accordingly, the first act of logothesis is a withdrawal from the sociolect, a voiding of the linguistic past and present. Barthes insists upon this: 'The new language must arise from a material vacuum; an anterior space must separate it from the other common, idle, outmoded language, whose "noise" might hinder it' (4). Within this 'material vacuum' the logothete is at the crossing, both outside and betwixt languages. Hence Barthes will stress the importance of the self-isolations, the retirements and preparations of these 'founders'. Like the Author, the logothete 'nourishes' the book: 'All these preparatory protocols, by eliminating from the field of the retreat worldly, idle, physical, natural language, in short other languages, are aimed at achieving the homogeneity of the language to be constructed, in a word, its pertinence.' (52) To invent language it is necessary to refuse it: 'All these protocols have the function of creating in the exercitant a kind of linguistic vacuum necessary for the elaboration and for the triumph of the new language.' (49) A linguistic break is thus achieved by the logothete, one that does not constitute a mutation of the system but the evolution of a truly closed and original writing practice. That such a desire for a new language should exist is no cause for surprise. What is unusual is Barthes's confidence that Sade, Fourier and Loyola all succeeded in this immense undertaking.[38]

Viewed from any standpoint, the idea of the logothete forces some realignment of the author-question both in Barthes's work and within the poststructuralist movement in general. The description is too powerful, too unsettling, to be glossed away as another instance of the loss of the subject in language.[39] The author-centred critics Barthes took issue with in *On Racine* talked of the Racinian universe, Racine's genius, (Barthes talks of 'Sade's genius') but nowhere do they talk of a 'founder of language'. Indeed, the logothetic description belongs to what we might call a 'meta-authorial' perspective. That is to say, one which characterises certain authors as having exceeded the parameters of conventional author-text relations. This is not an isolated aberration in the poststructuralist canon but a theme that is to occur in Michel Foucault and Jacques Derrida as well as in the work of avowedly author-centred critics such as Harold Bloom. These theorists will put forward powerful accounts of how influence and inscription can overrun even the most generous of geneticist models.

The idea of the logothete also necessitates the renewal of the concept of the oeuvre. 'Text' in *Sade Fourier Loyola*, we soon notice, means oeuvre. Specific citations themselves are rare: throughout Barthes talks of the 'Sadian text' as though *Justine, Philosophy in the Boudoir*, The *120 Days of Sodom* and so on, all form one indissoluble writing. And well he might. One of the principal theses of *Sade Fourier Loyola* is that the logothete is continually involved in a single project, that of constructing an autarkic language, and not least among Barthes's achievements here is his discovery of a manner of speaking about a body of writing without relapse to conceptual mapping or reduction to an arid homogeneity: the logothetic work is that of ceaseless difference within a single project. A recursive writing almost: infinitely generative of its own elements, but closed and oblivious to anything outside of itself. Indeed this closure has been affirmed not only of the outcasts Sade, Fourier and Loyola, but as the condition of all writing: 'All modes of writing have in common the fact of being "closed" ... writing is a hardened language which is self-contained.'[40] If indeed the logothetic language is closed – and *Sade Fourier Loyola* cannot work without this premise – then the possibility of its establishing a broad intertext is precluded, and it is perforce located firmly within the space of the oeuvre. For logothesis to make any sense at all, 'text' in *Sade Fourier Loyola* must mean oeuvre.

Of course, faith in the oeuvre is nothing less than faith in the author, or in his signature at least, and the constants and correspondences thereby contracted. In absolutely minimalist terms, the author is that principle which unites the objects – whether collusive or discrete – that gather under his proper name. And indeed a certain suspicion of the oeuvre is to be found in many forms of traditional criticism. Propositions of the order, 'the Ludwig Wittgenstein who wrote the *Tractatus* is not the Ludwig Wittgenstein of the *Philosophical Investigations*' are commonplace amongst commentators who otherwise have no particular hostility to the institution of the author. Yet Barthes, author of the author's death, has evinced considerable faith in the oeuvre, not only in the special cases of Sade, Fourier and Loyola, but at many points within his own oeuvre, and often with supreme indifference to disparities of content, ideas, positions. In *Writing Degree Zero*, style is proposed as the *etymon*, the silver thread which both unites a writer's work, and sets it off against that of others: a 'self sufficient language' which 'has its roots only in the depths of the author's personal and secret mythology, that subnature of expression where the first coition of words and things takes place, where once and for all the great verbal themes of his existence come to be installed'.[41] *Michelet* set out to 'restore to this man his coherence',[42] while *On Racine*, although reluctant to ground the oeuvre in the creativity and cohesion of the individual subject, nevertheless sought for structural and thematic unity within the Racinian tragedies. Even *S/Z* quite freely accepts Balzac's oeuvre and devotes a section to describing the pleasures of moving between various Balzacian characters and locales.

With *Sade Fourier Loyola*, however, Barthes subjects the notion of the oeuvre to a certain revaluation which had always been implicit in his earlier work. This revaluation consists in releasing the life's work from the wearisome and laborious chronological considerations of conventional oeuvre criticism. Barthes treats the oeuvre as an everpresent intertext, a space to be ranged forwards and backwards without progressional responsibilities. Oeuvre-reading is thus relieved of the programmatics of anteriority, development: the general organicist and teleological rationales which have formerly stood its surety are displaced by a fecund space, a space of coherencies and constellations, but not of syntagmatic order. Likewise, the flattening out of apparent contradictions, or the synthetic process of their assimilation into a greater whole have no place in this form of oeuvre-reading. No longer a forward march from fledgling texts to mature thought, the oeuvre becomes an arena or ellipse in which everything is rhapsodic, nothing sequential, in which themes, passages, ideas twist round upon each other in the manner of leitmotivs. When reading Sade, there is no call, say, to begin with the first version of *Justine* and to end with the last surviving work at Charenton, nor to take account of the two decades of revolution and counterrevolution that intervened between their composition: his texts belong to a common self-identical site, the site of their own recursive and idiorhythmic language which eludes the regimens of the linear, the temporal. What is augured here is (by an interesting reversal which combines concepts traditionally set at odds with each other) an *intertextualising of the oeuvre*, a freedom to traffic between an author's works that is perversely delimited by the narrative conventions of customary oeuvre-reading. Under the heading 'Rhapsody', Barthes writes of the 'Sadian novel':

> To recount, here, does not consist in developing a story and then untangling it, adhering to an infinitely organic model (to be born, to live, to die), i.e., to subject the series of episodes to a natural (or logical) order, which becomes the meaning imposed by 'Fate' on every life, every journey, but in purely and simply juxtaposing iterative and mobile fragments: then the continuum is merely a series of bits and pieces, a baroque fabric of odds and ends ... This construction frustrates the paradigmatic structure of the narrative (in which each episode has its 'correspondent' somewhere further on which counterbalances or rectifies it) and thereby, eluding the structuralist reading of the narration, it constitutes an outrage of meaning: the rhapsodic (Sadian) novel has no *meaning* or *direction*, nothing compels it to progress, develop, end. (140)

This passage speaks well also for the biographical innovations that *Sade Fourier Loyola* suggests. Barthes adds the author's life to the oeuvre in the 'Lives' section just as elsewhere he joins corpus to corpus by reading the body writing into the body of writing. Tomaschevsky had proposed the legend created by the author as 'literary fact';[43] Barthes makes the biographeme the basis of his writing of a life.

In the second preface to 'Philosophy in the Tragic Age of the Greeks', Nietzsche wrote:

> in systems that have been refuted it is only [the] personal element that can still interest us, for this alone is eternally irrefutable. It is possible to shape the picture of a man out of three anecdotes. I endeavor to bring into relief three anecdotes out of every system and abandon the remainder.[44]

In *Sade Fourier Loyola*, Barthes presents the life of Fourier in twelve anecdotes that span less than two pages. Like the Nietzschean biographer, he makes do with very little:

> 1. Fourier: a *shop steward* ('A shop steward who will refute political and moral libraries, the shameful fruit of ancient and modern quackeries'). At Besançon, his parents ran a cloth and spice store: *trade*, execrated, *spice*, adored in the form of a *body*, the aromale which (among other things) will perfume the seas; at the court of the King of Morocco, there is said to be a Director of the Royal Scents: aside from the monarchy, and the director, Fourier would have been enchanted by this title ...
> 9. His knowledge: mathematical and experimental sciences, music, geography, astronomy.
> 10. His old age: he surrounded himself with cats and flowers.
> 11. His concierge found him dead in his dressing gown, kneeling among the flowerpots.
> 12. Fourier had read Sade. (182–4)

The longer life of Sade consists of twenty-two entries which span material as diverse as the etymology of Sade's name, the wigs worn by his enemy Police Lieutenant Sartine, a declaration of the priority of the writing scene, as well as trifles such as, 'Suddenly transferred from Vincennes to the Bastille, Sade made a great fuss because he had not been allowed to bring his '*big pillow*..."The barbarians!"'.' (181) As the morpheme is to the linguistic analysis, the mytheme to myth, so the biographeme is the minimal unit of biographical discourse. Yet despite these scientific consonances, the biographical procedures it heralds are as far removed from structuralist methodologies as they are from documentary positivism. If anything, it is a poet's conception.

The biographeme obviously need not be an incident central to the life of the subject. As the 'Preface' to *Sade Fourier Loyola* says, Barthes is not concerned with the 'pilgrimages, visions, mortifications and constitutions' of the Ignatian life but with the saint's '"beautiful eyes, always a little filled with tears"'. (8) Often the biographeme would seem entirely tangential, not only to the life but to the episode in which it occurs. Whereas traditional Sadian biographers marshal evidence from every quarter in order to determine exactly what happened during Sade's accosting of Rose Keller, Barthes's interest is in the 'white muff' Sade wore at the time, 'an article obviously donned to satisfy the *principle of tact* which seems to have presided over the Marquis's sadistic activity'. (174) Similarly it is with 'that Provencal way in which Sade says "milli"', (8) with Charles Fourier's liking for 'little Parisian spice cakes' called 'mirlitons'. This is the 'chant of amiabilities', the 'plural of charms'. Yet the biographeme achieves more than Barthes says it will. These details – Fourier's cats and flowers, Sade's dislike of the sea – are crystalline moments in lives whose motion and totality are necessarily irrecoverable. While the conventional biographer will seek to mimic the impetus of a life, to register it according to certain representative proportions, the biographeme breaks with the teleology implicit in this lambent narrative movement. Events are not connected to imply any destiny or purpose in the course of a life, rather the biographemes are the shards of any such forward movement, those velleities that are passed over in the more frenetic, directed movement of the footprint-following biographer. The biographeme arrests the progressional narrative of biography proper, its insistence on reading themes of development and decline into the empirical contents of an author's life.

Consequently Barthes is not concerned with Sade's life as evil *grand seigneur* and *sansculotte*, viewed in all its tragic resonances as 'a man oppressed by an entire society because of his passion' nor with the 'solemn contemplation of a fate'.(8) The biographeme suspends narrative time and the *telos* that only such time can insure. Its ethos has affinities with the Proustian concept of 'involuntary memory' as it has too with the repertoires of ordinary memory. Those who have lost their nearest and dearest do not recall their departed in the manner of the monumental biographer, but through discrete images, a love of cats and flowers, a liking for particular cakes, watery eyes like Ignatius of Loyola. And those images, sufficient to themselves, are also images that (in the words of Yeats), 'fresh images beget'; they refer or expand to other images not by syntagmatic structuring but by association, invocatively.

For Barthes, never far from Proust, the biographeme reverberates with the pathos of lost time, and yet participates in its recovery. Barthes makes this clear in *Camera Lucida*: 'I like certain features which, in a writer's life, delight me as much as certain photographs; I have called these features "biographemes"; Photography has the same relation to History that the biographeme has to biography.'[45] Like the photograph of his mother so beautifully described later in that text, the biographeme is all that endures once a life has run its course: those moments that can be stilled, pictured – a bloated eunuch in a prison cell, a man dead among his flowerpots, a white muff worn on a night in 1768. What is modestly adumbrated here is a revaluation of biography, a new form of its writing which does not lie against time but accepts its conditions in a spirit of melancholy defiance. Where the death of the author had addressed itself to the timeless 'Author-God', the return of the biographical author is a return to transcience, mortality.

Following upon *S/Z*, which sought to work through and beyond structuralist categories, *Sade Fourier Loyola* makes the decisive break with the scientism Barthes practised in the 1960s, and along with *The Pleasure of the Text* makes a theoretical clearing for *Roland Barthes by Roland Barthes*, *A Lover's Discourse* and *Camera Lucida*.[46] A reworked conception of the author is the first move in this direction. To reintroduce the author and the author's life is to create a thaw in the cold dream of structuralist objectivity. Indeed, as the eudaemonist aesthetic comes to supplant the structural categories, the cohabitance of author and reader in the text becomes not only part of the text's pleasure but its 'index':

> Nothing is more depressing than to imagine the Text as an intellectual object (for reflection, analysis, comparison, mirroring, etc.). The text is an object of pleasure. The bliss of the text is often only stylistic: there are expressive felicities, and neither Sade nor Fourier lacks them. However, at times the pleasure of the text is achieved more deeply (and then is when we can truly say there is a Text): whenever the 'literary' Text (the Book) transmigrates into our life, whenever another writing (the Other's writing) succeeds in writing fragments of our own daily lives, in short, whenever a *co-existence* occurs. The index of the pleasure of the text, then, is when we are able to live with Fourier, with Sade. To live with an author does not necessarily mean to achieve in our life the program that the author has traced in his books ... to live with Sade is, at times, to speak Sadian, to live with Fourier is to speak in Fourier ... (7–8)

Much indeed is staked on the return of the author to this stage. With the founder of language, the acceptance of the author's life and corpus, 'The Death of the Author' seems almost to belong to a different era. Yet, of course, it does not. In many respects they are contemporaries.[47] It is perhaps because of the disruptions that these two texts work upon each other that they rarely if ever meet in readings of Barthes. Little in fact tends to be written about *Sade Fourier Loyola*. Commentators have generally been happy to move from *S/Z* to *The Pleasure of the Text*, thereby sidestepping the reopening of the authorship question that this text beseeches. Few, if any, of Barthes's critics will simultaneously countenance 'The Death of the Author' and *Sade Fourier Loyola* for to do so would seem to risk running into aporia or incoherence.[48] There is an unwillingness here to accept the very antilogism that is so lauded in Barthes, an unwillingness to relinquish the idea of order in his discourse. A discourse which, let it be remembered, could quite conceivably be grounded in uncertainty, in the confusion of a mind before the contradictory possibilities that its unbridled intelligence has opened up. Little heed is thus taken of that maxim of André Gide's which Barthes claimed has governed his own writing life – 'incoherence is preferable to a distorting order'.[49] There is, though, one very important sense in which the logothetic description is faithful to everything Barthes has written, a sense in which we might discover what is meant by the death of the author and his precipitous return.

MIMESIS AND THE AUTHOR

Barthes allows the logothetes privileges that extent far beyond those granted the author in traditional man-and-the-work criticism. What Barthes will not allow to his founders, however, is any representational significance in their discourses, any content: Sade without evil, Fourier without socialism, Loyola without God, these are the postulates upon which the study commences. In this we might find an explanation of Barthes's seemingly insurmountable inconsistencies on the author-question. Why is it that he will allow full authorial rights to some authors – a class to which belong, beyond the logothetes, Michelet, Proust, Bataille, Sollers and so on – and deny them to others, most notably Balzac? Why is it that Barthes can disparagingly write 'The *author* still reigns in histories of literature, biographies of writers, interviews, magazines',[50] and yet praise Painter's biography of Proust saying, 'I was very impressed by his Proust because Painter was the first to rehabilitate a real interest in the private life of Proust himself and no longer simply in the characters of his novel'?[51] Of Sade, Barthes writes:

> Although every creation is of necessity combinative, society, by virtue of the old romantic myth of 'inspiration', cannot stand being told so. Yet this is what Sade has done: he has opened up and revealed his work (his 'world') like the interior of a language ... [O]n every page of his work, Sade provides us with evidence of concerted 'irrealism' ... Being a writer and not a realistic author, Sade always chooses the discourse over the referent; he always sides with semiosis rather than

mimesis: what he 'represents' is constantly being deformed by the meaning, and it is on the level of the meaning, not of the referent that we should read him. (36–7)

And in the 'Preface' it is underlined that 'if Sade, Fourier, and Loyola are founders of a language, and only that, it is precisely in order to say nothing, to observe a vacancy (if they wanted to say *something*, linguistic language, the language of communication and philosophy, would suffice: they could be *summarised*, which is not the case with any one of them).' (6) Barthes, here as everywhere, is denying the reduction of language to any representational aesthetic. In *Criticism and Truth*, in 'The Death of the Author', in *S/Z* too, indeed whenever the removal, death or diminution of the author was called for, the disavowal of an instrumentalist conception of language was not far behind. Nor is this unique to Barthes. Anti-authorialism has always found itself in complicity with anti-representational poetics. The Russian Formalists and New Critics saw the removal of the author as part of the process which disemburdened literature of any dependence on extra-textual contexts, whilst in the structuralist movement this is taken to the further stage of seeing language as constitutive of both the 'reality' the text feigns to represent and the authorial subject who purports to be its source. Recently, too, in the poststructural phase of its development, feminist criticism has come to bracket together *auteurist* and representational aesthetics. Both the concept of the author, and that of a reality onto which textual language passively opens, are seen to be the products of a patriarchal politics of representation. At the centre of humanist criticism, Toril Moi writes,

> is the seamlessly unified self – either individual or collective – which is commonly called 'Man' ... In this humanist ideology the self is the sole author of history and of the literary text: the humanist creator is potent, phallic and male – God in relation to his world, the author in relation to his text. History or the text become nothing but the 'expression' of this unique individual: all art becomes autobiography, a mere window onto the self and the world, with no reality of its own.[52]

The ideologies of authorship and representation mutually reinforce one another, and in order to put an end to this mystified conception of language, Moi says, 'we must take the further step and proclaim ... the death of the author'.[53] From such a point of view, then, within 'subject of representation', the genitive is thought to be double: both the representing subject and the subject represented are to be detached from the plane of poststructural analysis so as to focus upon the reality of text and language. Such is also the basis of contemporary Marxist objections to the author, as too of many strands of deconstruction which maintain that extratextual realities such as 'author' and 'world' are miasmas generated by textual rhetorics. However, despite this common closure being a dominant theme in literary theory, the reasons why the author should be inextricably caught up in the demise of representation are rarely stated explicitly.

The concept of the author is by no means static or immutable. History provides ample evidence of changing attitudes to authorship from second-century BC. Alexandria through the exegeses of the Early Church Fathers to Medieval times.[54] Likewise, the role of the author varies from one aesthetic milieu to another. Within an era in which representational modes are in the ascendant, the author is called upon to perform certain specific functions. A text viewed as the achievement of a particular representational aim is necessarily tethered to its author in that it must pass through his figure to be referred to its alleged objects. A scene of representation is thus predicated of the text which becomes its adjunct and often the model by means of which commentary or explication is judged to have succeeded or failed in its operations. Thus *Oliver Twist* is referred to the Poor Laws, *Bleak House* to Chancery, a model of intention is extracted from Dickens's life, his activities in the law are researched and conjectures are made as to his state of mind at the time of writing. In this way, criticism is forced to be perpetually lagging behind the designs and dictates of the author whilst the work's language is seen as the simple means towards a referential end. Language is thereby devalued to the status of an instrument, a passive, mediative phenomenon which has no part to play in the construction of this anterior realm of reality-as-given.

Correspondingly, the break with the author effects a severance of the text from its putative referential obligations, and allows language to become the primary point of departure and return for textual apprehension and analysis. No longer reduced to a unilateral system of conformities with the 'world', no longer reduced to a 'single message', the text is opened to an unlimited variety of interpretations. It becomes, in short, irresponsible, a ceaseless braiding of differences in which any sense of 'the truth of the text', its original meaning in the world, is overrun by untrammeled significative possibilities. This is the message – indeed the 'single message' – of 'The Death of the Author'. To wit, that the abolition of the author is the necessary and sufficient step to bring about the end of a representational view of language, for it is only through the function of the author as the possessor of meaning that textual language is made obeisant to an extratextual reality. Barthes states this quite dramatically in *S/Z* under the rubric of 'The Mastery of Meaning':

The *author* is always supposed to go from signified to signifier, from content to form, from idea to text, from passion to expression; and, in contrast, the *critic* goes in the other direction, works back from signifiers to signified. The *mastery of meaning*, a veritable semiurgism, is a divine attribute, once this meaning is defined as the discharge, the emanation, the spiritual effluvium overflowing from the signified toward the signifier: the *author* is a god (his place of origin is the signified); as for the critic, he is the priest whose task is to decipher the Writing of the god.[55]

This nicely describes the futile shuttling between author and critic, encoder and decoder, when it operates in this rudimentary manner. But here, as in other instances, he must overstate his case, and, again, theological overtones supervene upon the author question. The acme of representation, the ideal of verisimilitude hearkened towards by the proponents of 'pure realism', casts the author in a role far removed from that of a textual divinity. As we have said, mimeticist criticism must pass through the figure of the author in order to arrive at the objects of representation, yet, in a purely mimeticist view, these objects are sufficient to themselves: the author is merely the conduit or point of passage in this procedure, that neutral 'someone' who records and observes without subjective biases or predilections of any kind. Marks of intention and desire will perforce taint this process which aspires to a state of pure immediacy, perfect translation, to the realisation of a language which acts innocently as a window onto the world. Authorial presence here constitutes a transgression, it can only cast a shadow on the text of *vraisemblable*, can only colour the window through which the reader looks. The purely mimeticist text could certainly do without the author; indeed its greatest good might be something like the self-effacement of the author in the act of writing. Witness Emile Zola formulating the theory of pure realism:

> The novelist is but a recorder who is forbidden to judge and to conclude. The strict role of a savant is to expose the facts, to go to the end of analysis without venturing into synthesis; the facts are thus: experiment tried in such and such conditions gives such and such results; and he stops there; for if he wishes to go beyond the phenomena he will enter into hypothesis; we shall have probabilities, not science ... the novelist should keep equally to known facts, to the scrupulous study of nature, if he does not wish to stray among lying conclusions. He himself disappears, he keeps his emotion well in hand, he simply shows what he has seen ... a novelist who feels the need of becoming indignant with vice, or applauding virtue, not only spoils the data he produces, for his intervention is as trying as it is useless, but the work

loses its strength; it is no longer a marble page, hewn from the block of reality; it is matter worked up, kneaded by the emotions of the author, and such emotions are always subject to prejudices and errors.[56]

Indeed realist theory only comes to assign a significant role to the author when it has drifted from the ideal of pure mimesis, as the represented field opens to admit the moods, personality and experiences of the author as a subjective being. Nor, indeed, is it difficult to imagine arguments to the effect that the decline of representation opens a space of greater authorial creativity as the writer becomes less and less bound to the objects of representation. We are, after all, more inclined to see creativity in a Picasso than in a Turner. Descriptive language, as Barthes is quick to point out, is an obstacle to creativity. Sade read for 'contents' becomes 'tedious' or 'abominable'. We could also, with little effort, imagine Barthes arguing for subjectivity against objective realism, arguing, that is, for the author against the kind of authorial abnegation promoted by Zola.[57]

It is not meant to suggest here that the concept of the author does not endorse a representationalist view of the text. What is clear, however, is that the author is not the *cause* of a representational apprehension of literature – this cause is, at risk of sounding imbecilic, an instrumentalist conception of language. Rather the authorial role is mediative in this process, that of a bridge or portal between text and world. Quite apart from being the God who dwells in the signified, the author is merely the *agent of verisimilitude*. This should give some pause to those – Barthes is by no means alone here – who would justify the death of the author in terms of the closure of representation. Given the secondariness of the author in this referential process, might not the proposition be reversed? Might not it be claimed, *a fortiori*, that the abandonment of a representationalist aesthetic renders the death of the author needless? Or, to put it another way, that the concept of the author exceeds the functions given within a representationalist aesthetic? Certainly, this would seem to be part of the meaning of the death and return of the author in Barthes's work. As we know, the deconstruction of verisimilitude continues long after the return of the author has been announced, author and Text being no longer set in opposition to one another. Moreover, the authors of texts which make no claim to a representational 'truth' – Mallarmé, Sollers, Bataille, Robbe-Grillet, and so on – are accepted without reserve. Their work is seen as the product of an intention to create the discontinuous, a-referential, pluralistic text. While Barthes will berate recourse to the intentions of a Balzac, he will accept the intentions of others while they are directed toward the creation of non-naturalistic modes of writing:

one can according to one's mood read Sade, Proust, by 'skipping', according to the moment, this or that of their languages … the plural of the text is based on the multiplicity of the codes, but it is ultimately achieved by the ease with which the reader can 'ignore' certain pages, this ignoring somehow being prepared for and legalised beforehand by the author himself who has taken pains to produce a *perforated* text so that anyone 'skipping' the Sadian dissertations will stay within the truth of the Sadian text. (135)

The dangers of intention are not intrinsic but in its objects. The text in which Barthes realised that the idea of the author is not a bane in itself is also the text in which the deconstruction of *vraisemblable* reaches its apogee. It is for this reason that *S/Z* is the text of the death and the return of the author.

'The Death of the Author', as we have remarked, was the early programme of *S/Z*. Indeed it might have been called 'The Death of Balzac' or 'The Death of the Realist Author'. In *S/Z*, the death of the author consists in reading against Balzac's intention to foist the illusion of the real upon the baroque and abyssal tale of the castrato and the sculptor. To this end, Barthes uses the considerable powers at his disposal to denature and denude 'Sarrasine', to unveil all the artifices and ruses through which it lies its way to 'naturalness'. Much has been written about the strategies Barthes deploys in this reading, and he is often called to account for the vagueness of the distinction between the readerly and the writerly, the lack of specificity in his articulation of the five codes, their overlapping, inexhaustiveness, and so on. But such criticisms are for most part cavils. That *S/Z* is a successful reading is borne out by the fact that it is impossible to read 'Sarrasine' innocently after Barthes. We might read Jacques Lacan's 'Seminar on "The Purloined Letter"', and admire its thesis (or, for that matter, Derrida and Barbara Johnson in reply to Lacan), but it is not difficult thereafter to approach Poe's tale from a non-psychoanalytic purview, Lacanian or otherwise.[58] With *S/Z*, however, Barthes justifies his opening hyperbole: 'We shall therefore star the text, separating, in the manner of a minor earthquake, the blocks of signification of which reading grasps only the smooth surface, imperceptibly soldered by the movement of sentences, the flowing discourse of narration, the "naturalness" of ordinary language.'[59]

Unlike any other of Barthes's texts, *S/Z* works accretively: it is a war of attrition against the 'reality effect' in 'Sarrasine'. It is perhaps because of this inexorable forward momentum that commentary on *S/Z* rarely rises above the level of merely 'adding pitiful graffiti to an immense poem'.[60] The best commentary on *S/Z* would indeed be its reproduction; it belongs to that class of writing that precludes any sort of faithful summary. What is interesting from our point of view, however, is that *S/Z* conjoins the two enduring principles of 'The Death of the Author', these being the refusal of an instrumentalist conception of language, and the promise of the 'birth of the reader', though it does so with unexpected results.

As Barthes journeys through 'Sarrasine' exposing the devices and conventions and the vast network of cultural assumptions that underpin and generate the 'naturalness' of Balzac's tale, he reveals that what calls itself the classic or readerly is a writerliness that dare not speak its name. What is also revealed here is that in removing 'Sarrasine' from its scene of representation and in lodging it in the realm of the 'already written', Barthes is, as he pledged, producing the text, rewriting it, so to speak, before Balzac, before the dead hand of the author began to overlay its narrative structures with a seemingly innocent rhetoric of naturalism. The deconstruction of representation and the birth of the reader thus run concurrently. What is retrieved from the real is rendered unto the reader; as the reading grows, representation recedes. And when Barthes has come as far as he can toward demonstrating that 'it is no longer possible to *represent*, to make things *representative*',[61] when he has come as close as anyone has to fulfilling the promise of the birth of the reader that closes 'The Death of the Author', we might be forgiven for anticipating the triumphal declaration of the death of the author as achieved both in theory and in practice.

Yet, this is precisely what does not occur. As with other mythical sacrifices, resurrection and rebirth are not long in coming. When a text no longer speaks the language of representation, the death of the author becomes gratuitous. This is why the death of the author need never be raised in connection with writerly texts, why Barthes does not explain what purpose authorial extirpation might serve in the cases of Genet, the later Joyce, Proust, Bataille and others. This is why, too, *Sade Fourier Loyola* can attempt to 'release Sade, Fourier, and Loyola from their bonds (religion, utopia, sadism)',(9) and talk about the return of the author in the same breath; why Sade, 'a writer and not a realistic author', Sade who 'always sides with *semiosis* rather than *mimesis*' is such an exemplary figure in the renewal of the author. If a text has been 'unglued' of its referentiality, its author need not die; to the contrary, he can flourish, become an object of biographical pleasure, perhaps even a 'founder of language'.

What Roland Barthes has been talking of all along is not the death of the author, but the closure of representation. We need not be surprised, then, that 'The Death of the Author' belongs to the earliest stages of *S/Z*. Nor that it is at the end of *S/Z* – when Barthes has amassed 210 pages and 89 divagations devoted to returning the readerly to the writerly, the real to the irreal – that the return of the author is announced. When the scene of representation has dissolved around him, Balzac can come back, an author of texts, no longer a scribe of reality; his work no more 'a channel of expression' but a 'writing without referent'.[62] It is for this reason that the death of the author and the annunciation of his return can occur in such perversely close proximity. With representation annulled, the crimes of the author are absolved, and even the arch-realist Honoré Balzac can receive a stay of execution. Barthes recognised as much over the course of a 'two-year seminar ... at the École pratique des Hautes Études',[63] a seminar that is itself the time of the death of the author, the interregnum between *S/Z* as work-in-progress and realised project; the time spanning divagation 74 ('The Mastery of Meaning'), and divagation 90 ('The Balzacian Text'), a mere moment.

Some forty years prior to Barthes's work of this period, the Russian theorist Mikhail Bakhtin clearly saw the need to oppose mimetic and univocal conceptions of the text. For Bakhtin, the traditional idea of authorship was entirely inapposite to the work of proto-modernistic writers such as Rabelais, Swift and Dostoevsky, whose novels he characterised as polyphonic, that is, works in which the authorial voice does not dominate other textual voices. Contrasting such texts to the monologic voice to be found in traditional and epic forms, Bakhtin believed that this multivalent or carnivalesque countertradition – which he terms Menippean – reflects a dissolution of hierarchies and the emergence of an anti-authoritarian discourse. Bakhtin was not, however, led therefrom to proclaim the death of the author, but instead reconceived the idea and function of the author in accordance with the modalities and structures of the polyphonic novel.

The author in this mode of writing was not to be conceived as a transcendent, annunciative being, but rather as that voice amongst the many which holds together the polyphonic strands of the text's composition, an author who 'resides within the controlling center constituted by the intersection of the surfaces'.[64] Nor either is the carnivalesque author in any way estranged from the workings of his text. Bakhtin's position, as he says, 'is not at all tantamount to asserting a kind of passivity on the part of the author'. To the contrary, within this Menippean literature, the 'author is profoundly active but this action takes on a specific dialogic character'.[65] The author does not need to be the God of epic monologism to be an author. Dostoevsky, he says, 'creates not voiceless slaves (as does Zeus), but rather free people who are capable of standing beside their creator, of disagreeing with him, and even of rebelling against him.'[66] The renunciation of the author-God does not do away with the idea of authorship, nor impede the creativity of the author and the intensity of his engagement with and within his text. Working with a distinction between types of literature which prefigures Barthes's delineation of the *lisible* and *scriptible*, Bakhtin thereby showed how the concept of the author can be renewed without compromising the anti-representational ethos of a writerly writing.

A similar path was struck out upon by Julia Kristeva who provided psychoanalytic frames for the historical bifurcation of literature into readerly and writerly modes.[67] Adapting Lacanian insight to Bakhtin's distinction between monologic and polyphonic literature, Kristeva delineates two orders of signification, the semiotic and symbolic. The semiotic is governed by the maternal influence at the pre-Oedipal stage and is characterised by the use of words not for their meaning or what they represent but for their rhythm, intonation, musicality. Semiotic language thus arises from a maelstrom of irrational signification to which Kristeva gives the Greek term *chora*. The symbolic language, on the other hand, is the linear, syntactic and representational discourse of socially constituted reality acquired during the abatement of the Oedipus complex. For Kristeva, the way in which the subject negotiates the Oedipal phase and the manner of its language acquisition determines which of these two modes of signification (or in her word *signifiance*) will characterise its discourse and the type of subject position subsequently adopted in relation to textuality. Where identification has entirely abandoned the semiotic flux of the maternal language in favour of the rational linearity of the symbolic order, the writer will take up the position of the epic author or unitary, self-present subject, whilst the writer who has retained a strong connection with the maternal *chora* will achieve a fluid and motile insertion in his or her texts.

Along lines parallel to those laid down by Bakhtin, Kristeva sees this demarcation emerge historically in epic modes of writing which presuppose a thetic, unitary consciousness expressing the logics of law and (symbolic) order, and in the sporadic irruption of a (semiotic) avant-garde writerliness which subverts the syntagmatic, meaningful plane of language via abrupt dislocations of syntax and literal meaning. This subversive tradition is best exemplified in Bakhtin's polyphonic novelist and in the modern semioclasty of Mallarmé, Lautréamont, Joyce and Artaud, all of whom have managed to recapture the musical, Dionysian illogicalities of language. Such writers take up the position of the 'subject in process', a subject unstable within the order of discourse but consequently free to change, to insert itself within textuality without acquiring the transcendental solitude of the epic author. For Kristeva, as for Bakhtin, this carnivalesque subject acquires revolutionary potentialities within discourse precisely because of its motility, its ability to take up new and transgressive subject positions.

Whilst neither Kristeva nor Bakhtin forwarded an exhaustive rewriting of the concept of authorship, they evolved a sense of the author which kept pace with a changing literary situation, thus admitting the crucial principle that author-text relationships are subject to variations both historical and structural. Moreover, in opposing both humanist and representationalist views of the text and at the same time allowing for the insertion of the subject within discourse, their work does not conflate the *methodological* project of foregrounding language with the *ontological* statement of the absence of the author from discourse. For the structuralists, and for the Barthes of this period however, the removal of the subject began as a means toward language and ended as its end. The dream of structuralism was to say 'this is what the world and its language are like' when all it had permitted itself to venture was 'this is what the world and its language would be like if there were not subjectivity'.[68] And in attempting – at the bridge of structuralism and poststructuralism – to dignify this exclusion, to confirm and justify it as a necessary absence which inheres in the world and the text, Barthes could find no path upon which to strike out. How indeed could the removal of the author function as anything other than a provisional reduction? How could it be asserted other than in the manner that a speculative science prescribes only what is true and not true *of itself*?[69]

The Russian Formalists likewise forbade recourse to the author in the interests of founding a science of literature which rejected the mimeticist view of language. By this exclusion they hoped to disemburden the text and criticism of the text of any answerability to 'contents', of any obligations to the aesthetics of representation. However, the further they progressed in the direction of a non-representational theory and criticism, the more they came to find that their researches put the validity, and even the efficacy of authorial exclusion under question. Thus, in time, the Russian Formalists were to seek ways of reinscribing the author without default on their commitment to the autonomy of literary language, a process which was continued by Bakhtin in the latter stages of that movement. What the Formalists came to realise – as Barthes did somewhat belatedly – is that the closure of representation neither necessitates the exclusion of the author, nor can be achieved on its basis. The removal of the author opens a provisional space wherein the methodology can be developed, but once the methodology has been established, it must either return to take stock of that which it has excluded, make reparations, revisions, or continue to neglect the question of the author at the cost of remaining regional, selective, inadequate to the literary object.

The representational aesthetic has been under attack at least since the time of Mallarmé, and the more radical critical schools to appear during this century, those of the Russian Formalists, the Anglo-American New Critics, the structuralists and deconstructionists, have – to greater and lesser degrees – rejected mimesis in favour of textual language in and for itself. Indeed, it would not be the boldest stroke to suggest that we have entered a postrepresentational era: certainly, in any case, no-one any longer takes seriously the ideal of pure realism. Correspondingly modernist and postmodernist fiction has moved further and further from representationalist modes.[70] The theoretical recognition of this development has not only proceeded on the high roads of structuralism and poststructuralism, but is also to be found in the quieter work of conventional aestheticians. John Hospers' *Meaning and Truth in the Arts* is as good a guide as any to the inherent contradictions in the doctrine of representation.[71] The decline of representation has been signalled also in the reworkings to which Marxist critical theory has been subject in the last quarter-century. Having moved beyond Lukács's reflection model, Marxist thought has come to assert that language is not so much expressive as constitutive of social and cultural realities, a position which maintains the text's interaction with its historical and infrastructural conditions whilst avoiding the corollary obligation to discover the principles of that interaction in the supposedly representational function of textual language. The later work of Michel Foucault is also of the greatest significance in the quest for non-representational structures by which textuality can be related to the social and ideological ground of its determination. With Jacques Derrida and Paul de Man the denial of representation takes the form of a thoroughgoing epistemological scepticism which relentlessly questions the basis and validity of imputing any properties of presence or re-presentation to textuality.

Barthes began his career by radically redefining the Marxist relation to textuality, and the work of recent Marxist revisionists can be retraced to *Writing Degree Zero*, as to the moment at which language rather than its objects was introduced as the determining factor in a literary text's engagement with the social and historical conditions of its emergence. Later in his career, Barthes's lifelong hostility to representation began to ally itself cursorily with the conclusions reached by Derrida and de Man, yet the reasons for Barthes's espousal of a language of pure differences could scarcely themselves be more different. As we have seen, Barthes's concerns are far from epistemological; if anything, his objection to representation is moralistic. That is to say, that what he spent a writing life challenging is what we might call the ethics of representation, the ways in which a society transforms culture into nature and thereby stamps its products with the seal of authenticity. Accordingly, he works to expose the concealed mechanisms by which representational ethos imposes itself, to dissipate *vraisemblable*, rather than to subject the philosophy of language underpinning such an aesthetic to rigorous scrutiny. This is the burden, too, of texts which have not concerned us here, *Mythologies* in particular. Advance pointing to your mask (*larvatus prodeo*), this is all Barthes finally asks of any system, any work of art or literature, and it is for this reason that his labours are finally more disentropic than iconoclastic.

In *On Racine* he had looked to criticism of the author, and had disputed its validity not on the grounds that the author was dead or irrelevant to criticism, but in point of its dishonesty in concealing the essentially subjective nature of such an activity. Author-centred criticism, he concluded, was as admissible as any other form of criticism provided that it no longer contorted in empty posturings of self-justification, so long as it became 'the mask of several living obsessions'.[72] In a way, the return of the author traces such an itinerary, a movement toward a freer, more figurative reading practice in which the former categories of consciousness, narrative, imagination and the real are displaced by the body, the fragment, the imaginary and the irreal, in which criticism of the author no longer foists the illusion of the natural upon itself and its readers. Like Bakhtin before him, Barthes's return of the author takes the form of a certain rewriting of our conceptions of authorship, but one which does not prescribe what can and cannot be said about the author, but rather calls into question the manner of our saying. Hence the return of the author can be a return to the cardinal points of *auteurist* criticism – creativity in language, the author's life and work. And Barthes was to submit the autobiographical to this revaluation as the birth of the reader and the *return* of the author came to find themselves in yet further complicity.

AUTOBIOGRAPHIES

…today the subject apprehends himself elsewhere, and 'subjectivity' can return at another place on the spiral: deconstructed, taken apart, shifted, without anchorage: why should I not speak of 'myself' since this 'my' is no longer 'the self'?

                                                    Roland Barthes[73]

In the parable 'Borges and I', Jorge Luis Borges describes a division between person and author, private and public self. The tale is ostensibly told from the point of view of the 'I' of its title, the everyday, empirical self, he who will 'walk through the streets of Buenos Aires and stop for a moment, perhaps mechanically now, to look at the arch of an entrance hall and the grillwork on the gate.'[74] This narrator regards Borges as the 'other one', the one who exists 'on a list of professors or in a biographical dictionary'.[75] He confesses that he lives 'only so Borges may contrive his literature'.[76] The parable ends as though these two aspects of the self, at once so near and so alien to one another, have finally come together: 'Years ago I tried to free myself from him and went from the mythologies of the suburbs to the games with time and infinity, but those games belong to Borges now and I shall have to imagine other things. Thus my life is a flight and I lose everything and everything belongs to oblivion or to him. I do not know which of us has written this page.'[77] And this ending contains a further twist. Perhaps, as with 'the games with time and infinity', Borges has wrested from the narrator the last of his belongings, the very voice of his autumnal lament, as 'Borges and I' becomes yet another work of the author, Jorge Luis Borges.

All this takes place over the course of a single page. *Roland Barthes by Roland Barthes* – the first of the trilogy of autobiographical works produced by Barthes in the late 1970s – signals a similar division in its title, and strives to maintain it over 188 pages. There is the Barthes who will 'eat a plum, take a piss', there is the 'R.B.', the 'he', and the 'I'. Much is made of these four selves, but in essence *Roland Barthes by Roland Barthes* is the book of the two subjects of its title – the Roland Barthes who is writing, and the Roland Barthes who is written about. Throughout, Barthes takes great pains to prevent the writer of the autobiography from merging with his subject/object:

> 'I had no other solution other than to *rewrite* myself – at a distance – a great distance, here and now ... Far from reaching the core of the matter, I remain on the surface, for this time it is a matter of 'myself' (of the Ego); reaching the core, depth, profundity, belongs to others. (142)

In insisting upon, in cultivating this dehiscence, *Roland Barthes* would seem to be breaking the timehonoured autobiographical contract – that the self writing and the self written on should be one and the same self. This has led many to see *Roland Barthes* as 'pseudo-autobiography', or as announcing the end of autobiography. The fragment, 'The Natural', relays this troublesome divergence of subjects as well as any other:

> The illusion of the natural is constantly denounced ...
>
> We might see the origin of such a critique in the minority situation of R.B. himself; he has always belonged to some minority, to some

margin – of society, of language, of desire, of profession, and even of religion ... who does not feel how natural it is, in France, to be Catholic, married, and properly accredited with the right degrees?

... Against this '*natural*', I can rebel in two ways: by arguing, like a jurist, against a law elaborated without me and against me ... or by wrecking the majority's Law by a transgressive avant-garde action. But he seems to remain strangely at the intersection of these two rejections: he has complicities of transgressive and individualist moods. This produces a philosophy of the anti-Nature which remains rational, and the *Sign* is an ideal object for such a philosophy: for it is possible to denounce and/or celebrate its arbitrariness; it is possible to enjoy the codes even while nostalgically imagining that someday they will be abolished: like an intermittent *outsider*, I can enter into or emerge from the burdensome sociality, depending on my mood – of insertion or of distance. (130–1)

This passage certainly poses a problem of reading in that it would appear to posit a multiplicity of subjects. Yet, were we to substitute first person pronouns for the third person, and to convert reported speech into direct speech, the above fragment would read quite simply as an autobiographical meditation distinguished mainly by its author's acuity, and gift for self-analysis. It is, therefore, in its pronominal economy that *Roland Barthes* is most markedly set off from conventional forms of autobiography: 'The so-called personal pronouns: everything happens here, I am forever enclosed within the pronominal lists: "I" mobilise the image-repertoire, "you" and "he" mobilise paranoia.' (168) However, in subverting this autobiographical etiquette, *Roland Barthes* does not break with the deep structures of the autobiographical *récit*. Rather, it engages with them in a more direct manner than does the customary autobiographer. That the author of the autobiography and the subject of the autobiography should cleave from one another is inevitable. The author of an autobiography cannot plainly *be* the subject of his past. As Mikhail Bakhtin puts it:

Even if the author-creator had created the most perfect autobiography, or confession, he would, nonetheless have remained, in so far as he had produced it, outside of the universe represented within it. If I tell (orally or in writing) an event that I have just lived, in so far as *I am telling* (orally or in writing) this event, I find myself already outside of the time-space in which the event occurred. To identify oneself absolutely with oneself, to identify one's 'I' with the 'I' that I tell is as impossible as to lift oneself up by one's hair ... [78]

Even given an ideal autobiographical scenario – that of the author who is engaged in a continual and self-reflexive autobiographical writing, a perennial diarist whose only concern is with the act of diarising – there would always be a hiatus, both spatio-temporal and ontological between he who writes, and what is written. This division is inescapable. Obviously, this is not to say that there is no possibility of commerce between the two subjects – far from it – only that these two subjects cannot be regarded as consubstantial in space and time. Bakhtin is not the first to realise this, nor is Barthes the first to incorporate this problematic division into the actual act of writing an autobiography. The great autobiographers, Augustine, Montaigne, Rousseau, Voltaire, all took some account of this bifurcation. Montaigne writes:

> I cannot fix my subject ... I do not portray his being; I portray his passage; not a passage from one age to another or ... from seven years to seven years, but from day to day, from minute to minute. I must suit my story to the hour, for soon I may change, not only by chance but also by intention. It is a record of various and variable occurrences, an account of thoughts that are unsettled and, as chance will have it, at times contradictory, either because I am then another self, or because I approach my subject under different circumstances and with other considerations. Hence it is that I may well contradict myself, but the truth ... I do not contradict.[79]

In order to stay within the truth of self-writing, Montaigne must accept that the self written about is no longer present to the self writing. If we take account of the personal pronouns in this passage, it is quickly apparent that they twist between Montaigne the author, and Montaigne the subject of the autobiography. The only substantial difference between this operation and the pronominal extravagances of *Roland Barthes* is that Montaigne does not deem it necessary to telegraph this separation by substituting 'M.d.M.', or such like, for those personal pronouns that signify the Montaigne as theme of the Essays. That Montaigne then sought to bring these two subjects into a certain accord does not mean that he had become any less aware of their requisite divergence, no more than Augustine ever lost sight of the fact that the writer of the *Confessions* was not of one substance with the seventeen-year-old who entered the cauldron of Carthage.[80] But whilst Montaigne sought to think his way through this division, and Augustine contained it within a narratorial distance, Barthes directs all energies to maintaining this breach at the level of the utmost visibility. The fragments or (auto) biographemes are subjected to the strategy of alphabetical ordering, and the alphabetical sequence is syncopated so as to ward off the possibility of any unintentional narrative emerging from the concatenation of fragments. This regimen of randomness is programmed to prevent any naive identification of the Bartheses. Yet the text admits that this strategy is not successful:

> I have the illusion to suppose that by breaking up my discourse I cease to discourse in terms of the imaginary about myself, attenuating the risk of transcendence; but since the fragment ... is *finally* a rhetorical genre and since rhetoric is that layer of language which best presents itself to interpretation, by supposing I disperse myself I merely return, quite docilely, to the bed of the imaginary. (95)

It is only at the close of *Roland Barthes*, however, that Barthes's text can relax its vigilance, and allow its two subjects to converge. Like virtually all autobiographies, *Roland Barthes* offers a final and dwindling promise of assignation, much like the one intimated at the end of 'Borges and I'. Conventionally, as the tale's telling draws to a close, the past of the subject and the present of the writing draw ever closer, the text begins to talk of here, now, for the future. Yet this moment is always already in recession, the vanishing point at which the two subjects meet and as soon slip away, as in Proust's *Recherche* which closes as its writing begins. This is one convention that *Roland Barthes* cannot but affirm:

And afterward?

> – What to write now? Can you still write anything?

> – One writes with one's desire, and I am not through desiring. (188)

It is at this point, and only at this point, that we can confidently say that we do not know which subject has written this page, as it is, too, when Augustine commends himself to his Lord God at the end of the *Confessions*, or Stephen Dedalus journeys into the exile in which James Joyce was to write *A Portrait of the Artist as a Young Man*.[81]

This division of subjects does precisely the opposite of disqualifying *Roland Barthes* as autobiography. The only autobiographies that can elude this division are those that proceed according to the conviction that all time is everpresent.[82] 'What right', Barthes asks, 'does my present have to speak of my past?', (121), and answers this question at another point in the text via another question: 'why should I not speak of "myself" since this "my" is no longer "the self" '? (168) As with biography, as with the idea of the oeuvre, Barthes has no objection to autobiography when it is uprooted from its naturalistic setting, whilst it is accepted that the past subject of the text cannot be spirited *in all its reality* into the here and now of the text's composition. It is again the duplicities of representation that are put under question; in this case, the legerdemain by which the hand that writes seeks to efface itself in the interests of re-presenting the past as an immediate reality. To see the demise of autobiography in *Roland Barthes* is quite simply to affirm a greatly simplified conception of the autobiographical act, as though once the autobiographical becomes troublesome it disappears, as though when a genre or mode of writing advertises its inherent problematics it is thereby denying or destroying itself. The foregrounding of the artifice in *Tristam Shandy* did not lead Victor Shklovsky to infer the death of the novel, rather he proclaimed Sterne's work 'the most typical novel in world literature'.[83] Jacques Derrida warned against the tendency to confuse the complexities of autobiography with its 'impossibility' or 'death':

> the line that could separate an author's life from his work ... becomes unclear. Its mark becomes divided; its unity, its identity becomes dislocated. When this identity is dislocated, then the problem of the *autos*, of the autobiographical, has to be totally redistributed ... one has to ask whether one will understand the autobiographical in terms of this internal border ... or instead rely on the standard concepts prevailing throughout tradition. Once again, one is faced with a division of the *autos*, of the autobiographical, but this doesn't mean that one has to dissolve the value of the autobiographical *récit*. Rather, one must restructure it otherwise on the basis of a project that is also biographical or thanatographical.[84]

Derrida made these remarks at a 'Roundtable on Autobiography' following a paper he delivered on Nietzsche, and, indeed, it is unfortunate that neither he nor any other of the participants discussed Barthes's text here, since *Roland Barthes* would seem to match, point for point the revaluation outlined: the division of the *autos*, the redistribution of the autobiographical in terms of the biographical and thanatographical – '*I am speaking about myself as though I were more or less dead*' (168) – and the crosscutting of corpora, the body of work and body of the writer. Indeed, this text would seem to be leading the way in the theory of the autobiographical, since, in raising rather than seeking to solve the problems of self-life-writing, it allows those problems to emerge with clarity, a clarity which is not to be found in attempts to submit the autobiographical to rigid generic definitions, nor in the resistance of those who find the problems of the autobiographical so vertiginous that they are led to conclude that no such thing exists. And where Barthes will always be a little ahead of the pure theoreticians of autobiography is in producing a text which is at once a rigorous critique of the conventions and undergirding assumptions of autobiographical discourse, and itself an autobiography of peculiar economy and richness. Those who are interested will discover that Barthes has never read the Hegel to whom his theoretical discourse made recourse, that he likes salad, cinnamon, Glenn Gould, having loose change, walking in sandals, that he doesn't like white Pomeranians, women in slacks, Miro, tautologies, telephoning; that he had at one time intended to write books with the titles *The Discourse of Homosexuality*, *A Life of Illustrious Men*, *Incidents*; that, for him, there is never self-restoration only self-writing, that several episodes of pre-pubescent sexuality occurred in his garden at Bayonne, that he dreams of arising in the early morning. All this, and more, without ever, finally, writing *Roland Barthes par lui-même*.

Derrida might also have had *Roland Barthes* in mind when he wrote of the enigmatic and fluid boundary between the writer's life and work: 'This divisible borderline traverses two different "bodies", the corpus and the body, in accordance with laws we are only beginning to catch sight of.'[85] From the first written page of *Roland Barthes*, where it is said – 'you will find here, mingled with the "family romance", only the figurations of the body's prehistory – of that body making its way toward the labor and the pleasure of writing' – to the concluding 'Anatomie', the ideas of writing the body, and the body writing, dominate the discourse. However, somewhat typically, Barthes, refuses to clarify either what is meant or what is at issue here. The fragment 'Ellipsis' is both a beautifully direct and elliptical example of this:

> Someone questions him: 'You wrote somewhere that *writing proceeds through the body*': can you explain what you meant? He realises then how obscure such statements, clear as they are to him, must be for many others. Yet the phrase is anything but meaningless, merely elliptical: it is an ellipsis which is not supported. To which may be added here a less formal resistance: public opinion has a reduced conception of the body; it is always, apparently, what is opposed to the soul: any somewhat metonymic extension of the body is taboo. (80)

The idea of the body of the writer had been with Barthes from the outset. In *Writing Degree Zero* it is said that style is biological;[86] *Michelet* is concerned with the themes of body in the historian's work; in *Sade Fourier Loyola*, the oeuvre is seen as a body of pleasure, and the biographeme is likened to cremation ashes; in *The Pleasure of the Text*, textuality is seen as the site of an erotic communion of the bodies of reader and writer. Barthes is well aware that this theme varies dramatically from text to text, though this instability, he feels, is an index of its significance:

> In an author's lexicon, will there not always be a word-as-mana, a word whose ardent, complex, ineffable, and somehow sacred signification gives the illusion that by this word one might answer for everything? Such a word is neither eccentric nor central; it is motionless and

carried, floating, never *pigeonholed*, always atopic (escaping any topic), at once remainder and supplement, a signifier taking up the place of every signified. The word has gradually appeared in his work; at first it was masked by the instance of Truth (that of history), then by that of Validity (that of systems and structures); now it blossoms, it flourishes; this word-as-mana is the word 'body'. (129)

Yet no sooner does Barthes disallow the word any fixed meaning than he makes the most daringly constative claim on its behalf: 'How does the word become value? At the level of the body.' (130) Once again 'body' arises via an 'ellipsis which is not supported': once again Barthes cunningly tempts us to ask what the 'body' means or what it does in his discourse.

Barthes declares that the prime influence on (or 'intertext of') *Roland Barthes* is Nietzsche, and the most influential Nietzschean text will be *Ecce Homo* with which Barthes's autobiography has decidedly elective affinities.[87] *Ecce Homo*, as well as being a text which forces a serious generic revaluation of the autobiographical, is also the text in which Nietzsche repeatedly recapitulates his insistence on the biologistic, physiological basis of the drive to knowledge. For Nietzsche, the emphasis on the body is avowedly autobiographical, as it is with Barthes, but it is also firmly tied to a primary philosophical objective. Nietzsche utilised the theme of the body to conduct a biologistic challenge to Christian idealism which he characterised as a slave morality, a fettering of the strong in health by the weak via the institution of otherwordly, spiritual ideals. Part of the revaluation of all values, as Nietzsche conceived it, was to deconstruct the duality mind-body, to assert the biological as the source of all thought, of all values and judgements. In asserting the body as the source of value, in mooting (with *The Pleasure of the Text*) a 'materialist theory of the subject', Barthes would seem to be continuing this aspect of the Nietzschean revaluation.

Yet, even on this point, Barthes is thoroughly inconsistent. Within *The Pleasure of the Text*, he maintains the opposition between mind and body which no materialism can suffer: 'The pleasure of the text is that moment when my body pursues its own ideas – for my body does not have the same ideas I do',[88] an idea that is perpetuated in various ways in *Roland Barthes*. One of Barthes's commentators, Roland Champagne, suggests that the insistence upon the body is an attempt to reverse the traditional privileging of consciousness over unconscious determinations in literature, as indeed we might expect it to be.[89] However, again nothing is to be that simple, for, of all contemporary theorists, Barthes is peculiarly uninterested in the unconscious, his concerns being rather with the surface play of signification rather than the depths from which it may have emerged. Furthermore, the body in his works dictates conscious scenarios, the fantasy rather than the dream. Champagne, though, also says that 'Barthes came to realise that writing is an attempt by the writer to make his body perpetual in time', and this is far more persuasive, particularly since *Roland Barthes* is the epic fulfilment of *Sade Fourier Loyola*'s desire: 'were I a writer, and dead, how I would love it if my life, through the pains of some friendly and detached biographer, were to reduce itself to a few details, a few preferences, a few inflections, let us say: to "biographemes" whose distinction and mobility might go beyond any fate and come to touch, like Epicurean atoms, some future body, destined to the same dispersion.'[90]

We notice that the return of the author came to be associated with the mortality of the author, just as 'The Death of the Author' never took account of the author as anything other than a strange deist abstraction inimical to high post structuralism. In attempting to conjoin the body of writing to the body writing – 'The *corpus*: what a splendid idea! Provided one was willing to read *the body* in the corpus.' (161) – *Roland Barthes*, for an instant, brings together those parts of the author that are destined to the most irrevocable sundering. Yet sunder they will – for an author's corpus outlives his body and its corpse – as they did in the case of Roland Barthes. Were we friendly, detached and painstaking enough, and were we to have written a 'Life of Barthes', we might at some point have said:

> *His body*: subject of inscriptions, of desire, of discourse, 'mana-word'; this body expired a few weeks after being run down by a laundry truck on a pedestrian crossing outside the Sorbonne.

Barthes's corpus is as alive and as well as that of any post-war writer, as is his biography. The theorist of the author's death became a celebrity in France, an enthusiastic interviewee on television, the radio, for newspapers; he went on to write two confidently autobiographical works, texts which were not autobiographies but autobiographical, books of feeling, impressions, of the self; he talked, we know, of writing a novel, a 'Proustian novel'.[91] Upon his death he became the subject of many obituaries, most gracefully those written by Susan Sontag who described his later work as 'the most elegant, the most subtle and gallant of autobiographical projects'.[92] Sontag, too, who had twelve years earlier declared that 'only if the ideal of criticism is enlarged to take in a wide variety of discourse, both theoretical and descriptive, about culture, language and contemporary consciousness, can Barthes be plausibly called a critic.'[93] Balzac did not die as a result of *S/Z*. He is as alive now as he ever has been since his death in 1850, yet – through *S/Z* – the idea of the reader as producer of the text was born. Harold Bloom may or may not be right when he says that personality 'cannot be voided except by personality, it being an oddity (perhaps) that Eliot and Barthes matter as critics because they are indeed critical personalities',[94] just as Oscar Wilde may or may not have been right when he proposed that criticism is the only civilised form of autobiography.[95] Yet might we not venture that the birth of the reader is not achieved at the cost of the death of the author, but rather at that of showing how the critic too becomes an author?

2

The Author and the Death of Man

Critical positions which argue the irrelevance of the author will invariably propose determinist theories if they are concerned to discover alternative models of the constitution of discourse. The work of Michel Foucault is no exception. Within his prodigious text, *The Order of Things* (1966), Foucault attempts the formidable task of presenting a history of thought within which the role of individual thinkers over some four hundred and fifty years of discourse is entirely subordinate to impersonal forces.[1] The determinism that Foucault promulgates is, superficially at least, akin to Marxist critique in that it is periodised into self-regulating historical structures. The statements, the texts, the philosophical systems and sciences of any given era will obey a prediscursive network of coherencies and rules of formation which constitutes the most fundamental level of knowledge. The similarities which we perceive in the discourses of a particular era, and which we rather vaguely interpret as the spirit or common purpose of an age, are, for Foucault, emanations of a strict, rigid, epistemological substrate. This substrate is not to be confused with *zeitgeist* or *weltanschauung*, which are simply its visible emanations, in the form of the atmosphere in which thought is conducted, or the community of moral, ethical and metaphysical perspectives at a particular time. So far from being a paradigm that has been superimposed upon an era, or an analytic reduction of the mass of discourse, the epistemological arrangement is the ground and possibility of thought itself, the potency of which the discourse of the age is an actualisation. To this system of relations Foucault gave the name *episteme*; to the science of its recovery, 'archaeology'.

It is not the surface structures of history that are the object of archaeological research, but the epistemological foundations upon which the great spectacle of Western discourse has been constructed. At this level, the role of individual authors is no more than that of *epistemic* functionaries. Once again Foucault's approach shows affinities with Marxist critique in that it sees ideas as the product rather than the motivation for historical change. But whilst many Marxists allow for a certain interplay between impersonal forces and immanent subjectivity, Foucauldian archaeology presents the work of individual thinkers as entirely determined by the *epistemic* configuration. As Foucault writes of the Classical *episteme*:

> it was the sign system that linked all knowledge to a language, and sought to replace all languages with a system of artificial symbols and operations of a logical nature. At the level of the history of opinions, all this would appear, no doubt, as a tangled network of influences in which the individual parts played by Hobbes, Berkeley, Leibniz, Condillac, and the 'Ideologues' would be revealed. But if we question Classical thought at the level of what, archaeologically, made it possible, we perceive that the dissociation of the sign and resemblance in the early seventeenth century caused these new forms – probability, analysis, combination, and universal language system – to emerge, not as successive themes engendering one another or driving one another out, but as a single network of necessities. And it was this network that made possible the individuals we term Hobbes, Berkeley, Hume, or Condillac. (63)

Like Foucault's first work, *Madness and Civilization* (1961), *The Order of Things* accepts the conventional demarcation of post-Medieval history into the Renaissance, the Classical age, and the modern age.[2] Nor, of itself, is Foucault's determination of the essential structures of knowledge in these eras particularly radical. The Renaissance is seen to be constructed around the scholastic theory of resemblances; the Classical age around the theory of representation and the system of signs; the modern age to be compassed by the ethic of subjectivity. What distinguishes Foucault's treatment is the absolute and reciprocal impenetrability he assumes between these eras, his refusal of the possibility of any significant influence carrying over from one *episteme* to another. The *epistemi* are fully coherent within themselves, and yet entirely discontinuous with each other. The homogeneity of the *episteme* is therefore a factor of the heterogeneity of the *epistemi*, and vice versa. There can be no thought of man in the Classical era, as equally there can be no thought within the modern age which is not, at base, thinking of man.[3] Likewise, the *episteme* of the Renaissance is constituted by the impossibility of thinking within the categories of representation, just as the Classical era is formed by the complete disappearance of the theory of resemblances from its horizons.

Consequently, just as the *epistemic* arrangement exercises absolute determinative power during the era which it undergirds, so too, when it disappears, it disappears entirely, leaving no residue but the remotest nostalgia for a lost order. It is here that *The Order of Things* swerves signally from dialectical histories in that such models imply some conservation of the forms of the superseded era through the synthesis of its contradictions, or the negation of the negation. For Foucault, however, the hiatus is absolute, irresolvable, acausal. Each *episteme* is the complete cancellation of the previous *episteme*. This point is axial, and all the more so in that it forms the basis for *The Order of Things'* most audacious and most memorable proposition, that of the death of man.

On Foucault's account, man only came into being as the subject of knowledge in 1800, and this opening is marked by Kant who introduced the anthropological question to philosophical reflection.[4] However, the centrality accorded to man in the new arrangement of knowledge estab-lished not the unity of the subject but his division. Indeed this division arises as soon as the Kantian question 'What is man?' is asked, for both an interrogated and an interrogating subject are immediately and inherently posited. The subjects occupy, respectively, the roles of the empirical object of knowledge, and the elevated subject who is the house or the condition of possibility for that knowledge. Within the phrase 'subject of knowledge' the genitive is therefore double but contradictory such that man becomes 'a strange empirico-transcendental doublet... a being such that knowledge will be attained in him of what renders all knowledge possible'. (318)

This conflict between the transcendental and the intraworldly is also reflected in man's precarious relationship with the unthought, for the further modern consciousness has probed the underlying reality of things, the more it has unearthed of its other in the forms of the in-itself, social determinations, and the unconscious. Through its advances, the sovereign *cogito* serves to illumine ever greater reaches of the darkness within which it is engulfed.[5] As Foucault puts it, in a sublime formula: 'modern thought is advancing towards that region where man's Other must become the Same as himself'. (328) But Foucault does not actually argue the end of man on the basis of these intrinsic contradictions in the anthropological arrangement: rather such contradictions are held to be inaugurally consti-tutive of the era of man. The argument for the death of man is to proceed on quite different lines. Simple lines, which run as follows. If man was only constituted in 1800, if he is a 'recent invention' contemporaneous with the modern *episteme*, then (archaeologically) it must be that once the modern *episteme* is over, man will disappear every bit as surely as did the Classical theory of representation at the end of the eighteenth century. In the 'Preface' this is stated directly:

Strangely enough, man – the study of whom is supposed by the naive to be the oldest investigation since Socrates – is probably no more than a kind of rift in *The Order of Things*, or, in any case, a configuration whose outlines are determined by the new position he has so recently taken up in the field of knowledge. Whence all the chimeras of the new humanisms, all the facile solutions of an 'anthropology' understood as a universal reflection on man, half-empirical, half-philosophical. It is comforting, however, and a source of profound relief to think that man is only a recent invention, a figure not yet two centuries old, a new wrinkle in our knowledge, and that he will disappear again as soon as that knowledge has discovered a new form. (xxiii)

However, this proleptic summary fails to register the force of implication in Foucault's text, its consistently subtle and guarded hints that this disappearance is in the offing. Even as he writes, signs are abroad (the unification of language in structural analyses against its dispersion in subjectivity, together with more arcane portents such as the irruption of desire in discourse) that another *epistemic* cataclysm is brewing, that the ground is once more stirring under our feet. If this is so – and Foucault does everything to suggest that it is – then man will be lost to knowledge in a movement not only inevitable but expeditious. Indeed at one point the text is moved so far as to say that: 'It is no longer possible to think in our day other than in the void left by man's disappearance.' (342) The thought of the 1960s thus finds itself at the crossing, poised in prospect of the end of anthropocentrism and the beginning of a counterhumanist age. It is at this point that the story of *The Order of Things* ends, and its writing begins.

The idea of man as the author of his own works is hereby prey to a double assault. In the first place, the role of individuals in the production of discourse is considered negligible in respect of the immanent rules of formation which govern the parameters and systematicity of the entire archive of a given historical period. For the second, the recently constituted *episteme* in which man is figured as the subject of his knowledge, of his writing, of his actions and their history, is seen to be coming to a close: 'Man', conceived of as subject or object, is 'in the process of perishing'. (386) Our concern will be with these two deaths – those of author and man – and later with the question as to whether they are one and the same death. Initially, though, we will be concerned to follow the transindividual precept as it functions within *The Order of Things*, and then to chart a re-entry of the author into this text. Two archaeological operations involving the author are thereby postulated, those of exclusion and inclusion, operations which we will mark by the indices 'Descartes' and 'Nietzsche' respectively. We will also attempt to argue that these operations – in principle so different – work toward a common end.

COGITO AND THE BIRTH OF MAN

> Up to Merleau-Ponty there is almost no French philosopher of the modern period who was not, in the most fundamental sense, 'Cartesian'.
>
> James Edie[6]

> Discourse ... is so complex a reality that we not only can, but should, approach it at different levels and with different methods.
>
> Michel Foucault[7]

Upon publication of *The Order of Things*, one of its passages in particular attracted considerable attention, an attention certainly in excess of its content and, perhaps also, of the seriousness with which it was intended. 'At the deepest level of Western knowledge', Foucault wrote, 'Marxism introduced no real discontinuity ... Marxism exists in nineteenth-century thought like a fish in water; that is, it is unable to breathe anywhere else.' (261–2) Marxism, he continues, 'may have stirred up a few waves and caused a few surface ripples; but they are no more than storms in a children's paddling pool.' (262) These contentions swiftly met with ample and indignant redress from the French left, as, too, Hegel's absence from archaeology was contested by certain parties. Foucault's dismissive treatment of Descartes, too, has often been noted, but has yet to be subjected to serious scrutiny.

Approaching *The Order of Things*, a central text by a thinker who – in his opposition to the constitutive role of consciousness, to dualism, rationalism, the autonomy of the subject – is so manifestly anti-Cartesian, we might be forgiven for anticipating some declaration of the necessity of breaking with the Cartesian influence that has for so long held sway over French philosophy. But the idea of a continuous tradition of Western thought is precisely what *The Order of Things* is contracted to resist at every turn. Descartes is a figure constituted in the interstices of a specific configuration of knowledge, the Classical system of representation, and there can be no transposition of the ideas of the *Discourse on Method* or the *Meditations* into any era not governed by this arrangement. The philosophy of Descartes is separated from the modern *episteme* by an unbridgeable rift in *The Order of Things* which occurred at the beginning of the nineteenth century when Classical representation disintegrated allowing the anthropological era to commence. If the thought of *The Order of Things* is then anti-Cartesian, it is not so in the sense of discovering a form of thought which evades or challenges the Cartesian epistemology, but rather in that it denies that there is any such thing as an enduring Cartesianism at all. It is, we might say, 'aCartesian'.

Foucault does pay a certain tribute to Descartes, though strictly as his discourse flourished *in situ*. The criticism, in the *Regulae*, of the Renaissance theory of resemblances is seen as an important and exemplary moment in the transition to the Classical system of representations.[8] But Descartes' contribution to the Classical order itself is held to be of no especial significance: 'This new configuration may, I suppose, be called "rationalism"; one might say, if one's mind is filled with ready-made concepts, that the seventeenth century marks the disappearance of the old superstitious or magical beliefs and the entry of nature, at long last, into the scientific order.' (54) Two pages later Foucault writes: 'Under cover of the empty and obscurely incantatory phrases "Cartesian influence" or "Newtonian model", our historians of ideas are in the habit of ... defining Classical rationalism as the tendency to make nature mechanical and calculable.' (56) The Cartesian and Newtonian discourses, so far from being central to an understanding of the Classical science of order are rather considered to be obstacles to the study of this arrangement at its deepest level. Foucault then proceeds to depose Descartes and Newton at a single stroke. Mathematics and mechanics, it is argued, had little impact on Classical science of order. What is claimed, simply, is that since there are no traces of mathematicisation or mechanisation in the emergent empirical sciences of general grammar, natural history, and the analysis of wealth, and since these new discourses did reflect the science of order, then the mathematics and mechanics of Descartes and Newton are lateral and nugatory in respect of the fundamental structure of classical science.[9] Foucault's reasoning here is woefully exiguous, and it is easy to see how this syllogism could be reversed to declare the irrelevance of the new empiricisms.[10] Nonetheless this disengagement is achieved (however tardily) and Foucault develops his compelling analysis of the Classical Age untroubled by the Cartesian question.

As it would happen, it is only when Foucault comes to depict the modern era that the ghost of this repression comes to haunt *The Order of Things*. This may seem surprising in that archaeology canonically rejects the possibility of conceptual exchange between *epistemi*, and the more so since Descartes belongs to the earliest stages of the Classical period and is therefore as far removed from modernity as a Classical thinker might be. Yet while it is ambitious enough to disconnect Cartesianism from the founding of a Classical science of order, it is still more so to declare its irrelevance to the narrative that Foucault imposes upon the nineteenth and twentieth centuries. What does it mean, in a text concerned with the birth and death of the subject of knowledge to disregard the Cartesian *cogito*? To talk of man arriving – as sovereign and transcendental subject – *only* in 1800 and with the Kantian analytic? To disconnect the *cogito* from any ideas we might have had about man-as-subject?

Absent throughout the discussion of the Classical *episteme*, the *cogito* is at last brought forward as Foucault locates the place of the King, the enthronement of man as sovereign subject and spectator within the lacuna left by the breakdown of Classical representation. But brought forth not as that which lay dormant for one and a half centuries, not as a principle that might have guided Immanuel Kant in his search for the transcendental conditions of knowledge: rather, these two subjects, the Cartesian *cogito* and the Kantian transcendental ego, are to be regarded as radically other, formulations whose similarities are entirely superficial:

> Classical language, as the *common discourse* of representation and things, as the place within which nature and human nature intersect, absolutely excludes anything that could be a 'science of man'. As long as that language was spoken in Western culture it was not possible for human existence to be called in question on its own account, since it contained the nexus of representation and being. The discourse that, in the seventeenth century, provided the link between the 'I think' and the 'I am' was accomplished in the light of evidence, within a discourse whose whole domain and functioning consisted in articulating one upon the other what one represents to oneself and what is. It cannot therefore be objected to this transition either that being in general is not contained in thought, or that the singular being as designated by the 'I am' has not been interrogated or analysed on his own account. Or rather, these objections may well arise and command respect, but only on the basis of a discourse which is profoundly other, and which does not have for its *raison d'etre* the link between representation and being. (311–12)

Given the immense difficulties of perpetrating an absolute dissociation of the Cartesian *cogito* and the modern idea of the subject of knowledge, and given the haste with which this thesis is dispensed, Foucault writes with considerable felicity. His argument, too, is clear. 'I think' is equivalent to representation; 'I am', naturally, to being. In the Classical *episteme* representations were inseparable from 'the living, sharp, perceptible presence of what they represent', (262) the order of words was fully transparent to the order of things, the structures of perception one with the forms of their percepts. In linking the *cogito* to the *sum*, Descartes is doing no more than link that which the *historical a priori* of Classical thought had conjoined in advance and in anticipation of Descartes, and of his 'Second Meditation'. For Foucault's Kant, however, the situation was of a completely different order. The transcendental subject arose from the abrupt, profound and irrevocable divorce between representation and being, consciousness and its objects. Thus any judgement passed upon the *cogito* which assumes a hiatus between the representing subject and the alleged objects of its representation belongs to a Kantian or post-Kantian epistemology, and thus thoroughly contravenes the essential *epistemic* conditions of the *cogito*'s articulation. For we of the nineteenth and twentieth centuries, we who live far beyond the unity of representation and being, it is no longer possible to conceive or imaginatively recapture such an order. Kant's critique submitted what was unproblematically assumed in Cartesianism – that 'nature and human nature intersect' – to the most emphatic scepticism. For Descartes, for whom representation and being, nature and human nature, were one, problems of this order did not exist. Not, that is, until we turn to the pages in which the *cogito* was first constructed.

The pages that form Descartes' 'Second Meditation' are probably the most scrutinised of all philosophical demonstrations, and it is therefore very perplexing that Michel Foucault should work this particular interpretation upon them. Far from resting on the simple identity of representation and being, the formulation of the *cogito* begins from subjecting the assumption that the mind has any objects to represent to absolute scepticism:

> Everything I have accepted up to now as being absolutely true and assured, I have learned from or through the senses. But I have sometimes found that these senses played me false, and it is prudent never to trust entirely those who have once deceived us.[11]

Such a scepticism does not halt at questioning the existence of the exterior world but elicits doubt as to the existence of the subject who doubts. But this second phase of doubt, in many respects the more drastic of the two, is the more remediable within the Cartesian theory of knowledge. The evil demon, as we know so well, is eluded because his deceits can only take effect upon a being who is being deceived; even if I am deluded as to the existence of everything around me, and to the form, nature and quality of my own existence, I am nonetheless the being which subsists, suffers and affirms itself in its deluded sense of selfhood. As it is written:

> I had persuaded myself that there was nothing at all in the world: no sky no earth, no minds or bodies; was I not therefore, also persuaded that I did not exist? No indeed; I existed without doubt, by the fact

that I was persuaded, or indeed by the mere fact that I thought at all. But there is some deceiver both very powerful and very cunning, who constantly uses all his wiles to deceive me. There is therefore no doubt that I exist if he deceives me; and let him deceive me as much as he likes, he can never cause me to be nothing, so long as I think I am something. So that, after having thought carefully about it, and having scrupulously examined everything, one must then, in conclusion, take as assured that the proposition: *I am, I exist*, is necessarily true, every time I express it or conceive of it in my mind.[12]

Nothing, whatsoever, is herein presupposed of the connection between representation and being. What the conjunction of the 'I think' and the 'I am' attests is that existence can be validated in complete independence of the veracity or even the existence of any representations at all. Even if this world, these hands, these eyes, this chair-beside-the-fire in which I sit, are all void, *I* nonetheless, as thinking subject, exist. The *cogito* does not begin from the connection between representation and being, nor does it (of itself) link representation and being. For this immense – if not impossible – task, an agency vastly more powerful is summoned, and it is thus that the meditating subject proceeds to construct an ontological argument for the existence of God.[13] Yet even from here, having established these two mighty certitudes, Descartes still did not feel that his representations were to be trusted. Only innate ideas, self-evident truths, such as those of mathematics, and ideas that possess clarity and distinctness (e.g. the laws of physical bodies) are vouchsafed by and for the subject since the senses are 'accustomed to pervert and confound the order of nature', the world they represent remaining 'most obscure and confused', and necessarily unknown to the knower.[14]

As is evident, the inverse of Foucault's proposition not only can, but must be averred by a reading of the *Meditations*: only a discourse which could not assume the unity of representation and being could be driven to link the 'I think' and the 'I am', for if representation and being were one, there could be no doubt as to the verity of the representations that the meditating subject makes to himself, and thus no necessity for the work of the *cogito* to get underway. Neither, if what Foucault says were the case, would the *cogito* require the *deus ex machina* to guarantee its representations, nor would non-representational truths be the only truths thus guaranteed. Indeed the *cogito*, in itself, questions whether there is any such thing as representation.[15] The subject doubts the existence of all phenomena outside itself, even the body in which it is purportedly housed, and representation, understood in whatever sense, obviously cannot be in the absence of objects. As *The Order of Things* itself prescribes: 'only judgements derived from experience or empirical observations can be based upon the contents of representation.' (242) And evidence, the empirical, is what the *Meditations* refuses at every stage. It is, Descartes says, by 'the light of reason' that he attempts throughout to proceed, a strictly non-empirical, self-evidencing reason which neither trusts nor recourses to the contents of representation. It is no coincidence either that, in seeking to prove the existence of God, the arguments forwarded by the 'Third Meditation' were not a posteriori – such as the argument from design by which it is asserted that God represents himself in the world – but *a priori* formulations.[16]

The Order of Things thus delivers a reading of the Cartesian *cogito* utterly at variance with its construction in the *Meditations*. The 'I think' is connected with representation when, in the Cartesian demonstration, the 'I think' is deprived of any necessary connection with its (presuppositional) objects of representation. Foucault knows these things as well as any, yet to grant Cartesianism its customary dues, to connect, as in the mass of philosophical histories, the Cartesian and Kantian subjects would disturb both the integrity of the Classical *episteme* in which the subject is necessarily absent, and that of the modern *episteme* in which sovereign subject 'Man' arrives as an absolutely unprecedented figure. If any continuity were to be allowed between the two subjects then either certain premonitory privileges would be accorded to Descartes, or the *epistemi* would relinquish their status as entirely distinct, historical structures: both of which, on the face of it, would seem to amount to one and the same concession. But Descartes, so casually passed over in the era to which he belonged, is to appear once more in Foucault's account of modernity. And we should not be surprised that this reappearance takes place in the context of Husserlian phenomenology, nor that it is the differences rather than the similarities between the *cogito* of Descartes and that of Husserl which *The Order of Things* is destined to declare:

> It may seem that phenomenology has effected a union between the Cartesian theme of the *cogito* and the transcendental motif that Kant had derived from Hume's critique; according to this view, Husserl has revived the deepest vocation of the Western *ratio*, bending it back upon itself in a reflection which is a radicalisation of pure philosophy and a basis for the possibility of its own history. In fact, Husserl was able to effect this union only in so far as transcendental analysis had changed its point of application (the latter has shifted from the possibility of a science of nature to the possibility for man to conceive of himself), and in so far as the *cogito* had modified its function (which

is no longer to lead to an apodictic existence, starting from a thought that affirms itself wherever it thinks, but to show how thought can elude itself and thus lead to a many-sided and proliferating inter-rogation concerning being). Phenomenology is therefore much less the resumption of an old rational goal of the West than the sensitive and precisely formulated acknowledgement of the great hiatus that occurred in the modern *episteme* at the turn of the eighteenth and nineteenth centuries. If phenomenology has any allegiance, it is to the discovery of life, work and language; and also to the new figure which, under the old name of man, first appeared less than two centu-ries ago; it is to interrogation concerning man's mode of being and his relation to the unthought. (325)

Like so much of *The Order of Things* this passage is compact, cleverly sculpted, and seemingly brimful with significance. However, the litotic argument is far from achieving the finality which it arrogates to itself. Adapted to syllogism, it states that: firstly, what appears to be a Kantian legacy 'has shifted from the possibility of a science of nature to the possi-bility for man to conceive of himself'; secondly, the Husserlian *cogito* differs essentially from that of Descartes in that it no longer leads 'to an apodictic existence' but to a 'many-sided and proliferating interrogation concerning being'; and thirdly, 'therefore', phenomenology does not repeat or synthe-sise Cartesian and Kantian themes, and has far more in common with the discourse on life, labour and language which appeared at the turn of the eighteenth and nineteenth centuries. Thus we are to think that what was said earlier – 'the modern *cogito* is as different from Descartes' as our notion of transcendence is remote from Kantian analysis' (324) – has been demon-strated. Yet even given these questionable premises, it is difficult to see how they could necessitate the conclusion, to see why we must therefore regard Husserl's *Cartesian Meditations* as having more common ground with the work of Cuvier, Bopp and Ricardo than with the *Meditations* of Descartes. A great deal more in the way of explanation is required, but what is offered is a further 'conclusion' from the above. Foucault directly continues:

This is why phenomenology – even though it was first suggested by way of anti-psychologism, or, rather, precisely in so far as, in opposi-tion to anti-psychologism, it revived the problem of the *a priori* and the transcendental motif – has never been able to exorcise its insidious kinship, its simultaneously promising and threatening proximity, to empirical analyses of man; it is also why, though it was inaugurated by a reduction to the *cogito*, it has always been led to questions, to the question of ontology. The phenomenological project continually resolves itself, before our eyes, into a description – empirical despite itself – of actual experience, and into an ontology of the unthought that automatically short-circuits the primacy of the 'I think'. (325–6)

The inference we are to make here is, presumably, that since the intentionality of consciousness, as understood by Husserl, must be consciousness of something, then phenomenology was bound to predicate an extramental, empirical realm. But the predication of such a realm is by no means tantamount to its empirical description, and to call a system 'empirical' which (however unsuccessfully) brackets off that realm in the interests of elaborating a pure philosophy of consciousness, involves a considerable extension of what we understand by an empirical science. By the same criteria, any system which incorporates some acceptance of a real, physical world exterior to consciousness would be empirical, or nearly so. Only pure mathematics, formal logic and extreme immaterialist and solipsistic theories would elude this definition. And Foucault shows no interest in explaining quite what is meant here; as earlier, the dissociation is hurried and didactic. Certainly there is nothing in this passage (whose two parts have been divided above) to suggest that phenomenology has any stronger allegiances than to the scheme of *The Order of Things*. Phenomenology is akin to the empirical sciences, and not to the *cogito* of Descartes, *because* Foucault wishes us to believe man and his empirical study commenced in 1800: beneath the curliques and clauses, there is no other proposition.

This is not to say that it is mistaken, or wayward to point up the differences between the *cogito* of Husserl and that of Descartes. It would, indeed, be naively ahistorical to regard transcendental phenomenology as a simple continuation, or worse, completion of the Cartesian project, and to thereby seal over the vast interregnum that separates the seventeenth century of the *Meditations* from the twentieth century of Husserlian phenomenology. And it would be equally foolish to suppose that the problems of the unthought that faced Descartes were of the same cast as those confronting theories of consciousness today. Yet to question this continuity is not to erase the wealth of irresistible similarities that persists: that both begin from the assumption that consciousness is, and then proceed to ask what consciousness can determine of the conscious being and its other; that Husserlian bracketing and Cartesian doubt both achieve a suspension of the empirical through a reduction which seeks to establish the field of pure consciousness; that eidetic intuition and clarity and distinctness, perform powerfully analogous functions in opening consciousness to the apprehension of essential external forms. And, most decisively, it does not prohibit the acceptance of differences far beyond those adduced by Foucault whilst articulating them on the basis of revisionism. A revisionism, moreover, expressed in all its aberrant fidelity by the founder of phenomenology himself: 'one might almost call transcendental phenomenology a neo-Cartesianism, even though it is obliged – and precisely by its radical development of Cartesian motifs – to reject nearly all the well-known doctrinal content of the Cartesian philosophy'.[17]

This inability to brook any degree of revisionism or influence outwith *epistemi* strikes at the heart of *The Order of Things*. Since Foucault cannot contain the homologies between the Cartesian *cogito* and the subjects of Kant and Husserl within a modest paradigm of essential conceptual appurtenances (and no less essential historical differences), he is obliged to pursue drastic strategies of dissociation. Phenomenology must be called an empirical science in order not to be Cartesian, the *cogito* must be misread in terms of representationalism in order not to be Kantian. These difficulties stem from archaeology's determination – at this stage – to promulgate absolutely rigid, internally coherent and reciprocally exclusive historical/*epistemic* structures. During its period of experimental development, the science of archaeology – like so many other emergent methodologies – attempts to totalise its own inceptive operations. In order to stake its ground, archaeology must refuse to confer, in whatever spirit of supersessive cooperation, with traditional approaches to the history-writing of ideas, though, in so doing, it is led to remould that history in a less persuasive way than if it had made certain concessions to conventional notions such as influence, revision.

The phenomenological issue exemplifies these difficulties acutely. Foucault is, on the one hand, contracted to review the phenomenological enterprise since it is the most splendid efflorescence of the subject in the modern, anthropological era and, at the same time, a theory of consciousness that is poised over the immense and threatening abyss of the unthought. The phenomenological *cogito* is thus at the pinnacle of the anthropological *episteme* yet perched before the greatest descent, thus speaking most acutely for the contradictory and hubristic situation in which modern man discovers himself. However, the Cartesian inheritance unsettles the very ground of the *epistemic* determinism upon which these beautiful and tenebrous formulations rest. Particularly so here since the further we move into modernity the greater the threat of Cartesianism becomes, a Cartesianism which can not only be taken up one hundred and fifty years after its founding in the form of a transcendental subject of knowledge, but also survives another century to be revived with Edmund Husserl. And these problems still further compounded by the fact that Descartes also has some stake in Renaissance thought.

For Foucault, the Renaissance began in 1500 and ended in 1660. 1650, we recall, was not the year Descartes was born but the year in which he died. If the *epistemi* are not vague conceptual abstractions but, as *The Order of Things* everywhere insists, firmly anchored historical units, then Descartes, as a matter of historical and archaeological necessity, belongs to the Renaissance and his thought – in so far as it is Classical – will therefore again be premonitory and precocious.[18] The author of the *cogito*, as critic of scholastic resemblance, as Classical rationalist, as harbinger of the Age of Man, would then impinge upon each and every one of the *epistemi*. Were this not ominous enough, there are further reasons why Cartesianism must be repelled.

For one – though this may seem somewhat incidental – the autobiographical framework within which the *cogito* is elaborated would pose certain problems for Foucault. The *Meditations* requires that for the time of the demonstration the reading subject insert himself into the Cartesian biography, that he follow Descartes in his quest of certainty, that he sit within that uncertain body by that uncertain fire and confront the evil demon. As Descartes suggests, the trials and triumphs of the *Meditations* are experiences which the reader must make his own. And indeed it is this purely autobiographical structure – which is the structure also of the *Discourse on Method* – that delivers the *cogito* from the brink of solipsism. If the reading subject installs himself within the meditating subject, if he becomes Cartesian, then the *cogito* effectively declares 'I think, therefore we exist'. While the *cogito* is true for Descartes, then it is also true for anyone who wishes to faithfully participate in its unfolding. And that an inalienably autobiographical act should become the founding act of the sciences of consciousness, this is an archetype that archaeology can scarcely afford to acknowledge. Jacques Derrida asks of Freud and psychoanalysis: ' how can an autobiographical writing, in the abyss of an unterminated self-analysis, give to a worldwide institution *its* birth?'[19] A similar question could be put to Descartes and the sciences of the subject.

Moreover, in lodging the philosophical dissertation within an autobiographical narrative, Descartes was not propagating an eccentric or eclectic mode. To the contrary, he was writing within a well-established discursive tradition, one which not only found monumental expression in the *Essays* of Montaigne, but informed the whole host of *mémoires* that appeared in the sixteenth and seventeenth centuries. This phenomenon, or discursive field, cannot (archaeologically or otherwise) be detached from the post-Medieval insurgence of interest in man, in bringing scientific and philosophical knowledge into harmony with personal experience and practical conduct. It also coincides with the seminally ethnological studies to be found in the records of generals, missionaries and explorers, an ethnologism which appears in Descartes' own work, particularly in this 'Second Discourse'. This is a rich area for archaeological delving, one which we might have expected Foucault to excavate. However, within the economy of *The Order of Things*, to do so would involve opening the very issue of Renaissance humanism which the text is determined to bypass.[20]

But the most serious threat that Descartes poses to *The Order of Things* concerns the death of man, for which his birth is perhaps only a preparation. If the ground of knowledge can only be changed by a sudden, seismic upheaval which entirely evacuates the previous *episteme* and provides the clearing for its successor, then the death of man – as the event that attends the close of the modern *episteme* – can only occur in like fashion. Just as man had no precedent in the Classical *episteme*, so too he will be irretrievably lost to futurity like a prisoner trapped in a forgotten tower. Even at the end of the text, when this point has been spelled out again and again, Foucault still deems it necessary to stress that the appearance of man

> was not the liberation of an old anxiety, the transition into luminous consciousness of an age-old concern, the entry into objectivity of something that had long remained trapped within beliefs and philosophies: it was the effect of a change in the fundamental arrangements of knowledge. As the archaeology of our thought easily shows, man is an invention of recent date. And one perhaps nearing its end. If those arrangements were to disappear as they appeared, if some event of which we can at the moment do no more than sense the possibility – without knowing either what its form will be or what it promises – were to cause them to crumble, as the ground of Classical thought did, at the end of the eighteenth century, then one can certainly wager that man would be erased, like a face drawn in sand at the edge of the sea. (387)

We cannot know how, when, or why the next cataclysm will take place, but we can 'certainly wager', and wager, too, with a quiet certainty, what its outcome will be. And on the basis of what? Of man's absolute absence before 1800, of his absolutely unique arrival with the modern *episteme*. As with all deaths, birth is the first, the necessary, and the sufficient condition, but with Foucault the precise date of parturition is also essential. Since, if man were as old as Descartes, if man dwelt where he did not (archaeologically) belong, what is to prevent him from perpetuating? If he lived before the last flood, how are we to know that he will not survive the next? *Epistemic* seclusion, *epistemic* coherence is – at this stage – all that indicates that man will disappear; and this seclusion is purchased at the price of the vigilant suppression of anything that could be called Cartesianism. It is for the same reason that there is no archaeological space for David Hume's still-radical proposal that the idea of the self has no epistemological foundation and denotes at best a mere consecution of sensations: for between Descartes and Hume, the birth and death of the subject of knowledge would seem to have been rehearsed long before man-as-subject is supposed to have come into being in the first place.[21] And as the counterhumanist theme comes more and more to dominate *The Order of Things*, Foucault shows himself strangely willing to sacrifice the corollary principle that no author can transcend *epistemic* determinations. To what end? That of man.

THE FOUNDER OF FUTURITY

> Beware when the great God lets loose a thinker on this planet. Then all things are at risk. It is as when a conflagration has broken out in a great city, and no man knows what is safe, or where it will end. There is not a piece of science but its flank may be turned tomorrow; there is not any literary reputation, not the so-called eternal names of fame, that may not be revised and condemned … The things which are dear to men at this hour are so on account of the ideas which have emerged on their mental horizon, and which cause the present order of things as a tree bears its apples. A new degree of culture would instantly revolutionise the entire system of human pursuits.
>
> Ralph Waldo Emerson[22]

> 'I have come too early', he then said, 'I am not yet at the right time. This prodigious event is still on its way, and is travelling …'
>
> Friedrich Nietzsche[23]

In a text which purports to be written neither by a subject, nor about subjects, who or what motivates its narrative, stands authority for its claims? By what means might such a text propose or dispose at all? How, indeed, is it possible for that text to say or do anything? And who or what, in this particular case, might narrate or author the death of man?

In an article entitled 'The Subject of Archaeology or the Sovereignty of the *Episteme*', David Carroll contends that *The Order of Things* is in fact organised around a subject, that in eliminating the subject, Foucault is led to make of the *episteme* itself a transcendental subject.[24] As Carroll sees it, the *episteme* is a presence, a consciousness, the constitutive ground of all events, and the encapsulation of 'pure experience'. Carroll's demonstration is saline, persuasive and perspicacious. It draws out the futility of dethroning one sovereignty only to coronate another in its stead. However, two points are neglected, and indeed must be neglected in this demonstration. Firstly, within Foucault's analysis of modernity, the idea of the death of man has no less claim to sovereignty. Why else should Foucault regularly reiterate the necessity of this theme when it has no place within the modern *episteme*? Why not be content to simply describe the modern arrangement of knowledge without prolepsis or prophecy? Secondly, *The Order of Things* does contain a subject in the traditional sense, a subject to whom, moreover, is accredited a sovereignty rare in any history of modern thought.

The central dilemma facing Foucault in his account of modernity is to find support for the theme of the death of man. That the death of man is a desideratum we can have no doubt. Foucault makes this very clear on numerous occasions. As one example among many:

> To all those who still wish to talk about man, about his reign or his liberation, to all those who still ask themselves questions about what man is in his essence, to all those who wish to take him as their starting-point in their attempts to reach the truth, to all those who, on the other hand, refer all knowledge back to the truths of man himself, to all those who refuse to formalise without anthropologising, who refuse to mythologise without demystifying, who refuse to think without immediately thinking that it is man who is thinking, to all these warped and twisted forms of reflection we can answer only with a philosophical laugh – which means, to a certain extent, a silent one. (342–3)

However, it is not for nothing that the archaeologist answers with a laugh, and a laugh that must be 'to a certain extent a silent one', for while archaeology might have drawn Foucault to the conclusion that man must soon disappear, it has also generated significant obstacles to the articulation of this inevitable disappearance.

Foucault's archaeology cannot but recall the historical dialectics of Hegel and Marx. In particular, *The Order of Things* will echo Marxist analyses in that it divides recent world-history into determined, self-regulating epochs, and anticipates the closure of the present epoch as a prospective consequence of the ruptures it has discovered in the past. However, though archaeology repeats this fundamental procedure, it differs from both the Marxist and Hegelian systems in one crucial respect. Archaeology is anti-dialectical, which is to say that it is also ateleological. Although the Marxist and Hegelian dialectics assert that historical change occurs oppositionally, nevertheless, every era contains, in *statu nascendi*, the elements which will participate synthetically in its supersession. Thus did Marx argue that bourgeois society, in its fissures, contradictions and internal weaknesses, engenders the forces whose full realisation will result in the institution of a globally communistic society. It is therefore only through an analysis of the structures and instabilities of bourgeois society that the dialectical materialist can divine the forms, qualities and historical necessity of the coming epoch.

The same economy is at work for the dialectical idealist. Within Hegel's *The Philosophy of World History*, the three great ages preceding the modern, and final age, contain within themselves the patterns and dynamics of their simultaneous closure and sublation.[25] For Foucault, though, epistemic change is blind, acausal and discontinuous, 'a profound breach in the expanse of continuities'. (217) Nothing in the modern *episteme* can be said to prefigure, or even insinuate the organisation of the succeeding *episteme*. Archaeology is contracted to inhabit a space outside all teleologies, and consequently must reject even the antithetical development of dialectic.

Consequently, Foucault cannot fully utilise his anthropological doubles, since any argument which sees the *cogito* becoming swamped in the unthought implies that the very force which is to be constitutive of the counterhuman future was already profoundly active within the Age of Man. The necessity of avoiding dialectical models becomes all the more urgent here, since, as Foucault stresses, along with anthropology, dialectic is the characteristic figure of the modern *episteme*. Having been constituted at the turn of the eighteenth century when dialectical and anthropological models supplanted the Classical arrangement, the figure of man can only disappear when dialectic has run its course.[26] Thus, whilst the double postulates, and inherent contradictions of anthropology may be registered, and drawn out at a certain length, they cannot be pressed in the counterhumanist direction in which they seem to be headed, for it would make little sense to drive man out of existence by way and by virtue of those forms of thought which brought him into being. To do so would only be to testify to the ubiquity and perdurance of the very system of knowledge which Foucault seeks to think beyond.

Moreover, and according to the same exigencies, there is no support to be found in the fact that for every assertion of a transcendental subjectivity over the last one hundred and fifty years, there is an equal if not greater weight of counterassertion.[27] Quite to the contrary, the existence of anything resembling a counterhumanist tradition so far from consolidating Foucault's thesis, unsettles its very foundations. A reading which sees a developing counterhumanism in Marx, Nietzsche, Freud, Heidegger, Lacan, Lévi-Strauss would not only reawaken an inimical dialecticism, but jeopardise the idea that it is not impossible to think in terms other than those of a transcendental anthropology in the modern *episteme*.

By this stage the archaeological axioms have begun to crowd in upon each other, and we might note the essential perversity of a antihumanist methodology which legislates against the factors most auspicious to its articulation. Foucault cannot base the death of man upon the contents of the modern *episteme*, for, as we have said, the death of man is most assuredly not an epistmime, nor can he admit the existence of a powerful countermovement against the transcendental subject within the epoch of subjectivity. The only authority that Foucault can fall back on is the suspect and inadequate proposition which underlies the *grandezza* of the book's close: man was born circa 1800 as the child of a particular configuration of knowledge, and when that configuration disappears (as it surely will do, soon), then man will be no more. This proposition – which holds only if we see nothing of man in Renaissance humanism, in the *cogito*, in antiquity even, if we consent to the absolute alterity of *epistemi* to each other – is scarcely sufficient, of itself, to persuade the most awe-struck archaeological votary of the imminent and inevitable demise of man.

It is at this point, and into this implex, that Nietzsche enters *The Order of Things*. Having devoted so much energy to resisting the insistent pressure that Cartesianism exerts on the borders of his text, having bound archaeology to study the discourses of particular authors as circumscribed and delimited by the arrangement of knowledge in which they emerge, Foucault nevertheless declares:

> Nietzsche ... took the end of time and transformed it into the death of God and the odyssey of the last man; he took up anthropological finitude once again, but in order to use it as the basis for the prodigious leap of the superman [übermensch]; he took up once again the great continuous chain of History, but in order to bend it round into the infinity of the eternal return. It is in vain that the death of God, the imminence of the superman, and the promise and terror of the great year take up once more, as it were term by term, the elements that are arranged in nineteenth-century thought and form its archaeological framework. The fact remains that they sent all these stable forms up in flames, that they used their charred remains to draw strange and perhaps impossible faces; and by a light that may be either – we do not yet know which – the reviving flame of the last great fire or an indication of the dawn, we see the emergence of what may perhaps be the space of contemporary thought. It was Nietzsche, in any case, who burned for us, even before we were born, the intermingled promises of the dialectic and anthropology. (263)

This depiction is quite obviously in the sharpest contradistinction to the central archaeological prescription that all discourses are *epistemic*ally determined. So far is Nietzsche from being enmeshed in the network of nineteenth-century thought, that his texts do not merely question, contest or undermine that order, but anticipate a new and ulterior configuration of knowledge which had not yet confidently begun in the middle of the twentieth century, and which is, it would seem, still to come. Nietzsche does not reject or bypass dialectic and anthropology, he sends them up in flames; the death of God, the übermensch and the eternal return do not merely throw down a challenge to Hegelian and Kantian conceptions of man and time, they represent the most significant signposts for the future of thought itself.

This passage – with scarcely perceptible modifications – is to recur four times in Foucault's text, and always at critical junctures. Early on in the axial chapter 'Man and his Doubles', Foucault asks of the contemporary preoccupation with language: 'Is it a sign ... that thought ... is about to re-apprehend itself in its entirety, and to illumine itself once more in the lightning flash of being? Is that not what Nietzsche was paving the way for when, in the interior space of his language, he killed man and God both at the same time, and thereby promised with the Return the multiple and re-illumined light of the gods?' (306) Midway through 'Man and his Doubles', as Foucault closes the decisive section 'The Empirical and the Transcendental', he does not allow his analysis to move directly to the natural conclusion, that this dual and contradictory conception of man signals an inherent instability in the anthropological conception of the subject. Rather, we find his text saying:

> It is easy to see why Nietzsche's thought should have had, and still has for us, such a disturbing power when it introduced in the form of an imminent event, the Promise-Threat, the notion that man would soon be no more – but would be replaced by the superman [übermensch]; in a philosophy of the Return, this meant that man had long since disappeared and would continue to disappear, and that our modern thought about man, our concern for him, our humanism, were all sleeping serenely over the threatening rumble of his non-existence. (322)

And in the midst of still another homage of this kind, Foucault states that: 'Nietzsche, offering this future to us as both promise and task, marks the threshold beyond which contemporary philosophy can begin thinking again; and he will no doubt continue for a long while to dominate its advance.' (342) In each of these passages, the package is the same. Firstly, in killing God, Nietzsche also killed man. Secondly, that the übermensch signals not the zenith of man but his death. Thirdly, that the eternal return dissolves man. Fourthly, that we are at the threshold of a Nietzschean *episteme*, that the mission of contemporary thought is to become Nietzschean. And this recourse to Nietzsche occurs at every point where Foucault directly declares the disappearance of man. Even the famous words that end *The Order of Things* cannot get along without the invocation of the precursor. Settling his accounts, the archaeologist's recourse to Nietzsche takes its most confident form yet:

> Rather than the death of God – or, rather, in the wake of that death and in a profound correlation with it – what Nietzsche's thought heralds is the end of his murderer; it is the explosion of man's face in laughter, and the return of masks; it is the scattering of the profound stream of time by which he felt himself carried along and whose pressure he suspected in the very being of things; it is the identity of the Return of the Same with the absolute dispersion of man. Throughout the nineteenth century, the end of philosophy and the promise of an approaching culture were no doubt one and the same thing as the thought of finitude and the appearance of man in the field of knowledge; in our day, the fact that philosophy is still – and again – in the process of coming to an end, and the fact that in it perhaps, though even more outside and against it, in literature as well as in formal reflection, the question of language is being posed, prove no doubt that man is in the process of disappearing. (385)

What 'absolute dispersion of man' could mean here is difficult to imagine, and is made no clearer by its identification with the eternal return. Moreover, how this summary and lyrical train of interpretation could ever 'prove no doubt that man is in the process of disappearing' is inconceivable. But what is even more troublesome is that Foucault could quite easily have brought Nietzsche into line with his principle of *epistemic* determinism.

Foucault is not compelled to read Nietzsche's texts as announcing the death of man, if anything the greater weight of interpretation and textual evidence tends in the opposite direction. What Foucault presents is a brief but ingenious inversion of customary Nietzschean exegesis, which has traditionally seen not the death of man as attendant upon the death of God, but the liberation of man from enslavement to an antithetical, other-worldly ideal. Similarly, the übermensch has been seen as the most strenuous awakening of the potential and propensities that have lain dormant within man during the Christian era. Is the übermensch the first appearance of man in his untrammelled essentiality? His fulfilment understood as triumph or cessation? His apotheosis? Antithesis? Closure? All of these? None of these? We have no final answer to these questions for the good reason that Nietzsche implies that the übermensch both is and is not man. At one moment Zarathustra will say, '*I teach you the Superman [Übermensch]*. Man is something that should be overcome',[28] at another that the übermensch is the realisation of all that is best in man. And later, in *The Genealogy of Morals*, that the übermensch is 'a man who will justify the existence of mankind, for whose sake one may continue to believe in mankind!'.[29]

Yet Foucault decides unilaterally and absolutely in favour of the anti-subjectivist reading which puts Nietzsche well beyond the pale of *epistemic* consistency. The eternal return, he claims (with a philosophic naïvety scarcely credible), means that 'man had long since disappeared and would continue to disappear', (322) when – as the recurrence of everything that has been, is, and will be – the eternal return equally means that man will reappear and continue to reappear, even given that he will disappear. 'Alas, man recurs eternally', Zarathustra laments.[30] Likewise, little obliges Foucault to heap such literality upon the idea of the last man. This notion occurs but once in Nietzsche, in 'Zarathustra's Prologue' and suggests entirely the opposite of Foucault's interpretation. '*The last man lives longest*', Zarathustra announces, implying that the liberal-Darwinist man here indicated outlives both the death of God and the übermensch.[31]

This is not so much to gainsay Foucault's reading here, still less to recommend that Nietzschean exegesis be returned to an aristocratic radicalism, or to existentialist interpretation. Foucault's counterhumanist appropriation, though partial and hyperbolic, has played its part in opening up the problematic of man and the subject in Nietzsche, a problematic within whose specific contours so much of the contemporary humanist-antihumanist debate has been conducted.[32] What is telling, though, in terms of *The Order of Things*, is that Foucault could well have read Nietzsche as confirming rather than subverting the archaeological theory of knowledge.

For one, the fact that the idea of the death of God did not originate with Nietzsche, but is indeed part of a general movement in nineteenth-century thought would seem to be very important from the perspective of an analysis contracted to study discourse in terms of clusters and networks rather than on the level of individual achievement. Yet Nietzsche is presented as the sole author of this idea, despite its emergence in situations so various as the discourses of Sade, Heine, Stirner and the Russian nihilists. Furthermore, if the general notion of the death of God intersecting with a certain death of man is to be asserted of Nietzsche, does this connection not emerge with every bit as much clarity in Marx?[33] Secondly, Nietzsche's ideas on the übermensch, on the higher and lower men, on the species ideal, on the religion of man and the earth, would appear to belong just as surely to the nineteenth-century preoccupation with the destiny and fulfilment of man, *even if it was Nietzsche's intention to proclaim the death of man*. Why then, we might ask, when numerous pathways were open to Foucault by which Nietzsche might be consistently and productively lodged within the archaeological description of the modern *episteme*, does he follow a reading entirely ruinous to the requisite transindividuality of his analyses?

As we have said, by this stage in his text, Foucault has written away almost all authority for the contention that the figure of man is disappearing. Such a thesis would present enormous difficulties to a methodology which had the full array of dialectical anticipation and teleology at its disposal, but in a text which has legislated against seeing the structures, instabilities and general tendencies of the past as indicative of the future configuration of knowledge, the redoubtable problematics of prediction become still greater again.

The most convincing demonstration of the necessity of the disappearance of man will always be that which exposes the contradictions and instabilities of the humanist discourse within which his figure is constituted. And Foucault's account of the anthropological doubles moves a good way in that direction. Yet it is here, precisely at the point where archaeology's counterhumanism is at its strongest, that Foucault is compelled to forestall his analysis, to fudge the issue as to whether the separation of man into distinct and incompatible characterisations does indeed prefigure the arrival of a de-anthropologised *episteme*. Having forced himself into this corner, the figure of Nietzsche proves of particular strategic significance to Foucault at this point. In grounding the entire counterhumanist thrust of the last hundred years or so in the solitary persona of Nietzsche, Foucault avoids the progressional series running from Marx through Nietzsche, Freud, Heidegger, Lacan, Lévi-Strauss, (Foucault) – a series which would strike at both the *epistemic* and anti-teleological bases of archaeology. In order to consolidate his thesis, Foucault resorts to a transepistemic author through whom he provides warrants for the death of man without sacrificing the coherence and autonomy of the *epistemi*; the notion of a transepistemic author possessing, as it will, the peculiar and tactical property of preserving the *episteme* whilst licensing departures from its determinations.

The valorisation of Nietzsche's discourse therefore belongs to the same economy that has suppressed the Cartesian *cogito*. Nietzsche's premonitions preside over the death of man in the same way as the deracination of the Cartesian influence ensures his unique birth with Kant. And the question of the death of man is, as we know, inseparable from the question of his birth: 'man is an invention of recent date. And one perhaps nearing its end.' (387) The absence of Descartes facilitates the first proposition, the presence of Nietzsche motivates the second. Indeed, as regards these two figures, the transindividual postulate of *The Order of Things* collapses on both fronts. Descartes and Nietzsche attest – by counterpoint – to the irresistibility of the author. The Cartesianism which Foucault denies can only be muffled not silenced; the Nietzscheanism he espouses will not make itself heard without the voice of the master.

This is neither the first, nor will it be the last time that Foucault will have recourse to Nietzsche in this precursive and foundational manner. Throughout Foucault's writing life the name of Nietzsche will always be one of the most important signposts for future work, the most significant point of return for modern thought. In *Madness and Civilization*, Nietzsche is presented as the great harbinger of the life of unreason, a modern hero who resists the 'gigantic moral imprisonment' of Western rationality.[34] Even *The Birth of the Clinic* turns to Nietzsche at a crucial point in its denouement.[35] In a 'Preface to Transgression', transgression itself – the thought of a futurity of which we can only glimpse the 'calcinated roots, … promising ashes' – is 'that form of thought to which Nietzsche dedicated us from the beginning of his works and one which would be, absolutely and in the same motion, a Critique and an Ontology, an understanding that comprehends both finitude and being.'[36] Indeed, this essay presents, in crystalline form, the dominant thesis of *The Order of Things*:

> Kant … ultimately relegated all critical investigations to an anthropological question; and undoubtedly, we have subsequently interpreted Kant's action as the granting of an indefinite respite to metaphysics, because dialectics substituted for the questioning of being and limits the play of contradiction and totality. To awaken us from the confused sleep of dialectics and of anthropology, we required the Nietzschean figures of tragedy, of Dionysus, of the death of God, of the philosopher's hammer, of the Superman [Übermensch] approaching with the steps of a dove, of the Return.[37]

Here again Foucault's attitude to Nietzsche is completely uncritical. It is assumed that Nietzsche achieved his intention to break with the Kantian system, and that in so doing he opened up the space of a non-metaphysical critique. As everywhere else, Foucault does not trouble to ask exactly what form such a critique might take, how Nietzsche actually 'within the interior of his language killed God and man both', nor does he wonder whether or not Nietzsche might have remained enmeshed within the categories he sought to escape, how there can be a Dionysianism without any of its dialectical counterparts (Apollonianism, Socratism, Christianity), and so on. But then Foucault does not regard such questions as particularly compelling, since, when Nietzsche is not being held up as a systematic philosophical critic of origins, dialectic, and anthropology, he is being recoursed to as mystical poet of futurity. At one time, Nietzsche is a mad transgressor of limits; at another, a patient, rigorous genealogist who soberly propounds the *philosophical* necessity of the end of subject-centred philosophies. Which of these two functions Nietzsche is serving in Foucault's work is usually signalled by the authors beside whom he is summoned. When it is a question of the transgressive Nietzsche, the names of Sade, Hölderlin, Artaud and Bataille will be quick in coming, when it is that of Nietzsche as the formulator of a radical and counterhumanist hermeneutic system, he will be invoked in the company of Marx and Freud.

Not that Foucault deems these two functions incompatible. Deleuze, another elect author in Foucault's work, is seen in both transgressive, anti-rationalist terms, and as a philosophical critic of such importance that 'perhaps, one day, this century will be known as Deleuzian', that through his labours 'new thought is possible. Thought itself is again possible.'[38] In *The Order of Things*, Nietzsche plays both these roles simultaneously. On the one hand, the death of God and man, the thought of the eternal return and the übermensch are blinding poetic flashes, figures of an essentially lyrical and Delphic vision, on the other elements of a critique which razes both dialectic and anthropology. Naturally, the result of this dual privilege is a valorisation of the Nietzschean discourse far in excess of anything to be found in traditional Nietzschean exegesis. Essentially, Foucault seems to be saying of Nietzsche what Nietzsche's final megalomania was saying of Nietzsche: to wit, that he is a destiny, will be born posthumously, and so on. Indeed, we might say that Foucault is never so Nietzschean as when he invokes Nietzsche, not on account of the thought thereby represented, but by the manner of his invoking, for Nietzsche throughout celebrated the view of history which sees great men – Socrates, Luther, Goethe, Napoleon, and others – succeeding each other across epochs. Every age, he will insist, is meaningful only in terms of its higher types. And it is these higher types who carry with then the promise of the übermensch. First and foremost, the übermensch is the untimely one, he who cannot be contained by his times, still less by an organising centre of prediscursive regularities. Within Foucault's textual history, this privileged, transhistorical status is bestowed upon Nietzsche himself.

Foucault nowhere considers why Nietzsche should be archaeologically unconstrainable, why there should be a thinker whose insights structuralism, hermeneutics and archaeology do not simply take up, revise and deploy, but to whose promise they hasten. Such a description would be troublesome enough to the most bountiful *auteurism*, let alone to a transindividual history of discourse. With a theorist often so meticulous before methodology and its aberrations some explanation might be expected, but none whatever is proffered. But then this is a problem which invades Foucault's thought at every stage. In one breath, he presents discourse as entirely subject to the rule, as thoroughly determined, constituted and circumscribed by the *epistemic* conditions of its emergence; in another, he wishes to sponsor, endorse and liberate a revolutionary or transgressive literature, a thought which defies any repressive system, which would break free of any categories, even those which archaeology has imposed upon discourse.

This tension is itself apparent in the tempers of his own writing, and the ways in which he structures his texts and their chapters. More often than not his method is to work from a cool, careful analysis toward hierophantic prognostications on the destiny of human knowledge. Even in a text like *The Archaeology of Knowledge*, which would seem entirely given over to the rule, Foucault will still conclude by seeing his elaboration of the enunciative function and rules of formation for statements as a challenge to the 'great historico-transcendental destiny of the West'.[39] This is perhaps what Gilles Deleuze meant in a wonderful oxymoron when he called Foucault a 'romantic positivist'.[40] As with the work of Marx, the most patient documentary analysis is driven to prophetic, even of occasion, heterotopian conclusions.[41] But whereas these forces achieve a certain fruitful tension in Marx, with Foucault the romantic and the positivist remain essentially impenetrable and strange to one another, so that as often as not it seems that either Foucault's visionary lyricism disrupts his coolly formalist analyses or, in another context, that he is the prisoner of his own archaeological categories.

Nowhere is this inconsistency more keenly registered than in *The Order of Things*, where, on the one hand, we might wish that Foucault had dedicated more energy to describing the conditions of knowledge within the modern *episteme* than to preparing the stage for its disappearance, and on the other that he had relaxed his *epistemic* structures to allow for obvious noetic appurtenances, an aetiology of concepts from one era to another, phylogenetic analyses, and so on. Certainly, in any case, little would have been lost by accepting a general principle of reciprocal interplay between what determines authors and what authors determine, even if this relationship were to be weighted heavily in favour of deep-lying rules of discursive emergence.

Of course, there are many reasons why Foucault should have encountered insurmountable difficulties in this text. *The Order of Things* is, after all, among the most ambitious histories attempted since Hegel, and is all the more ambitious in that it attempts to tell the story of four centuries without recourse to the idea of history itself, to the extent that history implies teleology, aetiology and influence, notions which not only provide the ground principles of historicity in general, but which also greatly facilitate the imposition of some form of narrative upon the proliferation of discourses. And we cannot but feel that had Foucault separated his *epistemic* researches from his attack upon the subject, perhaps even in the form of two discrete texts, that both theses would have gained in consistency from this distance. Foucault's subsequent work goes a certain way toward unpackaging these themes, though on the question of authorship his revision – like *The Order of Things* itself – both contradicts and reconfirms archaeological anonymity.

WHAT (AND WHO) IS AN AUTHOR?

As might be expected, *The Order of Things* became the subject of fierce controversy. Yet Foucault, generally so passionate in defence of his labours, tended to agree with many of his detractor's judgements. In the 'Foreword to the English Edition' of *The Order of Things* he isolated three problems to which his text had no satisfactory answers: the problems of change, causality and the authorial subject. Of these problems, it was the latter which seemed to have troubled Foucault most, and he returned to the author-question at length in a paper entitled 'What is an Author?'.[42] In the preamble to this monograph, Foucault explained the necessity for a reevaluation of his approach in *The Order of Things*:

> In proposing this slightly odd question, I am conscious of the need for an explanation. To this day, the 'author' remains an open question both with respect to its general function within discourse and in my own writings; that is, this question permits me to return to certain aspects of my work which now appear ill-advised and misleading. In this regard, I wish to propose a necessary criticism and reevaluation.
>
> For instance, my objective in *The Order of Things* had been to analyse verbal clusters as discursive layers which fall outside the familiar categories of a book, a work, or an author. But while I considered 'natural history', the 'analysis of wealth', and 'political economy' in general terms, I neglected a similar analysis of the author and his works; it is perhaps due to this omission that I employed the names of authors throughout this book in a naive and often crude fashion.

I spoke of Buffon, Cuvier, Ricardo, and others as well, but failed to realise that I had allowed their names to function ambiguously.[43]

Yet, from the list of examples Foucault forwards, it is clear that 'What is an Author?' is not destined to be an entirely open and candid critical reevaluation of *The Order of Things*. If, in fact, the names Buffon, Cuvier and Ricardo do function ambiguously in this text they scarcely do so with a breath of the mystery which surrounds that of Nietzsche. Indeed, 'What is an Author?' repeats many of the ambiguities that it seeks to dispel. As in *The Order of Things*, a spirit of hostility to the author is to encase a meta-authorial description. The essay proper opens with a line from Beckett, 'What does it matter who is speaking?', a line which tolls at the close as the indifferent answer to its own question, as Foucault hopefully envisions a society in which the author-function will have disappeared.[44] Indeed were we only to read the beginning and end of the main text, we should be forgiven for assuming 'What is an Author?' to be a no less intransigently anti-authorial tract than Barthes's 'The Death of the Author'. Yet having made a number of preliminary and schematic observations on the author function, Foucault introduces the centrepiece of his discussion:

> I seem to have given the term 'author' much too narrow a meaning. I have discussed the author only in the limited sense of a person to whom the production of a text, a book, or a work can be legitimately attributed. It is easy to see that in the sphere of discourse one can be the author of much more than a book – one can be the author of a theory, tradition, or discipline in which other books and authors will in their turn find a place. These authors are in a position which we shall call 'transdiscursive'. This is a recurring phenomenon – certainly as old as our civilisation. Homer, Aristotle, and the Church Fathers, as well as the first mathematicians and the originators of the Hippocratic tradition, all played this role. (153)

Foucault is here suggesting that the principle of authorship exceeds the bounds of the body of texts which bear his name. Thus the idea of an author exercising a jurisdiction over his own texts has not only been accepted in principle but is seen to be too narrow and restrictive in particular cases: Aristotle is, in a sense, the author of Aristotelianism, Euclid the author of geometry. It is easy to see that many authors could lay claim to a transdiscursive status. What is true of Aristotle in this context will be no less true of Plato, whilst Aquinas, Ptolemy and Descartes would all seem to have given rise to ideational spaces 'in which other books and authors will in their turn find a place'. Indeed, wherever an 'ism' attaches itself to a proper name, there some degree of transdiscursivity has arisen. Of course, in modern times, Marx and Freud are the most obvious examples of this phenomenon, but for Foucault they exert a still greater protectorship over the discourses they commence:

> Furthermore, in the course of the nineteenth century, there appeared in Europe another, more uncommon, kind of author, whom one should confuse with neither the 'great' literary authors, nor the authors of religious texts, nor the founders of science. In a somewhat arbitrary way we shall call those who belong in this last group 'founders of discursivity'. They are unique in that they are not just the authors of their own works. They have produced something else: the possibilities and the rules for the formation of other texts. In this sense, they are very different, for example, from a novelist, who is, in fact, nothing more than the author of his own text. Freud is not just the author of *The Interpretation of Dreams* or *Jokes and their Relation to the Unconscious*; Marx is not just the author of the *Communist Manifesto* or *Capital*: they both have established an endless possibility of discourse. (154)[45]

Like 'founders of languages' in Barthes, the phrase 'founders of discursivity' will sound strangely here, for it is the concept of the subject as founder which has earned Foucault's most consistent and enduring disapprobation. And Foucault is not merely acknowledging that Freud and Marx simply founded psychoanalysis and Marxism in the sense that they provided the concepts and procedures with which these discursivities could get underway, but that, as disciplines, dialectical materialism and psychoanalysis cannot go beyond the inceptive texts. However powerful or radical the work of subsequent Marxists or psychoanalysts, their revisions will always be legislated for within the primal corpus. For this reason, the founding of a discursivity is to be distinguished from the initiation of a science. Whereas the history of a science tends to be that of one paradigm replacing another in a linear or progressive series which moves ever further from the inaugural theorems or discoveries, that of the Marxist and Freudian discursivities takes the form of a perpetual return to the founder. Thus whilst the founding act of a science becomes inscribed as a necessary but now obsolescent stage within the development of the scientific field, 'the initiation of a discursive practice does not participate in its later transformations'. (156) As Foucault puts it, in a remarkable schema: 'the work of initiators of discursivity is not situated in the space that science defines; rather, it is the science or the discursivity which refers back to their work as primary coordinates'. (156)

We have therefore arrived at a position diametrically opposed to the archaeological thesis. So far from the work of authors being determined in their nature and very existence by the discursive formation, the entire discursive formation is hereby dependent on the work of an individual author. Foucault continues:

> In this way we can understand the inevitable necessity, within these fields of discursivity, for a 'return to the origin'. This return, which is part of the discursive field itself, never stops modifying it. The return is not a historical supplement which would be added to the discursivity, or merely an ornament; on the contrary, it constitutes an effective and necessary task of transforming the discursive practice itself. Re-examination of Galileo's text may well change our knowledge of the history of mechanics, but it will never be able to change mechanics itself. On the other hand, re-examining Freud's texts modifies psychoanalysis itself just as a re-examination of Marx's would modify Marxism. (157)

The phrase 'return to the origin' has its surprises also, and the quotation marks with which it is surrounded are unaccompanied by any precautions. As a direct consequence of these returns:

> To define these returns more clearly, one must also emphasise that they tend to reinforce the enigmatic link between an author and his works. A text has an inaugurative value precisely because it is the work of a particular author, and our returns are conditioned by this knowledge. As in the case of Galileo, there is no possibility that the rediscovery of an unknown text by Newton or Cantor will modify classical cosmology or set theory as we know them (at best, such an exhumation might modify our historical knowledge of their genesis). On the other hand, the discovery of a text like Freud's 'Project for a Scientific Psychology' – insofar as it is a text by Freud – always threatens to modify not the historical knowledge of psychoanalysis, but its theoretical field, even if only by shifting the accentuation or the center of gravity. (157)[46]

Despite beginning 'What is an Author?' with the question 'What does it matter who is speaking?' and concluding with the answer that it shouldn't really matter at all, Foucault here provides the most extreme example of why it does matter. The discovery of a text like Freud's 'Project for a Scientific Psychology' will modify psychoanalysis if and only if it is a text by Freud. Over and above the text's contents, the fact of attribution – in and of itself – is the primary factor in establishing its significance for the psychoanalytic field. Indeed so powerful is the disjunction between the declarations that surround 'What is an Author?', and the descriptions it makes, that it almost seems a Kierkegaardian exercise in collating antithetical texts.

On the one hand, Foucault is seeking out the specific conditions under which 'something like a subject [can] appear in the order of discourse',(158) whilst, on the other, he is presenting a meta-authorial figure who founds and endlessly circumscribes an entire discursivity.[47]

Something of the contradictory format of *The Order of Things* is certainly repeated in this paper, though Foucault does not, as promised, confront the ambiguous status of the author in that text. Surely in a discussion which sought to propose 'a necessary criticism and reevaluation' of the role of the author in *The Order of Things*, some mention of the Nietzsche who offered the archaeological 'future to us as both promise and task' might have been anticipated in the neighbourhood of a meta-authorial characterisation. But the name of Nietzsche appears but once, earlier, parenthetically, with no connection to the questions of either the transdiscursive author, or the founder of discursivity.[48] Foucault, too, has implied that Marx and Freud need not be the only examples, and he nowhere says that discursive initiation need be restricted to the human or social sciences. Furthermore, Foucault has many times grouped together Nietzsche, Marx and Freud as the founders of modern discourse. In particular, the essay 'Nietzsche, Marx, Freud' had not so long ago argued that these three figures opened up the entire field of modern hermeneutics, that they have established infinite interpretative possibilities.[49] Indeed, everything should have drawn Foucault to Nietzsche at this juncture and yet when Foucault was directly asked whether he considered Nietzsche to be a founder, the question was completely sidestepped.[50]

Naturally, there are many reasons why Foucault should wish to avoid the Nietzschean question in this context, for whatever statement he might make about the status of Nietzsche's authorship would necessarily raise the question of the authority of the archaeological discourse itself. On the one hand, were Foucault to present Nietzsche as a founder, or as a transdiscursive author, where then is archaeology, with its complex system of Nietzschean inheritances and dependencies, to be situated?[51] Is Foucault's work not to be seen in the same context of affiliation to the Nietzschean discourse as, say, the work of epigonous psychoanalysts entertains towards that of Freud? Does not Foucault aver the necessity of a return to the Nietzschean origin? Does he not refer back to the simultaneous deaths of God and man, to the übermensch, to the eternal return, as to 'primary coordinates'? In short, could it not be that the great labour of archaeology is but one fold within a generalised Nietzscheanism?

On the other hand, were we not to regard Nietzsche as a founding author, the problem of the archaeological recourse to Nietzsche would take on a particularly worrying aspect. For, if archaeology is not to be situated within the space of the Nietzschean discursivity, then what might the name Nietzsche signify in Foucault's project? Would not the superinscription of the Nietzschean subject appear as the most flagrant of (mis)appropriations, an appeal to authority – virtually an argument from authority – in the prosecution of the idea of the death of man? And like all appeals to authority, might not the appeal itself mask a more fundamental will-to-authority? Indeed, along such lines, might we not begin to read the archaeology of the human sciences as Nietzsche reread his own essay, 'Schopenhauer as Educator': 'what is being spoken of is fundamentally not "Schopenhauer as Educator" but his *opposite*, "Nietzsche as Educator"'?[52]

ALLEGORIES OF MISREADING

> I believe that it is better to try to understand that someone who is a writer is not simply doing his work in his books, in what he publishes, but that his major work is, in the end, himself in the process of writing his books … The work is more than the work: the subject who is writing is part of the work.
>
> Michel Foucault[53]

> I am told of a man who sets out to make a picture of the universe. After many years, he has covered a blank wall with images … only to find at the moment of death that he has drawn a likeness of his own face. This may be the case of all books; it is certainly the case of this particular book.
>
> Jorge Luis Borges[54]

Foucault was to say that the 'only valid tribute to thought such as Nietzsche's is precisely to use it, to deform it, to make it groan and protest', and that 'if the commentators say I am being unfaithful to Nietzsche that is of absolutely no interest'.[55] It is, of course, not at all surprising that commentators should make this observation of Foucault's work. His revision or misprision of Nietzsche is often so extreme as to be barely recognisable as Nietzschean at all. In the essay 'Nietzsche, Genealogy, History', for example, Foucault directly quotes Nietzsche some fifty times, and yet succeeds in presenting a Nietzschean history and genealogy almost entirely at variance with the careful explications of Sterne, Danto and Kaufmann.[56] Naturally, it would be churlish, and scarcely justifiable to call Foucault to account over this. Firstly, because at a very significant level this is entirely faithful to Nietzsche's ideas of strong revisionism, to the exhortations in *Zarathustra* that the faithful pupil repays his teacher poorly.[57] Secondly, because, as is so very often noted, the Nietzschean texts open themselves to antithetical interpretations on an astonishing number and variety of issues – on history, on genealogy, on politics, on feminism, on tragedy and so on. And also, as we have been concerned to stress, on the question of man.

Nothing compels Foucault to interpret Nietzsche as the avatar of a post-anthropological *episteme*, and from first archaeological principles, the reading of Nietzsche in terms of a radical and darkling humanism would seem positively *de rigueur*. Nor need Foucault have allowed Nietzsche to figure so largely here. *The Order of Things* shows no qualms before suppressing the anti-subjectivist elements in Marx, Freud and Heidegger. Yet Foucault presents an untimely Nietzsche who is absolutely identical with the counterhuman thesis of his text. In this sense, might we not wonder wherein the essential difference is to be discovered between the voice of Nietzsche in *The Order of Things* and that text's highest hope? Is Foucault not, here as elsewhere, using and (in suppressing the intrinsic undecidability of Nietzsche and the question of man) deforming Nietzsche's thought when, at every point at which archaeology announces the comfort, the profound sense of relief that accompanies the disappearance of man, he makes Nietzsche stand its surety? In the last analysis, as the author of archaeology himself would probably concede, it is of absolutely no matter if Foucault is really and truly presenting a revisionist Nietzscheanism, or whether he is using the name of the forefather in the manner of those Early Church authors who claimed as the work of John, doctrines they had themselves formulated.[58] In both cases, the ideas of 'Nietzsche' are those of the archaeologist.

Within *The Order of Things*, more than in any other text, it was necessary for Foucault to deflect attention from his own status as its author. By the very act of constructing the discourse of the prediscursive ground, archaeology indemnifies itself against the system of constraints which it enforces upon all other discourses. The archaeologist will therefore always be a detached overseer, and never part of the discursive configuration itself; as a matter of structural necessity he will be outside of time.

This situation differs with respect to the descriptions of the Classical and modern *epistemi*, though only to the point of modifying the quality of temporal transcendence which the archaeological discourse implicitly arrogates to its practitioner. Obviously, the description of the Classical era will of necessity take place outside that arrangement of knowledge, but neither can it issue from the vantage point of modernity, for Foucault would then be presenting not an understanding of the deepest stratum of Classical thought, but a history of the present as it views the past; an operation in which what are called the elements of Classical thought would be no more than merely material for allegory, for a revaluation of how our modern habits of thought negotiate the long distant past.

Moreover, and more worryingly still, the archaeological discourse of the modern *episteme* cannot itself belong to the modern *episteme*, for then it could only speak for, and not about the rules of formation for the anthropological arrangement. If it formed a part of the modern configuration, *The Order of Things* would represent another monument to the anthropological era, to the discourse on man, his destiny and ends. Kant writes of man as the end of all nature, Hegel of the end and fulfilment of man as that mystical journey of mind toward itself in time, Marx of the simultaneous dissolution and beatitude of man in classless society, Nietzsche of the übermensch, Husserl of an ultimate intersubjectivity, Heidegger of the shepherd of being – there would then be no reason not to see in Michel Foucault's thesis of the-death-of-man-as-the-end-of-man the latest instance of the modern preoccupation with the eschatological horizons of humanity.[59]

Yet Foucault insists that this is not the case. Archaeology is a radical break with anthropologism, it transgresses the limits of this era. What he does not say, however, is that in order to transgress these limits, it must also transcend the formal conditions which dictate to all other discourses the ground and limit of their possibility. The *episteme* must be described from the point of view of an ideal exteriority. Only from a mystical and privileged continuum alterior to all *epistemi* can the archaeologist range, circumscribe and re-present discursive history, and only from this place can he proscribe its future.[60] Foucault is therefore always already in possession of the transcendence which he bestows upon Nietzsche for in the last analysis, it is still Foucault who purportedly has unique access to the true historical mission and significance of the Nietzschean discourse, he who has ultimate powers of appropriation within an archaeology of the human sciences which is all his own. His is the discourse of all discourses, the one site from which the rules of formation of four centuries of writing can be revealed. Foucault therefore cannot avoid becoming the author of his own text, and it is precisely the monumental and totalising nature of that text which conspires to make the authority of the archaeologist unconscionably problematic.[61]

The whole range of texts which make more modest or local claims, those which are avowedly impressionistic, fictional or *subjective* will not imply transcendentally remote authors; rather such a subject tends to arise from high philosophical or theoretical texts, particularly in the case of texts which – like Foucault's, like Hegel's – attempt to tell the truth of history, for such a tale can only be told from the annex of a pure distance, an ahistorical alterity. And where the problems of ideal detachment are grave enough for Hegelian history, they are entirely calamitous for a text which seeks to lay the ghost of the idealist subject. Prime amongst the ironies of Foucault's project is that, even supposing that it had succeeded in its aim, history would still have been left to depose the subject of archaeology. Foucault has little enough success in ousting those authors whose influence he wished to deny. The one subject he could never in principle dislodge is Michel Foucault.

Archaeology offered no ways around this dilemma. Whilst Hegelian history might attempt to devolve its authority onto the world-animating Geist, in the archaeological science there can be no such *telos* which could assume the burden of its historical narrative: history, in its ruptures, its transformations, unfolds in the mind of the archaeologist, the mind which sees, recounts and motivates the story of language, knowledge, the birth and disappearance of man. Foucault might only have resisted becoming the transcendental subject of *The Order of Things* by inscribing his text within the determinism it promulgates. As such, this would require Foucault to constitute the archaeologist as a historical being responding to the circumstances of his day, on the understanding that the past as he presents it is delivered *sub specie modernus*, and not from the sanctity of an ideal omniscience. It would involve, that is, a situating of the speaker, an engagement with his material and his times, a perspectivism in the Nietzschean sense.[62] Yet to have done so would have been to admit the impossibility of there ever existing anything like an archaeology of the human sciences as *The Order of Things* construes this mission.

Ironically, however, it is as a historical document rather than as *the* text of documentary history that *The Order of Things* seems to have resolved itself. Foucault developed as an intellectual in an environment of intense neo-Cartesianism. Husserl's reformulation of the Cartesian *cogito* had an impact upon French thought comparable to that of Hegel upon German philosophy a century prior.[63] Recalling this era, Foucault has said:

> As all of my generation, I was … formed by the school of pheno-menology … And I believe that, as for all of those in my generation, between 1950 and 1955 I experienced a kind of conversion … we reexamined the Husserlian idea that there is meaning everywhere … And from 1955 we dedicated ourselves to the study of the formal conditions of the appearance of meaning.[64]

And we might wonder to what extent *The Order of Things*, in presenting a language-centred, subjectless era as in process of supplanting philosophies of consciousness, is the record of that conversion. Indeed, we have it on the best authority that the original subtitle of the work was *An Archaeology of Structuralism*.[65] Certainly, to us today, it will read more persuasively as an allegory of the transition from French phenomenologies and existentialisms to French structuralism than as an archaeology of the three great epochs of post-Medieval discourse. And like all allegories, its characters are proxy. For 'Kantian anthropology' we might read neo-Cartesianism, or even Sartre, for 'Nietzsche,' Foucault.[66] The story of *The Order of Things* is the (fabulous) story of the triumph of Nietzsche over Kantian anthropology, and the stations of this antagonism are precisely those taken up by Foucault and Sartre in their famous controversy following its publication.[67] Stephen Albert, in Borges's 'The Garden of Forking Paths', asks: 'In the riddle whose answer is chess, what is the only prohibited word?'[68] Foucault, we know, was ever anxious to deny any complicity with structuralism, and in response to one such charge replied that not once did he use the word 'structure' in *The Order of Things*.[69] Neither is the name of Sartre to be found among its pages.

After the work of 'What is an Author?', Foucault withdrew into a kind of *askesis*. When he reemerged, it was as a genealogist, a scientist of the self who no longer wished to dispense with the question of man under the rule of his disappearance, but rather to inquire into what makes man 'Man'. This decision was correspondent with a revision of his own relationship to knowledge. The genealogist speaks *dans le vrai* of his times (however stridently he might speak against it), he knows that he is part of the history he is writing, he knows that the interpretation is always, in some sense, the interpreter. Foucault also came to reread his earlier work in these terms, saying:

> Each time I have attempted to do theoretical work, it has been on the basis of elements from my own experience – always in relation to processes that I saw taking place around me. It is in fact because I thought I recognised something cracked, dully jarring, or disfunctioning in things I saw, in the institutions with which I dealt, in my relations with others, that I undertook a particular piece of work, several fragments of an autobiography.[70]

This decision is the decision between two conceptions of authorship, two conceptions of man.

TRANSCENDENTAL LURES: LACAN AND THE MASTERY OF LANGUAGE

The intense labour of archaeology taught its author that the end of man was in the strictest sense unsayable. Any radical eschatology of the subject would require the constitution of a subjectivity beyond man and time as harbinger of the disappearance of man in time. For Foucault there was no

way around this impasse and the relativisation of his own claims to knowledge was necessarily concomitant with a renewal of subjective categories
within his work. The Foucauldian discourse is by no means unique in
engendering insuperable contradictions through its attempts to dislodge
the subject; any determined discourse of the death of man will find itself
ensnared in a similar labyrinth of transcendental presuppositions. The work
of that other great anti-subjectivist of the modern era, Jacques Lacan, is as
surely implicated in the *folie circulaire* of *authoring* and *authorising* the disappearance of the subject, of *declaring* that no-one speaks.

Lacan likewise sought to speak for an order of discourse impenetrable
to conscious reflection. Where Foucault attempted to articulate a discursive
unthought underpinning four hundred years of scientific and philosophical
speculation, Lacan presumed to hold a mandate for a linguistic unconscious that determines all utterance, statement and text. According to
Lacan's lingocentric revision of Freudian psychoanalysis, the subject does
not think; rather language thinks and speaks the subject. In total contradistinction to the *sum res cogitans* of Descartes[71] ('I [am] a substance of which
the whole essence or nature consists of thinking'), the Lacanian subject is a
being whose proper essence is that it does not think. So far from deriving
existence from thought, as Descartes had done, the subject of structural
psychoanalysis moves from the (pre-Oedipal, imaginary) realm of the 'I am'
through the 'I think' only to discover that it *is not* where it thinks. Rather,
if the Lacanian subject exists at all, it exists there where it does not think,
in the unconscious which speaks before any subject has even the illusion of
thought.[72]

The language which emanates from the Lacanian unconscious is therefore absolutely anterior, alterior, and prerequisite to any conscious subject
whatsoever. This unconscious language, the discourse of the Other, is
adnascent with what Lacan calls the 'symbolic order', the domain of the
signifier which constitutes the subject and allows it entry into the systems of
society and culture. This entry into the signifying chain, however, is bought
only through denying the subject any authentic selfhood, through making
the subject nothing more than an effect of the signifier. The subject thus gains
the world of language – and therein its subjecthood – only through losing
its pre-linguistic state of imaginary oneness with nature and entering the
symbolic system of differences and arbitrary identifications through which
(for Lacan) all human society is constructed.

Hence Lacan will talk everywhere of the ex-centricity of the subject
to itself, of the absolute lack and loss of the subject in language, of 'the
supremacy of the signifier in the subject' and the 'pre-eminence of the

signifier over the subject'.[73] Like the archaeological arrangement of prediscursive regularities, the symbolic order would condemn the subject to derelict inarticulacy, to being a muted emissary of his language rather than its master, an agent of the letter rather than its signatory: 'the displacement of the signifier determines the subjects in their acts, in their destiny, in their refusals, in their blindnesses, in their end and in their fate … everything … will follow the path of the signifier.'[74] The law of the signifier is universal. No subject can possibly be exempt from dislocation, division and dispersal – from what Lacan calls *aphanisis* – in the proliferation of unconscious language.

Yet if no subject can transgress the law of the signifier, if all discourse is determined by the symbolic order, the problem of the status of the Lacanian text is posed from first principles. How can Lacan speak for the unconscious without speaking *ultra vires* of his own theory? How can he speak *of* rather than *in* a language prerequisite to any subject? Who can speak from a position aloof or tangential to the structures that determine all discourse? Who can speak for the defiles of the signifier without his own significations being defiled in the process? A profound contradiction therefore inhabits and inhibits the text of structural psychoanalysis as its very first page is turned. On the one hand, Lacan eludes his own structures and acquires the very mastery of discourse he deems impossible or, on the other, his discourse itself submits to the law of the signifier and loses any claim it might have to our attention as a description or metalanguage of the unconscious and of the corollary disappearance of the subject. Within the text *of* the unconscious, therefore, the genitive cannot be double. Either Lacan's text is a transcendent theory of the unconscious, *or* it is unconscious itself and has no more or less to say about the unconscious than any other text.[75] Both paths are, it would seem, equally perilous for the project of an anti-subjectivist psychoanalysis. The argument that Lacan merely 'reveals' the unconscious leads back into this set of problems. Lacan's revelation of the unconscious can enjoy exemplary status – over and above the free association, stream of consciousness, echolalia or automatic writing accessible to any literate individual – only by implicitly attributing some form of muse-bestowed privilege to itself. In other words, Lacanianism must call to itself one of the two perennial modes of authority – the rational or the poetic.

The Lacanian tradition itself has, by and large, upheld the former view, preferring to see his work as the testament of the unconscious rather than as an unconscious testament. Whilst endorsing the idea that no subject can acquire any degree of linguistic control, commentators will yet eulogise Lacan's astonishing understanding of the mechanisms and discontinuities

of language, the majestic facility with which he brings the play of signification to life in his texts. More than one critic even goes so far as to say that
Lacan's departures into the chthonic irrationality of unconscious language
betray a most awesome authorial control: 'Lacan's style attests to an incontestable mastery of the tongue. The associations and plays ... are never the
product of chance, but of a work of rare complexity.'[76] Catherine Clément
too has said: 'If he makes holes in his discourse, it's on purpose; if he splut-
ters, if he stammers, it's not infirmity ... it's total mastery of the play of
words.'[77] Such *maîtrise* thus makes Lacan not only the transcendent subject
of his text, but of language also. By way of mitigation, Clement has also
contended that structural psychoanalysis forced upon Lacan 'a mastery he
did not want'.[78] However, it would appear that if Lacan did repudiate this
status, he did so only in the manner of the Zen adept who seeks to achieve
mastery through its renunciation.

The sublimest thing, Wilde once remarked, is to set another before you,
and Lacan told his disciples on at least one occasion that, whilst they might
be Lacanians, he himself was a Freudian. Foucault, as we saw, attempted
to mask his own authority by the introduction of a prosopopoeic Nietzsche, and Lacan's insistent recourse to Freud offers similar tactical refuge
from the problem of assuming responsibility for his own text. By far and
away the most radical rereading of Freud ever proposed, the Lacanian
project displays the very reverse of any defensive anxiety of influence.[79]
Rather it insists, time and again, that the work of structural psychoanalysis
be inscribed entirely within the parameters of the founder's oeuvre. As he
declares in *The Four Fundamental Concepts of Psycho-analysis*, in terms that
foreshadow Foucault's idea of the founder of discursivity:

> no psycho-analyst can claim to represent, in however slight a way, a
> corpus of absolute knowledge. That is why, in a sense, it can be said
> that if there is someone to whom one can apply, there can only be one
> such person. This one was Freud ... He was not only the subject who
> was supposed to know. He did know, and he gave us this knowledge
> in terms that may be said to be indestructible, in as much as, since
> they were first communicated, they support an interrogation which,
> up to the present day, has never been exhausted. No progress has
> been made, however small, that has not deviated whenever one of the
> terms around which Freud ordered ... the paths of the unconscious,
> has been neglected. This shows us clearly enough what the function
> of the subject who is supposed to know is all about.[80]

It would of course be absurd to contest the inestimable debt borne by Lacan
to Freud (all the more pronounced because Lacan, better than anyone, knew

how to push the Freudian discovery within sight of its limits) but such recourse, legitimate as it is, serves the strategic purpose of allowing Lacan to speak as a master of language without accepting that mastery in name. Such in its more deceptive aspect is 'the function of the subject who is supposed to know'. From this subject, Lacan appeals for licence to discourse as master whilst simultaneously sheltering under the mantle of an ardent discipleship. Lacan can thereby propound freely and authoritatively whilst redirecting the problems of authorisation to the father of psychoanalysis.

The mask however can only be worn for so long, and this strategy, this *leurre* delivers Lacan no further from the problem of subjectivity *per se*. A mastery of the unconscious remains an implicit postulate; a transdiscursive, meta-authorial status needs be conferred somewhere within this anti-subjectivist text. A subjectivity is always at stake, then, be it that of Lacan or Freud and, in the latter case, structural psychoanalysis will always be left to explain how Freud could have so thoroughly defied the law of the signifier – an issue on which Lacan is conspicuously silent. And what is more, it matters but little whether Lacan is speaking in *propria persona* (and therefore in an improper persona) or in the name of the psychoanalytic father for in either case the Lacanian text has still authorized itself – whether through Freud or not – to opine from a position transcendent to the universal discursive conditions it describes. Nor indeed can any strategy divert attention from the fact that Lacan *did* speak, that he spoke to modernity with an authentic, strange and Orphic sonance about the unconscious and the contemporary crisis of subjectivity.

Lacan found himself caught within the same threadwork of transcendental lures that Foucault encountered in *The Order of Things*. The *aphanisis* of the subject could only be articulated in both its constative and performative aspects through the deliquescence of his own discourse, through his testimony of the muted subject losing itself in the very mutedness it describes. Like Foucault, Lacan could therefore only continue to announce the disappearance of the subject as a truth of discourse by staking his own subjectivity against the entire history of discourse. Which is again to say, that his text unravels not in the field of an abolished subjectivity but within the space of an uncertainty as to the nature and status of subjectivity, in particular that of the anti-subjectivist himself. Such indeed is the abyss awaiting any author of the death of man. The subject who announces the disappearance of subjectivity does so only at the risk of becoming – inferentially at least – the sole subject, the Last and Absolute Subject, left to face his subjecthood in the face an otherwise subjectless terrain, ever captive to a mirror of solipsism.

Confronted with this enigma whereby the discourse of the death of man either necessitates transcending its tenets or falls prey to its own thanatography, it is scarcely surprising that the anti-subjectivist has everywhere abandoned the choice and taken his place as one writing subject amongst others. Both Foucault and Lacan were consequently led to redefine and specify the subject under erasure, and hence reorganised their deconstructions around a specific instantiation of subjectivity, that of the Cartesian *cogito*. Doubtless with such considerations on his agenda, Lacan came to promote a sharply focused anti-subjectivism, generous in its exclusions:

> with the term 'subject', we do not designate the living substratum necessary for the subjective phenomenon, nor any other kind of substance, nor any being of knowledge in its primary or secondary affectivity ... nor even in the logos which is supposedly incarnated somewhere, but the Cartesian subject which appears the moment when doubt recognises itself as certitude – with this difference, that from our perspective, the foundations of this subject are seen to be much broader, but at the same time more subservient with respect to the certitude which escapes him.[81]

What such a reorientation bespeaks is that the death of man is unsustainable as a universal statement. Distinctions between the specific forms of subjectivity under assault must be made if an anti-humanist discourse is not to plunge headlong into *aporia* and inconsistency. Yet the work of Lacan, along with that of Barthes and Foucault is largely misread on the assumption that there is only one subject in question. The fact that – after the initial headstrong declarations had been made – their work does more to contradict than to corroborate indiscriminate anti-subjectivism is bypassed. Theorists continue to reiterate the idea that the concept of the subject has come to its end, and cursorily implicate the author in the same finitude without asking who or what dies in the death of man.

So many questions are repressed in this easy collocation of subjects. Does the death of man necessarily imply the death of the author? Is the author simply a specific and regional instantiation of the philosophical *anthropos*? Of the subject of knowledge? Of the *cogito*? Of the logos? What sense of the author disappears in the death of man? Intratextual author? Extratextual author? Psychobiographical signified? In view of the uncertainty, indeed the apparent ingenuousness contemporary anti-humanist critics show before these questions, we might wonder if the 'death of man' might not be an egregious neutralisation of the immense problematic and myriad compasses of subjectivity; a simplification such as Caligula dreamt of when he asked that his subjects have but one neck so he might dispose of them all at a single strike.

SUBJECTIVITIES

> The theory of meaning now stands at a cross-roads: either it will
> remain an attempt at formalising meaning-systems by increasing
> sophistication of the logico-mathematical tools which enable it
> to formulate models on the basis of a conception (already rather
> dated) of meaning as the act of a transcendental ego, cut off
> from its body, its unconscious, and also its history; or else it will
> attune itself to the theory of the speaking subject as a divided
> subject (conscious/unconscious) and go on to attempt to specify
> the types of operation characteristic of the two sides of this
> split; thereby exposing them, that is to say, on the one hand, to
> bio-physiological processes (themselves already an inescapable
> part of signifying processes: what Freud labelled 'drives'), and,
> on the other hand, to social constraints (family structures, modes
> of production etc.).
>
> Julia Kristeva[82]

> The philosophical self is not the human being, not the human
> body, or the human soul, with which psychology deals, but
> rather the metaphysical subject, the limit of the world – not a
> part of it.
>
> Ludwig Wittgenstein[83]

The death of the author has taken its place within a greater closure: that
of the era of subjectivity itself. Yet though Foucault and Lacan are seen to
be exemplary in signalling this common closure, nowhere do they directly
conjoin the issues of man and the author.[84] In their discourses, as in others,
the two deaths are used to casually evoke or amplify one another, but no
argument of any sort is presented as to why we should see 'Man' and the
author – in their lives, in their deaths – as one and the same subject.[85]

This might not seem of any particular significance in itself, but when
we consider few, if any other of the precursors of the death of man –
not Lévi-Strauss, Althusser, and emphatically not Nietzsche and Freud –
make this connection, then we might urge a little reserve and inspection
before assuming that the author is always and everywhere simply a specific
instance of generic 'Man'; and all the more so since the general closure of
subjectivity is so often cited to bolster anti-authorial theory. Speaking for
a revolution in thought, Jean-Marie Benoist declares:

> If the freedom of the text is asserted against the almighty rule of
> the 'author-generator', and the meaning is accepted as being simply
> relational, the inevitable result is a challenge to the very notion of the
> *subject*. The subjectivity of the author becomes of minor importance
> in the elucidation of the text, and the supposed subject of the work
> – 'what it is about' – disappears when the signifying plane is brought

into the foreground. This threat to subjectivity must however be seen outside the particular field of literary criticism. It relates to a widespread reaction on the philosophical level against a particular interpretation of the philosophy of Descartes. We might recognise in this modern tendency the 'end' or at least the exhaustion of the 'cogito epoch'.[86]

Benoist summarises this development as well as can be expected, yet in summarising he repeats the unreflective attitude which criticism and theory have brought to this issue. That is to say, it is always assumed, and never in any way demonstrated that the author is a simple subaltern or manifestation of the subject, and is therefore inscribed within the same finitude. For sure, this would seem obvious: both the author and the philosophical subject can be seen to enforce the primacy of human consciousness over the inhuman, the unthought; both play the role of the primary creative force, in respect of which language and the world of the in-itself are secondary, passive material. Furthermore, notions such as that of the omniscient author partake of the same sovereign detachment that is the first condition of a transcendental subjectivity. Indeed, the connection between these subjects will seem so obvious that it will be said, with the consonances of platitude: '"man" and "author" go hand in hand, the latter a particular instance of the former'.[87] That the destinies of man and author are entwined – and that they will become all the more inextricably so if our ideas of world and text increasingly cohere – is incontestable. What is by no means certain is that always and everywhere they are unproblematically reducible to one another.

The first meeting point of man and author in critical discourse is within the word 'subject'. And it is within the peculiar properties of this term itself that the commonality of their fate can be seen to unfold, since so much of contemporary thought seems to be directed toward restoring to the word its etymological purity whereby subject (*subjectus*: *sub*-under; *jacére*-thrown) denotes the one thrown under, the one who owes fealty to a greater power, be that power language, culture, discourse, history. Over the course of time, the word subject has acquired the status of an *enantioseme*, denoting the sovereignty of the transcendental ego of philosophies of consciousness, whilst retaining the original sense of vassalage, subordination, and so on. We might even say that no other word – in its plurisignificant fragility – has so enigmatically held the crises of an era within its semantic horizons. *Cogito*, logos, transcendental ego, self, topic, author, psychobiographical signified, even *episteme*, fall inside its compass. Correspondingly, we might expect adjectival precautions, qualifications, refinements, specifications as to the precise designation intended and so on, to herald its more portentous appearances in formulations of the order that 'recent poststructuralists have systematically deconstructed all received notions of the subject',[88] and indeed the very rare thinker will show him or herself scrupulous to alert the reader to the meaning intended in different contexts. All too often, however, we will find that the word has been used, over the course of a few short pages, to denote logos, *cogito*, and biographical subject, and used in such a way as to argue that the attack by Derrida on the first, and by Lacan on the second, leads to a dismissal of the third as though there has only ever been one subject in question. What is at work in this slippage is a global confusion of the intricate philosophical relations between self, *cogito* ego, transcendental ego, consciousness, knowledge, and creativity. Some will extend this still further, saying that the subject should be placed alongside 'God, logos, ousia, reason, being and so forth'.[89] Even, however, if divinity and reason are omitted, the amalgam is formidable. The death of the transcendental subject is consectaneous with the death of the subject of knowledge, is in turn consectaneous with the death of the author as a formal principle of textual meaning which is again consectaneous with the disappearance of the psychobiographical signified.

This chain of associations is the 'philosophical' grounding of the death of the author. What it states, at base, is that the denial of the *cogito* erases all forms of subjectivity and the predicates thereof. Certainly, it is undeniable that Lévi-Strauss, Lacan, Althusser, Derrida, Barthes, Foucault, have brought a concerted and epochal force to bear against the idea of an *a priori* subject situated outside the play of space and time, language, history, culture and *différance*. But does this onslaught collapse all senses of the subject as some will say? Is the concept of the author only tenable if a transcendental subjectivity is thereby designated? Or, to ask the logically prior and unasked question: how is the concept of the author distributed on the basis of a transcendental subjectivity?

First and foremost, any criticism which sees the author as a specification of the transcendental subject must detach the author as an empirical agency from the author as the purely ontological principle of the text. To be conceived in transcendental terms the author must be emptied out of all psychological and biographical content: a personalised, psychobiographically constituted transcendental subject is unthinkable. The classic formulations of transcendental subjectivity insist upon this from the outset. The subject of Kant's *Critique of Pure Reason* is transcendental apperception, the *a priori* unity of consciousness, a purely formal guarantee of objective knowledge: 'We can assign no other basis ... than the simple, and in itself completely empty, representation "*I*"; and we cannot even say that this is a concept, but only that it is a bare consciousness which accompanies all concepts. Through this I or he or it (the thing) which thinks, nothing further is represented than a transcendental subject of thoughts = X.'[90] The 'I' makes no claim to existence in the phenomenal world: it is a purely logical subject. Likewise the subject of transcendental phenomenology can have no empirical or psychological content, and is located outside of space and time. It must be extraworldly in order to be a transcendental subjectivity:

> Psychical subjectivity, the 'I' and 'we' of everyday intent, may be as it is in itself under the phenomenological-psychological reduction, and being eidetically treated, may establish a phenomenological psychology. But the transcendental subjectivity which for want of language we can only call again, 'I myself', 'we ourselves', cannot be found under the attitude of psychological or natural science, being no part at all of the objective world, but that subjective conscious life, itself wherein the world and all its content is made for 'us', for 'me'.[91]

A transcendental phenomenology is, therefore, to be distinguished from all psychologism: 'It would be much too great a mistake … to make *psychological* descriptions based on purely internal experience … a great mistake because a *purely descriptive psychology of consciousness is not itself transcendental phenomenology* as we have defined the latter, in terms of the transcendental phenomenological reduction.'[92]

Of course, as it has been translated onto the plane of literary criticism, phenomenological method has often failed to maintain the rigorous and austere purity of the transpersonal Husserlian subject, and has drifted into precisely the kind of psychologism that Husserl warned against. As Paul de Man says, in his earlier work: 'Some of the difficulties of contemporary criticism can be traced back to a tendency to forsake the barren world of ontological reduction for the wealth of lived experience.'[93] De Man urged a greater austerity among critics, a concerted vigilance against the 'almost irresistible tendency to relapse unwittingly into the concerns of the self as they exist in the empirical world'.[94] It is, however, possible to discern the influence of the Kantian and Husserlian subjects in certain operations to which the author is put, as a purely formal principle, in the verification of textual meaning. The work of E. D. Hirsch is instructive here.

Faithful to Husserl, Hirsch firmly opposes that scion of phenomenological criticism which 'mistakenly identifies meaning with mental processes rather than with an object of those processes', and sets about constructing a defence of the author which eludes a subjectivist psychologism.[95] For Hirsch, the author is a normative principle which ensures the objectivity of meaning. Along a somewhat circular path, Hirsch argues that since verbal meaning is determinate and determinable, then the postulate of a determining will is necessarily required, for in the absence of any such will there would be no distinction between what is meant, and what might be meant by a word sequence: 'meaning', he says, 'is an affair of consciousness', and there is no verbal meaning which is not '*a willed type*'.[96] Consequently, the author is necessary to the grounding of textual meaning in principles of validation, to the establishment of objective criteria in the work of interpretation: 'The determinacy and sharability of verbal meaning resides in its being a type. The particular type that it is resides in the author's determining will.'[97]

Kant and Husserl both found the postulate of a transcendental ego necessary to guarantee the objectivity of our knowledge about the world; only through such a postulate could individual knowledge be reconciled to the universal. It is easy to see how, in minuscule, Hirsch's use of authorial will as the ultimate principle of textual validation repeats this logic. Given the indeterminacy of textual meaning in the absence of any adjudicating norm, the premise of authorial will is a necessary epistemological condition of the existence of objective meaning. The author thus constituted is neither a locus of forces nor a psychobiographical site, but a metaphor for the text operating at the most consistent and plausible level of interpretation, a purely formal principle of the determinacy of textual knowledge. Intention is not here a vivid or agonistic struggle of an author with his material, but rather the ultimate tribunal at which criticisms vie, lay claim to their truths, and consent to be judged. The place of the author is therefore above and beyond the level at which textual meanings conflict and contest, and it is through his omnified agency that these conflicts can be neutralised in the interests of a higher, self-verifying 'truth', or determinate meaning.

Such a depiction can be said to be transcendental both in the sense that it is consistently non-empirical, and in that it asserts the authorial will as an absolute standard of authentification. It is to this aspect of the author-function, and the circularity implicit in its operation, that the movement against the author takes its strongest and most justified exception. As Barthes complains, the discovery of the author's intentions is all too often used to close rather than open the interpretation of a text.[98] For Foucault, too, the greatest reductions reside here: 'The author is the principle of thrift in the proliferation of meaning.'[99] Yet, whilst these objections warrant considerable respect, to affirm the counter-ideal of impersonality is to fall back into the very transcendental suppositions that Barthes and Foucault wish to evade. To repeat what was said above: there is no question of a transcendental author without the total abjuration of the psychobiographical signified. It is for this reason that the transcendental and the impersonal will always find a common purpose, a common absence. Despite their antithetical starting-points, both positions resolve in a shared ascetism. In Joyce's *A Portrait of the Artist as a Young Man*, Stephen Dedalus explains to Cranly:

> The personality of the artist, at first a cry or a cadence or a mood and then a fluid and lambent narrative, finally refines itself out of existence, impersonalises itself, so to speak … The artist, like the God of the creation, remains within or behind or beyond or above his handiwork, invisible, refined out of existence, indifferent, paring his fingernails.[100]

It is easy to see how readily the 'author-God' and the absence of the author meet one another, easy to see how this transcendental depiction could equally describe the disappearance of the poet-speaker in Mallarmé, the impersonalities of Eliot and Valéry. Similarly, but conversely, it is apparent how the doctrine of impersonality might imply the idea of a transcendentally remote author. Foucault himself warns against the transcendental idealism recrudescent in the concept of *écriture*: 'the notion of writing seems to transpose the empirical characteristics of the author into a transcendental anonymity'.[101] Indeed, with the impersonalist text, it is impossible to determine whether what arises is the transcendence of language or the transcendence of its author. 'Nearly every time you use the word *language*, I could replace it by the word *thought* almost without incongruity',[102] the phenomenologist Georges Poulet could say to Barthes, precisely because phenomenological subjectivity is conceived as an omnipresence of intentional consciousness which is superimposed upon the text like an invisible and perfectly isomorphic map onto the contours of a country. An ideal subject is posited in both cases, one under the auspices of a putative presence, the other as a no less artificial absence. From the point of view of interpretation, it matters little whether the author disappears into a transcendental annex or into the void: the text to be read is one in which the personality of the author is nowhere figured.

It would be the truest of truisms to say that impersonalist and biographicist conceptions of the text stand in resolute opposition. Yet given the proximity in which the impersonal and the transcendental must find themselves, it follows that not only are the biographical and the transcendental thoroughly distinct, but that these conceptions will also court a similar incompatibility. To constitute a biographical subject, or a subject of desire within a text which posits the transcendental uninvolvement of its author disrupts not only his sovereign detachment, but the very truth claims and objectivity that such detachment reinforces. As we have said, it is Foucault's failure to inscribe himself within the history he recounts which leads to the constitution of a transcendental subjectivity within *The Order of Things*. As we also remarked, the implication of authorial transcendence is all the more pronounced within texts whose aims are specifically constative. This is particularly true of philosophical discourse wherein impersonality tends to be a coefficient of the truth value of a system or critique. However, certain philosophers such as Montaigne, Descartes, and, to a lesser extent, Hume have attempted to narrow this distance by introducing autobiographical frames for their discourses, conversational intimacies, historical locales, and so forth. In modern times, Nietzsche, more than any other philosopher, has been keenly aware of these problems. The autobiographical in his text, his eccentric and highly personalised divagations and detours work against the philosophical ideal of lofty disinterestedness.[103] Moreover, Nietzsche did not just apply this strategy to his own texts, but sought to disillude the transcendental anonymity of philosophical discourse by opposing the personality and prejudices of the philosophical author to the ostensible objectivity of his system:

> What makes one regard philosophers half mistrustfully and half mockingly is ... that they display altogether insufficient honesty, while making a mighty and virtuous noise as soon as the problem of truthfulness is even remotely touched on. They pose as having discovered and attained their real opinions through the self-evolution of a cold, pure, divinely unperturbed dialectic ... while what happens at bottom is that a prejudice, a notion, an 'inspiration', generally a desire of the heart sifted and made abstract, is defended by them with reasons sought after the event – they are one and all advocates who do not want to be regarded as such, and for the most part no better than cunning pleaders for their prejudices which they baptise 'truths' ... [104]

Of course it is inconceivable that the philosophical labour could get underway without some attempt at disinterestedness. How indeed could a groundwork of the metaphysic of morals proceed along conative lines and still possess value and credibility as a contribution to the discipline of moral philosophy? But this is not Nietzsche's point. Philosophers present their conclusions as the outcome of strictly disinterested inquiries into the problems of truth, knowledge and morality, as consequences absolutely necessitated by purely rational procedures. In Nietzsche's view, however, this bourne is established from the outset. The text is written backwards; the philosopher reasons from conclusions to premises. Schopenhauer is by nature moribund and misanthropic, *thereafter* he weaves that wonderful vindication of pessimism and resignation known to us as *The World as Will and Representation*; Kant is a religious moralist, *therefore* he seeks to prove the existence of the 'starry heavens above and the moral law within'. For the critic of philosophical disinterestedness, the art of reading becomes that of retracing this primordial itinerary over and against the manifest structures of the text. To utilise such a strategy, to reread the author, his desires, prejudices, and drives, into the philosophical text, so far from consolidating the idea of the philosopher as the suzerain subject of his text, works rather to dismantle any such privilege. This insistence on the inescapably autobiographical element in any philosophy leads Nietzsche directly to the anti-transcendental theories of will-to-power and genealogy:

> It has gradually become clear to me what every great philosophy has hitherto been: a confession on the part of its author and a kind of involuntary and unconscious memoir; moreover, that the moral (or immoral) intentions in every philosophy have every time constituted the real germ of life out of which the entire plant has grown. To explain how a philosopher's most remote metaphysical assertions have actually been arrived at, it is always well (and wise) to ask oneself first: what morality does this (does *he* –) aim at? I accordingly do not believe a 'drive to knowledge' to be the father of philosophy, but that another drive has, here as elsewhere, only employed knowledge (and false knowledge!) as a tool. But anyone who looks at the basic drives of mankind to see what extent they may in precisely this connection have come into play as *inspirational* spirits … will discover that they have all at some time or other practised philosophy – and that each one of them would be only too glad to present *itself* as the ultimate goal of existence and as the legitimate *master* of all the other drives … In the philosopher … there is nothing whatever impersonal; and, above all, his morality bears decided and decisive testimony to *who he is* – that is to say, to the order of rank the innermost drives of his nature stand in relative to one another.[105]

As Nietzsche understood, perhaps better than any other, to affirm the impersonality of a philosophical system is the first step toward ascribing that system a transcendental value and vice versa. Consequently, Nietzsche rigorously inscribed the authorial subject within the system. Any criticism, and any theory which seeks to challenge the transcendence of a discourse will thus eventually find itself drawn to a form of *retrospective inference* 'from the work to its author, from the deed to its doer, from the ideal to him who *needs* it, from every mode of thinking and valuing to the imperative *want* behind it'.[106] So far from endorsing one another, from belonging to one another as aspects of the same subject, the transcendental subjectivity of philosophical systems, and the subjectivity of the author work against each other: the inscription of a biography, a biographical and biological desire within the text resists any theology of the idealist subject. Two markedly distinct subjectivities are in opposition: the one, transpersonal, extraworldly, normative and formal; the other intraworldly, biographical, a subject of desire, for want of a better word, a 'material' subject.

The misreception of Nietzsche as a proto-deconstructionist who advocates the disappearance of the author is the direct result of neglecting this distinction. Indeed, that segment of *The Will to Power* upon which the anti-authorial appropriation of Nietzsche is based, is directed exclusively against the Cartesian and Kantian subjects: an intensely focused philosophical critique of the onto-theological egology of philosophies of consciousness is directly misprised as an attack upon the author.[107] Indeed, no reading could be more erroneous, for – virtually alone amongst philosophers – Nietzsche insisted upon the most intimate links between man and his works, even, indeed, upon seeing this connection as an index of the value of a system of thought:

> It makes the most material difference whether a thinker stands personally related to his problems, having his fate, his need, and even his highest happiness therein; or merely impersonally, that is to say, if he can only feel and grasp them with the tentacles of cold, prying thought. In the latter case ... nothing comes of it: for the great problems, granting that they let themselves be grasped at all, do not let themselves be *held* by toads and weaklings ... [108]

The reinforcement of this connection, the *humanising* of knowledge, delivers thought from transcendental presuppositions; knowledge becomes relative, mediated, perspectival. This critique, whether it be thought as antihumanist or as a new humanism, was continued by Freud and Heidegger, who in very different ways, deconstructed the idea of a reified, unitary subjectivity in the interests not of the death of man or of the author, but of re-perceiving human subjectivity outside the domain of a transcendental subjectivity. For Heidegger, the rejection of humanism did not extend to anything resembling a rejection of the question of man. To the contrary, the question of man remained the question of philosophy; what is required, rather, is the redistribution of this question on the basis of a non-transcendental ontology 'in which the essence of man, determined by Being itself is at home ... '.[109] Such a redistribution does not involve the broad curtailment that humanists and antihumanists alike stake as the ground of their confrontation: 'Man is not the lord of beings. Man is the shepherd of being. Man loses nothing in this "less"; rather he gains in that he attains the truth of Being.'.[110] No impoverishment of man's unique existence, his rationality is implied here, quite the reverse: 'Humanism is opposed because it does not set the *humanitas* of man high enough.'[111]

The residual and enduring demand of these discourses is not to think without man but to rethink the question of man within a post-metaphysical ontology. The work of Nietzsche, Freud, Heidegger – Marx also – opens out onto a sense of the subject, of the author, which is no longer normative but disclosive, not timeless but rootedly historical, not an aeterna veritas but mutable, in process of becoming, not transcendent but immanent in its texts, its time and world. Indeed it would seem that all antihumanist discourse finally makes overture to a new form of humanism, that the rejection of the subject functions as a passageway between conceptions of subjectivity.

As the most recent representation of the movement against man, Foucault's work no more escapes the question of man than did that of Nietzsche, Marx, Freud or Heidegger. From *Madness and Civilization* where he attempted to give voice to unreason in man's experience through his studies of the constitution of the subject in power to *The History of Sexuality* in which discourse is recentred on the subject as a subject of desire,[112] Foucault's corpus can be read as a prolonged meditation on the question of subjectivity rather than on the absence of the subject; a meditation in which the death of man functions as a phase of hyperbolic doubt wherefrom the problem of man can be reassessed in the absence of transcendental presuppositions.

In 'The Subject and Power' Foucault in fact says that the goal of contemporary thought is 'to promote new forms of subjectivity through the refusal of the kind of individuality which has been imposed on us for several centuries'.[113] When we consider that *The Order of Things* had construed this individuality as essentially divided, not only from others but from itself, this task may well be read as that of promoting a de-alienated subjectivity no longer split between transcendental and empirical essences, between a sovereign *cogito* on the one hand and an impenetrable unthought on the other. Along these lines, we might even view Foucault's statement in *The Order of Things* that 'modern thought is advancing towards that region where man's Other must become the Same as himself' with a different eye, as the messianic mission of the Foucauldian project.[114] Certainly, from the vantage of any future humanism, Foucault's analyses of psychiatric, political, sexual and carceral modes of subjection, his genealogical sciences of the self – along with the thought of the 'antihumanist' movement in general – will seem of immeasurably greater value than the summary 'humanist' objections with which they have been confronted. There may be a certain irony in the fact that antihumanist discourse has provided the most significant directions in the theory of the subject, but there is not paradox: for the thought of the death of man cannot but be – in the most insistent, engaged form – the thinking *of* man *about* man.

3

Misread Intentions

Structuralism attempted to rescue language from the oblivion to which Western metaphysics had consigned it, but failed to pose the question of writing. For Jacques Derrida this omission was not just a simple oversight, but the last and latest reinforcement of a metaphysics of presence (as old as Plato) which has always and everywhere repressed the written sign and modelled language according to metaphors of self-presence and vocalisation. In order to uncover and contest this repression, Derrida devoted himself during the 1960s to profoundly intrinsic readings of philosophers such as Plato, Rousseau, Hegel, Husserl and Lévi-Strauss, destined to show that every attempt to subordinate writing to the immediate expressiveness and full self-presence of speech was obliged to presuppose a prior system of graphicity entirely at odds with the declared intent. In each of these readings, Derrida's method was to remain painstakingly faithful to the letter of the text, and the result was invariably a highly technical, inward analysis within which the relationship of these texts to the general history of metaphysics was constantly implied, but never stated in any systematic fashion.

In *Of Grammatology* (1967), however, Derrida locates his readings of Saussure, Lévi-Strauss and Rousseau within a historical and structural thematic of the metaphysical privilege accorded to speech over writing.[1] Within this text, and because of its concern with broad historical structures, the question of the author becomes most visible within the classic deconstructive period.[2] Naturally, if we are even to approach the philosophical context in which the author problematic is here inserted, then we will need to depart initially from specifically literary-critical issues. Moreover, it is only against the background of the deconstruction of metaphysics that Derrida's opposition to the author in *Of Grammatology* can be clearly appraised. In this expository phase, it will also be necessary to bypass numerous reservations and detours, in particular the issue of whether the deconstruction of metaphysics is not itself the most radical continuation of metaphysics, the last metaphysician always finding his work continued by the latest.

The movement against metaphysics was by no means new with Derrida. Indeed, it has been a recurrent theme in modern philosophy. Derrida does not, however, take his lead from the philosophers of the Vienna Circle who sought to dispel metaphysical questions on account of their unintelligibility, but from Nietzsche and Heidegger whose work directly engaged with metaphysical thought in order to disturb its very foundations. Derrida himself insists that his project is to be understood as a continuation of their critiques, particularly so in the case of Heidegger whose rereading of the history of philosophy functions as a continually invoked pre-text for the Derridean deconstruction. Following upon Nietzsche's identification of all metaphysical systems with the theological question, Heidegger came to conceive of metaphysics as onto-theology, the determination of being as presence. From Parmenides and Plato onward, says Heidegger, being has been conceived as a simple unity, a fully self-present origin and ground.[3] Heidegger accordingly saw the task of deconstructing metaphysics as a relentless interrogation of the notion of being such as it had been rendered by onto-theology, and the pursuit of a grounding of being more primordial than that of unitary and indivisible self-presence.

In his work subsequent to *Being and Time*, Heidegger explicitly sought this prior (and ungrounding) ground of being in what he called the ontological difference, or the difference between being and beings.[4] What the thought of being as presence neglects is that being in the abstract is not the same as the things-that-are, that existence is not one and the same as existents. Being is something toward which beings maintain a relationship, onto whose promise they open. The difference is both spatial and temporal. 'Spatial' because whilst we can say that beings are here and there, being itself is never anywhere, but beyond and transcendent of beings; 'temporal' because being is conceived as the timeless essence of beings whilst beings themselves are always subject to their seasons in that they can pass in and out of existence at any time.

This difference is then distributed into the difference between presence and the present in accordance with the ever-presentness of being and the finitude of beings. Ontological difference, Heidegger insists, is the primary unthought of metaphysics such that it cannot be thought within the horizons of Western onto-theology. To think the difference, therefore, is to think the end of metaphysics, of being-as-presence: 'The essence of presencing, and with it the distinction between presencing and what is present, remains forgotten. *The oblivion of Being is oblivion of the distinction between Being and beings.*'[5]

What for Heidegger is the finishing line is for Derrida somewhere near the start, in that he accepts the force and validity of both Heidegger's history of metaphysics as the history of the determination of being as presence, and the pursuit of a breach with that tradition via the uncovering of an originary difference. Presupposing, therefore, much that is deeply questionable in Heidegger's reading of the history of philosophy, the Derridean deconstruction becomes, and remains, the task of radicalising these two phases of the Heideggerian text. Derrida's first step along this road is to rework the history of presence in terms of the privileging of speech over writing. According to Derrida, the notion of speech, as it has been always and everywhere identified with fully self-present meaning, is related primally to the notion of presence in general: 'The system of language associated with phonetic-alphabetic writing is that within which logocentric metaphysics, determining the sense of being as presence, has been produced. This logocentrism, the *epoch* of the full speech, has always placed in parenthesis, *suspended*, and suppressed for essential reasons, all free reflection on the origin and status of writing.' (43) The basis of this system resides in the association of the signified with presence, and the signifier with the absence of a signified *presence*: 'The formal essence of the signified is presence', Derrida writes, 'and the privilege of its proximity to the *logos* as phone– is is the privilege of *presence*.' (18)

As its coinage suggests, logocentrism designates thought centred upon the *logos*, whereby *logos* designates not only the word of God, science and logic, but the broad conceptual system of Western metaphysics: the thing in itself, essence, origin, pure consciousness, identity, presence, being as presence. Where Derrida's thought here goes beyond Heidegger is in asserting that the metaphysical determination of being as presence could only have been produced as the outcome of the repression of writing, and that logocentrism is therefore the prior condition of onto-theology, the latter being produced as an effect of the valorisation of the *logos* or fully self-present meaning. Metaphysics could not have begun to install the thought of presence at the origin without having always already repressed the primacy of the signifier over the signified, the primacy of the sign representing presence-in-its-absence over presence itself. Logocentrism is not itself part of the metaphysics of presence, the metaphysics of presence is the effect of logocentrism. The reduction of writing is the necessary and sufficient condition, of the epoch of onto-theology; it has produced '*the greatest totality* ... within which are produced, without ever posing the radical question of writing, all the Western methods of analysis, explication, reading, or interpretation'. (46)

This recognition then prepares the way for the second phase of Derrida's attempt to pass through and beyond the Heideggerian deconstruction.[6] If the forgetting of writing, the sign, or 'trace' as Derrida often calls it, is the precondition of the epoch of metaphysics – behind and before the determination of being as presence – then the liberation of the signifier will unleash a pre-originary difference still more pristine than that between being and beings. Whilst it must be that all metaphysics rests upon the privileging of the *phonē* – via the erasure of writing, then the breaching of metaphysics will consist in the propagation of writing as a difference which precedes ontological difference as the unthought of metaphysics; a writing which, as we know, is thought as *différance*, a differing and deferring (non)principle which produces not only the illusion of presence, but the very possibility of differentiation in the first place. Such a writing, if it could be thought, if it could be written, would represent a breach with metaphysics, more powerful, more fundamental than the ontological difference which would then take its place as the final limit of metaphysical conceptuality and the first of the 'intrametaphysical effects of *différance*':[7]

> the determinations which name difference always come from the metaphysical order. This holds not only for the determination of difference as the difference between presence and the present (*Anwesen/ Anwesend*), but also for the determination of difference as the difference between Being and beings ... There may be a difference still more unthought than the difference between Being and beings. We certainly can go further toward naming it in our language. Beyond Being and beings, this difference, ceaselessly differing from and deferring (itself), would trace (itself) (by itself) – this *différance* would be the first or last trace if one could still speak, here, of origin and end.
>
> Such a *différance* would at once, again, give us to think a writing without presence and without absence, without history, without cause, without *archia*, without *telos*, a writing that absolutely upsets all dialectics, all theology, all teleology, all ontology.[8]

So very much indeed would seem to be at stake in the forgetting and remembering of writing. In the *Grammatology*, Derrida proposes a 'theoretical matrix' – a '*structural figure* as much as a *historical totality*' (lxxxix) – of this repression. And Derrida does not use the word 'totality' lightly here. Logocentrism, we are to believe, has controlled 'in one and the same *order*':

1. *the concept of writing* in a world where the phoneticisation of writing must dissimulate its own history as it is produced;

2. *the history of* (the only) *metaphysics*, which has, in spite of all differences, not only from Plato to Hegel (even including Leibniz) but also, beyond these apparent limits, from the pre-Socratics to Heidegger, always assigned the origin of truth in general to the *logos*: the history of truth, of the truth of truth, has always been … the debasement of writing, and its repression outside 'full' speech.

3. *the concept of science* or the scientificity of science – what has always been determined as *logic* … (3)

And, over the page, Derrida says that the subordination of speech to writing is 'the historical origin and structural possibility of philosophy as of science, the condition of the *episteme*.' (4)

Within such a vast, unified, and all-inclusive *episteme*, the work of individual authors will serve merely as indices, as regional instances of the infrastructural network of logocentric determinations. Thus, though half of the text is given over to a massively detailed reading of Rousseau, no especial significance is accorded to Rousseau's text as such; the reading is, as Derrida says, 'the moment, as it were, of the example' (lxxxix); what we are reading is not a text by a particular author, but one meeting point amongst so many others of the logocentric metaphysics which has governed Western thought from its beginnings down to the present day:

before asking the necessary questions about the historical situation of Rousseau's text, we must locate all the signs of its appurtenance to the metaphysics of presence, from Plato to Hegel, rhythmed by the articulation of presence upon self-presence. The unity of this metaphysical tradition should be respected in its general permanence through all the marks of appurtenance, the genealogical sequences, the stricter routes of causality that organise Rousseau's text. We must recognise, prudently and as a preliminary, what this historicity amounts to; without this, what one would inscribe within a narrower structure would not be a text and above all not Rousseau's text … There is not, strictly speaking, a text whose author or subject is Jean-Jacques Rousseau. (246)

The proper name is an improper variation on the common name. That the text has even to make provisional recourse to the names of authors is a regrettable expedience. For entirely preliminary purposes of concision and clarity, we locate a body of texts arbitrarily assembled under the signature 'Rousseau', but we do so on the understanding that the name 'Rousseau' is under erasure throughout, that, strictly speaking, it has no meaning, signifies absence.

Yet, from the very first, the *Grammatology* cannot be entirely secure on this issue. For is there not (even with the necessary precautions) a contradiction involved in continuing over hundreds of pages to talk about a Rousseauian text when no such thing properly exists? How can we, in all consistency, utilise that whose existence we contest 'at root'? As we know, Derrida has inherited from Heidegger numerous strategies with which to negotiate the saying of the strictly unsayable. Most notably the practice of writing under erasure (in tandem with the vigilant use of parentheses, quotation-marks) whereby words such as 'is', 'presence', continue to be deployed, not because we wish to reconfirm the metaphysic always inherent in their enunciation, but in despair of any other language with which to speak. And it would seem entirely *de règle* to allow this concession, for without it there would be either no possibility of Heidegger and Derrida writing, or of our reading their work. Yet to extend this concession to the *Grammatology*'s appropriation of Rousseau is not the same thing at all, for nothing in principle compels Derrida to the vast and disproportionate attention bestowed upon this single author. Within the 'age of metaphysics' he demarcates (Descartes to Hegel), he could have read the works of Descartes, Leibniz, Berkeley and so forth, and not exclusively those of Rousseau on trust that they most revealingly represent this epoch of logocentrism. And there is far greater unease on this issue than any other in the *Grammatology*. If we follow this important paragraph – which belongs to the 'Introduction to the "Age of Rousseau"' – in its shifting moods:

> The names of authors or doctrines have here no substantial value. They indicate neither identities nor causes. It would be frivolous to think that 'Descartes', 'Leibniz', 'Rousseau', 'Hegel', etc., are names of authors, of the authors of movements or displacements that we thus designate. The indicative value that I attribute to them is first the name of a problem. If I provisionally authorise myself to treat this historical structure by fixing my attention on philosophical or literary texts, it is not for the sake of identifying in them the origin, cause, or equilibrium of the structure. But as I also do not think that these texts are the simple *effects* of structure, in any sense of the word; as I think that *all concepts hitherto proposed in order to think the articulation of a discourse and of an historical totality are caught within the metaphysical closure that I question here*, as we do not know of any other concepts and cannot produce any others, and indeed shall not produce so long as this closure limits our discourse; as the primordial and indispensable phase, in fact and in principle, of the development of this problematic, consists in questioning the internal structure of

these texts as symptoms; as that is the only condition for determining these symptoms *themselves* in the totality of their metaphysical appurtenance; I draw my argument from them in order to isolate Rousseau, and, in Rousseauism, the theory of writing. Besides, this abstraction is partial, and it remains, in my view, provisional. Further on, I shall directly approach the problem within a 'question of method'. (99)

Singular difficulties have begun to emerge. What begins as a confident disclaimer of the author gradually lurches into hesitation and postponement. Though the passage seems to be asserting the redundancy of the author, it finally issues as an apology for the uses the *Grammatology* is subsequently to make of Rousseau. Not that the problem is sufficiently treated here – as Derrida says, its direct address is to be awaited. But nevertheless, we are asked to accept a text which will appear for all the world to be Rousseauian, and of unique importance in the history of logocentrism, on the conditions that it is not a text whose author and subject is Rousseau, and that it is no more than a mere instance of logocentrism.

The ambivalence of this position generates numerous contradictory statements throughout the *Grammatology*. Introducing the 'Age of Rousseau', we are told that Rousseau's text occupies 'a singular position' (97) in the history of metaphysics, whilst later it is said: 'Rousseau, as I have already suggested, has only a very relative privilege in the history that interests us'. (162) Similarly, though there is no text whose author is Jean-Jacques Rousseau, we are informed that 'something irreducibly Rousseauist is captured' (161) in Derrida's reading. Furthermore, when Derrida approaches the issue with a 'question of method', though much else besides is discussed, the question of Rousseau's status is treated still more exiguously, and is effectively closed no sooner than it is opened.[9]

What exigencies force Derrida into this awkward, and as he would say, embarrassed position *vis-à-vis* Rousseau? Why does he never attempt an answer to this question which everywhere presses upon the *Grammatology*? Another way of presenting this dilemma would be to ask: if logocentrism is all-pervasive why make one author stand surety for 'the reduction of writing profoundly implied by the entire age', (98) and examine this repression in the innermost recesses of his corpus? Derrida could surely have traced the logocentric arrangement symptomatically across that age of metaphysics between Descartes and Hegel. Not that there is insufficient space for such an undertaking. After all, a large section of the analysis of this age is given over to Lévi-Strauss, *on account of his fidelity to Rousseau*.[10] And, for that matter, why Lévi-Strauss rather than Descartes, Leibniz, or any other of those thinkers who actually belonged to the Classical Age?

Answers to these questions are pledged but postponed; much in the manner that impossible promises find their fulfilment assigned to the distant future in the hope they will then be forgotten. And for good reason, since these questions bear not only upon the deconstruction of logocentrism, but more primally upon its construction. What, then, is the status of Rousseau as an instance of logocentricity? What are the uses to which he is put in the *Grammatology*?

HORS–TEXTE

Derrida's analysis of Rousseau presented the critical establishment with a formidable and unprecedented model of reading, whereby the critic demonstrates at great length, and with exemplary rigour, that a text finally says quite the reverse of what its author intended. Rousseau's *Essay on the Origin of Languages* entirely turns back upon itself, his conception of writing as the supplement of speech issues, within the text itself, as more originary than speech both in spite, and because of its author's determination to say exactly the opposite. A counter-logic of supplementarity, traced with tenacious intricacy throughout the Rousseauian text, everywhere undermines the romantic thesis of a pure, immediate vocality prior to all inscription. While Rousseau wants to say that writing is an exterior addition to the self-presence of speech, his text continually presupposes that writing is also the 'supplement' of speech in a second sense whereby it is seen to compensate for a lack which has already appeared in the notion of originary presence. These two contradictory meanings or virtualities of the word 'supplement' co-inhere throughout Rousseau's analyses with an effect so disruptive that what his text inscribes at the origin of languages is a supplement at the origin, a 'writing that takes place *before* and within *speech*'. (315)

Within the course of this serpentine, and profoundly inward interpretation, Derrida also evolved a method of reading which combines the technical resources of both philosophical and literary criticism in a particularly fertile, sophisticated and challenging manner. Equally at ease with Rousseau's fiction and his philosophical discourses, the *Grammatology* takes up a unique position at the enigmatic threshold between literary and philosophical analysis, between these two disciplines which are so near and so occulted to one another. As we know, this significant achievement has had regrettable consequences for Derrida's reception in the philosophical community, but it has signally contributed to the excitement and enthusiasm which his work has inspired in literature departments. Yet, mirroring its divided reception, the text tends to be read literally in two halves.

Particularly in that the interpretation of Rousseau is often read aside from its context, as though it did not form 'Part II' of a text called *Of Grammatology*, as though it were not, as Derrida insists, to be connected to the theoretical proposals presented in the first half of the text.

Derrida opens his reading in a manner which will seem most unlikely if we consider the foregoing prescriptions concerning the absence of Rousseau as author. So far from commencing with a reading of the supplement in Rousseau's theory of language, Derrida devotes a chapter entitled 'That Dangerous Supplement' to tracing the supplement within Rousseau's (auto)biographical experience. Indeed the two, life and work, are to be thought as one:

> we must ... think Rousseau's experience and his theory of writing together, the accord and the discord that, under the name of writing, relate Jean-Jacques to Rousseau, uniting and dividing his proper name. On the side of experience, a recourse to literature as reappropriation of presence, that is to say, as we shall see, of Nature; on the side of theory, an indictment against the negativity of the letter, in which must be read the degeneracy of culture and the disruption of the community. (144)

Accordingly, 'That Dangerous Supplement' begins by endorsing the traditional psychobiographical interpretation which sees Rousseau's turn to writing as a means of compensating (supplementing) for his feelings of inadequacy in normal social life. That this is as *auteurist* an itinerary as can be followed does not detain or perturb Derrida, and he quickens his step along this path by connecting the psychopathological impulse that drives Rousseau to write with his masturbatory practices. Like writing, masturbation (when accompanied by object-fantasy) is a supplement or proxy of lived experience, an imago of an unattainable or unmasterable presence: in Rousseau's case of a morbidly feared plenitude enhoused in the acts of speech and copulation. Writing and masturbation alike are methods of mastering presence in the mode of absence, and with Rousseau they are so indissolubly linked that we can say: 'It is from a certain determined representation of "cohabitation with women" that Rousseau had to have recourse throughout his life to that type of dangerous supplement that is called masturbation, and that cannot be separated from his activity as a writer. To the end.' (155)

But the supplementary chain linking Rousseau's experience to his philosophy of language does not end here. Derrida then proceeds to co-implicate the absence of a 'real' mother in Rousseau's life with the logic of deferral and substitution. Having (it is widely supposed) lost his 'natural' mother in childbirth, Rousseau's life was thereafter populated by a chain of surrogates. In his relationship with Thérèse, which is itself supplemented via the dangerous vice of masturbation, Rousseau also discovers the supplement of his adoptive mother who is herself the supplement of the 'true' mother. And yet, for Derrida, even this natural mother is not outside the chain of supplementary substitutions: 'Jean-Jacques could thus look for a supplement to Thérèse only on one condition: that ... *Thérèse herself be already a supplement.* As Mamma was already the supplement of an unknown mother, and as the "true mother" herself, at whom the known "psychoanalyses" of the case of Jean-Jacques Rousseau stop, was also in a certain way a supplement.' (156)

The attempt to retrace this chain to any 'natural', or 'first' mother is therefore condemned in advance to the vain regress that Rousseau's text encounters in attempts to uncover the origin of language. At the wellspring there will always be another source, a pre-originary substitution, a further supplement of a presence itself irremediably absent like the lost mother. And it is easy to see how this endless and hollow supplementarity will resonate at the heart of Rousseau's political philosophy, wherein the quest of a pure state of nature will ceaselessly run up against proto-cultural forces. In all these areas, the thought of an originary presence is destined to discover a supplement at the origin, the supplement of an origin itself supplementary, a presencing absence, an absenting presence.

Naturally such an interpretation assumes the greatest degree of communication between Rousseau's life and work. Indeed its strength resides in the felicity with which Derrida evokes a purely Rousseauian world wherein sexual, social, and maternal neuroses, an essay on the origin of languages, and a political philosophy of uncorrupted origins are patterned and figured around the deviant logic of the supplement. As such, 'That Dangerous Supplement' repeats not only the content but the format and ethos of traditional psychobiography. But such an excursion is the last thing we have been prepared to expect from the *Grammatology*, or Derridean deconstruction in general. How is this chapter, with its troupe of biographical figures, to be reconciled to the injunction that 'the names of authors ... have here no substantial value', that they 'indicate neither identities nor causes'? No sooner does Derrida depart from the psychobiographical locale of the supplement than he raises a question of method.

Reading Rousseau in terms of autoeroticism and mother-substitutions cannot, we are told, be deemed psychoanalytic in the customary sense. Here Derrida's accents are distinctly Lacanian:

> Although it is not commentary, our reading must be intrinsic and remain within the text. That is why, in spite of certain appearances,

the locating of the word *supplement* is here not at all psychoanalytical, if by that we understand an interpretation that takes us outside of the writing toward a psychobiographical signified, or even toward a general psychological structure that could rightly be separated from the signifier. (159)

On one level this means, quite simply, that we are to regard the psychobiographical as but one form of writing or signification amongst others, for when we read biography or autobiography we are reading, as everywhere we must, nothing other than writing. And for all its banality, this is a necessary point, in that it provides the most direct route of return for the author as a biographical figure in criticism. The writer's (auto)biography is writing, and there is therefore no reason to either valorise its significance in the act of interpretation, or to outlaw its deployment on the grounds that it is somehow an improper form of textuality. Thus we can re-mobilise the autobiographical without lapsing once more into positivist or geneticist assumptions. Yet Derrida wants to take this further. In its most infamous hour, the text declares:

> *There is nothing outside the text* [there is no outside-text; *il n'y a pas de hors-texte*]. And that is neither because Jean-Jacques' life or the existence of Mamma or Thérèse themselves, is not of prime interest to us, nor because we have access to their so-called 'real' existence only in the text and we have neither any means of altering this, nor any right to neglect this limitation. All reasons of this type would already be sufficient, to be sure, but there are more radical reasons. What we have tried to show by following the guiding line of the 'dangerous supplement', is that in what one calls the real life of these existences 'of flesh and bone', beyond and behind what one believes can be circumscribed as Rousseau's text, there has never been anything but writing; there have never been anything but supplements, substitutional significations which could only come forth in a chain of differential references, the 'real' supervening, and being added only while taking on meaning from a trace and from an invocation of the supplement, etc. And thus to infinity, for we have read, *in the text*, that the absolute present, Nature, that which words like 'real mother' name, have always already escaped, have never existed; that what opens meaning and language is writing as the disappearance of natural presence. (158–9)

Derrida never quite says so, but he irresistibly implies it: life itself, in its materiality, even as it was lived, is writing. Subsequently, Derrida has on several occasions gone out of his way to correct the reading of this statement, to refuse the idea that 'there is nothing beyond language ... and other stupidities of that sort'.[11] Yet unjust as this idealist representation is, it does not take place on the basis of nothing, for Derrida is at his most ambiguous here, and all the important questions are left in suspension.

What are these 'more radical reasons'? Certainly they go beyond the commonplace assertion that the *Confessions* is a written text, and that there is no question of sustaining Mamma and Thérèse as natural, empirical presences in so far as they are biologically deceased and appear to us only as traces in Rousseau's text.[12] But where might we go beyond this? In declaring that there is nothing behind Rousseau's text are we saying that Mamma and Thérèse never existed except as textual figures even when they were alive? That for Rousseau they were supplements, and never presences, never more than textual figures even as he walked in their midst? And, most important of all, is this to be taken as peculiar to Rousseau, or as a principle of reading and writing in general? The text provides no elucidation here, even as it directly confronts its own methodological status. Once more, also, the unanswered question bears upon Rousseau's role as an instance of logocentrism.

Though it is not at all clear what Derrida means by this passage, what it *does* in the *Grammatology* is quite apparent. Once again it allows the text to thoroughly utilise resources whose validity it disputes. We may pursue the most generous psychobiographical thesis provided we bear in mind that the psychobiographical signified has never existed, just as we may have disproportionate recourse to the texts of Jean-Jacques Rousseau so long as it is recalled that there is 'no text whose author and subject is Jean-Jacques Rousseau'. That we summon Rousseau's autoeroticism, his relationship with Thérèse, Mamma, his discomfiture with the spoken word does not return us to the precepts of man-and-the-work criticism, for we are only dealing with writing, and here only with a certain collocation of texts which arbitrarily bear the name Jean-Jacques Rousseau, and whose very place in the reading is determined solely by their metaphysical and epistemic appurtenance. Yet in 'That Dangerous Supplement', so far from presenting that in Rousseau which is common to the age and to the *episteme*, Derrida is drawing upon a highly idiosyncratic network of circumstances in which an essay on the origin of languages, a political philosophy of uncorrupted origins, an obsessive autoeroticism and a psychopathology of mother-substitution all manifestly coincide with an exaltation of natural presence and a denunciation of supplementarity as negativity, evil, exteriority.

The fortuities of this situation are not the stuff and substance of epistemic exemplarity, yet they have been proffered as such. In accordance with the classic deconstructive trope we could say that a lacuna has opened up between statement and gesture here. The 'Introduction to the "age of Rousseau"' has told us that Rousseau is simply an example of the logocentric ensemble. 'That Dangerous Supplement' has shown us that what the author of the *Essay on the Origin of Languages* exemplifies most perfectly is the contorted psychopathology of Jean-Jacques Rousseau. The next move which the *Grammatology* makes is still more unlikely.

A HISTORY OF SILENCE

But, first of all, is there a history of silence?

Jacques Derrida[13]

The succeeding chapter of the *Grammatology* is entitled 'Genesis and Structure of the *Essay on the Origin of Languages*'. 'Genesis' will be a peculiar word in the *Grammatology* since the weight of its thesis is directed toward problematising the existence of anything like genesis, whether it be that of language, society, humanity. But the genesis Derrida has here in mind is extremely narrow and local. His concern is with the precise date of the composition of the *Essay*,[14] and he analyses this question over the course of a long subsection entitled 'The Place of the *Essay*'. In the absence of any absolutely authoritative external evidence as to the time of its composition, Rousseau scholars have been divided as to whether the *Essay* was written before or after the second *Discourse (Discourse on Inequality)*.[15] Speculation ranges over a period of fifteen or so years, the mid-1740s being the earliest possible time, 1761 the latest. The second *Discourse* (1754) occupies such prominence in this debate because it is considered the first of the great Rousseauian works, and thus forms the opening of the primary canon. Scholars have largely consented in the view that the *Essay* is not the equal of these great discourses, that a certain want of structure and immaturity of philosophical reasoning are incompatible with the later work. Correspondingly, the themes of the later works have been discovered in inchoate and fledgling form in the *Essay*. This position has also the added advantage of explaining why the text was never published during Rousseau's lifetime. Publication was withheld, it is assumed, because the author realised that this work would not do justice to the great philosophical project he was about to undertake.[16]

Derrida contests this position vigorously, and in an argument that throughout respects all the protocols of classical textual scholarship. With an attentiveness and rigour all his own, he argues that in terms of external evidence, there is no progression in philosophic thematics between the

Essay and the second *Discourse*, if anything the reverse. There is thus no question of the *Essay* predating the second *Discourse* on these counts. With regard to the external question, Derrida claims that the debate was settled in favour of the posteriority of the *Essay* as long ago as 1913, and quotes a Rousseau scholar at great length to this effect.[17] The intricacies of Derrida's argument are of no especial interest here. The more compelling question is why the *Grammatology* should concern itself with this issue at all. What motivates Derrida to depart from the theme of the supplement for a full and valuable twenty-five pages immediately after having introduced it in the most spellbinding fashion? And to do so in the interest of pursuing the most *auteurist* and positivistic of exercises? What could be more irrelevant to a broad-based intertextuality than the question of whether the *Essay* was written six years before the second *Discourse* or six years after?

Derrida's commentators are silent on this issue. As well they might be, for not only does this section command precious little interest for anyone who is not a Rousseau scholar, but it would appear, also, to be thoroughly counterintuitive. Gayatri Chakravorty Spivak is rare, perhaps alone, in mentioning 'The Place of the *Essay*', and she does so only in the offices of a translator's introduction. For her, it 'is engrossing to watch the bold argument operating in the service of a conventional debate', an opportunity to savour the 'taste of a rather special early Derrida', and the section is to be read as a piece of 'rather endearing conservatism'.[18]

However, true as this may be, the implication is that we are to regard the relationship of 'The Place of the *Essay*' to the rest of the *Grammatology* as purely contingent. Yet one thing we quickly learn from reading Derrida is that nothing is a simple digression, undertaken for no apparent reason. Rather such moments, like fault-lines in the text, will appear marginal and extrinsic, but to rigorous investigation in fact reveal an economy, or strategic wager, vital to the entire system. It is upon such moments, a footnote, a harmless *entr'acte*, a casual metaphor, a seemingly directionless chapter, that deconstructive reading will begin its work of unsettling the structures and presuppositions of the text. Why then does Derrida want us to agree that the *Essay* postdates the second *Discourse*? Spivak also says: 'I do not believe that Derrida ever again devotes himself to this sort of textual scholarship.'[19] However, when we consider that Derrida undertakes a very similar mission in 'Plato's Pharmacy', the necessities which dictate 'The Place of the *Essay*' begin to emerge.[20]

By a coincidence, perhaps uncanny, Plato's *Phaedrus* has also been relegated by tradition to a place among the works of its author's immaturity.[21] The use of myth to illustrate the problem of writing (an explanatory tactic generally censured by Plato), and ill-construction in the exchanges between Phaedrus and Socrates, have led scholars to suppose that it was Plato's first dialogue. In the early twentieth century this view persisted but took a curious turn as scholars now began to assert that it was Plato's last work, the same defects now explicable in terms of declining rather than nascent critical powers. Here again Derrida plays the dutiful advocate: 'We are speaking of the *Phaedrus* that was obliged to wait almost twenty-five centuries before anyone gave up the idea that it was a badly composed dialogue ... We are no longer at that point.'[22] To sufficiently sensitive expiscation, Derrida argues, the *Phaedrus* will surrender all the logical rigour of the great Platonic dialogues. It is only really necessary to *read* this text to see that, in its denunciation of writing, it is not only compatible with the Platonic system in general, but actively and urgently necessitated by that system. 'Plato's Pharmacy' thus gives over its first twenty pages to defending the *Phaedrus* against the tradition

Of course this will seem a little puzzling, since from a prima facie point of view, the tradition is very much in agreement with what we might expect deconstruction to avouch here. Platonic scholars themselves, far from upholding Plato's denunciation of writing have found it somewhat inconsistent, and in explicit contradiction with Plato's own practices as a writer. Indeed, we might say, that in certain respects, the critical basis on which deconstruction might take place here has been prepared long in advance. Yet what presents itself here as the deconstruction of logocentrism here, is in fact responding to the far more onerous pressures of constructing that tradition.

Over and above the necessities of undoing the text, and as their indispensable condition, the *Phaedrus* must be seen to belong fully to the great Platonic metaphysics, for within the deconstructive narrative this text – of which only four pages deal negatively with the question of writing – forms the origin of logocentrism. And the stacks are laid high against Derrida here, since it is not just that the *Phaedrus* as a whole is thought to belong to a prodigal immaturity, but it is thought to do so primarily on account of the very section which introduces the myth of Threuth to illustrate the argument that writing, as an artificial mnemic device, would subvert the living presence of natural memory.[23] Furthermore, additional support for the condemnation of writing only comes from a *Seventh Letter* whose authenticity is widely contested.[24] Derrida *must* insist upon the 'rigorous, sure, and subtle form'[25] of the *Phaedrus*, he *must* argue with a supremely patient vigour, that the *Phaedrus* is absolutely essential and axial to the primary Platonic canon, that the very system of Platonic idealism relates *eo ipso* to the the repression of writing, for it is only from this point that the seemingly lateral question of speech/writing can be wedded to the vast tradition of Western metaphysics. It is only from here that Derrida can say that the metaphysics of presence came into its being with the repression of writing, only from here that his text can begin to use these terms interchangeably within its history of Western thought.

Likewise, in the case of Rousseau's text. Having allotted to a short, little read and posthumously published tract the onus of representing an entire age of metaphysics between Descartes and Hegel, the redoubtable problems of exemplarity[26] that this raises would be still further compounded if – following tradition – we were to see in the *Essay* a work not even itself properly Rousseauian.[27] This would not have presented such problems to Derrida had he merely wished to discuss the *Essay* on its own terms, as though it could have come from anywhere. But in order to lend the theme of supplementarity its full breadth the *Grammatology* has been obliged to trace it across Rousseau's entire corpus, and to read it in the deepest reserves of his experience, thereby evolving a Rousseauism from which the *Essay* is thenceforth in principle inextricable. Furthermore, within the complex economy of the *Grammatology*, supplementarity must be traced through the *Confessions* if it is to be a determinant psychic force; as, too, the *Essay* must intertextualise from a position of parity with the great discourses, for it is in this hour that the question of writing as supplementarity conjoins itself to the discourses on nature, culture, politics; and indeed having established the posteriority of the *Essay* to the second *Discourse*, grammatology will spare no effort in reading the question of writing as tacitly implied in the entire Rousseauian philosophy.[28]

There is then a very definite sense in which deconstruction is in complicity with the texts it deconstructs. As a general principle, preparatory labours of construction must accompany any deconstructive act, for the reading must propose a model of order even if only in the interests of finally unsettling that order; and in this sense Derrida's work acquires a rare analogue in its industrial counterpart, for which a certain work of consolidation is sometimes necessary if a building is to collapse according to pre-established patterns. Yet, though this initial phase of construction is common to all the deconstructive readings, its urgency is somewhat greater in the cases of the *Phaedrus* and the *Essay* than elsewhere. That Derrida will exert such efforts of sponsorship on their behalf is primarily due to the peculiar fragility of the history he recounts. For this reason, too, he has no answers to the question of Rousseau's exemplarity.

If we reconstitute the history of logocentrism, we will see that – in its exemplary moments – it leaps directly from antiquity to Rousseau's *Essay on the Origin of Languages*. And it is not in the interests of brevity or momentum that Derrida should move so expeditiously between the *Phaedrus* and the Rousseauist dream of a pure, originary voice. 'If the history of metaphysics is the history of a determination of being as presence, if its adventure merges with that of logocentrism, and if it is produced wholly as the reduction of the trace, Rousseau's work seems to me to occupy, between Plato's *Phaedrus* and Hegel's *Encyclopaedia*, a singular position.' (97) Yet the singularity of Rousseau's position is determined by the singular silence of the Classical Age on the priority of speech, repression of writing: 'Within this age of metaphysics, between Descartes and Hegel, Rousseau is undoubtedly the only one or the first one to make a theme or system of the reduction of writing', the text says, but feels compelled to add that this reduction was 'profoundly implied by the entire age'. (98) However, Derrida does not show how the reduction of writing was profoundly implied by Descartes, nor any other of the philosophers of the Classical era. Indeed, grammatology is here forced into a position exactly the reverse of Foucault's analysis of the Classical *episteme*. Whilst *The Order of Things* devotes its longest, most evidenced and persuasive analyses to demonstrating the Classical pre-occupation with the system of signs, *Of Grammatology* must enforce the repression of the sign during this epoch, and on the basis of very little evidence or argumentation.

Furthermore, the 'age of metaphysics' that Derrida demarcates becomes all the less propitious to the logocentric thesis in that those areas in which the question of writing was raised – general grammar, the Leibnizian project of the *characteris universalis* – exerted energies more accommodating to a nascent grammatology than metaphysical phonocentrism. Indeed, in this era we would anticipate that grammatology, as the science of writing, would do everything to draw forth the efflorescence of interest in the sign system, the mathematicisation of knowledge, in the Chinese ideogram, the burgeoning disciplines of pasigraphy and so forth, rather than pressing the dour and negative thesis that we behold here only the illusion of writing's liberation, that at the most fundamental level writing was still shackled, lateralised, debased. Yet Derrida is contracted to this position, since – as the Classical era is itself the great epoch of metaphysics – it is essential that the logocentric arrangement will be seen to hold undivided sway during this period. Not surprisingly, Derrida is forced into defensive, almost rearguard actions here. Most markedly in the case of Leibniz:

> In spite of all the differences that separate the projects of universal
> language or writing at this time (notably with respect to history and

language), the concept of the simple absolute is always necessarily and indispensably involved. It would be easy to show that it always leads to an infinitist theology and to the *logos* or the infinite understanding of God. That is why, appearances to the contrary, and in spite of all the seduction that it can legitimately exercise on our epoch, the Leibnizian project of a universal characteristic that is not essentially phonetic does not interrupt logocentrism in any way. On the contrary, universal logic confirms logocentrism, is produced within it and with its help, exactly like the Hegelian critique to which it will be subjected. I emphasise the complicity of these two contradictory movements ... (78–9)

Putting to one side the question of whether the simple absolute or characteristic does lead so easily to infinitist theology,[29] as well as the suspicion of circularity in his argument here (that universal logic is produced within logocentrism is precisely what is in question), it is clear that the terms of the grammatological thesis have been deftly shifted at this point. The principal contention of the *Grammatology* has been that the repression of writing is the universally prior condition of the logocentric *episteme*, 'the historical origin and structural possibility of philosophy as of science, the condition of the *episteme*'. (4) Now, however, Derrida is saying that the Leibnizian sign system is logocentric even though it does not privilege the *phonē*. Even if we accede to everything Derrida says about the connection between the simple absolute and infinitist theology, nothing is redeemed in this respect; if anything the questions raised take on a still more worrying aspect. How is it that a universal language which privileges neither speech nor writing, and which is proposed in the form an arche-writing logically prior to both, should, indeed *could* be logocentric without respecting the sole and sufficient condition of that *episteme*? Are we to accept a logocentrism which is not phonocentric? How, in grammatological terms, is that possible? *Of Grammatology* has much to clarify at this point, but the text moves quickly away from the Leibnizian question, as also from the issue of the widespread classical research into Chinese writing, a project which is dismissed as 'a sort of European hallucination'. (80)

The problems that the Classical era present to grammatology, then, are immense, for not only are overtly logocentric texts conspicuous in their absence, but Derrida has also to contend with a movement in thought which appears, for all the world, to interrupt or breach the great epoch of logocentrism. Of course it might be said that such a silence consolidates the deconstructive insistence on the presuppositional inherence of logocentrism in Western discourse, that though so much in this epoch would suggest the contrary, these forces merely register superficial or illusory displacements, and that the repression of writing continued to operate at the deepest level. And this is not quite as eristic a point as it might seem. The agency of repression, as we know, is at its strongest when it operates unawares. But since logocentrism can, and does surface every now and then, we might expect some historical account of why it enters discourse at a manifest level at some times and does not at others. Moreover, even if we allow the verity of each and every grammatological proposition, the absence of explicitly logocentric texts will still present Derrida with enormous expository difficulties in that there are precious few points at which deconstruction can seize upon logocentricity and contest its assumptions.

That deconstruction must take place upon a construct is obvious, and to oppose a tacit and sedimented nexus of phonocentric assumptions across an *episteme* as old as thought itself would be a task so problematic as to be all but inconceivable. As a result, Derrida is obliged to exalt those brief and historically isolated moments of logocentric clarity in which the grounding assumptions of two-and-a-half millennia surface as a theory of the primacy of speech over writing. Indeed, the tendency of deconstruction to work so assiduously on the margins – with four pages of the *Phaedrus*, a hybrid text like the *Essay*, Freud's tiny 'Note on the Mystic Writing Pad', a footnote to *Being and Time*, with one citation from *De Interpretatione*, with the implicit, the scarcely said, the *lapsus scribendi*, and so forth – all this may well be largely attributable to the fact that the question of speech's ascendancy over writing had never entered the philosophical mainframe. From Rousseau onward, it is true, phonocentrism becomes a little more explicit in the philosophical text, and we owe it to Jacques Derrida that we now know exactly where to look in Hegel, Husserl, Saussure and Heidegger to find its express formulations. Yet even with these thinkers phonocentrism does not force a dominant theme at any obvious level: not a text, nor a chapter of a text is given over to the subject in any direct manner. Thus to the questions Derrida asks – 'Why accord an "exemplary" value to the "age of Rousseau"? What privileged place does Jean-Jacques Rousseau occupy in the entire history of logocentrism?' (97) – we might reply that without Rousseau there would be neither a single example of logocentrism between Plato and Hegel, nor a logocentric text of any length in the history of logocentrism. Indeed, we might wonder if it is correct even to talk of privilege in this context. When a text is *sui generis*, there is no valorisation, only tautology involved in allotting it a unique class. What we can say, though, is that without the *Essay*, the history of logocentrism would be all but inaudible. Whether it is possible to write a history of silence – which would also be a silent history – is extremely doubtful. Certainly it would not have the density imposed upon it by *Of Grammatology*.

The *Grammatology* catches Derrida in a position of unaccustomed vulnerability, since rather than interrogating the systems of others, we find him constructing a certain theoretical structure and history of his own, as he is obliged to do if the more specific analyses of logocentrism are to have anything more than a regional significance. All the other works of this period constantly presuppose the necessity of the logocentric *episteme*, but nowhere do they forward any substantial account of its constitution and history. Everything proceeds as though this history were given, and the deconstructor bringing a decisive moment in its articulation into the sharpest focus. The *Grammatology* therefore functions very much as the groundwork since it stands as reference for the *episteme* to which these essays have constant recourse. Thus the *episteme* acquires an indispensability in deconstruction which it does not have in Foucault's thought, since Foucault could abandon the concept as an explanatory device whilst continuing his project of seeking out the rules of formation for discourse.

For Derrida, however, logocentrism, as the privileging of speech, must be the first condition of two-and-a-half thousand years of metaphysical thought if the thought of writing as *différance* is to have the power to force some sort of breach in the metaphysical enclosure. Just as *différance* must be (conceptually) older than ontological difference, and (from the revisionist point of view) younger than Heidegger, so too the privileging of the *phonē* must be older than presence for *différance* only acquires its counter-metaphysical force in so far as it derives from and against a concept of metaphysics which originates not in presence but (before and as the cause of presence) in the ideal of full speech. And the difficulties facing Derrida here are immense for unlike the critiques of metaphysics made by Nietzsche, by the logical positivists, or Heidegger even, the Derridean deconstruction of metaphysics does not proceed from an easily communicable or comprehensible characterisation of metaphysics, his idea of metaphysics as the privileging of the *phonē* having no support in the movement against metaphysics and very little within the thought of metaphysicians themselves. Furthermore, what Derrida, for all his labours, cannot establish is why the opposition speech/writing is anything more than one opposition amongst others, why, that is, it should have inaugural and all-institutive status within the history of metaphysics. It is easy enough to follow Derrida in seeing that the speech/writing opposition is related to the opposition presence/absence which Heidegger regarded as constitutive of all metaphysical thought, but it is not clear why it should do so as the condition of the metaphysical tradition rather than as its effect. And Derrida would seem, against his interests, to confirm that the phonocentric question is secondary or subordinate to that of presence, since in showing that speech is always determined as full presence to itself, and is *therefore* metaphysical, the idea of presence is from the outset assumed to be logically prior to the idea of speech. It is difficult to see how, from this position, Derrida can convincingly argue for the logical priority of speech over presence and the entire chain of deconstruction which takes place on the basis of (and in opposition to) this supposed priority. At very most the deconstructive critique might open up a certain undecidability on this question, yet even in so doing, the central claim that phonocentrism is the primal condition of the *episteme* – and writing therefore its primal repression – would remain unsatisfied.[30]

Naturally, that Derrida cannot produce transcendental arguments for the priority of logocentrism should not deter or invalidate the grammatological project. But what it does do is to place the burden of the demonstration on the role of logocentrism within the historical development of metaphysics. Which is to say, that the text must furnish examples of the repression of writing if deconstruction is to have any leverage within the elusive tradition which it opposes. But examples, as we have seen, are at a premium, and, needless to say, when the number and range of instances of what is held to be a universal phenomenon are severely limited then the problems of exemplarity are redoubled. And when the weight of exemplifying an age falls so heavily upon one author, then it is questionable whether we are dealing with exemplarity at all. Is Rousseau an example? Can one example represent an age? Precisely because it is the key issue of the *Grammatology*, the question of exemplarity must be short-circuited whenever it arises, and most commonly and conveniently in the shape of denying that 'Jean-Jacques Rousseau' means anything. Doubtless the problem of exemplarity is one facet of the problem of the author. The need to instantiate will exert signal stresses on any deauthorised history, particularly when one or two authors will serve to exemplify what thousands cannot. However, in the *Grammatology*, quite apart from this constituting a reason for accepting the role of individual authors in the history of discourse, it forces Derrida into the most awkward of positions whereby his text must deny the author precisely *because* of the exorbitant recourse it makes to Jean-Jacques Rousseau as author, logocentrist.

The claim that the author does not exist is unique to the *Grammatology*, and subsequently Derrida has made certain efforts to say the opposite on this question.[31] Indeed, with this in mind, we might wonder if the opposition to the author that arises here has anything more than a strategic value. There is, however, one area, in which Derridean deconstruction will seem to consistently confront the author: that of intention. Things here will not be as clear cut as many wish to suppose, but the necessity of deconstructing intention is to be found in virtually all Derrida's readings, not only as a principle of method, but as their remainder, their identity, their justification.

DOUBLING THE TEXT: INTENTION AND ITS OTHER

The gain-of-anxiety, for the strong poet and the strong reader, is the certain location of a place, even though the place be an absence, the place-of-a-voice, for this setting of a topos makes a poem possible ... We mark the spot by wishing to slay the father, there, at that crossing, and we then know the spot because it becomes the place where the voice of the dead father breaks through. The marking, the will-to-inscribe, is the ethos of writing that our most advanced philosophers of rhetoric trace, but the knowing is itself a voicing, a pathos, and leads us back to the theme of presence that, in a strong poem, persuades us ever afresh, even as the illusions of a tired metaphysics cannot.

Harold Bloom[32]

In a certain way ... I am within Rousseau's text.

Jacques Derrida[33]

Between the publication of Wimsatt and Beardsley's 'The Intentional Fallacy' (1946) and Steven Knapp and Walter Benn Michaels' 'Against Theory' (1982), literary theory has been entirely divided on the question as to what relevance authorial intention has to the interpretation of the literary text.[34] Curiously enough, though they take up diametrically opposed positions on intentionality, the two articles are more striking for their similarities. Beyond the fact that they are co-authored – a consideration which raises certain intriguing questions as to whose intentions are whose and as to how a corporate intention can be distributed – 'The Intentional Fallacy' and 'Against Theory' both sought to put an end once and for all to critical quibbles about intention and did so in the name of the New: in the former, that of the 'New' Criticism; in the latter, that of a 'New' Pragmatism.

Wimsatt and Beardsley, as is well known, thought to do away with tiresome speculation about what such and such a poet meant by such and such a poem on the grounds that what the poet meant is both unknowable and, in any case, irrelevant. The poem only means on the level of the poem and once it is written its author's intent in writing it is to be discounted entirely. Knapp and Michaels, on the other hand, seek to achieve an equally

spectacular simplification of critical practice. For them, there is no difference whatsoever between meaning and intention. The text means exactly
what its author meant it to mean. There is therefore no purpose whatsoever in even trying to establish intention as a condition of communicable
meaning. To attempt, as E.D. Hirsch has done, to ground meaning in intention is tautological: intention is meaning, meaning *is* intention.

Intentionless meaning is thus for Knapp and Michaels as fallacious as
meaningful intention was for Wimsatt and Beardsley. Strange as it might
seem then, 'Against Theory' finds itself in full agreement with 'The Intentional Fallacy' on at least one issue. Both articles maintain that it is fruitless
to enquire into an author's intention, that there is never any need to step
outside the text in search of an author: on the pragmatist case, because
what the author meant is everything the text means; for the New Critics,
because what the author means cannot find its way back into his or her text.
The critical field is thus simplified in one of two antithetical modes: either
the text is fully governed by an immanent authorial intention, or by the
immanent meanings that absent intention uncovers.

This critical stalemate has been played out in the thirty-six years that
intervened between the two articles. On the one hand, New Critical, Structuralist, poststructuralist and practical schools of criticism have generally
assumed that authorial intent is ruled out of court from the start, leaving
the critic free to pursue intrinsic readings without any regard for what the
author might have meant to say. On the other hand, phenomenologically
influenced critics such as E.D. Hirsch have elevated authorial intention
to the highest interpretive norm, finding certain support in the work of
speech act theoreticians such as J.L. Austin, John Searle and H.P. Grice
who have all variously asserted that the speaker's intentions are a necessary condition of any meaningful communicative act.[35] Between these two
positions there is little or no compromise, and the question of intention
has rarely been distributed in terms of a middle ground. At its simplest,
intention is deemed either necessary or unnecessary, and absolutely so in
both cases.

Derrida's reception on the issue of intention has tended to reflect this
divide. Both those critics who would uphold intention and those who
would do away with it altogether have assumed that his work denies the
category of intention outright, and often this assumption has been made
in overtly polemical interests. For deconstructive anti-intentionalists, this
construal of Derrida's work has often served as an expedient justification
for abandoning interpretive norms in the pursuit of abyssal or freeplaying
criticism, whilst for proponents of a more orthodox and *auteurist* criticism,

it has constituted one more reason to dismiss deconstruction as a kind of rootless textual nihilism. Within the contemporary critical forum, these positions have, in their conflict, a certain reciprocity, the one gaining strength from the other, whilst the actual, literal and reiterated statements Derrida has made about authorial intention have been neglected.

Indeed, when the opportunity for debate clearly arose in the famous exchange between Derrida and John Searle in 1977, it misfired largely because of the intemperately polemical tone of Derrida's response to Searle's critisisms, but also as a consequence of the Anglo-American tendency to take up absolutist positions on intention. In an energetic paper, Searle claimed that from Derrida's text we must infer that intentionality is 'entirely absent from written communication'.[36] However, if, as Derrida prompts us, we return to 'Signature, Event, Context', we find something quite different:

> Rather than oppose citation or iteration to the non-iteration of an event, one ought to construct a differential typology of forms of iter-ation, assuming that such a project is tenable and can result in an exhaustive program … In such a typology, the category of intention will not disappear; it will have its place, but from that place it will no longer be able to govern the entire scene and system of utterance.[37]

As is abundantly clear this is not at all the same thing as disputing the actuality or necessity of intention, rather what is put in question is the absolutely determinative hegemony of intention over the communicative act. Intention is to be recognised, and respected, but on condition that we accept that its structures will not be fully and ideally homogeneous with what is said or written, that it is not always and everywhere completely adequate to the communicative act. There will be times at which crevices appear in its hold, at which language resists, or wanders away from the speaker's determinate meaning. Consequently, though the dominion of intention over the textual process is to be rigorously refused, intention itself is not thereby cancelled but rather lodged within a broader signifying process. Intention is within signification, and as a powerful and necessary agency, but it does not command this space in the manner of an organising *telos*, or transcendental subjectivity. That Searle should so misread Derrida on this issue is perhaps explicable in terms of the common mistake by which the denial of absolute authority to a category is confused with that category's total evacuation.

Of course another explanation might be that Searle was not sufficiently familiar with Derrida's work, for this medial position on intention also coincides at the most apparent level with the practice of many of the deconstructive readings. In the *Grammatology*, for instance, it is written:

> Rousseau's discourse lets itself be constrained by a complexity which always has the form of the supplement of or from the origin. His declared intention is not annulled by this but rather *inscribed* within a system which it no longer dominates. (243)

Indeed, even at the stage of the most preliminary acquaintance with Derrida's work, it is clear that intention is not opposed in the classic New Critical manner of asserting that it is irrelevant and unknowable. Quite the reverse: if authorial intentions are to be deconstructed it must be accepted that they are cardinally relevant and recognisable. The deconstructor must assume that he or she has the clearest conception of what the author wanted to say if the work of deconstruction is to get underway. The model of intention culled from the text must be especially confident and sharply defined since the critic undertakes not only to reconstitute the intentional forces within the text, but also to assign their proper limits. It is only in terms of this reconstruction that the deconstructor can begin to separate that which belongs to authorial design from that which eludes or unsettles its prescriptions. Accordingly, deconstructive procedure takes the form of following the line of authorial intention up to the point at which it encountered resistance within the text itself: from this position the resistance can then be turned back against the author to show that his text differs from itself, that what he wished to say does not dominate what the text says, but is rather inscribed within (or in more radical cases, engulfed by) the larger signifying structure. Again the *Grammatology* states this with perfect transparency:

> the writer writes *in* a language and in a logic whose proper system, laws, and life his discourse by definition cannot dominate absolutely. He uses them only by letting himself, after a fashion and up to a point, be governed by the system. And the reading must always aim at a certain relationship, unperceived by the writer, between what he commands and what he does not command of the patterns of the language that he uses. (158)

The text is thereby stratified into declarative and descriptive layers,[38] the former relating to what the author wanted to say and the latter to that which escapes intention, a division which might be expressed in other critical languages, *mutatis mutandis*, as that between the constative and performative, the manifest and the latent, or in contemporary parlance as the difference between the programmatic intention (what the author set out to say) and the operative intention (what his text ends up saying).[39] This stratification then in turn relates to the critical text itself which is necessarily divided into explicative and deconstructive phases, whereby authorial intention is first reconstructed and then deconstructed via that which has escaped its jurisdiction.[40]

Derrida thus recommends an interesting compromise between intentionalist and anti-intentionalist views, since he neither identifies intention with the entirety of textual effects (as have many neo-pragmatists), nor moves to the other extreme of denying the necessity of intention as a factor in generating and shaping what is written. There is, therefore, no way in which Derrida's work can be assimilated to anti-intentionalism as it is commonly conceived. However, the Derridean position will seem anti-intentionalist in a second and less severe sense, since as a practice of reading the critic sees it as his responsibility to turn the text against its author's programmatic intentions, thus establishing an opposition between the reader and writer. Furthermore, as part of the same movement, the author is estranged from a specifically demarcated area of his text, for whilst the authority of the writer is accepted over the declarative aspect of what he writes, his intentions hold no sway over the descriptions he makes.

We find ourselves therefore still, in a certain sense, within the movement against the author but no longer in the mode of his death or disappearance. The author is to be opposed, but not dismissed: a somewhat dramatic scene of criticism is set in which the critic sets out to show that he or she is a better reader of the text than its author ever was. The critic will attempt not only to outpace the author along his or her pathways, but will turn those very pathways back on themselves, thereby discovering within the text all the reserves by which its author is to be opposed. Deconstruction will evoke in order to revoke, accepts the author, but on condition that the critic can produce the text as a broader signifying structure within which the author's determining will is inscribed as one factor amongst others. The critic thus establishes a constant priority over the author. No longer is it a question of the critic seeking to adequate his intentions to those of the author, but of the author finding his intentions allowed only on condition that they will be secondary, nowhere equal to the writing that wrote itself through and against him. That this is a profound reversal is undeniable. How true it is of the deconstructive critiques in general is, however, another matter, as are the exigencies by which this doubling of the text is sometimes motivated.

Derrida does not always and everywhere rigidly adhere to this model, but the variations he makes tend not to further circumscribe the role of intention but to accommodate a greater acceptance of the validity and force of what the author wanted to say. In fact, in many instances Derrida is not deconstructing authorial intentions but the received interpretation of a work, and his itinerary is here classically intentionalist in that the reading proposes to restore the first intention against reductive construals put upon it by the critical tradition.[41] In still other cases, when addressing thinkers whose aims are largely consistent with the deconstructive enterprise – Nietzsche, Freud, Levinas, and most especially Heidegger – what is forwarded is not at all the deconstruction of the primary intent but its radicalisation, the interrogation not so much of what they wanted to say as what they failed to say. Deconstruction will here take the text beyond itself, not in the interests of overhauling the intent with which it was written, but in those of showing how it stopped short of pursuing its most radical directions.[42] In such places, Derrida's work bespeaks a distinctly revisionary impetus, opposing Heidegger in those places where Heidegger is insufficiently Heideggerian, taking the further step on the countermetaphysical pathways cleared by the Heideggerian project.

Two distinct attitudes to intention thus prevail, depending on whether Derrida is reading one of two broad categories of text. On the one hand, it can be said that the intention is not adequate to the text, that the text says things which cannot be encompassed by the author's determinate designs (the pattern which Derrida adopts with metaphysical writers such as Rousseau, Hegel, Plato). On the other hand, the inverse is avouched, in that it can be said that the text itself is not adequate to its governing intent (the pattern Derrida adopts with counter-metaphysical writers: Nietzsche, Heidegger, Levinas). The same basic premise that the author does not have full control over his language is constant in both cases, but the latter approach cannot be readily reconciled to an anti-authorial position, since it conforms to a classically revisionist paradigm whereby the aims and conceptual resources of a precursor are inherited, and carried forward in accordance with new conditions and imperatives. To see anything of the death of the author in Derrida's work here is to utterly misconstrue the nature of revisionism for which a certain conflict of means is necessary if thought is to continue toward the same ends. It is, for example, only through showing how the Heideggerian intent was not fully effectuated by the work of *Being and Time*, *Identity and Difference*, that is to say, *exhausted* by him, that deconstruction can inherit from his legacy, that the intentions of the Heideggerian project can have a life beyond the death of their author. Derrida himself makes this clear on numerous occasions.[43]

In the former case, though, deconstruction remains in strict opposition to authorial intention, and once more it is in the *Grammatology* that this opposition is at its most vigorous. Indeed, the reading of Rousseau differs from Derrida's work on other metaphysicians, if not in kind, then certainly in the intensity with which the critic pursues the author into antinomy and aporia. It is here, too, that Derrida found it necessary to incorporate the theory of intention into the reading at the most explicit level, and to enforce the hiatus between meaning-to-say and saying on virtually every page of the deconstructive reading. Rousseau *declares*, but Rousseau *describes*, this formulation dominates the text from 'The Place of the *Essay*' onwards. And the inflexible urgency with which the distinction is prosecuted is at all times apparent. Every priority which Rousseau attempts to set up, whether it be that of speech over writing, nature over culture, melody over harmony, literal over figural meaning, the languages of the South over those of the North – is seen to be expressly contradicted in his text.

Derrida employs numerous strategies to open up this gap between gesture and statement. At one time he will look to the figurative and metaphorical in Rousseau's text as to guilty locutions which betray the repression of writing, at another to the modes and tenses of Rousseau's verbs, at yet another he will produce classically consequential arguments to show that Rousseau's presuppositions logically entail conclusions at odds with the manifestly intended conclusion. Indeed the *apparatus criticus* Derrida brings to Rousseau is wide-ranging, concerted, even awesome in its relentless invagination. The text is cleaved throughout:

> *Articulation is the becoming-writing of language*. Rousseau, *who would like to say* that this becoming-writing *comes upon the origin unexpectedly*, takes it as his premise, and according to it *describes in fact* the way in which that *becoming-writing encroaches upon the origin*, and arises from the origin. The becoming-writing of language is the becoming-language of language. He *declares* what he *wishes to say*, that is to say that articulation and writing are a post-originary malady of language; he says or *describes* that which he *does not wish to say*: articulation and therefore the space of writing operates at the origin of language. (229)

> Rousseau *would wish* the opposition between southern and northern in order to place a natural frontier between types of languages. However, what he *describes* forbids us to think it … the languages of the north are *on the whole* languages of need, the languages of the south, to which Rousseau devotes ten times the space in his description, are *on the whole* languages of passion. But this *description* does not prevent Rousseau from *declaring* that the one group is born of passion, the other of need … (216–17)

> Rousseau's entire text *describes* origin as the beginning of the end, as the inaugural decadence. Yet, in spite of that *description*, the text twists about in a sort of oblique effort to act *as if* degeneration were

> not already prescribed in the genesis, and as if evil *supervened upon* a
> good origin. (199)

Rousseau saw without seeing, said without saying.[44] For all his attempts
to gain control, Rousseau witnesses his *Essay* plunge into contradictions
which it cannot circumvent. And all of this confirms what Derrida has
said. The text recoils from its author's control: the further intention pushes
against its marches, the more it engenders of its other; contradictions and
impasses emerge which problematise and finally overhaul its thesis.

Yet often in the *Grammatology* this division seems forced, arbitrary of
occasion, insecure even. Rather than allow the reading to progress at its
own pace, Derrida takes every conceivable opportunity to remind us that
Rousseau is not saying what he wants to say, that what the *Grammatology*
is saying is entirely irreducible to the intentional structure of the *Essay*.
And this reminder is obsessively italicised, well beyond the point at which
it has become stupefyingly clear. Furthermore, there are times at which
Derrida exaggerates the distinction, and not only by his critical inventiveness in teasing out hidden textual implications, but also via a somewhat
rigid and constraining interpretation of what Rousseau actually means to
say. That there might be a speculative side to the *Essay*, that Rousseau
might be asking that we chance a journey to the origin of languages, and
in the expectation of discovering all sorts of things on the way, is never
taken into account. Rather the text must always and everywhere be interpreted with an ungenerous, and intractable literality; Rousseau's failure to
perceive the supplementary threadwork in his text must be absolute, never
partial, and the *Grammatology* never once questions the status of its ascription to Rousseau of such regimented and unilinear designs. Nor either
does Derrida once venture why it is so important, why it is *the issue* of
the reading that Rousseau is unaware of what his text is saying. Of what
account is it that Rousseau did not know that he was describing the play
of a supplementarity prior and catastrophic to all origins? Why insist upon
so rigorously policing this border between statement and gesture? Even to
the extent, as we shall see, of ending his text by contrasting the oneirism
of the logocentrist with the wakefulness of the logocentrist? Something of
the answer to these questions lies not in the distance that separates Derrida
and Rousseau, but in the closeness of their conflict. Were we to cancel the
gap between declaration and description in the manner of an experiment,
we would find not a different story, but exactly the same story. At the same
time, however, the roles of its protagonists would be significantly altered.
For, like the *pharmakon*, Rousseauism is the cure for its own poison.[45]

Systems, Hegel says, sow the seeds of their own destruction, and though the *Essay* is tendered as the logocentrist text *par excellence*, it is also the first serious and sustained meditation *on writing*. Rousseau's text marks a considerable advance on the *Phaedrus* not only because of its length and focus, but also because of its radicality. Whilst Plato takes it somewhat for granted that writing is derivative of speech, seeking primarily to demonstrate the moral and ethical superiority of the spoken word, the *Essay* refuses the assumption of speech's priority at least whilst it remains an assumption. That Rousseau does everything to confirm the logocentric prejudice alters nothing in this respect. The possibility that it might be otherwise has been admitted. And it is within this very possibility, and according to its specific terms, modalities and irresolutions that the entire grammatological critique unfurls.

It is not that Rousseau argues badly in the *Essay*; had he done so his work would not have the fecund grammatological significance that Derrida discovers. Rather, his attempts to unearth the origin of languages are driven from problematic to problematic, and if Rousseau's text runs into difficulties, it is because of its author's refusal to suppress the growing menace of supplementarity to the integrity of the origin. And it is precisely through the ardour with which he pursues an infinitely regressing origin through layers of supplementarity that Rousseau uncovers all the resources with which the *Grammatology* opposes the manifest drift of the *Essay*. Both Derrida and Rousseau inquire into the origin of languages and uncover a voice without grain, a writing before the letter. Rousseau describes a voice within whose warp and woof a system of pre-vocal articulation is already inscribed, Derrida describes what Rousseau describes and calls this voice which has never spoken, this writing which has never been written 'arche-writing'. That Derrida's characterisation of this matinal language prejudices 'writing' and Rousseau's 'speech' is not so great a difference as it might seem, if indeed it is a difference at all.

For Derrida is not to be construed, here or anywhere else, as asserting the primacy of writing in so far as writing is commonly conceived as words upon a page. What Derrida attempts to show, rather, is that any detailed argument for the priority of speech is compelled to presuppose a system of prior differences which cannot be circumscribed by the category of speech or that of writing whilst the latter is conceived in opposition to the former. As is obvious, an argument for writing conducted on those terms would be destined to the same impasses as that for the *de jure* priority of speech.[46] That which is named 'arche-writing' could equally be called 'arche-speech' for it precedes speech, writing and their opposition. And as Derrida insists, this arche-writing is to be found in Rousseau's text itself. It is another name for the logic of the supplement, for *différance*: 'Rousseau does not declare it, but we have seen that he describes it. From here on, I shall constantly reconfirm that writing is the other name of this *différance*.' (268)

The situation regarding intention is therefore double-edged, for, looking in another light, we could say that Derrida is opposing Rousseau at those points where the deconstructor and logocentrist are at their closest, where the one is most in danger of being taken for the other, there where Rousseau '*declares* the absolute exteriority of writing but *describes* the interiority of the principle of writing to language.' (313) This is why the question of intention takes on such significance within the reading, for since Derrida insists upon inscribing nothing that is not to be found always already in Rousseau, then it is only through doubling Rousseau's text into intention and its other that the *Grammatology* can carve out its own precarious self-identity. Should it have been that Rousseau saw *whilst* seeing, said *whilst* saying, then the logocentrist would have prepared in advance everything that the grammatologue himself wishes to say: 'Rousseau … says what he does not wish to say, describes what he does not wish to conclude: that the positive (is) the negative, life (is) death, presence (is) absence.' (246) Viewed in this way, the reading would no longer be production but explication, however novel a form that explication might seem to have taken. The distinction between meaning-to-say and saying, the doubling of text between critic and author is thus indispensable if the commentary and text are not to reverse into one another, if the critic is to have a guard against the threat of the autodeconstructive text, if it is not at least to *seem* that the 'critic … has his uses, though this use may be no more than to identify an act of deconstruction which has always already, in each case differently, been performed by the text on itself.'[47]

The idea of the autodeconstructive text is most easily associated with the identification of authorial intention with the text in its totality, with the assertion that everything within is circumscribed by what the author wanted to say, that (as certain pragmatists might say) textual meaning is authorial intention without surplus or shortfall. But the complete evacuation of intent promotes the idea of autodeconstruction every bit as surely, for without the category of intention there is nothing whatsoever to proscribe against the recuperation of all textual effects for the text itself over and above its interpretation.[48] In the former case, everything in the deconstructed text belongs to the author's intention, in the latter, the deconstruction belongs to neither author nor critic but to the text itself. In both cases, however, there is nothing that can properly be appropriated for the critic.

Consequently, whilst the rigid and rigorous division of the text into two stratas, or textual voices, serves to steer a path between the transcendental presence of intention and its no less transcendental absence, it simultaneously demarcates a space of criticism protected against reappropriation for either author or text. Through introducing the author, via intention, and through then setting very specific limitations on what authorial intention can govern, Derrida guards against the threat of autodeconstruction, and against the corresponding domestication or neutralisation of his own labours: the *Essay* can be read as neither the product of an idealised author, nor as an ideal structure which always and everywhere takes account of its own operations. The critic here needs intention, but no longer as a yardstick by which to evaluate his interpretation, but because he needs its other, something to oppose to it, to say to his own account.

The undoing of intention in the *Grammatology* therewith inhabits an almost paradoxical structure of conflict and complicity in that those times at which Rousseauian intention is most vulnerable to deconstruction are also those at which the *Grammatology* is most at risk of losing itself in the *Essay*. Which is not at all to say that Derrida's text is indefinitely recuperable for Rousseauian intention,[49] but that once again opposition to Rousseau signifies nothing so clearly as the massive recourse made to Rousseau; as logocentric exemplar, and, in Derrida's hands, proto-deconstructionist. What offers itself in the form of aggression will at one and the same time be a distancing and defensive process, the repulsion of a dangerous proximity, sundering Rousseau and Derrida when their texts are most reconciled. The distinction between declaration and description primarily effects the division of textual voices in a critical area of reading so introjective that there is often no immediate way of telling text and interpretation apart: everywhere it underscores that what we are reading at these times is a production and not a reproduction.

Earlier in the text Derrida had said that the work of deconstruction implies 'neither an unconsciousness nor a lucidity on the part of the author', and that reading 'should … abandon these categories – which are also … the founding categories of metaphysics'. (163) In the very next sentence he says that the *Grammatology* is not a doubling commentary but is 'certainly a production because I do not simply duplicate what Rousseau thought.' (163) As the reading ploughs deeper and deeper into the Rousseauian text, this second sentiment progressively overwhelms the first, since it is only through insisting that the reader is more conscious of what the text was doing that the *Grammatology* can mark its advance on Rousseau. With heavier and heavier stresses the text must tell us that *Rousseau declares but Rousseau describes,* and in statements which often have recourse to the rhetorics of consciousness and unconsciousness, of Rousseau 'travelling along the system of supplementarity with a blind infallibility, and the sure foot of the sleepwalker'. (203) At the close of the *Grammatology,* when this monumental critical agon finally comes to a close, Derrida writes:

> Rousseau could not think this writing that takes place *before* and *within* speech … Rousseau's *dream* consisted of making the supplement enter metaphysics by force. But what does that mean? The opposition of dream to wakefulness, is not that a representation of metaphysics as well? And what should dream or writing be if, as we know now, one may dream while writing? And if the scene of dream is always a scene of writing? At the bottom of a page of *Emile* … Rousseau adds a note: '… the dreams of a bad night are given to us as philosophy. You will say I too am a dreamer; I admit it, but I do what others fail to do, I give my dreams as dreams, and leave the reader to discover whether there is anything in them which might prove useful to those who are awake.' (315–16)

Has deconstruction forced a breach in the metaphysics of presence, and thus awoken from Rousseauism? Or merely pursued the dream of an origin of languages a little more consciously, in the manner of reverie? So much Derridean work issues in this uncertain hour, balanced between revision and rupture, when the voices of critic and author vie and coalesce in such a way that we are never sure who is speaking, or if the reader has ever emerged from the text he was reading.

THE MYTH OF WRITING

> … it seems to me that 'the history of metaphysics' was a *bad* name. Derrida never really finished, or even undertook, that much-promised deconstruction. He hasn't been Son of Heidegger in that respect.
>
> Gayatri Chakravorty Spivak[50]

The father of metaphysics himself *dreams* throughout 'Plato's Pharmacy'. He dreams all of philosophy as an idealised speech; he dreams of a memory with no sign. Here Derrida engages with the inaugural text of that enigmatic history which *Speech and Phenomena* and *Writing and Difference* and *Of Grammatology* have attempted to surprise.[51] He will also seek to repay the substantial line of credit these texts have drawn on Plato's *Phaedrus*[52] in their appeals to an 'epoch of logocentrism', to a history of the devaluation of writing: 'what seems to inaugurate itself in Western literature with Plato will not fail to re-edit itself at least in Rousseau, and then in Saussure.'

(158) Referring to these cases as 'three 'eras' of the repetition of Platonism', and to his path of reading as 'a new thread to follow and other knots to recognise in the history of *philosophia* or the *epistēmē*' (158), Derrida affirms that 'the "linguistics" elaborated by Plato, Rousseau, and Saussure must both put writing out of the question and yet nevertheless borrow from it, for fundamental reasons, all its demonstrative and theoretical resources'. (158–9) Derrida identifies protocols familiar from the earlier readings: 'the texture of the text, reading and writing, mastery and play, the paradoxes of supplementarity'. (65) Supplementary play in Rousseau discovers a Platonic equivalent in the *pharmakon*, a similarly exorbitant figure which derives from and yet defies authorial intention. Replaying the 'Question of Method' outlined by *Of Grammatology*, Derrida declares:

> The word *pharmakon* is caught in a chain of significations. The play of that chain seems systematic. But the system here is not, simply, that of the intentions of an author who goes by the name of Plato. The system is not primarily that of what someone *meant-to-say* [*un vouloir-dire*]. Finely regulated communications are established, through the play of language, among diverse functions of the word and, within it, among diverse strata or regions of culture. These communications or corridors of meaning can sometimes be declared or clarified by Plato when he plays upon them 'voluntarily', a word we put in quotation marks because what it designates, to content ourselves with remaining within the closure of these oppositions, is only a mode of 'submission' to the necessities of a given 'language'. None of these concepts can translate the relation we are aiming at here. Plato can *not* see the links, can leave them in the shadow or break them up. And yet these links go on working of themselves. In spite of him? thanks to him? in *his* text? *outside* his text? but then where? between his text and the language? for what reader? at what moment? To answer such questions in principle and in general will seem impossible; and that will give us the suspicion that there is some malformation in the question itself, in each of its concepts, in each of the oppositions it thus accredits. (95–6)[54]

The peculiar significations that collect around the word '*pharmakon*' emerge as a general principle of reading, one which authorises the reader to bypass (non-pharmaceutical) moments of altogether less ambiguity. What seems 'voluntary' will not translate into what is intended; the involuntary, on the other hand, will not rule out the possibility of desire on Plato's part. Furthermore, the notion of volition is maintained whilst also being identified as '"submission" to the necessities of a given "language"' – as though such submission disallows voluntarism within the play of those necessities.[55] Derrida will indeed play off his own reading against a model of Platonic intention which appeals to the disputed *Seventh Letter* as a definitively Platonic moment.[56] Having seemingly suspended the distinction between voluntary and involuntary signification, 'Plato's Pharmacy' follows *Of Grammatology* in utilising the ambiguities of 'dream' (*rêve*) as it combines desire with unconsciousness, volition with the involuntary, purposiveness with inadvertency. Derrida also uses the impersonal case to this end: when he wants us to think of what Plato demands, what Plato wants-to-say, his essay tells us that the *Phaedrus* demands, that *philosophy* wants-to-say. The model of deliberate organisation is required, but it cannot be affirmed as the intention of an author called Plato: 'The hypothesis of a rigorous, sure and subtle form is naturally more fertile', Derrida declares at the outset. (67) On the next page, he will inform us: 'At the precisely calculated center of the dialogue – the reader can count the lines – the question of *logography* is raised.' (68) Clearly there is no calculation without a calculator: something or, more likely, someone, for example, *calculatedly* placed the issue of *logography* at the precise midpoint of the *Phaedrus*.

The question of intention raises itself tellingly in Derrida's lengthy attention to the myth through which the trial of writing is instituted. 'Our intention here has only been', he says – in a statement which also affirms a Platonic intention – 'to sow the idea that the spontaneity, freedom and fantasy attributed to Plato in his legend of Theuth were actually supervised and limited by rigorous necessities.' (85) One might expect Derrida's interests to settle here on the coexistence of *muthos* and *logos* in Plato's discourse, but the essay does not tend that way. Instead, Derrida uses the myth to lock the *Phaedrus* into a by now familiar network of oppositions:

> Plato had to make his tale conform to structural laws. The most general of these, those that govern and articulate the oppositions speech/writing, life/death, father/son. master/servant, first/second, legitimate son/orphan-bastard, soul/body, inside/outside, good/ evil, seriousness/play, day/night, sun/moon, etc., also govern, and according to the same configurations, Egyptian, Babylonian and Assyrian mythology. (85)

Perhaps Derrida might even indeed have chanced that Plato also *intended* his tale to conform to those laws: this will indeed be the unstated assumption on which the reading of the myth of Theuth proceeds. Derrida notes, with some patience, the many faces worn by the god – his associations with the moon, with recognition and learning, his later appearance in the Cycle of Osiris as the god charged to weigh the hearts of the deceased at their judgements – but it is the association of Theuth with death which is taken as axial to the *Phaedrus*'s determination of writing.[57] Having already introduced the equation of speech with life in the form of a Platonic *logos-zōon* (also established via the *Sophist*[58]), the figure of Theuth then provides the countervailing figure of 'writing-death'. Nothing of course forbids the association: Plato may have expected his audience to foreground Theuth's connection with death. He may also have anticipated that the whole range of mythic reverberations would sound from the name of the god; then again, he might have been drawn by an unconscious logic to that which in 'Theuth' is moribund. But the claim that 'structural laws' are betrayed in this 'choice' strains credibility. Any appeal to what Derrida himself characterises as '[t]he discordant tangle of mythological accounts in which [Theuth] is caught' (86) will be too haphazard to fall under the rule of law: nor will there be any guarantees for proceeding to the claim that 'it goes without saying that the god of writing must also be the god of death'. (91) Quite mundanely, dramatic exigencies would have guided Plato in his displacing of the Greek benefactor by the Egyptian god: Prometheus being the inventor of writing in Greek mythology, it is unlikely that any audience envisioned by Plato would credit King Thamus as an adversary of the great Titan.[59] In thematic terms, the question of whether Plato intended the amalgam 'Theuth-writing-death' is impossible to answer: the more fruitful inquiry would centre on why Derrida should wish mortification to claim centre stage in the *Phaedrus*'s discussion of writing.

In seeking to connect the reading of Plato's *Phaedrus* to that of Rousseau, 'Plato's Pharmacy' faces a number of difficulties. Where Rousseau's *Essay on the Origin of Languages* argues the 'proper' primacy of speech and presence, the *Phaedrus* is not concerned with issues of origin – considered *de jure* or *de facto*: placing writing's origins in Theuth's hands doubtless respects a tradition whereby divine intervention is used to explain civilisation's beginnings, but it will also ensure that the hierarchical equations of speech with nature and writing with culture do not complicate this debate.[60] This is not to say that the *Phaedrus* does not borrow its imagery and oppositions from the natural order. The section on speech/writing is indeed studded with such figures, many of which Derrida himself has taught us to read there. Images of gardens, of suitable soil, of boundary, defence, enclosure, and cultivation do their work alongside the procedures of rational enquiry: all of which express healthy constraint, controlled growth, supervised development, in an economy of domestication which also defends (*boētheia*) and nurtures that which is being tamed. On the other side, Derrida's figure of dissemination serves eloquently to mark writing insofar as it drifts, it rolls, (*kulindeitai*: 275e) exceeds domestication, breaks out of the closed and controlled spaces the dialogic forum, the ideal speech situation. However, what the text does not provide is a system of imagery configured on the axis of life/death. Indeed, the figures of rolling, drifting, of disseminating express just as much animation – albeit in a wild, untrammelled and profligate sense of living, of being animate, of moving. Whilst the comparison of writing to painting (*Phaedrus*, 275d) registers the fixed nature of written *logoi*,[61] it is quickly succeeded – in the same speech – by the image of drifting. (*Phaedrus*, 275e) Far from being cadaverous or petrified, this wandering free-floating energy places itself on the disreputable side of a distinction between two modes of vitality: one controlled, enclosed and cultivated; the other, aleatory, wanton and wandering.

Derrida, though, is determined to discover the life/death opposition in these four Platonic pages, and it is no coincidence that he begins to talk of writing substituting 'the breathless sign for the living voice' (92) only when Theuth has been boxed into the corner of death:

> As a living thing, *logos* issues from a father. There is thus for Plato no
> such thing as a written thing. There is only a *logos* more or less alive,
> more or less distant from itself. Writing is not an independent order
> of signification; it is weakened speech, something not completely
> dead: a living-dead, a reprieved corpse, a deferred life, a semblance
> of breath. (143)

Presumably this claim does not wish to be taken in any historical sense in seeking to exploit the idea of writing as *eidōlon*, as Hadean shade of the living word, but the metaphoric insistence could be read as an attempt to have the *Phaedrus* say what a Rousseau *would* have it say as much as what a Socrates or Plato did say. Certainly, the missions of the *Phaedrus* are no more romantic than they are in quest of a noble primitivism embodied in speech: Plato's text does not export the network 'speech/writing, life/death' into western conceptuality so much as Derrida's mythological excursus imports a Rousseauian sense of writing into a dialogue which is concerned with the ethical and epistemological status of discursive media. Indeed, the *Phaedrus* condemns the spoken in the same terms as the written. (*Phaedrus*, 277e)[62] Altogether banally, we shall find that statements are evaluated through the validity of their *logoi* rather than their *lexis*, for their proximity to 'justice and honour and goodness'. (*Phaedrus*, 278a)

A second area of difficulty in Derrida's treatment of the myth of writing centres on his identification of the Platonic view with the pronouncement of King Thamus. Talking of the play of signification set in motion by the *pharmakon*, Derrida asserts: 'It is precisely this ambiguity that *Plato*, *through the mouth of the King*, attempts to master, to dominate by inserting its definition into simple, clear-cut oppositions'. (103: my emphasis) The significance of this statement to the essay's construal of authorial intention need hardly be underlined. The 'voice' of a mythic character is given by Derrida as an authorial 'voice': Thamus becomes the place from which the Platonic wisdom speaks. In tracing the intricate chain of the *pharmakon*, Derrida neglects to consider the vertiginous play of signatures in this scene: in a dialogue written by Plato, King Thamus 'speaks' the judgement on writing within a myth which is 'spoken' by Socrates. Narrative, mimetic and technical considerations militate against declaring that it is Socrates or Plato who speaks in the King's words; and all this before one even begins to ask how mythic *logoi* accommodate to dialectical *logoi* in a tale whose authorship is immediately challenged by Phaedrus. (*Phaedrus*, 275b) Even were the judgement of Thamus shown to be in consort with the Socratic viewpoint – a task which is rendered counterintuitive when weighed against that recapitulatory statement at 278b–d (which we shall consider in due course) – Derrida would still be called upon to balance the delicate scales of the Socratic problem.[63]

Moreover, the first axiom of judgement established by Thamus is in clear contradiction with what Derrida justly takes to be a central argument of the *Phaedrus*. The strongest objection Plato makes to writing specifies its separation of a discourse from the subject who produced it, a separation which orphans a piece of writing, leaves it helpless before incompetent, malign and abusive readers: 'the composition ... drifts all over the place ... it doesn't know how to address the right people, and not to address the wrong. (*Phaedrus*, 275e) However, the mythic discourse prescribes the contrary:

> ... the king answered and said, 'O man full of arts (*technikōtate*), to one it is given to create the things of art, and to another to judge what measure of harm and of profit they have for those that shall employ them. And so it is that you, by reason of your tender regard for the writing that is your offspring, have declared the very opposite of its true effect. (274e–275a)

Writing as *technē* is separated from the father; creator and creation, inventor and invention, are sundered because the filial bond precludes objective evaluation. According to Derrida, speech is praised for maintaining the unity of philosophical speaker and statement in the present; written words are condemned for their parricidal usurpation of the father-author.[64] While Theuth is not separated from a written discourse but from the medium of writing he has invented, the sanctity of the paternal relation is here desecrated by King Thamus. The art of writing would be defended with all too much parental solicitude by the father of writing (*patēr ōn grammatōn*). It is universally the case, Thamus declares, that the father will never judge impartially; of all people, therefore, the father is the only one to be debarred by right from the court of judgement. The regal defender of speech here introduces the very breach – the separation of son from father, of creation from creator – for which writing is later to be condemned: any discourse 'when it is ill-treated and unfairly abused … always needs its parent (*patēr*) to come to its help.' (*Phaedrus*, 275e) So stark is the contradiction between mythical account and ensuing dialectical exchange that were we to look for a Platonic 'mouthpiece' in this overdetermined scene, there would be no more and no less justification for reversing the Derridean identification to see the dialectical position as represented by the god of writing.[65]

In any case, it can never be the purpose of the ensuing dialogue to echo or simply elaborate King Thamus's judgement: the regal rejection is amply ironised by the fact that writing had *not* been refused to the human world in which the *Phaedrus* was written. Indeed, from this position, the reader who reads Plato alongside Derrida might begin to wonder if the *Phaedrus* wishes to set itself against writing in anything like the regal or Derridean manner. There is Platonic scholarship which sees the *Phaedrus* as a defence of Plato's own practice of philosophical writing, one in which the Socrates who speaks is continually ironised and undercut by the Plato who writes.[66] We need not go this far, though, to challenge Derrida's conviction that this dialogue bears first witness to 'the exclusion and the devaluation of writing'. (158)

One of the peculiarities of 'Plato's Pharmacy' is that its argument travels some 110 pages to arrive where the *Phaedrus*'s reflections on writing begin. The admirable movement whereby writing is reappropriated is the movement by which the text of Derrida glides under that of Plato.[67] Derrida is of course aware of this: he will be conscious that his text has not been read when commentators take 'Plato's Pharmacy' to undo an opposition which the *Phaedrus* sets up in classical terms. The by-now standard proposition that 'Plato shows a *metaphysical* preference for speech over writing' is not adequate to the work of the *Phaedrus*. One might risk, at most, the banal suggestion that 'Plato shows an ethical preference for speech insofar as the medium of speech is the medium *par excellence* of dialogue' but even such a qualified distinction is not drawn by the *Phaedrus* with determining force. Nothing, indeed, is of a piece here, and the relationship between speech and writing will be one of distribution and overlap rather than of antinomy. Plato discriminates between good and bad speech in such fashion that the latter finds itself in the place of a repudiated writing. Enigmatic on first inspection, this textual economy becomes entirely coherent if the reader registers how the *Phaedrus* is governed by the opposition between monologic and dialogic discourse.[68] Socrates' first objection to writing alights on its unresponsive and monologic nature:

> The painter's products stand before us as though they were alive, but if you question them, they maintain a most majestic silence. It is the same with written words; they seem to talk to you as though they were intelligent, but if you ask them anything about what they say, from a desire to be instructed, they go on telling you just the same thing for ever. (*Phaedrus*, 275d)

It is not absence of life that carries over from painting to writing so much as the inability to hear or reward questioning. All discourse which offers itself to debate, to question-and-answer, is approved in Plato's text in the same movement by which all unresponsive, univocal communications are condemned. These latter discourses will include both writing and non-dialogic speech. It is not speech (as a *logos* present to the individual) but *dialogic speech* that Plato upholds in opposition to *both* writing and unresponsive speech. (*Phaedrus*, 277d–e)[69] Oratory or orally-delivered poems are equally rigid productions if their subjects are unavailable or incapable of responding. As Socrates remarks elsewhere: 'if one asks any of them an additional question, like books they cannot either answer or ask a question on their own account'. (*Protagoras*, 329a)[70] As we will see somewhat later, the dominance of the monologic/dialogic opposition will also explain how it is that the *Phaedrus* by no means decides against inscription but favours a writing which is made dialogically answerable to philosophy.

Indeed, so far from being opposed in metaphysical terms, speech and writing are considered under the same heading during the lengthy discussion of rhetoric (259e–274b) which precedes the myth of writing. What distinctions the *Phaedrus* makes cut across both categories. Good *writing* is equated with good *speech*, bad *speech* is equated with bad *writing* – just as the later section on the inferiority of the written word will equate non-dialectical *speech* with non-dialectical *writing*. The question of whether one speaks or writes is irrelevant to discursive propriety:[71]

> SOCRATES : ... do you suppose that anyone ... and whatever his animosity toward Lysias, could reproach him simply on the ground that he writes?
>
> PHAEDRUS : What you say certainly makes that improbable, for apparently he would be reproaching what he wanted to do himself.

SOCRATES   : Then the conclusion is obvious, that there is nothing
             shameful in the mere writing of speeches.
PHAEDRUS   : Of course.
SOCRATES   : But in speaking and writing shamefully and badly,
             instead of as one should, that is where the shame comes
             in, I take it.
PHAEDRUS   : Clearly.
SOCRATES   : Then what is the nature of good writing and bad? Is
             it incumbent upon us, Phaedrus, to examine Lysias on
             this point, and all such as have written or mean to write
             anything at all, whether in the field of public affairs or
             private, whether in the verse of the poet or the plain
             speech of prose? (258b–d)

To write *in* plain speech. The distinction between vocality and inscription is
not drawn. To the contrary, it is superseded. From its beginnings in a discussion of the merits of Lysias's speechwriting, the text has moved to the utmost
generality in its concern with all modes of discourse.[72] Through to the elaboration of the myth of writing (259e–274b), *legomenon* – usually rendered as
'thing said' – must be taken in the sense of 'thing *written* or spoken'.[73]

   That 'Plato's Pharmacy' should overlook this passage is surely significant.[74] The trial of logography closes the gap between speech and writing in
advance not only of the trial of writing, but of the Derridean reading itself.
In so minutely focused a reading, this omission will not smack of careless-
ness. Nor should we be blind to the fact that 'Plato's Pharmacy' does not
see fit to cite the concluding remarks of the *Phaedrus* (277a6–279b5). In a
reading which closes its voyage into the mythological *hors-texte* of Theuth
by saying '[l]et us return to the text of Plato, assuming we have ever really
left it', (95) the exclusion of the *concluding* section can only astonish. Some
reconstruction, however, of the close of the *Phaedrus* suggests that Derrida's
essay is increasingly threatened by the text it is reading. Let us identify the
point at which 'Plato's Pharmacy' desists from any further citation of the
Phaedrus.

   Derrida has reached the point where his text can declare that '[t]he
dividing line now runs less between presence and the trace than between
the dialectical trace and the nondialectical trace, between play in the "good"
sense and play in the "bad" sense of the word.' (155) To exemplify which, he
cites the exchange (276d–277a) in which Socrates allows writing as amusement (*paidia*), as a 'store of reminders' (*hupomnēmata*) to assuage declining
memory. The citation then allows Derrida to explore the asymmetrical
opposition of seriousness/play (*spoudē/paidia*) in a closing section entitled

'Play: From the Pharmakon to the Letter and from Blindness to the Supplement'. Although lengthy extraction is made from numerous other dialogues, the *Phaedrus* plays no further part.[75] This *terminus* will suit the pharmaceutical reading which can then analyse 'the Platonic repression of play' as analogous with the repression of writing: to this end, Derrida insists on translating *paidia* by 'play'.[76] Captivating as it is, Derrida's discussion of play serves to cancel the operation by which the *Phaedrus* reconsiders the repression of writing. Prior to that moment – perhaps preparing for it – Socrates declares: 'nothing that has ever been written whether in verse or prose merits much serious attention – and for that matter nothing that has ever been spoken in the declamatory fashion which aims at mere persuasion without any questioning or exposition'. (*Phaedrus*, 277e) It is not speech *qua* speech that is at issue but a particular form of *dialogic* discourse, one whose terms the 'spoken' can transgress as readily as the 'written'. The contest of 'speech' and 'writing' is not here conducted through the metaphysical category of 'presence'. Rather it is addressed to ethical and epistemological issues which split the notion of speech into responsible, truth-seeking dialogue on the one hand, and dogmatising monologism on the other. Naturally it will be first and foremost a matter of the validity of what is said *or* written; of whether Plato considers the communication to be a truthful discourse (*alethinos logos*). Where the reception of *logoi* is concerned, it is not the fact of speech itself but the presentation of a discourse within a pedagogic framework of question-and-answer that determines its value. Thus when Derrida, in a later work, describes idealised speech as embodying the speaker's 'absolutely current and present intention or attention, the plenitude of his meaning',[77] he is superimposing a metaphysics of intention on a Platonic corpus which shows the deepest suspicion toward the adequacy of any natural language – written or spoken – to intention, consciousness or meaning. The very insistence on question-and-answer derives from Plato's conviction that spoken discourse cannot be transparent to intention. The *Cratylus* would have something to say on this point, and in the Euthyphro, the *logoi* run off like the statues of Daedelus (*Euthyphro*, 11c–d).[78] So far from speech housing a conscious, private and self-present intuition of the speaker's, it is the public processing of discourse rather than any supposed coincidence of thought and expression that dictates the *Phaedrus*'s preference for a dialectical method which can select the recipients of its discourse or silence itself when the audience seems inappropriate.

The conjunction of speech and writing under a negative aspect at 277d–e is followed by a recapitulation in which the critique of writing is qualified:

SOCRATES   : Do you now go and … deliver a message, first to Lysias
              and all other composers of discourses (*logoi*), secondly to
              Homer and all others who have written poetry whether
              to be read or sung, and thirdly to Solon and all such as
              are authors of political compositions under the name of
              laws – to wit, that if any of them has done his work with
              a knowledge of the truth, can defend his statements
              when challenged, and can demonstrate the inferiority
              of his writings out of his own mouth, he ought not to
              be designated by a name drawn from those writings, but
              by one that indicates his serious pursuit.
PHAEDRUS   : Of course. Then what names would you assign him?
SOCRATES   : To call him wise, Phaedrus, would, I think, be going
              too far; the epithet is proper only to a god. A name that
              would fit him better, and have more seemliness, would
              be 'lover of wisdom', or something similar. (*Phaedrus*,
              278b–d)[79]

When orally supplemented, writing is acceptable (albeit in an inferior case):
if its author answers lucidly to philosophy, he answers to the name of philosopher. To be sure, the 'writing' Socrates describes above is very far from the
'pathbreaking writing' Derrida promotes. Writing is both contained and
constrained by dialectical philosophy; always under *sub poena*, the written
word awaits favourable judgement from the dialectical court before it may
travel. Like dialogic speech, it cannot disseminate, move beyond the watch
of philosophy. Nor can it treat itself as a fixed or finished entity but must
ever adapt and renew itself as spoken supplement and in accordance with
the demands of Socratic interrogation.

Nonetheless, all such objections can be met whilst acknowledging that
writing is here tolerated in a manner one would never suspect were 'Plato's
Pharmacy' the window through which the *Phaedrus* was perceived. Only
just indicted on the general ground of an unresponsiveness that covers
much of that which is spoken, writing is never for a moment interdicted in
this movement. Writing can participate in a 'serious' pursuit (and here the
potential relevance of this passage to Derrida's meditation on 'play' should
be noted) if only insofar as the (written) critique of writing is serious.
More importantly, the fact that we do not find here a 'Plato who maintains
both the exteriority of writing and its power of maleficient penetration,
its ability to affect or infect what lies deepest inside' (110) authorises us in
asking why Derrida does not attend to a closing statement which bears
upon all the themes of 'Plato's Pharmacy'.

'Plato's *Pharmacy*' has set out to discover 'new chords, new concord-
ances ... in minutely fashioned counterpoint ... a more secret organisation of themes, of names, of words'. (67) A reading with such an emphasis
on 'newness', on revelation, can have no room for an explicit drawing-
together of speech and writing. By neglecting to cite such passages (258b–d;
278b–d), Derrida obscures the problematic of writing in Plato altogether
more than the dialectician who is accused here of 'drawing the curtains over
the dawning of the West'. (167) The pharmaceutical reading deconstructs
the opposition between speech and writing on the basis of a sundering
which never takes place. There is a narrative strategy in certain philosophical
works whereby a postulate is hidden from the demonstration so as to make
its presentation the more conclusive in closing; somewhat similarly, 'Plato's
Pharmacy' only shows how the speech/writing opposition is insupportable
within the *Phaedrus* by insisting on a classic form of the opposition which
Plato's text does not propagate. The claim that '[t]he dividing line now runs
less between presence and the trace than between the dialectical trace and
the nondialectical trace' (155) amounts to little more than saying that for
Plato there is good and bad discourse independently of the media through
which they are articulated. The Derridean performance thus depends on the
suppression of those moments when philosophy (wisely) refuses to inaugurate any epoch of logocentrism. These tensions are abundantly evident
when Derrida chooses to remind us of the epochal significance of both the
Phaedrus and the reading of it which 'Plato's Pharmacy' has produced:

> According to *a pattern that will dominate all of Western philosophy*,
> good writing (natural, living, knowledgeable, intelligible, internal,
> speaking) is opposed to bad writing (a moribund, ignorant, external,
> mute artifice for the senses). And the good one can be designated only
> through the metaphor of the bad one. Metaphoricity is the logic of
> contamination and the contamination of logic. Bad writing is for
> good a model of linguistic designation and a simulacrum of essence.
> And if the network of opposing predicates that link one type of
> writing to the other contains in its meshes *all the conceptual oppositions
> of 'Platonism'* – here considered the dominant structure of the history
> of metaphysics – then it can be said that *philosophy is played out in the
> play between two types of writing*. Whereas all it wanted to do was to
> distinguish between writing and speech. (149: my emphases)

All the conceptual oppositions of Platonism are contained in the play between
two types of writing; Platonism dominates the history of metaphysics;
therefore the *Phaedrus* establishes the contradictory pattern which both
stabilises and destabilises the history of philosophy. What might it mean for

an opposition of this kind to dominate *all* of philosophy? For philosophy to be played out in the play between two types of writing? For all the themes of the west to be reducible to a good writing which masquerades as spoken presence and a bad writing which obscenely writes itself? On an empirical level, and one clearly not intended by Derrida, we could summon Aristotle, who, though dependent on thought as *logos*, castigates the idea of an ideal speech situation in the scene of dialectical instruction; the very same who sees speech as unscientific, ill befitting the proper practice of philosophy.[80] A scholasticism could also be invoked in which the paradoxical structure of devaluation and dependence is found not in relation to writing but in the attempts of Ockham, Abelard and others to escape *speech* as the model for the determination of meaning.[81] Numerous other pathways could be followed – including those leading to and from a Baconian rationalism which explicitly defines itself in terms of the ethos and *episteme* of writing – all of which would reveal that the problems encountered by Derrida's phantasmatic history derive from his desire to graft the technological onto the metaphysical in such a way that the media of speech and writing are deconstructed long before their adequacy to the categories of presence and absence has been assessed. As media, speech and writing are largely exiguous to a tradition which concerns itself with a *ratio* and not an *oratio*: the mimetic subordination of writing to speech occurs only in an exteriority or 'realm of expression' which is not an object of primary concern to the metaphysician. That this *ratio* is sometimes portrayed as a 'writing in the soul' does not imply any contradiction with the mimetic subordination of writing to speech: if anything, it shows how far tradition is from identifying speech with *logos*. Indeed, as Martin Elsky suggests, 'for many Scholastic logicians, speech and thought are at odds': 'The act of speech is a moment of struggle between the mental articulation of a thought and its expression in the sounds of convention-bound speech.'[82] What Derrida uncovers as an *archē*-writing is already for the metaphysician a language of purely mental concepts which exists prior to its phonetic or graphic expression: if this language is best described as an interiorised writing prior to its inscription as marks-on-the-page, it is because speech and writing are not set in opposition by the quest to describe what Ockham called 'mental words' which 'reside in the intellect alone and are incapable of being uttered aloud'.[83] That the metaphor of a 'writing in the soul' served best to capture this mental language reveals a tradition which, so far from being in contradiction with itself, has never demonstrated a significant or consistent hostility to writing. Once more, then, the failure of transcendental arguments or empirical evidence for his 'history of metaphysics'

drives Derrida to an exemplary author for the postulation of all pervasive
fear of writing in western conceptuality, and we should not be surprised at
his unwillingness to unveil the logographic or recapitulatory phases of the
Phaedrus. Given the insecurity of the history of logocentrism announced in
Of Grammatology – a history which constructed itself on the promise and
collateral of the *Phaedrus* – we find a Platonic logocentrism only definitively
articulated in a *Seventh Letter* whose authenticity remains far from secure.[84]
We would also find a Platonism which also speaks in favour of writing, as
in the *Laws* when the text declares that writing 'will be a most valuable aid
to intelligent legislation because Regal prescriptions, once put into writing,
remain always on record as though to challenge the question of all time to
come.' (*Laws* X, 891a)[85] Reading quite casually, we would also encounter
a Platonism which – so far from dreaming of 'a memory with no sign'
(109) – wants, and in all equipoise, in all respite from contradictory play,
to write *mnēmē* independently of *hupomnēsis*, to read writing as the truth of
memory. In writing:

SOCRATES : It seems to me that at such times our soul is like a
book.

PROTARCHUS : How so?

SOCRATES : It appears to me that the conjunction of memory with
sensations, together with the feelings consequent
upon memory and sensation, may be said as it were to
write words in our souls. And when this experience
writes what is true, the result is that true opinion and
true assertions spring up in us ... (*Philebus*, 39a)

We would find, in short, a history of the repression of the written sign
which does not commence until Rousseau, a symptomatic history which, by
committing itself to the 'all' of philosophy – 'a pattern that will dominate
all of Western philosophy' (my emphasis) – has a totalising relation to the
very tradition whose deepest presuppositions it claims to have revealed.
'Plato's Pharmacy' gives us no options but those of assent or dissent in terms
of this myth of rationalism's origin in the privileging of speech. To this
extent, we find ourselves at a considerable methodological distance from
the Derrida who (in the words of Derek Attridge) sees the text as 'radically
situated – written and read and re-read at particular times and places – and as
possessing a singularity (each time) which can never be reduced by criticism
or theoretical contemplation.'[86] Although attentive to Plato's relation to the
Sophistic discourses of his day, 'Plato's Pharmacy' major drive is to situate
the *Phaedrus* in the rarefied, stratospheric context of a history of logocentrism. If reading involves a play between the general and the singular, then

the attempt to locate Plato's text at the opening of a history of the repression of the written sign does not affirm the singularity of an act of writing (Plato's *Phaedrus*) and an act of reading ('Plato's Pharmacy'): or, rather, the reading works itself out in the contest between the singular force of a reading and the generalised structure which that reading is forced to inhabit. The reading, *qua* reading, respects singularity in a finely calibrated manner, but the grandiose expectation that it will identify the conceptual origin of the *episteme* cannot withstand that distinctive idiom, that signature to which 'Plato's Pharmacy' is the most arresting countersignature. For this reason, Derrida does indeed raise the *Phaedrus* to a level of 'interest and complexity unglimpsed by more orthodox commentators', [87] and this in spite of his claims concerning the 'history of metaphysics'. Yet, this achievement can neither be the product of the singularity of its reading alone: 'An absolute, absolutely pure singularity, if there were one, would not even show up, or at least would not be available for reading. To become readable, it has to be *divided*, to *participate* and *belong*.'[88] This structure of participation and belonging is overwrought in 'Plato's Pharmacy' and prompts us to look for another level of generality within which the essay belongs. Is there, then, an alternative way of acknowledging the power, the originality and claim upon generality of an essay which fails to establish the opposition between speech and writing as a dominant, if repressed, theme of western philosophy?

In glancing comments, in his attention to the detail of the Platonic myth, Derrida hints at a third term in his analysis. Along a relay of deferrals without conclusion, he promises to speak of '[t]he kinship of writing and myth, both of them distinguished from *logos* and dialectics'. (75)[89] One might come closer to a pattern which dominates all of philosophy through seeing the good discourse of *logos* – whether considered as philosophy or science – as seeking to found itself on the systematic exclusion of *muthos*; just as Plato's œuvre would indeed be the founding moment of this exclusion, 'the most powerful effort to master it, to prevent anyone's ever hearing of it, to conceal it by drawing the curtains over the dawning of the West'. (167) One could also argue, contentiously but with resonance, that Plato could not master the play of *muthos* within his own text, that, whether in the founding myth of the *Republic*, or of the cicadas and writing in the *Phaedrus*, *logos* had not fully separated itself from the mythical writing which it sought to supplant. One might do this whilst respecting Socratic emphases on the responsiveness of discourse, on *logos* as expressed through question-and-answer to show that what Plato fears in writing he fears also in the orality of the epic tradition, in any discourse which might solidify into an unresponsive, 'unquestionable' body of received opinions, of dogma.[90]

Less an awkward attempt to revise the history of metaphysics, 'Plato's
Pharmacy' might then reveal itself as a startling contribution to the ancient
quarrel between poetry and philosophy – a *Birth of Tragedy*, if you will,
for the twentieth century, an argument which enacts its own challenge
to poetic banishment in the form of a pathbreaking and literary writing
that writes itself beyond the vigil of philosophy. Such a reading would
note how Derrida's most spectacular effects are poetic: his pushing of the
Socratic images of seeds, of scattering, of dissemination to the limits of
their endurance; his anthropomorphisms which proceed from the slightest
textual suggestions; the resonant pathos he reads beneath the dialectical
treatment of writing:

> [Writing] rolls this way and that like someone who has lost his way,
> who doesn't know where he is going, having strayed from the correct
> path, the right direction, the rule of rectitude, the norm; but also like
> someone who has lost his rights, an outlaw, a pervert, a bad seed, a
> vagrant, an adventurer, a bum. Wandering in the streets he doesn't
> even know who he is, what his identity – if he has one – might be,
> what his name is, what his father's name is. He repeats the same thing
> every time he is questioned on the street corner, but he can no longer
> repeat his origin. Not to know where one comes from or where one
> is going, for a discourse with no guarantor, is not to know how to
> speak at all, to be in a state of infancy. (143–4)
>
> Writing is the miserable son. *Le misérable*. Socrates' tone is sometimes
> categorical and condemnatory – denouncing a wayward, rebellious
> son, an immoderation or perversion – and sometimes touched and
> condescending – pitying a defenceless living thing, a son abandoned
> by his father. In any event the son is *lost*. (145)

Here we would see a Derrida adding his own inimitable touch to this
quarrel between poets and philosophers, a reader working only at the level
of language and at its limits, a defender of poetry who drives Dionysian
play through the Socratic rationalism of Plato's text. We would then read
the pharmaceutical reading as a myth, as a fabulous history which uses
the text of philosophy to spectacularly place itself beyond reach, beyond
account to the norms of objectivity and methodological prudence. May
one *read* Derrida's reading in this way? As a supersubtle text in which *logos*
and *muthos* masquerade, if only for an hour, as speech and writing?

At the very close of 'Plato's Pharmacy', Derrida shifts register in a
dramatic and – for many – embarrassing fashion. Narrating a myth which
perversely renounces the poetic effects achieved by the reading in its more
formal guise, he bids us enter the mind of philosophy at its inception:

After closing the pharmacy Plato went to retire, to get out of the sun. He took a few steps in the darkness toward the back of his reserves, found himself leaning over the *pharmakon*, decided to analyse.

Within the thick, cloudy liquid, trembling deep inside the drug, the whole pharmacy stood reflected, repeating the abyss of the Platonic phantasm.

The analyst cocks his ears, tries to distinguish between two repetitions.

He would like to isolate the good from the bad, the true from the false.

He leans over further: they repeat each other.

Holding the *pharmakon* in one hand, the calamus in the other, Plato mutters as he transcribes the play of formulas. In the enclosed space of the pharmacy, the reverberations of the monologue are immeasurably amplified. The walled-in voice strikes against the rafters, the words come apart, bits and pieces of sentences are separated, disarticulated parts begin to circulate through the corridors, become fixed for a round or two, translate each other, become rejoined, bounce off each other, contradict each other, make trouble, tell on each other, come back like answers, organise their exchanges, protect each other, institute an internal commerce, take themselves for a dialogue. Full of meaning. A whole story. An entire history. All of philosophy.

Is Derrida here miming the origins of his fabulous history of logocentrism, just as Plato mimed the myth of writing as a gift refused? Is this section to make good the earlier claim that 'if reading is writing ... the *is* that couples reading with writing must rip apart'? (64) Perhaps Derrida is performatively undoing the *muthos/logos* opposition or working it as non-opposition into a mixed discourse where *muthos* and *logos*, literature and philosophy do not find themselves in conflict, where the play of genre plays itself not out of the philosopher's hands but into those of the reader.

Simultaneously, perhaps, we find a Derrida hinting here – in the final chapter of his 'entire history' – that the logocentric epoch of philosophy is itself a fiction, a Rousseauian dream. Given that Derrida will later say 'we should no longer let ourselves be taken in by the somewhat *trivial* opposition between speech and writing'[91] we might think of philosophy as trivialised by the act of reading speech/writing into the heart of its enterprise and wonder who was so taken in by this opposition in the first place – certainly not a Plato, nor any tradition which followed him. We might ponder these matters while recognising that Derrida's essay restores a certain poetry to philosophy but does not do so *as* philosophy. No more than reading here becomes writing at any expense of an author called Plato.

READING AND (SELF-) WRITING

Harold Bloom claims that all reading is 'defensive warfare', and whatever validity this statement possesses in general, it would certainly serve as an accurate description of the deconstruction of logocentrism.[92] What deconstructive opposition to the author reveals as it conceals, in its double figure of conflict and complicity, is that primarily Derrida's work is revisionist, and like all revisionism, its highest stake is that of marking some advance upon the revised text. And the distance to be marked – as Derrida sometimes concedes – is often all but imperceptible, regardless of whether deconstruction is reading the texts of metaphysicians or counter-metaphysicians. With Hegel, for Derrida the most typical of metaphysicians, it can nonetheless be said that the thought of *différance* works an 'infinitesimal and radical displacement' on the Hegelian difference.[93] Similarly, but from the other direction, Derrida's rereading of Heidegger is at once a radicalisation and a scarcely audible refinement of ontological difference, moving beyond Heideggerian (and Hegelian) difference only by a hair's breadth, the ineffable 'a' of *différance*. And the same again is true of the Freudian and Levinasian notions of the trace,[94] of Plato's *pharmakon* and Rousseau's supplement. All Derrida's readings of the 1960s reflect this basic principle: that the deconstructive and deconstructed texts will find themselves – like *différance* and Hegelian difference – at 'a point of almost absolute proximity'.[95]

What distinguishes Derridean revisionism from any other, however, is that this proximity is not necessarily the outcome of a continuity between Derrida's 'ideas' (if indeed there are such things), and those of the authors he reads, but that it arises rather from a unique approach to the act of philosophising. If Derrida is to be remembered as a great philosopher, it will be as the individual in whom – for the first time – the philosopher becomes exclusively a reader-critic. All philosophy begins with the reading of philosophy, most philosophers take the work of another philosopher and begin their careers with a critique of that work even if it is not explicitly proffered in this form. Yet, with Derrida, the task of philosophy was an interminable rereading in the closest possible manner, a constant working into the already-written. Unlike the philosophers he deconstructs, Derrida never elects to reach that stage when his texts discuss problematics on their own terms, but rather must formulate, interrogate, and deconstruct those problematics through other eyes, hear their resonances with another ear. Even the essay 'Différance', which appears to be offered up without anchors, finally issues as a reading of Heidegger, grounded in a number of subordinate readings (that of Saussure most notably).[96] Indeed, Derrida has himself said that his work is 'entirely consumed in the reading of other texts', and the word 'consumed' should be given its full emphasis here, for no other philosopher, or critic even, has ever buried his work so deeply in the resources, conceptuality, and language of the texts he reads.[97] In boring so far within, in taking up so fully the terms, strategies and aporias of the authors with whom he contends, in refusing to bring external criteria to bear, in respecting 'as rigorously as possible the internal, regulated play of philosophemes,'[98] all in all, through the thoroughly empathetic quality of his deconstructions, the Derridean text is always at risk of disappearance into the world of the other.

Opening '*Cogito* and the History of Madness', Derrida writes: 'The disciple must break the glass, or better the mirror, the reflection, his infinite speculation on the master. And start to speak.'[99] But this, to 'start to speak', with a voice of his own, is what Derrida never quite risked; and as a failure which arises directly out of the strength of his reading. Rather his text *liaises*, speaks in tongues, folds over the voices of critic and author like the figures of a fugue, at times ventriloquising, at others miming the voice of the author it reads, whether this takes the form of a thoroughly Husserlian refutation of Husserl, a supra-Heideggerian Heideggerianism, Plato's deconstructive dialogue with himself in the pharmacy, or the most eerie Augustinian conversation concerning the death of the (North-African) mother.[100] For deconstruction, as criticism, never speaks in *propria persona*, but only with a voice borrowed from the author. Or, put differently, finds its own voice in the hollow of an Other's.

After the arduous, and exhaustive philosophical readings of the 1960s, Derrida's work took a distinct turn, not a break in his thought such as that which separates, say, the early from the later Wittgenstein, but a change in mood, approach, outlook and style. His reading becomes less inward, delving, and is happy to play around the fringes of the text, to glance off its surfaces. He becomes preoccupied with the question of signatures.[101] The philosopher of language who had said that the 'names of authors … have here no substantial value' was to pen some of the most beautiful words ever written on authorship, biography, life, its loss and legacy: 'A man's life, unique as his death, will always be more than a paradigm and something other than a symbol. And this is precisely what a proper name should always name.'[102] He also devotes himself obsessively to autography, to the paraph, the signet and seal. *Glas* is concerned with Hegel (eagle/*aigle*) and Genet (flowers/*genista*), Dissemination with Sollers (sun/*soleil*), *Signsponge* with Ponge (sponge/*éponge*).[103] He presents a lecture entitled 'Otobiographies: Nietzsche and the Politics of the Proper Name', and in the midst of the most exorbitantly *auteurist* reading in the recent history of criticism, *The Post Card* announces its thesis that psychoanalysis is the science of Freud's proper name.[104] In these texts, he proposes interpretations of Nietzsche and Freud in terms of the interpenetration of work and life, and calls for deconstruction to take itself to the enigmatic line between these corpora.[105] Having asked, in 'Freud and the Scene of Writing', 'what is the scene of writing?' he answers a decade later that it is signed, sealed and delivered as the scene of autobiography, of desire, of the subject. Without saying so, Derrida was to revisit his reading of Plato in a finely suggestive analysis of the 'destinational structure' of the Nietzschean discourse. Derrida argues that an absolute falsification of Nietzsche's text – or any other for that matter – is not possible: at some level and to some extent, Nietzsche's discourse itself cannot be distanced from the monstrous appropriations made of it by the propagandists of National Socialism. Having demonstrated that Nietzsche did little within his texts to discourage aberrant readings, Derrida searches for the principles of reading and writing which gave rise to an appropriation that Nietzsche himself would surely have discountenanced in the strongest terms. 'One can imagine the following objection,' Derrida says:

> Careful! Nietzsche's utterances are not the same as those of the Nazi ideologues, and not only because the latter grossly caricaturize the former to the point of apishness. If one does more than extract certain short sequences, if one reconstitutes the entire syntax of the system with the subtle refinement of its articulations and its paradoxical reversals, et cetera, then one will clearly see that what passes elsewhere for the 'same' utterance says exactly the opposite and corresponds instead to the inverse, to the reactive inversion of the very thing it mimes. Yet it would still be necessary to account for the possibility of this mimetic inversion and perversion. If one refuses the distinction between unconscious and deliberate programs as an absolute criterion, if one no longer considers only intent – whether conscious or not – when reading a text, then the law that makes the perverting simplification possible must lie in the structure of the text 'remaining'...[106]

To such lucidity we can have little to add except by way of noting that we are here at precisely the opening of the Platonic interrogation of written discourse, of Plato's objections to writing's unauthorised dissemination, its vulnerability to serious or savage misappropriations.[107] We are also confronted, once again, with the baroque figure whereby the most telling insights on authorial responsibility issue from authorship's hollow.

This movement in turn communicates with Derrida's increasingly explicit investment in his own texts. He devises manifold ways of encrypting his name in the texts he writes. In *Glas* he inserts fragments from his own biography between the columns; *The Post Card* tenders a cautiously autobiographical 'satire of epistolary literature'.[108] Indeed, in these texts, Derrida seems to hold himself at the limit of criticism and the opening of literature. *Glas*, in particular, displays a scintillating inventiveness with language, but everything must be overlaid upon, or realised through, Hegel and Genet. As Derrida's commentators are fond of saying, this is a tactic which prevents any one authorial voice from gaining control, as indeed it is.[109] But does it not also, simultaneously, indicate a reticence about taking control, about risking the proper name? The need to *approach* literature through criticism, writing through reading? In an interview with Irme Salusinsky, Derrida intimated:

> since I've always been interested in literature – my deepest desire being to write literature, to write fictions – I've the feeling that philosophy has been a detour for me to come back to literature. Perhaps I'll never reach this point, but that was my desire even when I was very young. So, the problematics of writing, the philosophical problematics of writing, was a detour to ask the question, 'What is literature?' But even this question – 'What is literature?' – was a mediation towards writing literature … And then I had the feeling that I could write differently. Which I did, to some extent, in writing *Glas* or *La Carte Postale*. But right now I have the feeling that I'm always in that preliminary stage or moment, and I would like to write differently again. Differently: that would mean in a more fictional, and a more (so to speak, in quotation marks, many quotation marks) 'autobiographical' way.[110]

Are we then to see Derrida as Foucault saw Barthes: 'I do believe that in his eyes, his critical works, his essays, were the preliminary sketches of something which would have been very important and interesting'?[111] Unlike Barthes and Foucault, Derrida's majestic canon is not yet settled. But might not the absolutely singular 'literature' that now posthumously bears his name *be* itself the search for a voice, for a form of expressiveness no longer tied to the programmatics of reading, and those of reading over the author's shoulder? In other words, is it, strictly speaking, impossible to read *The Post Card* literally when it declares to its anonymous addressee: 'I have never had anything to write. You are the only one to understand why it really was necessary that I write exactly the opposite, as concerns axiomatics, of what I know my desire to be, in other words you: living speech, presence itself'?[112] Or to hear a lament in the opening words of *Mémoires*: 'I have never known how to tell a story'?[113]

Conclusion: Critic and Author

> when what has been repressed returns, it emerges from the repressing force itself ...
>
> Sigmund Freud[1]

Like the poets whom Plato wished to remove from the ideal city, the author lives on within and without theory.[2] The death of the author emerges as a blind-spot in the work of Barthes, Foucault and Derrida, an absence they seek to create and explore, but one which is always already filled with the idea of the author. A massive disjunction opens up between the theoretical statement of authorial disappearance and the project of reading without the author. What their texts say about the author, and what they do with the author issue at such an express level of contradiction that the performative aspects utterly overwhelm the declaration of authorial disappearance. Everywhere, under the auspices of its absence, the concept of the author remains active, the notion of the return of the author being simply a belated recognition of this critical blindness. A similar pattern of inscription under erasure could be assiduously traced in other deauthorising texts. The work of Lacan is entirely organised around the enigma of subjectivity even as the subject is declared absent; Paul de Man's *Allegories of Reading* harbours a massively inscribed Rousseauian subject quite against its stated anti-authorialism.[3] In texts which had somehow passed beyond the author, the death of the author would not be at issue. Direct resistance to the author demonstrates little so much as the resistance *of* the author.

It may well be that the question of the author is not a special case in this regard. Every theory will be haunted to some extent by that which it seeks to methodologically exclude.[4] The question of history will always exert signal stresses on any formalism; all historicisms will eventually have to confront the problem of form. However, what distinguishes the death of the author as a particularly acute form of critical blindness is that the arguments proposed for the eradication of the author often have very little bearing on the problem of authorship *per se*. So much in deauthorising discourse takes place at a remove, the death or disappearance of the author finding its justification only in the manner of an epiphenomenal consequence of other epochal 'events'. If, so the 'argument' runs, we are witnessing the deaths of God, Man, representation, metaphysics, the book, bourgeois humanism, then the death of the author will necessarily follow as an inevitable result of these closures. Everything proceeds as though the author was simply identifiable with God, Man and so on, as though authorship can only be conceived on a plane of metaphysical and idealist abstraction, as if these closures are in process of occurring, and as if we can clear the horizons of Western knowledge in one concerted movement of thought.

Even when the question of the author is addressed somewhat more directly, when specific contentions are tendered as to why we should no longer regard the author as a relevant category of modern thought, anti-authorial positions founder on unwarrantable suppositions and false antinomies. As often as not, the conceptual network proposed in the stead of *auteurist* criticism serves to reawaken the very categories it would vitiate. Intertextuality, for example, as it has been formulated and put into practice, returns quite compliantly to notions of influence and revision. The field of intertextuality is not generalised and unfurrowed: it exists by virtue of constellations, overlap, relays. Nietzsche never read Kierkegaard, and it would doubtless be possible to read him as though he had, but immeasurably stronger intertextual currents open up between Schopenhauer and Nietzsche, Nietzsche and Heidegger, precisely because there is influence, continuity, succession, recession and revision, withal, an act of strong reading between their work.

Within the archaeological version of intertextuality, as we have seen, the artificial distance between author and *episteme* cannot long be sustained. It is not enough to read Schopenhauer on the will as no more than epistemically coincident with Nietzsche on the will, thus discounting Nietzsche's reading of Schopenhauer, his debate and dialogue with *The World as Will and Representation*, any more than it would be sufficient to see Nietzsche's doctrine of the will solely in terms of the Schopenhauerian influence, and in hermetic independence of historical and epistemic contexts. At a broader level of interpretation, the insights of archaeology cannot but rejoin those which they set out to supplant. Even whilst we accept the hardest deterministic arguments of archaeology, that individual discourses are purely the product of anonymous epistemic forces, nothing within archaeology can outlaw the subsequent influence of the discourses thus constituted. Should it be that the Kantian discourse is simply an epistemic event perchance articulated through a particular Königsbergian citizen, we are still forthwith left with the question of the Kantian influence over modern philosophy, with the problem that the Kantian discourse was constituted in such a profound and inaugural fashion that the thought of two centuries has discovered so many of its most significant directions, and points of departure from that discourse. This influence, however it may have originally been wrought, remains as something to be assessed, considered, explained.

In many respects, it matters little what species of determinism is used to argue the death of the author. Whether we see the subject as constituted in and through language, history or *episteme*, the postulation of a prior consti- tutive cause does not deny the constituted entity its existence, nor does it prevent that entity in turn causing something else. Joyce is not the father of *logos*, but this does not mean that in *Finnegans Wake*, he did not recon- figure language in a textual construct without precedent in the history of writing. Naturally, we must agree with Barthes, Lacan, and others, that no subjectivity precedes a language that has evolved for millennia before the subject utters its first inchoate words, but this in no way impedes the ability of an author to work – like the logothete – innovatively with and within language.

The blindness of all determinist models of the literary text is that they eschew any possibility of compatibilism, that they refuse the continua- tion of the causal chain beyond the ground prescribed. Once something is identified as an effect of language, the *episteme*, or whatever, the possibility of that effect becoming a cause at a later stage of development, of its engen- dering significant events in its train is abjured, even to the point of calling into question the very existence of that effect on the ground that is an effect. Yet whilst subjectivity is the outcome, the effect of the impersonal Other (in any of its poststructural forms), it still remains as subjectivity, as something to be located and specified. Nor is there indeed any reason why the subjectivity thus constituted need be uniform or purely functional. If the author is the site of a collision between language, culture, class, history, *episteme*, there is still every reason to assume that the resultant subject should be constructed in each case differently, the psyche thus forged being irreduc- ible to any one of those forces in particular. Short of taking this line of reasoning to the ludicrous extreme of asserting that subjects are constituted homogeneously, the difference between subjects remains to be explained.

Of course all such deterministic arguments represent an attempt by critical theorists to promote authorial absence as an inherent property of discourse rather than as merely one approach amongst others to the problems of reading and interpretation. The general aim of extreme anti-authorial discourses is to show how the absence of the author can be upheld not only as a stipulation but also as a descriptive definition of the discursive field. Much confusion, in fact, arises from the neglect of this distinction, from confounding the death of the author as a speculative experimental approach to discourse with authorial absence as the truth of writing itself. Two statements drawn from Barthes serve aptly to illustrate this difference:

> We must ... decide to rearrange the objects of literary science. The author and the work are only the starting-points of an analysis whose horizon is a language: there cannot be a science of Dante, Shakespeare or Racine but only a science of discourses.[5]
>
> Flaubert ... achieves a salutary discomfort of writing: he does not stop the play of codes (or stops it only partially), so that (and this is indubitably the *proof* of writing) *one never knows if he is responsible for what he writes* (if there is a subject *behind* his language); for the very being of writing (the meaning of the labor that constitutes it) is to keep the question *Who is speaking?* from ever being answered.[6]

The first statement is *ad hoc*, heuristic. Given that we wish to found a science of literature, and given that the institution of such a science is feasible and desirable, then we shall be compelled to put the question of authorial involvement within parentheses. In the manner of classical science, we will circumscribe and delimit the field, reduce it to manageable proportions, thereby opening our analyses only to those objects which admit of scientific description. Having thus established our object, and the range of our investigations, we will have nothing to say about what lies outside the scientific domain, whether it exists or does not exist, what properties or qualities the excluded phenomena may or not possess. The second statement is of a completely different order. The death or disappearance of the author is no longer a point of method but the proof of writing, its revealed truth, a matter of cognitive certitude rather than a strategic hypothesis.

The death of the author operates in the hiatus between these two statements, its goal being to bridge the distance between the methodological and ontological questions of authorial disappearance. Yet faced with this challenge, proponents of the death of the author have done little but blur the distinction altogether. The critic will say that we might productively explore the openings made by removing the author, and this proposition will slide – over a certain distance – into the claim that the text *demands* to be read without an author. In an interesting reversal of the old fallacy, critics move from the *de jure* to the *de facto*, from a point of principle to a point of fact. Thus Barthes will suggest that we bracket the question of the author awhile, and shall then say that writing is in essence the 'space where our subject slips away, the negative where all identity is lost.'[7] Foucault will provisionally recommend an anonymous history of discourse by way of an alternative to positivist history, only then to announce – *in medias res* – that anonymity is the proper essence of discourse and its history.

Anti-authorialism thus begins in the manner of a scientific reduction and reemerges as the end to which it purported to be the means. The death of the author 'proves' the death of the author: subjectivity is put to one side, therefore subjectivity does not exist. What such circular 'arguments' themselves confirm is that their are no 'proofs' of writing which necessitate authorial disappearance. The decision as to whether we read a text with or without an author remains an act of critical choice governed by the protocols of a certain way of reading rather than any 'truth of writing'. Which is to say that authorial absence can never be a cognitive statement about literature and discourse in general, but only an intra-critical statement and one which has little to say about authors themselves except in so far as the idea of authorship reflects on the activity and status of the critic.

CRITIC AND AUTHOR?

The Yale critic, and *poet manqué*, Harold Bloom, has devoted a career to the development of a theory of the poetic anxiety of influence.[8] Every poet of the post-Miltonic era, he contends, begins his poetic life in dread of having nothing to say. Confronted by the grand and oppressive tradition, the newcomer senses his harrowing belatedness before the enormous weight of the already-written. In an attempt to discover a poetic voice, the newcomer or ephebe cathects onto the work of a great precursor, and – whether consciously or not – begins producing imitations of the predecessor's work. A scene of instruction is underway which will remain with the ephebe throughout his poetic life, one which at various stages the ephebe will attempt to break free of, seeking here to withdraw entirely from the precursor's work, there to discover ways in which this work might be continued in an original or deviant manner. Caught within an essentially Oedipal, psychopoetic pattern of enthralment and denegation, affirmation and denial, the ephebe will at some stage attempt the symbolic, ritual slaying of the Father in an attempt to carve out a space of authentic self-expression. But as with all gestures of this kind, the rejection of the precursor serves only to reconfirm the influence of the precursor. The only outroute for the ephebe is to reach a stage of poetic maturity in which the influence of the poetic father can be harnessed and mastered through the rewriting of the primal work in such a powerfully revisionist fashion that it comes to seem the ephebe's own. Thereafter, and only thereafter, the *agon* abates, the newcomer becomes a poet in his own right, a strong poet.

It is not difficult to see how Bloom's theory maps every bit as comfortably – if not more so – onto the relationship between critic and author such as it has been played out in recent times. We have seen that the death of the author is promulgated in agonistic terms, in the form of usurpation, as we have seen also that it is inseparable from a strong act of rewriting by all these critics: Barthes rewriting Balzac, Foucault making literally what he will of four hundred years of philosophical thought, Derrida rewriting Rousseau. The seizure, from the author, of the right to produce the text is the motivating thrust behind all these extirpations. Yet in all these cases – that of Barthes in *S/Z* most immediately – once the act of rewriting has been achieved, the desire to eradicate the authorial subject recedes, the author is returned. So far from consolidating anti-authorialism, this rewriting leads in its turn to a certain distancing of these critics from the critical field itself. Barthes more or less abandons reading to produce his own forms of autobiographical fictions, Derrida departs from philosophical criticism to interscribe autobiography with Joycean tapestries on writers such as Hegel, Genet, Ponge. Having rewritten the canonical text, the critic goes on to produce texts of his own.

This development from strong reader to rewriter to writer has led many poststructuralists to suggest that criticism itself has become a primary discourse. And this notion commands a certain respect, for the weakening of the boundaries between creative and critical is not only a development within criticism, but also a powerful and necessary extension of modernism in general. As the literary text becomes more self-reflexive, as its artifices and narratological structures come to dominate the foreground, as the work of fiction becomes autocritical, autodeconstructive even, it is entirely concinnous that the critical text should become increasingly creative, interpretable, and like the work of Wilde and Mallarmé, a realm with charms, mazes, and mysteries of its own.[9] However, what has opened up as the space of a possible convergence between literature and the most innovative forms of literary criticism has been pushed to the limit by some theorists who see, in Derrida's work especially, evidence that criticism, whatever its cast or quality, can be no longer demarcated from primary discourses, that it can no longer be constrained within a passive, handmaidenly capacity, that source and commentary, origin and supplement, traverse the discursive field on an equal footing. The boundary is no longer operative; the secondary becomes primary, the supplement is at the origin; criticism finds itself within literature.

Yet, whilst acknowledging the force and enticements of such an idea, when turned against the author this line of argument becomes entirely self-defeating. Barthes, Foucault and Derrida have not problematised the distinction between primary and secondary discourses by diminishing the primary text to a state of servile dependence. Quite the contrary. If anything, their readings restore to us the adventure of reading these source texts. Barthes on Sade, Derrida on Husserl, open and revivify the text, uncover layers of significance, draw forth possibilities of reading and rereading that a more humble criticism would surely bypass. But more importantly still, in this context, it is only by elevating their own work to a pitch of creativity with language that they resisted – and continue to resist – domestication as secondary writers. They *created* oeuvres of great resonance, scope and variety. They became more than critics: a vast body of secondary literature has grown up around their work, one which generally has sought not to contest or deconstruct what they say, but rather has re-enacted precisely the predominance of source over supplement, master over disciple, primary over secondary. They have been accorded all the privileges traditionally bestowed upon the great author. No contemporary author can lay claim to anything approaching the authority that their texts have enjoyed over the critical establishment in the last twenty years or so. Indeed, were we in search of the most flagrant abuses of critical *auteurism* in recent times then we need look no further than the secondary literature on Barthes, Foucault and Derrida, which is for the most part given over to scrupulously faithful and almost timorous reconstitutions of their thought.[10]

Even such a strong-minded critic as Geoffrey Hartman is prey to this tendency, and in the course of critical discussions wherein he seeks to challenge the primacy of the creative over the critical text. In many of his texts – 'Literary Commentary as Literature' in particular – Hartman takes *Glas* as an exemplary text in the dissolution of the distinction between literature and criticism.[11] From the outset therefore, Hartman's case is suspect, for no work could be less typical of criticism either at its best, worst, or most journeyman. Hartman then proceeds to argue as though this monumental, ageneric and thoroughly maverick text imports criticism-in-general into the primary sphere. And he does so by means of a polemic whose terms are unremittingly axiological, that is, hierarchical. *Glas*, for Hartman, is plainly *too* creative, *too* labyrinthine, *too* good to be a distant cousin of literature, so much so that he predicts for it a destiny comparable only to *Finnegans Wake*.[12] Derrida's text, in short, possesses all the attributes by which we have conventionally recognised the great literary work. In his fervour to dissolve the distinction between primary and secondary, Hartman plays squarely back into its clutches. By writing so sensitively, so well, so expli-

catively about *Glas*, he makes of it a canonical text but only at the price of
declaring his own work secondary, parasitic, sponsorial. Hartman's position
thus leads in one of two parallel directions. Either we accept that Derrida's
work has left the homelands of criticism, has passed over into literature – as
Hartman contends, he speaks even of 'crossing the line'[13] – or we evolve a
tripartite distinction between authors, primary critics, and deutero-critics.
In other words, we ask: is the Overreader an author? If we answer in
the affirmative, we maintain the distinction between the primary and the
secondary via admitting the elect amongst the latter into the former: if in
the negative, then we are faced with a certain refinement in our classifica-
tions or with the construction of a gradient of creativity within criticism.
In all events, this is not an argument – nor even the ghost of one – for the
death of the author.

Whether Derrida, Foucault and Barthes are authors is prohibitively
difficult to determine and, in many respects, beside the point. Certainly,
they would seem to be neither authors nor readers in any stable sense,
in so far as we might say that their work passes between these categories
at different stages of development. *A Lover's Discourse* and *Camera Lucida*
are undoubtedly works of an author, *On Racine*, a critical text written
by a critic. Derrida, introducing Husserl's *Origin of Geometry*, or reading
Edmund Jabès[14] is functioning as a critic, whilst writing *Glas* he plays the
roles of critic and author simultaneously. Foucault, promoting the work of
the Surrealist author, Raymond Roussel, is quite consciously and deliberately writing in the service of his chosen author,[15] though when criticising
the vast matrix of power systems, his work departs entirely from criticism understood as an intersubjective process. There would seem no way
of doing justice to the life's work of these three writers via either term.
Critic or author? Critic *and* author? It might be necessary to arrive at a new
writerly category, or to revive the notion of a classical pedagogy in order
to adequately describe their situation. What is assured, though, is that they
did not force this rethinking of the relationship between critic and author
through declaring the death of the author. Rather, they have expanded and
revised our notions of both criticism and authorship by writing their way
out of criticism in the only way one can: that is, toward authorship.

MISRECEPTIONS: PHENOMENOLOGY INTO DECONSTRUCTION

Naturally, the question remains to be asked as to why the death of the
author should have exercised an influence so far in advance of its articulation. Its appeal to a criticism eager to elevate itself to a point of parity with

primary discourses is immediately apparent, but such an explanation falls short of accounting for the widespread impact that radical anti-authorialism has exerted, particularly upon the Anglo-American tradition.[16] Indeed, the reception of the death of the author has been a profoundly complicated and confused affair. In America especially, many critics have responded to the death of the author in Barthes, Foucault and Derrida as though it were amongst the most compelling statements that their discourses have to offer, and the prevailing weight of counterassertion has been all but ignored. Moreover, as replayed by American critics, the death of the author has an unmistakably belated quality, being evoked in the manner of a distant event whose original import and energy have been lost in transition. In this received form, the death of the author has retained its characteristic hyperbole without recapturing the sense of epochal necessity which motivated its initial formulations. The specific historical and ethnological circumstances in which Barthes, Foucault and Derrida promulgated extreme anti-subjectivism have not been taken into account, and the discourse of the death of the author has been imported into the Anglo-American critical programme without essential modifications, without having been *translated* in the broader sense of that term. As such, the death of the author has revealed itself as another casualty of the stammered and asymmetrical exchange between continental and Anglo-American thought.

The death of the author − as argued above − is inseparable from the massive reaction in France against the resuscitation of the Cartesian *cogito* in Husserlian phenomenology, it being only as a particularly vigorous form of anti-phenomenologism that French structuralism and poststructuralism can be properly understood. However, the situation in the Anglo-American tradition during the 1960s could not have been more different. While Derrida, Foucault, Lacan and others sensed the exhaustion of phenomenological categories, and whilst Barthes was urging the necessity of breaking the traditionally strong institutional hold of the author in the French academies, anti-subjectivism was somewhat etiolated in Anglo-American scholarship due to the long ascendancy of the New Criticism. For the younger generation of critics eager to move beyond the, by then, rather tired ideas of the intentional fallacy, the aesthetic monad, words on the page and so forth, phenomenology had a completely different aspect: exotic, juvenescent, systematically intentional and oeuvre-centred, it represented the most challenging outroute from formalism. Largely through the mediative figure of Georges Poulet, the avant-garde at Yale was introduced to a philosophically based criticism of consciousness, centred upon an all-inaugurating authorial *cogito*, a methodology which in the sharpest contradiction to New Critical objectivity, chose to 'annihilate ... the objective contents of the work, and to elevate itself to the apprehension of a subjectivity without objectivity'.[17] Nowadays it might be difficult to imagine the exciting promise of a phenomenological criticism, but for a tradition which had worked under the influence of Eliotism for more than thirty years, it was received in the manner of a liberation. Under the tutelage of Poulet, two of the most influential critics in the recent history of American criticism – Paul de Man and J. Hillis Miller – began the movement out of the formalist impasse and toward the apprehension of a transcendental subjectivity conceived, in Poulet's words, as ideally 'anterior and posterior to any object'.[18]

Paul de Man, whose links with continental philosophy were obviously well developed, devoted much of his work in the 1960s to arguing against the New Criticism from a phenomenological perspective. Chief amongst de Man's contentions are the neglect of the self in formalism and its refusal to allow for the determining role of intention in the literary act. The New Criticism only succeeded in treating the poem *qua* object through ruling intentionality out of court: the 'partial failure of American formalism, which has not produced works of major magnitude, is due to its lack of awareness of the intentional structure of literary form'.[19] For de Man, intentionality, like subjectivity, is transcendental: 'the concept of intentionality is neither physical nor psychological in its nature, but structural, involving the activity of a subject regardless of its empirical concerns, except as far as they relate to the intentionality of the structure'.[20] In direct opposition to the New Criticism, the intentionality of a transcendental consciousness is proposed as *the* question of literature. Through establishing the distinction between an empirical and an ontological self, phenomenological criticism, de Man claims, 'participates in some of the most audacious and advanced forms of contemporary thought'.[21] Even the formalist doctrine of impersonality is to be read in phenomenonological terms as another expression of this purging from the self of all empirical content in the constitution of a purely ontological literary selfhood.[22]

The phenomenological orientation of Hillis Miller's work during this period is no less explicit. Over the course of a few years, he shifted from fledgling New Critic to critic of consciousness, and produced interesting studies of Dickens and Hardy in terms of the most thoroughgoing transcendental *auteurism*. Literature is defined as 'a form of consciousness, and literary criticism is the analysis of this form in all its varieties.'[23] The role of the critic, Miller declared, is to penetrate the authorial *cogito* as profoundly as possible, to mould his consciousness in the likeness of that of the author. The 'genius' of the critic resides in the 'extreme inner plasticity' whereby he can 'duplicate within himself the affective quality of the mind of each of his authors'.[24] The author, conceived as a 'naked presence of consciousness to itself', becomes the 'true beginning ... the ground or foundation of everything else',[25] the critic a self-effacing figure entirely in thrall to this primary *cogito*. Reading, at its best, can aspire to,

> glimpse the original unity of a creative mind. For all the works of a single writer form a unity, a unity in which a thousand paths radiate from the same center. At the heart of a writer's successive works, revealed in glimpses through each event and image, is an impalpable organising form, constantly presiding over the choice of words.[26]

Within American criticism, Miller's work seemed to represent the beginnings of a massive upheaval, the introduction of continental philosophies of consciousness into a tradition whose philosophy and criticism had never before seriously engaged with the idea of transcendental subjectivity. Miller's role in this movement was ambassadorial, seeking at once to educate the critical establishment as to how the ideas of phenomenology could be transposed onto the critical plane, and to urge a new receptivity of American thought to continental influences. To this end, Miller published an important essay in 1966 entitled 'The Geneva School', an accessible introduction of the ideas of the European phenomenologists, which was eagerly ingested by critics seeking to gain an understanding of continental philosophy and its pertinence to the study of literature.[27] And, in the same year – 1966 – the opening of channels of communication between continental and American thought was marked by an event whose effects are still being felt today – the Johns Hopkins symposium on 'The Languages of Criticism and the Sciences of Man'.[28]

The event was planned as an exchange between continental and American thought, but the influence was entirely one way, as the vast preponderance of French speakers itself testifies. Furthermore, the Anglo-American critical scene was completely ill equipped for what was in store, for not only had French theory effectively passed over into a structuralist methodology largely unknown outside Europe, but certain of the participants – Derrida in particular – were taken up with the necessity of moving beyond both phenomenology *and* structuralism. Of the very many and startlingly varied papers delivered, it was Derrida's 'Structure, Sign, and Play' which was destined to have the greatest impact upon subsequent American theory.[29] In his paper, Derrida managed, with an incomparable deftness, to unsettle the concept of centre both as it operated as the anonymous mainstay of structural analyses, and as it appears in the form of an all-organising phenomenological *cogito*. To a critic such as Miller, the twin themes of decentring and interpretative freedom which 'Structure, Sign and Play' argued must have seemed an uncannily prescient deconstruction of the tenets of authorial centre, and absolute critical fidelity to the *cogito* upon which his work was consolidated. Consequently, as American criticism was taking its first uncertain steps toward comprehending a recently arrived phenomenological criticism, it was presented with the most powerful, well-informed and technically intimidating critique of Husserlian phenomenology and the structural anthropology of Lévi-Strauss. The challenge with which Derrida confronted the American avant-garde was to think through and beyond a phenomenological methodology which had not yet been properly assimilated or understood, and to do so not in the interests of passing into structural analyses, but in pursuit of that critique of metaphysical conceptuality known to us now as deconstruction.

The effect of Derrida's arrival was massive, devastating we might almost say. Paul de Man began to rewrite his position, claiming that the Pouletian subjectivity he had previously adhered to was only, in reality, a metaphor for language.[30] In 'The Rhetoric of Blindness' he conducted a rearguard attack upon Derrida's reading of Rousseau in terms of a transcendental conception of intentionality, an attack however which confirmed little so much as the growing influence of deconstruction upon his criticism.[31] A few years later, de Man emerged as a frontline deconstructionist, and began work on a massive reading of Rousseau according to anti-intentionalist strategies culled directly from the *Grammatology*.[32] For Hillis Miller, Derrida's influence was radical in the extreme. In the space of a few years, and in what must appear today as a virtual allegory of the changing lights of American criticism, he inverted his entire itinerary. He now emphasised a radical textuality where before he had insisted upon the utmost fidelity to the authorial *cogito*. Where the author had functioned as an all-centring presence, he now posited a vast absence, a presence lost and retreating *en abîme*. Where before he had declared the ideal transparency of language to authorial intention, he now denied the ability of mind to exercise any authoritative control whatsoever over textual effects; rather the critic puts 'the notions of mind and of the self' under the most emphatic erasure, 'and sees them as linguistic fictions, as functions in a system of words without base in the *logos* of any substantial mind'.[33] Absolute centre reverses into absolute absence of centre: the text is entirely governed by centre: or it is entirely ungoverned and ungovernable. The idea of the author – we note once again – must be that of total centre or no idea at all.

What the alacrity and extremism of Miller's reversal of perspective illustrate is how the ascription of total control to the authorial centre necessitates that any displacement of the centre is experienced as total, infinitely abyssal. Such is the consequence of failing to recognise that the denial of an absolute authorial centre implies not the necessary absence of the author, but the redistribution of authorial subjectivity within a textual *mise en scène* which it does not command entirely. That deauthorisation and a vulgar idea of decentring should have been taken up so enthusiastically by Miller, and the American deconstructionists generally, is the outcome of espousing an anti-phenomenological poststructuralism without properly thinking through Husserlian phenomenology or structuralism. Decentring takes place so joyously, so blithely because the centre has not been fully comprehended: the unsettling of centre is misconstrued as erasure rather than as displacement and relocation. Explaining his position in the discussion following 'Structure, Sign and Play', Derrida insisted: 'The subject is absolutely indispensable. I don't destroy the subject; I situate it ... I believe that at a certain level both of experience and of philosophical and scientific discourse one cannot get along without the notion of the subject. It is a question of knowing where it comes from and how it functions.'[34] Indeed, in the paper itself Derrida had said that deconstruction 'determines the non-center otherwise than as loss of the center'.[35] What is at issue, rather, is rethinking the question of the subject outside the realm of a transcendental phenomenology, of seeing the subject actively engaged as one principle amongst others in the evolution of discourse. As Derrida says, in a much miscited passage: 'The "subject" of writing does not not exist if we mean by that some sovereign solitude of the author. The subject of writing is a system of relations between strata: the Mystic Pad, the psyche, society, the world. Within that scene, on that stage, the punctual simplicity of the classical subject is not to be found.'[36]

What has occurred in the American reception of Derrida's thought is that the deconstruction of the ideal, extraworldly self-presence of the Husserlian transcendental ego has been hastily misconceived as an attack upon subjectivity in general, and the subjectivity of the author in particular. Fragments of a specifically directed, rigorous, and highly technical critique have been put to the service of a freeplaying literary criticism eager to sideline the question of the author rather than to debate and contest the issues it raises. The crossing over, not only from one intellectual culture, one 'region of historicity' to another, but also from one discipline, one set of critical problematics to another, has been achieved only at the inevitable cost of distortion and misappraisal.[37] Commenting perceptively upon the precipitous effects of Derrida's arrival on the Anglo-American critical forum, Christopher Norris writes:

The result has been a kind of radical euphoria, much like the consequence of reading Nietzsche before one got round to reading either
Kant or Hegel. It has also produced a one-sided account of Derrida's
texts whose partiality can best be shown up by returning to those
texts and reading them afresh with a view to what is often passed over
on the standard 'deconstructionist' view. Then … there emerges the
outline of a counter-interpretation more rigorous in its 'philosophic'
bearing and far less amenable to the purposes of straightforward
literary-critical use.[38]

And in transposing the Derridean critique of philosophical conceptuality
onto the literary-critical plane, the euphoric American deconstruction
loses much of the radicality of the Derridean interrogation, for there is
considerably less at stake in exposing the rhetorical ruses and metaphoricity
of a medium such as literature which is often concerned to foreground the
undecidability of truth claims. What leverage the deconstructive method
exerts upon the philosophical text, with its claims to objectivity, its suppression of the figural and tropological nature of language, is considerably
weakened when deployed in the analysis of a mode of writing for which
the perils of metaphor are – *ex officio* – a source of celebration. Indeed, it
is often argued that in their analyses of the undecidable nature of literary
language, American deconstructionists such as Hillis Miller, Hartman, and
de Man have returned to a position not so radically different from the New
Critical perspective from whence they emerged.[39] For all its ludic and abyssal
qualities, American deconstruction can be viewed as the restoration of an
ethos of reading no less formalist than the old New Criticism which it
thinks to have left behind. In its habit of scrupulously close reading, in its
suspension of the extratextual referent, of history, and – most importantly
for our purposes – of the authorial subject, the school of American deconstructionists would seem not to have moved beyond formalism, but to have
developed formalist reading to an unprecedented pitch of rhetorical and
tropological sophistication.

Many objections, naturally, might be made to this recuperative reading
of deconstruction in general, but in so far as the placement of the author
is concerned, it is clear that the rhetors of Yale have made precious little
advance upon American formalism. Intention and personality, and the
whole host of epistemological problems they raise have been evaded by
critical prescriptions not themselves noticeably different from those of the
intentional fallacy and the personalist heresy. The absence of the author is
taken for granted as though it belongs to the *vita ante acta* of contemporary
theory. The movement against the author in the France of the 1960s there-

fore fulfils very much the same function for American deconstruction as Wimsatt and Beardsley's formulation of the intentional fallacy did for the New Critics, in that it is taken as a well-established theoretical *donnée* which leaves the critic free to pursue entirely textualist readings without regard or responsibility for what those readings exclude or short-circuit. Derrida, along with Barthes and Foucault, is evoked as though he has demonstrated and *achieved* the disengagement of the author from the text and from the critical field such that it is properly improper to speak of the author in our day and age. To argue or justify the death of the author is deemed trifling, otiose: these familiar arguments need no further recitation, it being the task of criticism to proceed in the imperturbable assurance of authorial disappearance.

Naturally, such an enduring rejection of intention and authorship could not pass by entirely unchallenged, and yet the few worthy attempts to restore literary intention have been isolated productions and consequently without significant influence. And when, as in the New Pragmatism (in its literary rather than linguistic manifestations[40]), a more concerted assault has been made on the theoretical position, the central arguments proposed have shown themselves strangely complicitous with certain aspects of formalist and textualist thinking. In fact, the pragmatic intentionalist challenge made by Steven Knapp and Walter Benn Michaels adds a new chapter to critical resistance to the author under the title of authorial return. If followed through to the letter, their programme for restoring an intention isomorphic with textual meaning would diminish the author to even more skeletal proportions than the notions of an 'author-function', a 'decentred subject'. As we have argued earlier, there is no effective difference between identifying the text with its own meanings or those of its author, whilst that identification takes place in absolutist terms. The notion of 'author' simply collapses into that of 'text' in the articulation of an intentionality which, as Knapp and Michaels themselves happily concede, is *theoretically* irrelevant, '*methodologically* useless', and *practically* null and void.[41] The return to the author here is thus a return only to intention, and to a concept of intention that has no place within either the theoretical, critical, *or pragmatic* enterprises.

So far from forcefully unsettling the tradition of Anglo-American formalism, such a pragmatic gesture serves as one more way of keeping authorial subjectivity in abeyance. What the New Critics called 'objective meaning', the poststructuralists 'textuality', and Knapp and Michaels' 'intention' – for all their differences in ethos – serve the common purpose of emptying out the author-problematic. Consequently, from the era of Eliot onwards, the dominant critical methodology in the Anglo-American tradition has turned away from the problems posed by authorship, or has turned toward them only occasionally, and only by way of the most drastically impoverished descriptions. No attempts to consolidate, revise or redefine anti-authorial theory have been made, nor has any decisive and broadly-based interest been shown in the project of authorial renewal.

THE GHOST IN THE MACHINE: AUTHORIAL INSCRIPTION AND THE LIMITS OF THEORY

Beneath and behind the continuing theoretical refusals and reductions of authorial subjectivity lies a model of textual simplicity which seeks to keep 'life' at bay. For the best part of the twentieth century, criticism has been separated into two domains. On the one side, intrinsic and textualist readings are pursued with indifference to the author, on the other, biographical and source studies are undertaken as peripheral (sometimes populist, sometimes narrowly academic) exercises for those who are interested in narrative reconstructions of an author's life or the empirical genealogy of his work. The proximity of work and life, the principles of their separation and inter-action are neglected by the representatives of 'work' and 'life' alike. Work and life are maintained in a strange and supposedly impermeable opposi-tion, particularly by textualist critics who proceed as though life somehow pollutes the work, as though the bad biographicist practices of the past have somehow erased the connection between *bios* and *graphē*, as though the possibility of work and life interpenetrating simply *disappears* on that account.

Needless to say, work and life are not opposed, not even in the casual manner by which night is opposed to day. The principles of any such counter-poise are themselves impossible to imagine. Nor either is an author's life necessarily contingent, something which can be summarily extricated and reduced to a position of irrelevance or inferiority in the reading of a text. The grounding assumption of theoretical objections to 'life' is that through appealing to the biographical referent, we are importing phenomena from one realm into another wherein it is alien, improper, incongruous. Yet, even whilst suspending reservations about this demarcation between life and an abiotic writing, what does a pure textualism or formalism do with a text which incorporates the (auto)biographical as a part of its dramaturgy, a text which stages itself within a biographical scene? A text, for instance, like Nietzsche's, which continually refuses the idea that his life can be jettisoned into a separate sphere?

In *Ecce Homo*, Nietzsche insists that his whole life, his entire oeuvre to date, are indispensable preludes to the text's unfolding. The supposed forcefield between his writing and his life is undermined at every turn, even to the extent that his previous works – critically reviewed by the author himself – become chapters of the Nietzschean autobiography. From the outset, the revaluation of values is an act of self-revelation, the 'self-overcoming of morality through truthfulness, the self-overcoming of the moralist into his opposite – *into me* …'.[42] To understand the Nietzschean philosophy, its texts declare, is first and foremost to understand and behold the man. Having interiorised the history of knowledge in such a profound and unsettling way, the forces represented by Christ and Dionysus (or any other 'subjects' invoked by the text, Voltaire for example[43]) are at work within the autobiographical, philosophising subject himself. By telling the story of his life, as he has done throughout his philosophical career, Nietzsche is telling the story of the overcoming, of the passage from idealism to affirmation, Christ to Dionysus. There is no telling life and work, text and subject apart – 'Have I been understood? – *Dionysos against the Crucified*'[44] – still less of cleaving one from the other in the interests of a more 'rigorous', 'proper' or 'textual' reading. Any reading which ignores the theatricality, the autobiographical performance of the Nietzschean subject simply turns away from the text.

Of course it is not at all easy for a textual theory to take on the performance of a subject within his text, not only an awesomely complex and transgressive subject such as the author of *Ecce Homo*, but any subject who ardently inserts herself into her writing. It is problematic enough for tropes, rhetorics, narrative structures, signs, and so on, to become objects of a critical science without theory having also to confront the interplay between work and life, the shifting instabilities of their borders, the modes of inscription by which a subject appears in her text. Once an authorial subject is admitted into the theoretical picture of a text, that text becomes more difficult to govern and delimit, its identity, its separation from other entities is gravely undermined. The neat demarcations by which biography is separated from a literary or a philosophical text, or even from a general intertextuality are immediately under threat. We see, for example, what happens to *Beyond the Pleasure Principle* – a work hitherto offered only to immanent and thematic readings – when Derrida reads Freud's dreams of legacy, his own troubled family romance into the formulation of a metapsychology.[45]

In the second chapter of this later, speculative, work, Freud recalls seeing a baby boy (in fact, and in principle, his grandson, but this is suppressed in the text) playing a game with a wooden reel attached to a piece of string.[46] The game consists in throwing the reel out of his cot and then retrieving it with evident pleasure and relief, actions accompanied respectively by the exclamations *fort* (gone), *da* (there). Freud interprets this as an attempt by the child to negotiate his mother's absences, to create the illusion of her inevitable return at his will and behest. Throughout the account, the text adopts the neutrality of scientific description; the narrator is simply that anonymous, disinterested spectator who observes, and ventures hypotheses on the psycho-aetiology of the game. However, retracing, or rather reconstituting the text in terms of the Freudian (auto)biography, Derrida discovers multiple levels of subjective inscription: 'there are at least three instances of the same "subject", the narrator-speculator, the observer, the grandfather.'[47] And there is to emerge one further persona – the founder of psychoanalysis deftly pulling all the strings of the analytic movement in order that the science of psychoanalysis become the legacy of his proper name, the inheritance of his daughter Anna, his grandson Ernst, the property of the family name 'Freud':

> Just as Ernst, in recalling the object (mother, thing, whatever) to himself, immediately comes *himself* to recall *himself*, in an immediately supplementary operation, so the speculating grandfather, in describing or recalling this or that, recalls *himself*. And thereby makes what is called his text, enters into a contract with himself in order to hold onto all the strings/sons [*fils*] of the descendance. No less than of the ascendance. An incontestable ascendance.[48]

Reinscribed with its subject, the text becomes mysterious, overloaded, oneiric: vivified by the name and biography of Freud, by the children of whom he has such dreams, by his dreams of a familial destiny of the analytic movement generally, by the grandfather of the grandchild, by the jealous grand-father of psychoanalysis, *Beyond the Pleasure Principle* becomes a rebus in which nothing remains simply constative, theoretical, in which what we think of as a work and a life lose the identity of their separateness, in which the force of desire, the Freudian *conatus*, unsettles any objectivity. The entry of the author, and the author's biography into the text multi-determines the scene of its writing, dissolves any putative assumptions that an author's life does not belong with his work, or belongs to it only improperly. Reading biographically is not a neutralising, simplifying activity. So far from functioning as an ideal figure, from figuring as a function of Cartesian certitude, the author operates as a principle of uncertainty in the text, like the scientist whose presence invariably disrupts the scientificity of the observation. More than any rhetorical solicitation, the re-entry of the subject into the writing disrupts its claims to objectivity, allows energies and forces that exceed and elude its reading in programmatic or linguistic terms. 'A "domain" is opened', Derrida writes, 'in which the inscription ... of a subject in his text ... is also the condition for the pertinence and performance of a text ... The notion of truth is quite incapable of accounting for this performance.'[49]

Critical theory, as we say, has shown itself no more capable of accounting for authorial performance, of negotiating the overlap of work and life, since all theory is finally predicated upon an idea of order and systematicity, a reduction of the idea of text to a clear uncluttered field, to a given whose genealogy is suspended. Though criticism can in practice read a text in terms of its tropes, aporiai, rhetorics, words on the page, and also read in terms of biography, psychological dynamics, authorial inscription, and do so without obvious contradiction, the propagation of a theory of reading and of writing which takes stock of all these determinants is awesomely difficult to conceive. The question of the author tends to vary from reading to reading, author to author. There are greater and lesser degrees of authorial inscription, certain authors occupy vastly more significant positions than others in the history of influence, the attraction of the biographical referent varies from author to author, text to text, textual moment to textual moment. Each new act of reading itself presupposes a different or modified philosophy of the author. A theory of the author, or of the absence of the author, cannot withstand the practice of reading, for there is not an absolute *cogito* of which individual authors are the subalternant manifestations, but authors, many authors, and the differences (in gender, history, class, ethnology, in the nature of scientific, philosophical, and literary authorship, in the degree of authorship itself) that exist between authors – within authorship – defy reduction to any universalising aesthetic.[50]

Yet the promulgation of a textual theory can no more elude the question of the author than contain it. As we have seen, the essential problem posed by the author is that whilst authorial subjectivity is theoretically unassimilable, it cannot be practically circumvented. The processes of intention, influence and revision, the interfertility of life and work, autobiography and the autobiographical, author-functions, signature effects, the proper name in general, the author-ity and creativity of the critic, all these are points at which the question of the author exerts its pressure on the textual enclosure. Notions such as the Dead Author, the over-prosecuted fallacies of intention, personalism and genesis, function as little more than defensive strategies against the essentially overdetermined nature of the text, an overdetermination which lies outside the compass of any extant theoretical programme or charter. Indeed a concerted programme of authorial reinscription may well be inconceivable under the banner of literary theory;

it could even be that since theory became possible with the exclusion of the author, the author signals the impossibility of theory. This is a conclusion to be resisted, and one that can only be resisted by theorists themselves, for the question of the author poses itself ever more urgently, not as a question within theory but as the question *of* theory, of its domains and their limits, of its adequacy to the study of texts themselves, to the genealogy and modes of their existence. And it does so in the manner of an interminable haunting, as that unquiet presence which theory can neither explain nor exorcise.

Epilogue

TECHNOLOGY AND THE POLITICS OF READING

With data systems for user interactivity and geometrically variable hypertext, the reader is no longer simply spectator, one who looks at meaning through the page's window in rectangle, *from the outside*, but coauthor of what he reads, a second writer and active partner. He can enter *into* the landscape of meaning and modify its architecture as he wishes. Once monologue, the text becomes dialogue. It loses its mass, is privatized. It is no longer a static invariant, a road travelled in a given direction, recorded once and for all. Rather, it is a moving mosaic (text, image, sound), an unpredictable sequence of bifurcations, a nonhierarchical, unpredetermined crossroads where each reader can invent his own course along a network of communication nodes ... Perhaps in fact, hypertext will be *the* ultrademocratic, fatherless and propertyless, borderless and customs-free text, which everyone can manipulate and which can be disseminated everywhere.

Régis Debray, 'The Book as Symbolic Object'[1]

'Cemeteries take what they are given', Victor Hugo warns in *Les Misérables*, and just as literary studies seemed to be developing away from the anti-authorialism of the 1960s, technological visionaries attempted yet another premature burial of the author. In 1992, George P. Landow's *Hypertext*[2] alerted the literary-theoretical and technological communities to a 'remarkable convergence of social, technological, and theoretical pressures'.[3] Landow argues that hypertext technology constitutes a literal embodiment of theory's textual concepts. The fact that the theoretical questioning of the culture of the book undertaken by Barthes, Foucault and Derrida proceeded in independence of technological developments is central to Landow's claim that a paradigm shift, a revolution in thought has occurred which takes us far beyond the book. In a *prima facie* sense, Landow's case in arresting: from the first hint, the reader who is acquainted with both cultures can easily construct parallels between the more extreme claims of poststructuralism and the resources of digital technology for reconfiguring text, author and reader. Barthes's freedom of the reader translates into technological as well as *scriptible* terms, the lexia prefigures the item of digitally liberated text (reconfigurable via markup languages), Derridean *débordement* becomes an operational feature of digital environments, Foucault's attempt to reconceive the unities of discourse beyond those of book and author is literally enacted by hypertext programmes. The fixed everywhere gives way to the fluid, centres and margins are dissolved, meaning is seen as illimitable, textuality becomes an open sea; authorial intention and the order of the book are swept aside by intertextuality and the interactivity of the reader. A more theoretical assembly of terms such as 'network' (*réseau*), 'interwoven' (*s'y tissent*), along with slogans such as 'the end of the book', 'the death of the subject', 'the text as mosaic of citations' are taken to be uncannily prescient of these developments, almost as though the mysterious Foucauldian claim that the 'ground … is once again shifting under our feet' was unconsciously referring to this technological paradigm shift.[4]

This paradigm shift is announced via a rhetoric of determinism, supersession and liberation.[5] Taking discontinuities in the past to herald those of the future, advocates of the digital revolution envisage that its influence on intellectual culture will be comparable to the shifts from speech to writing, from the scroll to codex, from textual scarcity to superabundance with the invention of moveable type. Beyond their debts to McLuhan, the visionary arguments for digital culture also depend upon the interiorisation theses propounded in relation to the cultural assmiliation of writing.[6]

Walter Ong argues that writing restructures consciousness, while Eric Havelock attributes the great cultural intellectual shift that occurred in fifth-century Athens to cognitive changes in the human psyche produced by its adaptation to the written word. In freeing culture from the immense burden of memorising the archive, writing provided a means of storing information outside of the mind: this freedom, Havelock argues, created an analytic subject in relation to information. Where it is supposed that the transition from orality to literacy allowed for the fundamental assumption of western rationalism – a subject of knowledge is separated from an object of knowledge – hypertextual visionaries claim that the passage beyond the book will dissolve such categories as authorship, selfhood and subjectivity. In relation to authorship, it is premised that the concept of the author derives from the culture of the book and that the collapse of the latter necessarily vitiates the former. Such arguments again have a Janus-faced quality. Rather like the dubitable trajectory which McLuhan followed in seeing a secondary orality in the technologies of radio and television, digital votaries find affinities in the pre-technological world of primary orality. Interactivity is seen to restore the immediacy and copresence of the speech situation: a dialogic or polyphonic anti-authoritarianism is promised in the 'scripted speech' which contemporary technology facilitates. At the same time, the model of unitary authorship is challenged by a collaborative model which seeks distant antecedents in the accretional construction of 'Homeric' epic, the open text of the Medieval period, or the work of the *confabulatores nocturni* of *The Thousand and One Nights*. Pretechnological necessity is thereby associated with a virtuously democratic futurology. The unifying functions of book and author are rethought as imprisoning and monologic impositions on a discursive sphere which is properly without closure or respite. From a pastoralised world in which 'the text is handed over to the reader in a state of perfection', digital technology constructs a realm where 'in the near future it will be difficult – even impossible – to say who is the author of a text.' Just as 'the closed and protected text will be a thing of the past', so too 'the boundary between reader and author should largely disappear'.[7] As Michael Heim writes in *Electronic Language*: 'digital writing turns the private solitude of reflective reading and writing into a public network where the personal symbolic framework needed for original authorship is threatened by linkage with the total textuality of human expressions'.[8]

In considering these claims, nothing could be further from the point to declare oneself for or against technology. Its progress will not be delayed or indeed expedited by any 'ought': both the first word of prophecy and the last word of reaction are equally out of place. One can, however, call into question a representation which purports to speak from elsewhere. Reflections on the technology lag behind the technology itself, but the argument insists that we inhabit an ideal vantage point which has yet to be realised. How, for example, are we to take the constructions of multiple authorship and the idea of the reader as co-author within this postlapsarian culture? In what kind of world will the reconfiguration of the canonical text be a compelling act – whether in aesthetic or political terms? If interactivity allows the reader to become the co-author of, say, *Paradise Lost*, are we to expect that this 'new' text – reconfigured and replete with readerly interpolations – will be a document of widespread cultural interest? The utopian nature of this vision need hardly be stressed. One need not be an unreconstructed advocate of objective aesthetic value to perceive that while I may become free to interact with and co-compose Bach's *Mass in B Minor*, I would also expect to be the sole auditor of my act of co-composition. A seemingly less contentious construal would take the claims of interactivity to mean that 'the active reader necessarily collaborates with the author in producing a text by the choices he or she makes'. If this is the case, however, then the number of texts produced by readers are innumerable, just as Scotus Erigena once said that scriptural meanings are without limit. There may well be as many Bibles as its readers, but there are not innumerable versions of The Bible in circulation. As Borges's 'Pierre Menard: Author of the *Quixote*' wryly demonstrates, the *ne varietur* form of the book does not inhibit rewritings by the reader; the same form of words can constitute different texts in different times.[9] For us, the *Iliad* and the *Odyssey* are objects of aesthetic pleasure and historical speculation; to the presocratic Greek they constituted guides to practical action. The words of the *Tempest* have not changed substantially but they compose today a text different to the one experienced by an inhabitant of Elizabethan England. However, a multitude of readings implies a stable entity on which such readings take place (and here much confusion would be avoided if advocates of the digital revolution attended to Roman Ingarden's argument that the literary work of art must be distinguished from its concretisations, its mundane reproductions and the multiple acts of readerly consciousness that it promotes[10]): a tiny proportion of those readings enter public consciousness and less still endure as acts of reading which have an ongoing influence of the interpretation of the primary text. Any achieved act of criticism reconfigures the text by proposing a singular channel and set of links to other texts. It is quite possible that extraordinary documents of creative criticism will one day be produced using digital technology just as extraordinary readers are once or twice produced in a generation in the forms of an Oscar Wilde, a William Empson. What is certain, however, is that the new technology will not produce an ultrademocratic world in which a significant proportion of linked-up readers produce compelling readings.

The more modest variant of this claim asserts that hypertext provides a unique cultural window through which we might revisit and reconsider our notions of textuality, reading and authorship. Certainly, there is much to be said for any event which brings our cultural assumptions into clear focus and – like the theoretical calls for the death of the author – digitalisation rescues the issue of authorship from a place of indifference or easy acceptance. However, the opportunity has been somewhat spoiled by the sponsorial zeal through which digital culture is seen as a radical break with all that has come before. In *Zeros and Ones*, Sadie Plant declares:

> ... all notion of artistic genius, authorial authority, originality, and creativity become matters of software engineering ... Retrospectively, from behind the backlit screens, it suddenly seems that even

the images most treasured for their god-given genius were themselves matters of careful composition and technical skill.[11]

'Careful composition and technical skill' instantiate into 'software engineering', creativity is reduced to a naive model of inspiration ('god-given genius'). From the privileged vantage of the digital present ('behind the backlit screens'), the entire tradition of literary and aesthetic criticism appears as the history of an error. Supersession often reduces the past to pastoral, a tendency to which contemporary technological discourse has surrendered in opposing itself to a stereotypical picture of both authorship and a literary institution deemed to 'uncritically inflate Romantic notions of creativity and originality to the point of absurdity'. As casualty, authorship is seen as pure causality. Addressing *'the preeminence of the author'*, Raffaele Simone says:

> If the text is closed, it generally has an author (or a definite number of authors). Not only is the author the *pure and simple generative source of the text* but he or she also acts judicially, as it were, because he or she assumes specific rights and duties by the *pure and simple fact* of making him or herself the author of that text.[12] [my emphases]

Caricature of this kind guarantees that any item in a intelligent reflection on textuality will serve to dislodge the author. In this manner, pioneers of hypertext technology adduce the resources offered for multiple author-ship as a further reconfiguration of the discursive field. However, the phenomenon of multiple authorship has only ever been problematic to the notion of authorship when the latter is romantically conceived in terms of solitary genius.[13] Our acceptance that Eliot's *The Waste Land* was shaped by Ezra Pound has never interfered with our sense of Eliot as the author of *Four Quartets*; Conrad will be the author of *Under Western Eyes* even as he co-authored *Romance* with Ford Madox Ford and benefited from the latter's lendings to *Nostromo*. *De Sophisticis Elenchis* remains a text of Aristotle, even while we will never know who authored the *Iliad* and the *Odyssey*, or, indeed, the extent to which the Peripatetic school collabo-rated in the 'final form' of what we readily accept as *Aristotelis Opera*. The Japanese renga or *The Thousand and One Nights* compose coherent works in spite of being produced by numerous individuals; Malcolm Lowry's *Under the Volcano* and James Joyce's *Finnegans Wake* are the uneven works of single authors. Digital technology only threatens to reconfigure authorship by (i) associating authorship with absolute aesthetic coherence and (ii) level-ling out complex discriminations between primary authorship, secondary authorship, multiple authorship, compilation, editorship, and scholarly annotation. Witness Landow's description of the creation of *The Dickens Web*:

The Dickens Web, a sample Intermedia document set published by IRIS in 1990, exemplifies the kinds of collaborative authorship characteristic of hypertext. The web, which contains 245 documents and almost 680 links, takes the form of 'a collection of materials about Charles Dickens, his novel *Great Expectations*, and many related subjects, such as Victorian history, public health issues, and religion'. Creating *The Dickens Web* involved dozens of 'authors' and almost that many kinds of collaboration.[14]

So too, we may assume, does the construction of a housing estate, but pseudo-problems of this order are negotiated by way of corporate identity: similarly, the academic journal has got along quite well through its adoption of a unique title. Numerous other examples of this kind of hypertextual collaboration will emerge, all of which may prompt us to make more able (and inevitably hierarchical) discriminations between levels of involvement, degrees of authorship. Rather than acting against the idea of authorship, *The Dickens Web* confirms Foucault's expansion of the concept of the author in terms of a creating a field – here marked by 'Charles Dickens' – in which other texts and authors will find a place. *The Dickens Web* fully consorts with idea of a great author as an individual who creates a discursive space beyond the confines of an individual life. Indeed, more sanguine hypertextual enthusiasts actually envisage a cooperative relation between cyberspatial redaction and the labours of authorship:

> ... we can stop to consider the extraordinary usefulness of an instrument which can provide us with not only different readings of a text, but also with the possibility of being able to grasp the progressive coming into being of a text, considering all the aspects it contains or implies, an instrument which which can equip the reconstructed text, as far as possible, with its various layers, each one worthy of being read. This is by no means a simple operation, given the often insurmountable difficulty of identifying the precise moments and chronology of corrective interventions on the part of an author, but one which can certainly be realised at the level of the macrostructure, and this itself can facilitate the successive work of sectional restoration.[15]

Having shuffled off its apocalyptic airs, hypertext might facilitate editions which combine genetic criticism, manuscript variants, source studies, histories of the *textus receptus* etc., and in a technology which permits unprecedented scope and readability.

One need not pause long to recognise the altogether greater benefits of constructive collaboration with an authorial document rather than pseudo-creative linking. Hypertext enables the *representation* of links. Broadly speaking, these links will be made in the diachronic and synchronic spheres. In the former case, the value of those links will depend on the coherence of the field in which links are made; in the latter, value will derive mainly from the competence and intelligence of the linker(s). Nothing is much changed in conceptual terms by the passage from print to digital culture: the difference resides in the literalisation that hypertext provides of these operations. As Georges Poulet reminds us, a book is not just an object among others: it gains its essential life only when read.[16] No text is 'a space that resists all intrusion'[17] and the only closed text is one that has never been opened. Once read, a book has a life beyond its physical or authorial confines, and that life is always interactive, even when the reader lives with the memory of the book, constructs him or herself as the dialogic counterpart of its author. At this stage, hypertext vividly illustrates the complex network of processes by which an active reader *reads* a work: it provides an external correlative for patterns of thought established in a culture of print. Proponents and visionaries of the new discourse would do well to emphasise these continuities: the genius of hypertext resides in its unprecedented facility for making exterior mechanisms of consciousness which have been developed over the millenia since the invention of writing. Here one would want to add to the interiorisation thesis a related thesis of exteriorisation.

The radical argument for digitalised writing depends not upon hypertext as external technology but upon its capacity to restructure human consciousness with an revolutionary effect comparable to the interiorisation of writing. Yet, even if accredited, the interiorisation thesis proscribes that such restructuring takes place over many centuries of psychic adaptation to the new technology. When one considers how radical Augustine found St Ambrose's habit of silent reading, it is clear that writing was long considered the servant of *vox*, just as it was more common to *write down* than to write in an intransitive fashion: only with the advent of print culture did it become customary to proceed from the silent signifier to the concept signified and without the mediation of the voice.[18] In projecting an interiorised digitalisation, the radical hypertextualist argument comes too early. If writing was only slowly and jaggedly interiorised as a constructive component of the human psyche, then one may not speak of the interiorisation of hypertextual technology from this matinal point in its history. Thus the digital argument again appeals to possible and projected futures, to a culture where digitalisation has been thoroughly interiorised as a component of the human psyche. The stronger argument — acknowledging also the ease and celerity with which culture has embraced digitalisation — would see the new technology as an exteriorisation of cognitive processes developed in a culture of writing. The capacity of the literate mind to establish links and intertexts is itself the foundation upon which a technology of linking has been established. As Hillis Miller points out, Georges Poulet's *Les Metamorphoses du Cercle* is a proto-hypertextual operation, and one of great distinction since Poulet's unique cartography depends not only upon sublime connections but also an elegant selectivity.[19] The book maps both the image of the circle and the mind which maps that image's recurrences. Equally, the impressive work of reconfiguration undertaken by Roland Barthes's *S/Z* may well prefigure hypertextual deconstructions, but the worth of this *exposé* of 'natural' narrative depends upon the critical brilliance of a Roland Barthes. To this extent, the most (and 'most' is here a great deal) that can be said about digital technologies is that they exteriorise those synthetic and analytical processes which the human mind developed in its adaptation to a world of written text. So far as *our* horizons extend, digital technology is the bountiful correlative of graphic culture.

The interiorisation thesis upon which radical conceptions of the digitalised future depend itself condemns visionaries to falsify a paradigm shift whose promised contours and countries are necessarily inconceivable. Caught within the ever-recurrent paradox whereby a determinism cannot be articulated by those who live within its frames, the theorists of hypertext have no substantial point of recourse except to politicise cyberspace. By way of claims which conflate readerly and political empowerment, the new technologies are presented as the material embodiment of the 'Copernican overturning' by which texts revolve around the reader rather than the author. The 'ultrademocratic' freedom of the reader is opposed to a tyrannically author-centred literature which forces the reader down a pre-determined and linear path imposed by authorial intention. As Landow presents the case:

> ... [the] liberating and empowering quality of hypertext appears in the fact that the reader also writes and links, for this power, which removes much of the gap in conventional status between reader and author, permits readers to read actively in an even more powerful way – by annotating documents, arguing with them, leaving their own traces. As long as any reader has the power to enter the system and leave his or her mark, neither the tyranny of the center nor that of the majority can impose itself. The very open-endedness of the text also promotes empowering the reader.[20]

Whilst no-one would dispute the right of the reader to choose his or her own path of reading, it is credulous to see this as 'empowerment' in the political sphere: the notions of freedom and empowerment are traduced or trivialised by an 'antihierarchical' argument which never addresses the economic issue of access, nor the possibility that technoculture might further widen the gap between affluent and impoverished cultures.

Even when taken on its own – textualist – terms, the argument for the political value of displacing the author fails to persuade. Authorial ordering is more a way of guiding the reader through a particular experience than a sovereign claim upon the textual centre. Would we, for example, see a Dante 'empowered' through being relieved of Virgil in his negotiation of the Inferno, a Theseus as 'liberated' in the labyrinth by the removal of Ariadne's clew of thread? The 'empowerment' of the reader is a political act only within a institutional world which takes its own storms and seasons for *the* world. In associating itself with a politics of reading, the 'theorisation' of digitalised technology – something altogether different from the work of those who construct and refine technologies – disinters some of the most egregiously falsifying arguments for the removal of the author. Sadie Plant, in the feminist variant on Landow's convergence theory, politicises techno-culture by establishing its essential charateristic as the (essentially feminine) art of weaving. On the basis of a metaphorical connection between the terms used to describe digital systems and the specific (industrial) practices of the loom, Plant draws on Irigaray to suggest that technological change marks a break between a manned past and an unmanned future: 'Just as weavings and their patterns are repeatable without distracting from the value of the first one made, digital images complicate the questions of origin and originality, authorship and authority with which Western conceptions of art have been preoccupied.'[21] Does it not betray a poignant sense of political ineffectuality for literary criticism to allegorise its own activities in terms of an oppressive author, an oppressed reader and a politics of reading *qua* reading? Do we not detect here an obsession with the politics of the sign which has erased all signs of the political? One can see the politicisation of reading as symptomatic of a breach – growing since May 1968 – between the world of the institution and the world of external political realities (whose existence so-called political critics have effectively denied on the grounds of representation being humanist and illusory). Digital technology represents the latest addition to this tendency: its 'politics' rest on the assumptions that the medium is the message and that the message is inherently political. Fredric Jameson, himself a stern critic of technological pretensions to political radicalism, admits the very principle that allows institutional self-regulation to mask as a political act. If indeed one accepts that the 'only effective liberation … consists in the recognition that there is nothing that is not social and historical – indeed, that every-thing is 'in the last analysis' political', [22] then nothing can be *falsely* political: political significance can be claimed for debates which have not the slightest relevance to economic, racial, social or sexual equalities, including even that melancholy shift from the active case of a politics of writing to the passivity of a politics of reading. With admirable directness, Gayatri Spivak says: 'We are not discussing actual political commitment but our fear that students and colleagues will think we are old-fashioned if we produce a coherent *discourse about* political commitment after the postwar critiques of Modernism and, indeed, of Sartrean humanism.' [23] In the name of little more than fashion, and from the era of Sartre, De Beauvoir, Russell et al., to that of poststructuralism, political engagement has been surrendered by the world of letters. In this sallow retreat from authorial engagement to readerly empowerment, the death of the author marks a point so iconic that the reconstruction of the political may depend in considerable measure upon the rematerialisation of the author.

'HALF DUST, HALF DEITY': THE MIDDLE WAY OF SITUATED AUTHORSHIP

Digital constructions of authorship and reading replace the Kantian 'view from nowhere' with a 'view from everywhere'. [24] No attempt is made to situate either the technological argument or the specific practices of reading and writing to which it refers. In this sense, the theoretical appropriation of digital culture provides a negative reminder of the need to treat authorship as a situated activity. Given the immense difficulties involved in attempting any theorisation of authorial practices, it is not possible here to do more than state the necessity of installing the human within the subject and to outline some of the challenges this project would face. In addressing such a need there would seem to be only one tenet that can be stated with any confidence: to wit, that authorship is *the principle of specificity in the world of texts*. So far from consolidating the notion of a universal or unitary subject, the retracing of the work to its author is a working-back to historical, cultural and political embeddedness.

The need to ground authorship should be felt most intensely within political forms of literary criticism. Feminist adoptions of the death of the author/subject have led to something very close to the death of feminism as an ethical, social and political movement. Recognising as much, Seyla Benhabib writes: 'The situated and gendered subject is heteronomously determined but still strives toward autonomy. I want to ask how in fact the very project of female emancipation would be thinkable without such a regulative ideal of enhancing the agency, autonomy and selfhood of women.'[25] Understandably, Benhabib's *Situating the Self* is only able to declare the necessity of such a rematerialisation of subjectivity: confronted with the issue of how such a situating might proceed, her text is silent. Perhaps beyond *any* theorisation, the problems of situating the self are compounded in feminism by its mission to generalise subjectivity at the level of sexual identity. One cannot call a feminism which claims half of the human race – cutting across sexualities, nationalities, ethnicities and class positions – a specifying or situating operation in the same way as identifying an African-American female poet from Alabama or a male, Protestant novelist of Northern Ireland signals a full departure from the generalised subject position. Breaking the autonomy of the humanist subject in two does not break it sufficiently, and for that reason gender would seem to be one form of authorial specificity amongst others. To this extent, the role of a dispersed feminism in informing current critical returns to singularity, to specificity and historical overdetermination would seem more historically appropriate than the attempt to propose a unified field of female subjectivity.

However, while feminism addresses the question of situatedness with direct reference to subjectivity and authorial placements, much of contemporary critical discourse refuses to frame its contextual returns within any kind of authorial lexicon. Postmodern emphases on locality, on little narratives, on singularity; neo-ethical concerns with respecting the Otherness of the Other; postcolonial specifications of the subaltern, of national and historical contexts – all these drives within contemporary critical discourse pass from the text to its histories without properly acknowledging that an authorial life and its work allow such a passage to be made. The author will be exceeded but never bypassed in the critical movement to the time, the place, the social energies and structures in which the text was constituted. In historicist readings, also, it will be through letters, biographical details, documents relating to the writer's life and dealings that we arrive at 'whatever in a poem is most concrete, local and particular to it'.[26] Even strong New Historicist readings which utilise information about which the author could have no knowledge (for example, the use of French provincial legal history in the interpretation of *Twelfth Night*) will recognise, if not be ruled by, the relation of an author to his or her times: among the 'many voices of the dead' is also the voice of a dead author.[27] The contrary movement by which twentieth-century criticism has sought 'to lift the poem out of its original historical context', only achieves this deracination through downplaying the role of the historical author.[28] Aesthetic autonomy is claimed insofar as the text is separated from its authorial circumstance, its *res gestae*. In saying that 'the critic places himself in a position from which he can treat the literary work as if it were a timeless object, unconnected with history', Jerome McGann fails to recognise that such idealisation arises from a lack rather than excess of attention paid to its historical author.[29] Similarly, Greenblatt's recognition that 'the apparently isolated power of the individual genius turns out to be bound up with collective social energy', covertly installs a situated authorial subjectivity.[30] Authorial placement may well be a methodological by-product of political readings whose aim, rightfully, is to construct a nexus of power relations in which the author is only one element, but there are also institutional reasons why an explicit return to the author has been absent from contextual criticism. An embarrassment before the author remains, and one which derives from the association of authorship with an absolutist picture of intention. As I have tried to argue, this isomorphic model of intention specifies no intention at all: in their shared determination of the text as autonomous and *perfectum*, transcendental intention and the notion of the autotelic text have the effect of thoroughly impersonalising literature. Conversely, while intelligent critical practice will use the faultlines or competitions within authorial intention so as to open the text to its contexts, such criticism is construed in anti-authorial terms even as its actual itineraries use the author to break up the ideal unity of the work. Here criticism fails to overtly recognise that the author is that one category which clearly overlaps – one might even say conjoins – text and context. Yet again, all too heavy an investment in the concept of the author as transcendental subject forbids methodological returns to the author in those more fecund areas of will, relevant biographical detail, the relations of works in an oeuvre to one another, the issues of ethical responsibility and so on. The transcendental/impersonal reflex[31] thus continues to delay any concerted reappraisal of authorial roles and prevents contemporary criticism from acknowledging the model of authorial situatedness buried in the movement from the text to the cultural energies of which it is both product and *exemplum*.

Moreover, grave problems arise from the inadequacy of theoretical or methodological language to describe the situated subjectivity implicit within contextual criticism. We all know that texts are written by people with histories, desires, with glorious imperfections and dismaying prejudice. Yet the attempt to picture such an authorial subject leaves us in the quandary of that St Augustine who confessed to knowing what time is only until asked 'what is time?' Situating the author may involve a return to that conflation of philosophical and literary subjectivity whereby modernity transferred the theological property of transcendence from the subject of

knowledge to the authors of texts. This return would be to German Idealism's extension of critical philosophy to literary theory, to the foundations
of romantic aesthetics as to the great dilemma Kant bequeathed to modernity by emptying the 'I' of the unity of apperception of all existential
substance. The Kantian postulation of a subject both transcendental but
nowhere figured in the world – an ahistorical 'I' which is the precondition
of experience but is devoid of all experiential content – has been mistrans-
lated into literary criticism.[32] Either ideally aloof from the creation in the
manner of the theological authors of Schiller and Flaubert, or ideally absent
after high Romantic, modernist, New Critical and theoretical models, one
finds a text drained of all reference to the living, historically circumscribed
person whose name it bears. Restoring that person, that unique face which
Plutarch tells us will never occur again, involves a return to Kant so as to
turn away from the model of transcendental subjectivity and its mistrans-
lation in terms of literary authorship. The point of such an incursion was
suggested by Heidegger as that moment in the Kantian schematism when
transcendental philosophy briefly opened itself to an occluded power
within the human subject through which imagination organised space and
time.[33] As Heidegger recognises, no sooner did the possibility of filling out
the empty subject of the transcendental deduction present itself, than the
author of critical philosophy drew back into the sanctuary of his formal
and existentially hollow system. Amidst the brilliant architecture of the
first critique, the question was closed as to what or who the 'I' through
which experience is organised might *be*. To this extent, those seminal texts
which have attempted to humanise the subject of knowledge may prove
the most productive guides in an attempt to situate this empty subject, the
ghostly 'I' of modernity and its inertly unknowable objects. Here we will
think of Nietzsche's perspectivism, whereby the author, artist or philosopher is a part of the picture he or she paints; Heidegger's notion of 'being
in the world', of existence and of its expressions as a groundedness: Sartre's
engaged and historically situated subject. Retrograde though this loop from
postmodern thought to 'existential' views of selfhood and authorship may
seem, it is clear some re-turn is needed in a critical culture which is wary
of approaching its authors, its *ethos*, even itself. Literary thought would
once again be faced with redoubtable problems of translation, not this time
from a philosophical to literary transcendence, but from a philosophical
immanence to a literary situatedness.

   This prospect is one peculiar horizon of the contemporary temper we
label the 'postmodern'. Perhaps also, the route toward a theory of situated
authorial subjectivity will be compelled to announce itself in the form of a

New Humanism. Whatever the event, this return must attend to the spirit, if not the letter, of Harold Bloom's affirmation of embattled subjectivity. It will need to capture:

> the agonistic image of the human which suffers, the human which thinks, the human which writes, the human which means, albeit too humanly, in that agon the strong poet must wage, against otherness, against the self, against the presentness of the present, against anteriority, in some sense against the future.[34]

Among the manifold tragedies and blasphemies of the human is that the terms of our thought are still so explicitly theological as to allow us to grasp transcendence and absence altogether more surely than the distinctively human, that ever-singular place of desire, will and history from which spring all acts of authorship. In capturing that distinctively human, we might confront afresh the fact of our own mortality. Cicero echoes the Socrates of *Phaedo* (67d) when he says that philosophising is preparing for death. Montaigne makes of this a pedagogic imperative in saying that 'To philosophise is to learn how to die' and adds that a life is always complete when it is over.[35] Authorship is the most spectacular and doomed defiance of this wisdom: it is the limit of an expressive world and the striving we make toward a beyond. If, as Wallace Stevens intimated, 'the theory of poetry is the theory of life', the theory of authorship too has its tenebrous place in our sense of human destiny and its narratives.

Appendix 1: The Biographical Imperative

To judge from recent publications and conference papers, 'biography' is once again a word and concept that can be freely owned by critics and theorists concerned to reinvestigate the always vertiginous relationship between a life and a work. Fashion notwithstanding, this development follows upon some twenty years in which criticism has sought recontextualisation under such various headings as New Historicism, Cultural Materialism, Identity Politics and Postcolonial Studies. A renewal of interest in the authorial life was inevitable in that new contextualisms have depended upon a biographical recourse that has failed to incorporate itself at a methodological level. *Tel arbre, tel fruit*, in Sainte-Beuve's famous formulation, still does a certain justice to the contemporary contextualising impulse, however theorised it might seem on the surface.

Twenty-five years ago, and during his brief Althusserian phase, Terry Eagleton observed:

> It is not, naturally, that the organicist modes of Eliot's novels are the 'expression' of her authorial ideology. As a literary producer, George Eliot delineates a 'space' constituted by the insertion of 'pastoral', religious and Romantic sub-ensembles into an ideological formation dominated by liberalism, scientific rationalism, and empiricism ... The phrase 'George Eliot' signifies nothing more than the insertion of certain specific ideological determinations – Evangelical Christianity, rural organicism, incipient feminism, petty-bourgeois moralism – into a hegemonic ideological formation ... [1]

Even did the 'phrase' signify this 'nothing more', without that life lived as Mary Ann Evans – and then as the textually purer 'George Eliot' – neither these 'certain ideological determinations' nor this 'hegemonic ideological formation' would have taken shape. Here, as in contemporary contextualising criticisms, the biographical subject is simultaneously invoked (as a bridge between the text and its materialised conditions of production) and cancelled (as the product of humanist ideology). This simultaneous reliance upon and embarrassment before the biographical subject stems from a poststructuralist legacy whereby authorship is construed as a transcendental category even within critical movements which seek to demystify universalist assumptions via historical specificity. The New Historicist Louis Montrose reiterated the need to resist 'a prevalent tendency to posit and privilege a unified and autonomous individual – whether an Author or a Work – to be set against a social or literary background'.[2] Similarly, Identity Politics and postcolonial criticism situate subjects whilst disclaiming the very authorial and biographical categories that make such an interpretative strategy possible. We are asked to accept a 'name-under-erasure', say that of 'St Augustine', as though our movement from the texts of the *Confessions* or *On Christian Doctrine* to the North African plains, to the life of a colonial outsider, a sexual transgressor, a speaker of patois, did not draw on the credit of an authorial signature. Neo-contextual criticism has thus participated in a reduction comparable to that practised by twentieth-century formalisms. As with its apparent opposite 'aestheticism', it has turned away from the vexed categories of biography and 'lived experience': a hazily expanded notion of textuality being used to keep life – in all its barbarity – from the gates. But life, as ever, presses and pulses, asserts itself on the margins of the insecure discipline of literary studies. Impossible to assimilate, it shadows critical enquiry like a dark interpreter.

'We fall prey', says Paul de Man, 'to an almost irresistible tendency to relapse unwittingly into the concerns of the self as they exist in the empirical world.'[3] Yet, the concerns of the personal self might equally be a cause for celebration rather than lament, for witting rather than unwitting relapse. As Virginia Woolf says in *A Room of One's Own*:

> fiction, imaginative work that is, is not dropped like a pebble upon the ground, as science may be; fiction is like a spider's web, attached ever so lightly perhaps, but still attached to life at all four corners ... when the web is pulled askew, hooked up at the edge, torn in the middle, one remembers that these webs are not spun in mid-air by incorporeal creatures, but are the work of suffering human beings, and are attached to grossly material things, like health and money and the houses we live in.[4]

Woolf's elegant commonsense turns upon what might be called 'the biographical imperative'. Just as everyone knows that poems come out of a head not a hat, so too it is universally acknowledged that, however supernal their final cast, literary works emanate from the human-all-too-human. No sooner, though, is that recognition granted than an equally valid impulse overtakes us. To retrace the work to its author's life strikes us as unconscionable reduction. Like the Platonic and Freudian model of the soul or ego as a chariot pulled in contrary directions, literary critic and philosopher alike wonder how to reconcile the ideals of disinterest and objectivity with the quotidian realisation that a work or indeed a judgement upon a work arises from a specific perspective in a specific set of circumstances. The biographical imperative thus finds itself disowned as soon as owned, invalid in the very instant of its validation. But how did the real world become a lie, life a pollutant, a poor relation of literary criticism? How did biography, the authorial life as lived, become the shadow self, the wraith of literature?

Borges's beseiged Funes must devote an entire day to the recollection of an entire day. Those impossible cartographers who wish to practice 'Exactitude in Science' must contrive unobtrusive maps that are one with the size of the kingdom. The mind of God, Borges tells us elsewhere, would see the footsteps taken by a man during his lifetime with the same intuitive certainty with which the finite mind recognises a triangle, square or circle. The perfect biography is a similarly inconceivable figure. As the Evangelist puts it: 'And there are also many other things which Jesus did, which, if they should be written every one, I suppose that the world itself could not contain the books that would be written' (*John*, 21:25). Borges's Pierre Menard puts his own quandary in terms applicable to the ideal biographer: 'My task is not difficult, essentially ... I should only have to be immortal to carry it out.'[5]

Locked into a correspondence theory of truth, biography-as-genre is untheorisable. Even in the purely agraphic instances of Socrates and Christ where we divine a perfect unity of life and teaching, the biographical imperative has proved parabolic or indeed tendentious. No work of representation can be complete but incompletion is the very essence, the art or sullen craft of the biographer. A haiku or lyric poem might be incomplete according to an aesthetic measure, but will never be incomplete in the manner of a biography. An epic poem or novel (to take the harder cases) may well be an imperfect actualisation of a grander authorial vision but, to invert the eighteenth-century metaphor, we cannot know the stone in which the ideal sculpture resided. However, the raw materials of a biography – irrecoverable as they often are – once constituted broad events in the concrete world. Hence the virtue of necessity that characterises antique biography. Lacking the range of information available to the modern biographer, authors such as Plutarch were free to take the shimmering instant, the resounding anecdote, as emblematic of a life, a time. A depleted archive enforced proto-photographics: Alexander of Macedonia resting his head on his left shoulder and gazing absently as though his eyes would deliquesce into space; Zeno of Elea basking in the sun whilst eating figs. Indeed, Plutarch saw fit to draw attention to his method:

> For it is not histories that I am writing, but lives; and in the most illustrious deeds there is not always a manifestation of virtue and vice, nay a slight thing like a phrase or jest often makes a greater revelation of character than battles where thousands fall. (*Alexander*, 1.ll.1-2)

Plutarch's instinct would be formally realised by the division of late-antique biography into *praxēis* and *ethos*, a division within which the latter was accorded the higher value.[6]

Revived in the twentieth century, this minimalist search for *ethos* was recommended by Boris Tomasevskij, for example, through a redrawing of boundaries whereby the literary legend constructed by authors could be encompassed within the aesthetic realm. It also informs Barthes's neo-classical notion of the biographeme as encapsulation, the paradigmatic instant in an authorial life that somehow calls back to being the embarrassed essence of a life as lived.[7] Stasis and portraiture replace the monumental biographies of the post-Johnsonian era. But even here, in this most modest of accounts, the biographical does not lend itself to theoretical extrapolation. This legendary reduction can posit only a vanishing point, a moment that scarcely happens in time at all. From the predicated infinity of empirical biography, we move to an eerie crystallisation, an ephiphanic moment or revelatory feature that can only define a life in the manner of snapshot, a hostage, a lie against time.

It is a commonplace to remark that the pioneers of impersonality were writers themselves. In one of many hygienic strictures, Coleridge spoke of a necessary aloofness on the part of the poet, Keats of negative capability, and Byron of the ideal of an aestheticised selfhood. Baudelaire, Proust and T.S. Eliot all formulated versions of the *moi profond*, a transcendental self that speaks over and above the personal voice: the self insatiable for non-self ('*un moi insatiable de non-moi*'), as Baudelaire put it in a resonant paradox (one which Eliot would rewrite in 'Tradition and the Individual Talent'). Intriguingly, the repudiation of the prosaic, biographical self hearkened back to a romantic view of the author as a solitary, sage-like, Olympian figure – as far elevated above the cares of everyday life as the visionary Nietzsche who, on the heights of Sils Maria, declared himself to be '6,000 feet above man and time'. Like Caspar David Friedrich's cloaked Wanderer, or Byron's Manfred, this shamanic figure gathered status in proportion to its radical alienation from the empirical world.

T.S. Eliot's attempts to formalise this tendency took an overtly anti-romantic line which is nonetheless belied by the figures of suffering, sacrifice and alienation that consort with the impersonalist thesis. The true poet, in fact, suffers from insupportable emotion which he would escape (hopefully, through transmutation into art): 'Poetry is not a turning loose of emotion, but an escape from emotion; it is not the expression of personality, but an escape from personality. But, of course, only those who have personality and emotions know what it means to want to escape from these things.'[8] This *prima facie* paradox serves not to dislodge but to restore the romantic image of the imprisoned artist grounded in a mortal world of toil from which he would fly. Furthermore, personality and emotion are here the precondition for impersonality, the poetic 'self' only transcending the empirical with a backward glance at the personal. One need only look to tense (for example, 'only those who *have*') to recognise that impersonality is a wish not a realisation, an absence premised on a disturbing presence that the poet is compelled to affirm in the very moment of renunciation. We can see here something of the irony of the Joycean/Dedalean will-to-exile. Resolved to fly by those cultural nets, the young artificer has still to take flight, can only define *anomie* in terms of entrapment. In a silence that cannot but speak, the cunning of a weaver of nets, this Dedalean deracination depends upon the rooted, just as Eliotic impersonality is a stage in the homecoming of the poet's self. The flight from the self, as ever, leaves behind the distinctive signature it longs to disown. The atheist may indeed accord the highest praise to creation insofar as its perfect cast does not require a creator; not so, though with the onymous work which bears the signature, the date and place of its maker. What is exhausted in the act of writing is not personality but intent. A work's final form, whether completed or – as Valéry would have it – abandoned, testifies to that exhaustion. Draft-upon-draft, the writer acts as a privileged reader of his work: so many acts of intention and interpretation are recycled into the 'work' and its relinquishment.

This notion of finished form (*forma formata*) led Wimsatt and Beardsley to believe that where the privileges of the author end, those of the reading public begin. In surrendering the work from the private to the public sphere, the author abrogates any right to act as its most sapient reader. It is assumed that every last word the author has to say about the work disappears into the work, *becomes* the work and its final intention. The novel or poem is therefore the *summum bonum* of authorial intention; it is because of this plenitude rather than any poverty of intention that any subsequent statement by the author is deemed both *de trop* and a hindrance to the activity of criticism.

Written within the last days of genuine *belles lettres*, 'The Intentional Fallacy' suited and served writers well. The essay provided a critical foundation for the modernist writer's conviction that the work is composite, unretraceable, a free-standing entity which should speak only for and of itself. Gentlemanly in its formulation, this critical move nonetheless lent itself to antagonistic development. Following upon the decline of a culture of letters, the *caveat* against intention was always open to radicalisation through an ethos and rhetoric of assassination ('the death of the author'). Albeit unwittingly, Wimsatt and Beardsley had set the stage for the loneliness of the contemporary author and the retreat of the academy into a pseudo-professionalism that has become increasingly ungrateful, arcane and mystificatory.

Wimsatt and Beardsley allow that intention presides over the inception of a literary work but deny it any claim on the work's reception. To retrace the poem to authorial psychology or to evaluate it using intention as a yardstick is to misprize the object of study: 'The poem is not the critic's own and not the author's (it is detached from the author at birth and goes about the world beyond his power to intend about it or control it). The poem belongs to the public.'[9] The publication of a poem is thus an act of radical dispossession comparable to Barthes's notion of *écriture* or Derrida's of dissemination. Indeed Wimsatt and Beardsley close by putting the author somewhat in the position of the transcendental signified: 'Critical inquiries are not settled by consulting the Oracle.'[10] This seems at first glance to insist that no transcendental signified (author, intention) can close down interpretation. However, oracular statements are those upon which intention and biography cannot supervene. Of all sequences of words, those of the Oracle intend exactly what they mean, mean exactly what they intend. Lacking provenance, too, the Oracle cannot find its words retraced to an interpretative source: the testament of an Oracle is one which craves no contexts. Though directed ironically at certain romantic conceptions of authorship, the oracular metaphor actually harmonises with the arguments against biographical or intentionalist interpretation.

Their contention that words are 'detached from the author at birth', and go about the world free of authorial control or intention, affirms the very condition of writing that Plato denounced in *Phaedrus*. However, Wimsatt and Beardsley fail to take account of the threat posed by this dissemination to textual autonomy. Their essay assumes that the poem will move around as an unbroken, monadic and self-sufficient 'entity'. One wonders, then, how Wimsatt and Beardsley would respond to the problems posed by what Derrida calls 'iterability': that is, the propensity of words to wander away from their original context and to garner new and unforeseeable meanings in alien habitations. Do the Psalms travel as a unity? Or, indeed, Nietzsche's *Zarathustra* – snippets of which were infamously misappropriated by Nazi propagandists? Or the 'Proverbs' of Blake's *Marriage of Heaven and Hell*? Surely in such iterative cases there is an ethico-biographical imperative through which the work can be traced to fuller authorial contexts. This applies not only to iteration and fragmentation but also to the authorial *corpus*. Might we not have a duty to relate *Ecce Homo* not only to other works by Nietzsche but also to the circumstances of its composition, to its author's gravely declining mental health? I strongly suspect that Wimsatt and Beardsley would themselves encourage such recourse when appropriate, but their article leaves ethical considerations aside.

Evaluation is not at issue when we take into account Nietzsche's impending collapse: *Ecce Homo*'s status as a good, bad, or damnably curious species of autobiographical writing is not compromised when we ask whether or not its author was in a state of diminished moral responsibility at the time of writing. In a context of discovery such a move seems incumbent upon us just as a context of validation would forbid any such move. Deranged mathematics ceases to be mathematics; confessional writing, however *outré*, remains confessional writing. 'Evaluation' in the aesthetic realm does not provide an equivalent to 'verification' in the scientific realm and a species of category error arises when literary criticism seeks to model itself on disciplines which proceed from axiomatic foundations. The meaning of a literary text does not admit of proof or disproof as does a mathematical equation: the choice between incompatible literary readings can only be made on the basis of aesthetic or ethical criteria.

According to E. D. Hirsch: 'We can depend neither on metaphysics nor on neutral analysis in order to make decisions about the goals of interpretation.' The moment of decision is stark, made without consolation or support from either scientific or metaphysical precedents: 'We have to enter the realm of ethics. For, after rejecting ill-founded attempts to derive values and goals from the presumed nature of interpretation, or from the nature of [Heideggerian] Being, what really remains is ethical persuasion.'[11] Like Wimsatt and Beardsley, Hirsch finds his first inspiration in Kant's *Critique of Judgement*. Whereas the authors of 'The Intentional Fallacy' developed Kant's notion of aesthetic 'disinterestedness', Hirsch's ethic takes its bearings from the categorical imperative. He argues that neglect of authorial intention makes the author a means rather than an end: 'When we simply use an author's words for our own purposes without respecting his intention, we transgress ... 'the ethics of language', just as we transgress ethical norms when we use a person merely for our own ends.'[12]

Like Plato, Hirsch is worried about the propensity of words to meander away from biographical source and authorial intention. But whereas Plato's concern is pragmatically directed towards the ethical dangers of misreception, Hirsch's more austere ethic insists that a strenuously dutiful contract should be honoured between critic and author: '... an interpreter, like any other person, falls under the basic moral imperative of speech, which is to respect an author's intention'. Thus, Hirsch argues, 'original meaning is the "best meaning"'.[13] But how to discover 'original meaning'? The phrase itself is hesitantly poised between meaning recovered from intention and meaning recovered from biographical contexts. Just as 'The Intentional Fallacy'' might equally have been published as 'The Biographical Fallacy', so Hirsch's ethic of intention is as much an ethic of biography as of intention. How do we get to original meaning other than by way of biographical recourse? Hirsch would argue that 'biographical information is ethically valid insofar as it assists in divining an author's original meaning'. There is, however, a real danger of circularity here. Either we must know the author's original meaning in order to be certain that the biographical information we invoke pertains to that meaning, or we must construct original meaning from biography, according to the latter the priority ascribed to the former. Moreover, an ethical shift occurs when we move from intention to biography. If we respect an author's original meaning (given that we can both find and validate it), then we do indeed adhere to a literary version of the categorical imperative. However, if we search for that meaning amidst biographical detail, then we are in danger of treating an author as a means rather than an end. Psychobiographical criticism is doubtless the most florid instance of such an abuse, but all biographical investigation will to some degree run this risk. Using a life as lived in search of an author's original meaning is a vexed issue in ethical terms, as is any breach of privacy in the interest of public ends. Treatment of the authorial life as a means to a critical end (a construction or hypothesis of original meaning) remains ethically problematic, if not in quite the same way as the neglect of authorial intention.

Here, one might set against ethical intentionalism what Tobin Siebers, in *The Ethics of Criticism*, calls 'the ethics of autonomy'.[14] In a work that imputes positive intention to the authors of 'The Intentional Fallacy', Siebers argues that the so-called fallacy served a mission more protective that puritanical. The author could no longer be held to account for his work: the biographical and the intentional were inadmissible. Gregory the Great said that it was as futile to ask who was the author of Job as to ask with what pen a writer inscribed his work; likewise, the denial of intention accords the work an unretraceable, even transcendental status. Textual autonomy leads to personal autonomy, and the repudiation of authorial intention takes on an ethical as well as aesthetic dimension. Should it function as an effective guardrail against reprisal, the intentional fallacy would, by extension, vouchsafe the imaginative freedom of authors (even should that freedom remain open to ethical question both in its generality and in uses to which it is put).

If the biographical imperative cannot assert itself without calling its opposite into view, how might we decide? Nothing straight, as Kant said, was ever made out of the crooked timber of humanity and there cannot be a general theory of the ethics of biography. The ethical critic can only proceed text by text, author by author, circumstance by circumstance. But the need to inhabit this contradiction between the transcendental and the empirical engages us in every moment of decision. Not just as critics, but as human beings, we feel the obligation to transcend our personalities and prejudices whilst being compelled to acknowledge that this very need abides within, and arises from, a limited, personal and situated perspective. The relation between criticism and biography is not merely a methodological issue but reflects an unresolved dilemma within modernity. How, as the philosopher Thomas Nagel puts it, might we 'combine the perspective of a particular person inside the world with an objective view of that same world, the person and his viewpoint included'? As Nagel adds: 'It is a problem that faces every creature with the impulse and the capacity to transcend its particular point of view and to conceive of the world as a whole.'[15]

In a typically poised essay, 'The Sublimation of the Self', Paul de Man sets the empirical or personal self against a transcendental or ontological form of selfhood that speaks in the literary work. De Man's conclusion reveals what has all along been his starting point: 'Literary criticism, in our century, has contributed to establishing [the] crucial distinction between an empirical and an ontological self; in that respect, it participates in some of the most audacious and advanced forms of contemporary thought.'[16] But what is this 'ontological' self, one which de Man treats as synonymous with a transcendental self? De Man seems concerned to distance himself from a neo-Kantian vocabulary, but it is clear that this self is to be seen in epistemological rather than aesthetic terms, as closer to the 'I' of the *Critique of Pure Reason* or the phenomenological *cogito* than to literary notions of impersonality, the writerly mask or negative capability.

The close of de Man's essay covers over a perplexity which might have more candidly served as a point of departure. De Man has already declared that 'because it implies a forgetting of the personal self for a transcendental type of self that speaks in the work, the act of criticism can acquire exemplary value'.[17] Is this transcendental self a third self that arises from author and reader in the act of proper critical attention – the result of some intersubjective flash of illumination as described in the *Seventh Letter* commonly attributed to Plato? Or the mysterious process posited by Georges Poulet in which author and reader are conjoined in the textual 'I'? The essay avoids such questions. Of what self, de Man might have asked, can we speak when the personal, unique self has voided itself? What is this self which is neither an author, a person, nor a catena of historical and biographical circumstance?

One must question why literary theory elected, in the twentieth century, to replicate the Kantian gesture whereby the subject is reduced to a purely formal function. In treating a textual subject as analogous to an epistemological subject, theory implicitly denies the specificity of the literary experience as well as the specificity of individual literary works. Indeed, at this point, one might be tempted to restore the formulaic Lukácsian distinctions that de Man has already demoted: 'Contrary to the theoretical subject of logic, and contrary to the hypothetical subject of ethics, the stylized subject of aesthetics is a living unity that contains within itself the fullness of experience that makes up the totality of the human species.'[18]

Yet there *is* a sense in which the act of reading presupposes a self or subject of the work which can never coincide with the personal self of the author of that work, still less with a reified, living unity of the species. In reading Eliot's *The Waste Land*, the presupposition of a transcendental self – which has shored up poetic fragments against the ruin of the empirical self – assures the readability of a poem which moves through so many seemingly incompatible subject positions. But to treat this emanatory self as an ontological entity would seem an immodest move, a multiplication of entities beyond necessity, a flouting of the Occamite principle of parsimony. What J.L. Mackie says of objective values or Platonic Forms applies equally to the presupposition of a transcendental self: to wit, that such notions are notions *per se* and 'not part of the fabric of the world'.[19] The 'transcendental type of self' does not abide; it is an alien entity whose composition conforms to no other sublunary object of experience. The transcendental subject of literary theory thus presents itself as a fiction of a fiction, a ghost of the Kantian ego which Nietzsche sought to expose in all its insubstantiality. Toward that end, Nietzsche often adumbrated a biographical critique of philosophical objectivity according to his conviction that 'most of a philosopher's conscious thinking is secretly directed and compelled into definite channels by his instincts'.[20] However, it is difficult to imagine the extrapolation of this perspectivism without the most gross and egregious reductions. Using the biographical fact of Kant's piety in the context of a critique of the transcendental deduction may tell us a great deal about Kant's personal inclination toward austerity, but it would not impinge one jot upon the viability or intelligibility of the deduction itself. The retort 'he would say that, wouldn't he?' can offer us no guidance on the truth or falsity of what has been articulated. Criticism of such kind does not amount to a deconstruction of philosophy so much as a refusal to do philosophy at all.

Nevertheless, Nietzsche's recognition of the human-all-too-human wellspring of philosophical systems needs to be acknowledged at one and the same time as we accord to those systems the right to be judged in rational, impartial terms. As Thomas Nagel says: 'The personal flavor and motivation of each great philosopher's version of reality is unmistakable, and the same is true of many lesser efforts.'[21] Nagel wishes to maintain the realism of this 'view from somewhere' precisely because of its tension with the attempt to transcend personal concerns that he calls the 'view from nowhere'. As both Christianity and the categorical imperative teach, morality is founded upon the normative act whereby we attempt to stand outside our own interests and prejudices. Although the word 'biography' is not used in Nagel's *The View From Nowhere*, the thesis of a necessary conflict between the contingent self and its duty to transcend its contingent nature accurately captures the dilemma faced by literary theory as it negotiates between a crude but realistic recognition of the text's unavoidable connection with the 'grossly material' and the ideal of a transcendentally purified literary subject. As Nagel puts the matter for epistemology:

> What really happens in the pursuit of objectivity is that a certain element of oneself, the impersonal or objective self, which can escape from the specific contingencies of one's creaturely point of view, is allowed to predominate. Withdrawing into this element one detaches from the rest and develops an impersonal conception of the world and, so far as possible, of the elements of self from which one has detached. That creates the new problem of reintegration, the problem of how to incorporate these results into the life and self-knowledge of an ordinary human being. One has to *be* the creature whom one has subjected to detached examination, and one has in one's entirety to *live* in the world that has been revealed to an extremely distilled fraction of oneself.[22]

This process of incorporation is akin to the work of biographical reading which, at its best, consists in reintegrating the authorial 'view from nowhere' with the particularities of authorial experience. Only those who wish to see literature *sub specie aeternitatis*, or who would mire text and author in a Funes-like stream of unconceptualised becoming, will not feel this tension between the creatural origins and loyalties of the literary work and the understandable desire on the part of the literary author to transcend those origins. The biographical imperative is thus the reflex of the transcendental imperative: it seeks commerce between contrary but parallel depictions of authorship. In a formulation reminiscent of the Woolfian image of the 'web', Nagel writes:

> A succession of objective advances may take us to a new conception of reality that leaves the personal or merely human perspective further and further behind. But if what we want to understand is the whole world, we can't forget about those subjective starting points indefinitely; we and our personal perspectives belong to the world.[23]

Custodians of literature and tradition work between these competing claims in the hope that from this dialectic without synthesis, new energies and ideas will ensue. What Nagel says of epistemology and ethics, we might also say of literary studies:

> the correct course is not to assign victory to either standpoint but to hold the opposition clearly within one's mind without suppressing either element. Apart from the chance that this kind of tension will generate something new, it is best to be aware of the ways in which life and thought are split, if that is how things are.[24]

One need only substitute 'literature' for 'thought' here to arrive at the problems confronting any serious critic who treats a text neither as a historical record nor an *objet trouvé*.

It is tempting to keep faith with the notion of 'things as they are' to the exclusion of the transcendental position. The Kantian 'view from nowhere' cannot answer the issue of specificity. Yet, as critics of Kant must themselves acknowledge, the transcendental deduction could not have been achieved without the absolute refusal of all particulars, passions and humours. It would have been an undertaking both absurd and impossible to elaborate a system of thought in which there were as many theories of perception as perceivers. A theory of the subject can only base itself on the form rather than the content of experience:

> Unity of synthesis according to empirical concepts would be altogether accidental, if these latter were not based on a transcendental ground of unity. Otherwise it would be possible for appearances to crowd

in upon the soul, and yet to be such as would never allow of experience ... The appearances might, indeed, constitute intuition without
thought but not knowledge; and would consequently would be for
us as good as nothing.[25]

The problem posed by the biographical imperative, however, is to allow
that appearances 'crowd in upon the soul' even as the soul searches for
transcendental clarity. A fully empirical subject, Kant says, 'would be for us
as good as nothing', and, as he adds a little later, 'less even than a dream'.[26]
Human beings are, indeed, in Marjorie Greene's memorable phrase, 'the
upsurge of time'. Activity of mind, she says, 'is not a bare event, but a
doing, and it must be done by *someone*. [And] some one is always some one
in particular, born somewhere at some time of some parents, possessing
some innate aptitudes, moulded somehow by the setting of his family,
society, time.'[27]

The biographical imperative enjoins us to remain within this contradiction, to dwell in 'uncertainties, mysteries, doubts'. To be negatively
capable in this fashion will not lead to any immediate result but ensures
that criticism remains realistically suspended between the poles of the
transcendental and the empirical, just as Byron in his *Manfred* recognised
that humankind lived within tragic division: 'Half dust, half deity, alike
unfit / To sink or soar ...'. Rather than forgetting the personal self for
an ontological literary self, or refusing the latter in favour of a multitu-
dinous, ungovernable specificity, the critical impulse should say 'yes' and
'no' simultaneously to both alternatives when confronted by that moment
Kierkegaard called 'the madness of decision'. It should do so with embattled
patience and in the hope, as Nagel says, that something new will emerge.

Appendix 2: The Author as Reader

In the study of literature, the question of the self appears in a bewildering network of often contradictory relationships among a plurality of subjects ... From the start, we have at least four possible and distinct types of self: the self that judges, the self that reads, the self that writes, and the self that reads itself. The question of finding the common level on which all these selves meet and thus of establishing the unity of a literary consciousness stands at the beginning of the main methodological difficulties that plague literary studies.

Paul de Man[1]

Authorship is as much an activity of reading as writing. This is particularly apparent in autobiographical literature. The author becomes a privileged reader of his or her erstwhile self: 'the self that reads itself'. The authorial self divides into subject and object of study; the former attempts to gather up the fragments of a past self into a coherent, even teleological narrative. Writing at a temporal and epistemological remove from the experiences recounted, the author becomes the interpreter of those experiences. In any conventional autobiographical *récit*, the author splits into a detached subject who reads a past self from a vantage of superior knowledge and the past self who lives through experiences without realising what place they will occupy in narrative reconstruction. This split can be rendered in formalist terms as the difference between an extradiegetic and intradiegetic subject or, epistemologically, as the gap between a subject of knowledge and of experience. Along either register, the author becomes a reader through recognising that the self read is no longer his or her self. Any author of autobiographical works must assume a degree of detachment from the self and its trials, but in modernist theory, impersonality became theoretically entwined with a literature which turned toward the self as object of aesthetic exploration while rejecting traditional autobiography as an inartistic genre. Through impersonality, the untidy genre of autobiography was distilled into the purer mode of the autobiographical just as *Stephen Hero* was remodelled into the artistically cleaner *A Portrait of the Artist as a Young Man*. Of course, rare indeed is the literature that is without biographical residue, and it is always possible – if not always desirable – to discern traces of the authorial psyche in literature whose *histoire* is remote from the 'personal' self (for example, in the retellings of myths). But a Balzac or Dickens will less feel the need of an impersonalist theory of literature. The self and its idiomatic concerns will doubtless be present in *La Comédie humaine* or *Little Dorrit*, but their mode of writing does not incorporate the problematic of self-representation at the level of practice, aim, ideal or genre. When, however, the Augustinian themes of selfhood, memory, time and language become the foregrounded material of art, literature will be conscious of the need to defend against an excess of personality or subjectivity.[2]

Obviously our concern is not with reading modernist texts autobiographically in the sense of reducing a great text (the work itself) to an inferior text (the life, including 'the bundle of accident and incoherence that sits down to breakfast').[3] It is rather with the assumptions about the self, the narratological, poetic and epistemological burdens that the autobiographical impulse places on authors as they attempt to transmute personal experience into literary knowledge. Various gestures were made by modernist writers to negotiate the problem of self-division in the act of writing: the positing of epiphanic or extratemporal experiences in which subject and object are grasped as a totality; Eliot's notion of the 'still point' of understanding; Proust's involuntary memory in which the past self is apprehended as pure presence; Woolf's 'moments of Being'. Recourse was also made to late-romantic *savants* such as Bergson, Bradley and the Nietzsche of *The Birth of Tragedy*, all of whom posited primordial realms in which subject and object, past and present, the fire and rose were conjoined in a pre-rational unity. Yet this drive in modernism was countered by the doctrine of impersonality which implicitly acknowledged that there is no Edenic or Dionysian realm in which the self could recover its lost unity, no epiphanic or extratemporal experience in which the writing self would be one with the recollected self. Between the desire for such an experience and the recognition that the artist must be aloof from *any* experience – refined out of his textual world, consciously shaping the *prima materia* of his art – emerged the specific epistemological tensions of modernist writing.

Literary modernists realised that so far from closing the breach in Being made by self-consciousness, the act of writing further separated the recollecting and experiencing selves. Authors such as Proust, Eliot and Woolf strove toward self-presence whilst fully recognising the impossibility of that ideal. In this *agon*, modernist failure to close the gap between the self writing and the self written about showed itself more subtle, complex and aesthetically rewarding than postmodernist or poststructuralist consecrations of the impossibility of uniting literary selfhood. The work of Samuel Beckett can be situated at the crossroads of these two movements. In *The Unnamable*, Beckett abandons the quest of uniting past and present selves by absorbing the discourse of the self into the present act of enunciation. By moving beyond the impasse of temporal disjunction and finding division in the self even in the 'here-and-now' of narration, *The Unnamable* marks a crucial point in the shift from a rhetoric of consciousness and temporality to one of language, of a metalingual epistemology. In a text that is both repository and seminal, we find both the culmination and *reductio ad absurdum* of modernist discourse on the self and the opening of that belated literature we call the postmodern.

KNOWLEDGE AND EXPERIENCE IN AUTOBIOGRAPHICAL ACTS

> I cannot say what portion is in truth
> The naked recollection of that time,
> And what may rather have been call'd to life
> By after-meditation.
> > William Wordsworth[4]

To understand experience is to be an experiential and temporal remove from that experience. Understanding takes place but what is understood is no longer experience. Indeed, *the only experience we understand is the experience of understanding*. The only unity of the two concepts is to be found when understanding forms the sole content of the experience. Where there is understanding there is not experience; where there is experience there is not understanding. This is the movement of the Cartesian *cogito* wherein understanding is only achieved by the most radical impersonalisation and disembodiment. In the curious species of autobiographical prose that is Descartes's *Mediations*, the narrator's past, memory, his body, sensory evidence and experience are hyperbolically reduced to the present act of attention. The narrative 'I' enters into its own death rather like the Barthesian author who disappears into the act of writing. The *cogito* is true only in the instant, the moment, event of epiphany or intuition. It is performative, instantaneous, fleeting, a virtual point when understanding or intuition guarantees the self – a moment of no greater duration nor less significance than the Platonic flash of illumination in which master and ephebe, author and reader are united not in understanding experience, but rather in experiencing understanding.[5]

Although autobiography itself treats of the self over vast tracts of experienced time, it too arrives only at a fractional instant in which the written 'I' and recollected 'I' coalesce. The pre-conversion self of Augustine is providentially tracked to the converted Augustine who ends his book at the end of time, in the standing present of eternity. Rousseau closes the account of his life in the context of reading that life to a 'private' gathering. Cyclically, Proust's Marcel narrates his life up to the point at which the narration of his life becomes possible, thus turning closure into opening. Yet these are narrative strategies rather than genuine acts of unification. They are similarly fleeting, like the fractional intuition of the *cogito*.

Autobiographical acts remain haunted by Hume's notion that the self is a consecution of sensations as too by the Heraclitean dictum 'you shall not go down twice to the same river': the thing experienced (the river) and the thing experiencing (the self or subject) are both discontinuous.[6] Where the cogito achieves self-presence through the negation of the past self, autobiographical and lyrical works enact the wound in being (overscored by Hegel in his recognition that the distinctively human property of self-consciousness opens a tragic gap between knowledge and experience) in making man both the subject and object of study. Autobiography thus 'veils a de-facement of the mind of which it is itself the cause'.[7] To narrate the self issues in cognitive disfigurement between a 'knowing' subject and a subject it can only 'know' as an abstraction. Conversely, to experience the self one must cease from narrating the self. Beckett's Unnamable protagonist declares, 'to stop speaking, I should have spoken of me and me alone'.[8] Self-representation thus brings the cognitive and experiential orders to a pitch of mutual exclusivity. In their refusal to neglect the experiential in the interest of the cognitive, and vice versa, modernist writers sought the discourse of the self in an impersonality which cast the author as a scrupulous and detached reader of a past subject, a 'reticent autobiographer'.[9] However, so far from resolving the epistemological problems raised by autobiography, impersonality only served to widen the epistemological lacuna between knowledge and experience to a breadth of artistic crisis. Eliot's distinction between 'the man who suffers' and 'the mind which creates' is rightly read as a call for the author to cleanse or refine his work of the overly personal concerns of the self.[10] However, it can also be read as a recognition of the impossibility of ever capturing the 'unity in division' that is posited as the self. This impossibility becomes clear when we register the disjunction between the suffering (experiencing) self and the creative self in temporal and epistemological rather than aesthetic terms. In a lyrical passage nearly contemporaneous with 'Tradition and the Individual Talent', the poet-speaker reminisces:

> ... when we came back, late, from the hyacinth garden,
> Your arms full, and your hair wet, I could not
> Speak, and my eyes failed, I was neither
> Living nor dead, and I knew nothing,
> Looking into the heart of light, the silence.[11]

The epistemological problem is apparent. The poet-speaker is concerned to revisit a moment of immediate experience. Immediate experience does not belong to the cognitive order ('I knew nothing'). But now, from a cognitive distance, the poet knows at least that he knew nothing. He is no longer part of the experience. When he experienced this moment, he was neither living nor dead, neither self nor non-self, there was no difference between subject and object. But later, in trying to capture that moment, in trying to understand that experience, he perforce splits himself into the subject of that experience and the object of that experience. As poet, he understands something but what he understands is not experience. Primarily, he understands the impossibility of understanding experience in the Kierkergaardian sense that whilst life can only be understood backwards, it must be lived forwards. The self strives to narrate, to gather up experience and the self into a meaningful order; yet that order is achieved by an author now alien to the recollected subject.

A parallel interpretation, with different inflections, would declare that the passage attempts to communicate the incommunicable. The pure, Bergsonian experience is inaccessible to conscious thought, yet without the interventions of retrospective consciousnesses and language, the experience would forever remain in 'the heart of light, the silence'. This reading, too, would put stress on both the validity of the mystical experience and the poet's detachment from that experience in his search for a metalanguage adequate to a potential meaning produced between the poles of (formerly) self-present experience and its re-presentation in the antithetical present of its poetic articulation. In a replaying of the antique distinction between form and energy, criticism would seek for a dialectical synthesis of mastered energy, experience artistically shaped.

Yet there is no such synthesis. The passage is lyrical, affective, readable only on both sides of the antinomy it engenders. From his work on Bradley, Eliot learned that feeling cannot transmute into thought, that experience or 'finite centres' cannot be absorbed into knowledge since knowledge breaks up unity of feeling. As Bradley writes: 'there is nothing beyond what is presented, what is and is felt, or rather is felt simply. There is no memory or imagination or hope or fear or thought or will, and no perception of difference or likeness. There are, in short, no relations and no feelings, only feeling.'[12]

The aesthetic strives toward a higher intuition, an uplifting or synthesis which Bradley calls the Absolute: an impersonal realm to which thought, having broken up primary feeling, seeks to return. Impersonality becomes detachment from experience, an attempt to find a cognitive-poetical order in which relations can be perceived. Yet without this leap of idealist faith in the Absolute – one which Eliot was not prepared to make – the poet is condemned to write in full consciousness of the incommensurability of thought and feeling, knowledge and experience.[13]

IMPERSONALITY AS THE QUEST OF THE SELF

T. S. Eliot's precocious conversion from the 'meretricious captivation' of Bergson to the 'melancholy grace' of Bradley seemed to ensure that at least one school of modernist thought would not succumb to the oceanic resolution of self-division offered by the concept of *la durée*. However, in positing an Edenic realm of pure feeling inaccessible to thought, Bradley's philosophy has affinities with both the Bergsonian *durée* and Nietzsche's Dionysian ecstasy in which personal consciousness dissolves into a primordial union of subject and object which is inaccessible to rational/Socratic thought. In his poetry, Eliot continues to yearn for an undifferentiated order of being even as he sharpens his sceptical awareness that the written self will never be present to the self writing. 'You are not the same people who left that station/Or who will arrive at any terminus,' the Eliot of the 'Dry Salvages' can write in anticipation of the 'still point' of a logos which looks for all the world like a baptised Bergsonianism.[14]

Commendably, criticism has during the last two decades moved away from the irrationalist influence by giving due emphasis to the values of cognitive detachment and scientific rationality in the writings of Proust, Woolf and, by extension, the modernist 'movement' itself. Such revision should allow, however, for the temperate readmission of the historically demonstrable Bergsonian influence in a paradigm which acknowledges the dynamic interplay between detachment and immersion in modernist construals of literary selfhood. Opening Quentin's narrative in *The Sound and the Fury*, Faulkner plainly restates Bergsonianism: 'Father said clocks slay time. He said time is dead as long as it is being ticked off by little wheels; only when the clock stops does time come to life.'[15] However, it is no more reasonable to assume that the text thereby stops still at a Bergsonian reading than to claim that Woolf's foregrounding of the issue of '[s]ubject and object and the nature of reality', her repeated references to impersonality in art in *To the Lighthouse*, or her normative ideal of a world viewed without a self preclude the Bergsonian influence.[16] One should instead see patterns of oscillation, of strong misreading, influence and critique. When, in solitude, Mrs Ramsay recognises herself as 'a wedge-shaped core of darkness', it would be reasonable to suppose the influence of Bergson's theory of a core self.[17] With the hard-won leisure 'not even to think', Mrs Ramsay becomes the thing she looks at: '[her] self having shed its attachments was free for the strangest adventures'.[18] She experiences the self beyond relationality – the Bergsonian core self – and yet what arises from the lake of her being is a mist, a deliquescence. This self whose 'horizon seemed to her limitless' is a self without boundaries.[19] Woolf's text poses the question 'what sort of self has no boundaries?' The episode points up a contradiction that the time-philosophy generates and never quite resolves. Bergson claims that in duration we find the core self, the real self – yet that self is only found when its boundaries are broken down, when it merges with the past, when one loses personality. There is no sense that one gains personality when losing it; the core self begins to look like the dispersal of the self. This is the kind of objection that Eliot and Wyndham Lewis made to the time-philosophy.[20] The gain of the real self is the goal and justification of the time-philosophy and yet the self that it gains is dissolved, unrecognisable, starting here and ending nowhere.

Similarly, despite Proust's disingenuous attempt to disclaim the Bergsonian influence altogether, *A la Recherche du Temps Perdu*'s most celebrated reflections on time, memory and selfhood learn from and implicitly critique the time-philosophy.[21] Marcel initially presents the madeleine experience as pure Bergsonianism: 'all the efforts of our intellect must prove futile'.[22] As Kristeva points out in her psychoanalytic reading, the madeleine episode begins in primary orality with the sensation of taste.[23] This itself suggests that involuntary memory belongs to a pre-rational order of experience: 'An exquisite pleasure had invaded my senses, something isolated, detached, with no suggestion of its origin … It is plain that the truth I am seeking lies not in the cup but in myself' (1:48). Truth is to be sought in a core self, one immune to the fragmentations of mechanical or spatialised time. In the succeeding discussion of method, Marcel says: 'I decide to attempt to make it reappear … And so that nothing may interrupt it in its course I shut out every obstacle, every extraneous idea, I stop my ears and inhibit all attention against the sounds from the next room' (1:49). From a Bergsonian premise, the text proceeds to enact a form of mini-Cartesianism as Marcel brackets off all extraneity in the attempt to apprehend a pure sense of the self. Like the Descartes of the *Meditations*, the narrator resolves 'to clear an empty space' (1:49) in front of the mind, an experiential hollow in which rather than discover itself as if for the very first time as auto-cognitive self-presence, the past self can resurrect itself as existential plenitude.

The self he seeks is not the self in the present (the temporality is Bergsonian rather than Cartesian) and it might be argued that, on a thematic
level, Proust here traces the movement from Cartesian reflection to a
pre-reflective imaginary. However, the text itself does not *perform* any such
movement. Rather, the madeleine episode is cognitively structured. It takes
the form of a *discursus* rather than a surrender to the imaginary, to the realm
of undifferentiated experience. The 'episode' is organised and patterned in
a logical fashion. Metaphors are subordinated to the logic of the demonstration. The crowning simile of the Japanese water bowls – in which are
steeped 'little pieces of paper which until then are without character or
form, but, the moment they become wet … take on colour and distinctive shape, become flowers or houses or people, solid and recognisable'
(1:51) – seems to express immersion in experience, a metaphoric expansion. But, as Kristeva notes, it effects a displacement.[24] At the point of
maximal presence, the episode must be troped by way of a metonymised
Japan which is antipodean to the experience of 'involuntary memory'.
The taste of the *pétit madeleine* is 'experienced' by Marcel as character; it
is organised at the level of *récit* by the retrospective narrator and patterned
in terms of figuration by the authorial intelligence. At both the narratological and thematic levels it serves to reopen and complicate the problem
of the divided self even as it would manifestly present itself as a resolution
or union of the subjects of knowledge and experience, recollection and
feeling. The effect of presence is fleeting, evanescent; expanded beyond the
moment of Cartesian certitude but nonetheless ephemeral. Memory hints
at a unified self but needs supplementation. In *Les Temps Retrouvé*, Marcel
realises that he has neglected the role of art in the process of unifying the
self. However, if art does unify the self in this way, then one must presume
that the artist gets closer to the experiences of the past self of Marcel than
can Marcel as narrator. The assumption of a meta-narratorial subject – an
ever-present, never-visible author – is required by the epiphany. So much
is made clear toward the close of *Les Temps Retrouvé*: 'the being within me
which had enjoyed these impressions had enjoyed them because they had
in them something that was common to a day long past and to the present,
because in some way they were extra-temporal' (3:904).

If Marcel and Proust have become indistinguishable at this point, then
the unity of the self is indeed realised *a posteriori* in the *Recherche*.[25] However,
an *a posteriori* unification is no unification at all in terms of the temporal
disjunction we have been discussing. No less than three 'selves' inhabit
the 'I' of this inexhaustible novel: the young Marcel; Marcel as narrator;
Proust as author. This third self is not immediately readable; it is a secretive

voice which whispers that the project of the *Recherche* is doomed, that the
truth of life is death.[26] This voice knows that knowledge and experience
will not be united; that past and present selves, written and writing selves
are doomed to disunion. It is the voice of a latter-day romantic irony, one
similar to the voice that transcends the speaker of Keats's 'Ode on a Grecian
Urn' to confirm that truth and beauty can never be reconciled even as the
words on the page appear to tell us that the great imaginative synthesis is
not only possible but vouchsafed. In such spirit, Paul de Man writes:

> Marcel is never as far away from Proust as when the latter has him say:
> 'Happy are those who have encountered truth before death and for
> whom, however close it may be, the hour of truth has rung before the
> hour of death.' As a writer, Proust is the one who knows that the hour
> of truth, like the hour of death, never arrives on time, since what we
> call time is precisely truth's inability to coincide with itself.[27]

What de Man calls 'truth' could equally be rendered as 'the self'. Proust's
great project tells us altogether less obliquely that time is the *self*'s inability
to coincide with itself. Hence, did the *Recherche* not embrace impersonality, it would have impersonality thrust upon it: its ethos is one of cognitive distance, of perception and analysis. The 'self' is not lost through
the Dionysian or thaumaturgical; if it is lost, it is not to oceanic absorp-
tion but to rational scepticism. Genette writes that the *Recherche* is 'a story
and analysis of the perceptive activity of the observing character, of his
impressions, gradual discoveries, change of distance and perspective, errors
and connections, excitement and disappointment'.[28] Behind the figure of
Marcel, a third self rouses, the author as reader of the narrator, his 'analysis'
demarcating an activity between authoring and reading – the perspective of
an author interpreting *a* self which has ceased to be *the* self.

In Proust's work, as in any species of autobiographical literature, an impersonalising split in the self is the first condition of articulating the self. Of
Rousseau, Derrida writes: '[he] neither wishes to think nor can think that
[the] alternation [presence/absence] does not simply happen to the self, that
it is the self's very origin'.[29] Modernist writers wrote in full cognisance of
this necessary division and of its artistically generative rather than destruc-
tive potential. Foreshadowed in Keats's negative capability, Wordsworth's
pre-theoretical recognition that two consciousnesses inhabited *The Prelude,*
in Coleridgean impersonality, this aesthetic-poetic dilemma of romanticism was revisited by modernist writers as a challenge set by epistemology
to the aesthetic imagination. In order that the self overcome its alienation
not only from the world but its own history, it became the mission of a

philosophically-attuned literature to achieve the epiphany wherein knowledge and experience are no longer separated, where life is no longer lived forward but, for an instant of aesthetic apprehension, is understood as it is lived, lived as it is understood. If rationalist philosophy worked toward an experientially empty knowledge, then it fell to literature to reconcile the demands of experience and knowledge. However, if the hour of truth is the hour when knowledge and experience are indistinguishable, then the hour of truth is indeed – as de Man says – the hour of death. The reflective artist was posed with a choice between repeating the mystical conceit of ineffability, whereby the unity between knowledge and experience cannot pass into articulation and accepting that the gap between knowledge and experience is the precondition of science as well as philosophy, of literature as well as communication in general.

The acceptance of this unbridgeable gap and of the henceforth double demand of impersonality explains Eliot's paradox or seeming confusion toward the close of 'Tradition and the Individual Talent'.[30] The necessity of impersonality is generated in direct proportion to the imperative to express personality. Personality calls to impersonalisation, and vice versa. Immersion in raw experience could not communicate itself; pure cognition would have nothing to communicate beyond itself. The self is not a communicable given until approached as an object external to itself, until an author cultivates towards his or her personality the detachment of a reader, a covert and careful interpreter of experience. *Cognitive* distance is essential if recounted experience is to take a re-*cognisable* form. Hence impersonality and ironic distance act as ushers by which the self comes forth as process and project into the public world, the public work. Impersonality does not subvert so much as serve the personal, the self-revelatory, the autobiographical. So far from being a flight from the self, impersonality allows for the expression of a self that is always in flight. It permits the story of the self to be told on condition that the self becomes other to the author. In this auto-detachment, the poetics of impersonality confirm a coeval commitment to a cognitive as well as an experiential realm. Literature becomes a unique way of knowing, a necessary and even corrective supplement of philosophical accounts of subjectivity.

'THE LONG SONATA OF THE DEAD'

> I ought to give a different name to each of the selves who subsequently
> thought about Albertine; I ought still more to give a different name to each
> of the Albertines who appeared before me, never the same, like those seas –
> called by me simply and for the sake of convenience 'the sea' – that succeeded
> one another and against which, a nymph likewise, she was silhouetted.
>
> Marcel Proust[31]

> All these Murphys, Molloys and Malones do not fool me. They have made me
> waste my time, suffer for nothing, speak of them ...
>
> Samuel Beckett[32]

Like Proust, Beckett knew that any autobiographical act will gather not a sole
self but a rendezvous of persons. But, whereas Proust strove toward unity
and closure in terms of 'how one becomes what one is', the Beckett of *The
Unnamable* recognised that writing can do no more than foist the fleeting
illusion of being upon the river of becoming. No more a source of deep, if
sceptical investigation, the 'self' becomes the arbitrary site of enunciation
which unremittingly reflects upon its own lack of foundation. The 'He' of *The
Unnamable* speaks not of time but of fragmented alienation through language:
'I'm in words, made of words, others' words ... I'm all these words, all these
strangers, this dust of words, with no ground for their settling' (390).

   The Beckett of this text is not the one who formerly declared: 'We
are not merely more weary because of yesterday, we are other, no longer
what we were before the calamity of yesterday.'[33] The Beckett of *Proust*
is speaking from a Heraclitean/Humean scepticism in which the notion
of continuous selfhood is made unsustainable by temporal rather than
linguistic dislocation, one to which he would return in *Krapp's Last Tape*.
A dark postscript to the modernist quest of a unified subjectivity, *Krapp's
Last Tape* parodies the idea that a past self can be resurrected in the present.
Technology supplants primary orality; in place of the *pétit madeleine*, a
tape recorder opens the possibility of a channel between a past self and
a present self.[34] The close of the play brings together these two subjects
even as it separates them through the most cruelly ironic distance. So far
from drawing the nominal selves into cohesion, the technological bridge
across time has served to fragment the self irretrievably: the past self is
scarcely recognisable to the present self; the two beyond any possibility
of commerce. The artistic self-affirmation made by the younger Krapp in
the act of recording leads to the most desiccated alienation in the dramatic
present by the 'return' of a self now strange.

   Like all parody, *Krapp's Last Tape* must provisionally re-inhabit the
conceptual universe it parodies. The division within the self takes place

against a backdrop of expectation that the name 'Krapp' might signify a core self which persists in spite of physical, mental and circumstantial vicissitude. In the universe of *The Unnamable*, Krapp's bewilderment would be incomprehensible. Any notion of self-division over time itself is fundamentally nostalgic in postulating the ideal of a unity that could be divided in the first place. Although remorselessly determined to inhabit temporal disjunction, *Krapp's Last Tape* still works within the lyrical thematic of a past self lost to the present which led Eliot to accept that self-presence is only achievable in a redemptive death or which prompted Proust's observations that he might have more accurately assigned different names to 'the phalanstery of selves' that gather under the 'I' of the *Recherche*.[35] 'Only that name remain', said an exiled Coriolanus, and – in simultaneously invoking and refusing the offices of a proper name – the very title of *The Unnamable* repudiates even the illusion of continuity conjured by a proper name. We need names for things to create the illusion of permanence, says Heraclitus, and it is the very property of the name that allows us to say that the Krapp of one time is not that of another, that the Marcel who obsesses over Albertine is not the Marcel who recounts that obsession. No such negotiations are incumbent upon *The Unnamable* whose scepticism is that of a negative Cartesianism. As with the *Meditations*, it is an all-inclusive first-person, this unnamable 'I/Not I' of everyone and no one, inhabitable by any thoughtful, competent reader for the time of the reading. The 'I' of *The Unnamable*, however, is not that of the achieved *cogito* but an 'I' marooned in the phase of pre-emptive Cartesian doubt.

If the discourse of the *cogito* is the autobiographical abnegation of a philosopher seeking certainty, *The Unnamable* is the paradoxical autobiography of a writer who can neither own nor disown the self. The unnamable discourse unfolds in the present tense of the enunciation. The temporal split between subjects does not intrude upon the articulation at a thematic or grammatical level. Even so, the self cannot speak of itself. Forever asking 'who speaks?', the text retorts with a feverish 'Not I' that is not a simple negation of the 'I' but its lengthening shadow, its mantric disease. Having announced early on that he should speak of himself (305), the narrator of *The Unnamable* questions this experiment which is also an expedient and an economy: 'But enough of this cursed first person, it is really too red a herring. I'll get out of my depth if I'm not careful. But what then is the subject? Mahood? No, not yet. Worm? Even less' (345). Abandoning both belief in the creation of fictional characters (or 'vice-existents') and the ability of the self to express itself, Beckett's text marks one transition from the modern to the postmodern in its rejection of '[s]tupid obsession with depth' (295). The syntagmatic everywhere excludes metaphor and symbol: aporetics, antitheses, ephetics, negations which are in turn negated, motivate the discourse. The pursuit of 'depth' through third-person characterisation or the unification of the narrating 'I' with the experiences of a past self gives way to a *fort/da* which can cease only *in articulo mortis* and that final wordless exoneration from its 'sin against the silence'.[36] In *The Unnamable*, such a performance is the self-writing of the instant at which subject separates from sign: the very mark of the 'I' or 'Je' fractionally prior to its attendant negation. In this forestalling, *The Unnamable* points to the end of any autobiographical act, to what Simon Critchley calls the 'unrepresentability of death'.[37] When the narrator of *Malone Dies* declares that 'my notes have a curious tendency ... to annihilate all they purport to record' (261) the only thing that is 'spared' annihilation in that instant is the enunciating subject.

The Unnamable seems like an exhaustion or end of literature not because of its thanatographical impulses – the least self-conscious and literary of autobiographies invoke death at their close purely in so far as they look to the future and thereby to finitude – but because it refuses literary temporality along with characterisation.[38] It denies itself the consolation of closure because the representation of death would involve the restoration of the diegetic temporality which it has subjected to unremitting scepticism. The writer of autobiography or a philosophical work denies him or herself the possibility of recounting his or her death. Death as closure can only be recounted through an extradiegetic narrator or a fictionalised first-person intradiegetic narrator. The death of the writing subject could have as its instantaneous record no more than a random mark (a dash, a secretion, a stain) made upon a scroll, sheet of paper or screen at the moment of expiry.

The pretheoretical impulse that would read the 'death' or 'exhaustion of literature' into *The Unnamable* found its counterpart in the relatively hospitable prima facie case that Beckett was here working through or toward the death or disappearance of the author into language. For Barthes, the 'modern scriptor' who succeeds the author is 'born simultaneously with the text'. While the voice that speaks in the unnamable has a few hazy, disjointed recollections (of fabricating other 'characters' and thereby hinting that his is the authorial consciousness that brought the first two novels of the *Trilogy* into existence), he is 'in no way equipped with a being preceding or exceeding the writing'. In the unnamable discourse, as with the text of the modern scriptor, there is effectively 'no other time than that of the enunciation' and one feels, at least, that the text is 'written eternally *here and now* ' (one may approach the novel as a circle, that is, one may enter it at any point without experiencing significant disorientation). Certainly, too, the impression created by the unnamable discourse is that it is composed 'by a hand cut off from any voice, by a pure gesture of inscription (and not of "expression")' and that it 'traces a field without origin – or which has no origin other than language itself'.[39] Indeed such is the 'fit' between text and theory, and the influence of Beckett upon the postwar Parisian conception of an avant-garde *écriture*, that it is reasonable to suppose the influence of *L'Innommable* on Barthes's description of the 'modern scriptor'. However, if Barthes reads the *Unnamable* as the epitome of an authorless writing, it is with a far more unsettling force that *The Unnamable* reads through to the fault line in Barthes's conception of authorship.

In an act of sheer writerly honesty or infinite literary exhaustion (which are perhaps indistinguishable), Beckett literally gives up on all pretence at literary artifice or mediation. One consequence of this privation is to minimise the distance between the writer and his writing: one cannot radically dissociate Beckett and the Unnamable as one does the 'voice' that speaks in *The Adventures of Huckleberry Finn* and the language and perspective of its author. 'I can't go, I'll go on': the tragic affirmation of old re-echoes in this elementary paradox, as does the structural inevitability that the text will go in the absence of its author. Relieved of any obligation to represent, to acknowledge a past or future of writing, devoid of anything to express, the text comes as close as any literary work to 'pure expressivity'. The eternal now of an intransitive writing may be that of the modern scriptor, but it is also the unmediated, pure and purely autobiographical opening of the (ad) venture of the authorial trace. Barthes's notion of pure enunciation does not allow room for a narrator (which would here only be the contrivance of a supposedly bygone 'realism'). Indeed, the unfurling of the text in the 'eternally here and now' only permits the unmediated authorial discourse of a micro-autobiographical or subjectively performative writing. Everything lost to the narrator, as to a life, is the name's inheritance. The *sum res cogitans* becomes 'something is writing and this is necessarily true every time something gets written'.

The structure 'I/Not I' does not divide the name that signs to its play. What distinguishes the narrator from the author of *The Unnamable* is that the latter could and did bear a name and that he could and did bestow upon the novel what he withheld from the narrative. In this regard, the fact that he chose to bestow the same name upon heterogeneous works spanning half a century is anything but contingent. The considerable scepticism maintained toward the *corpora* did not extend to the corpus, or from self to the authorial signature. The 'Not I' could be the voice that distances author from narrator. The 'Not I' cannot, in any case, repel the 'I' anymore than the latter can sustain itself through appeal to the law of non-contradiction. True, this signature does not sign to an identity but it does sign across the invisible line between the 'I' and the 'Not I'. One cannot say that this name is simply appended, that it does not both prepare the space of reading and remain as its repository. The 'I' that 'can't go on' is the subject of experience, the corporeal figure of a Samuel Beckett, a Jacques Derrida or a Roland Barthes. The 'I' that will 'go on' names the authorial repository which inherits from the deeds, the words and works of the experiencing subject.

Indeed, once the name of an author is properly construed as mark of an originary absence, it only remains to ask by what reckoning the living words of logocentrism are to be distinguished from deathless acts of deconstructive writing. This disappearance of the subject of experience – relieved of antecedent commitments to represent, read or render a past 'self', the outer circumstance or inner nature of a 'subject' which can no more know than escape 'itself' – opens the space of unmediated inscription: the trace it leaves is not of 'images', 'scenes', external 'events' but of the untrammelled act of authorship itself. There is, quite brutally, nothing else left, no possibility of closure beyond the cessation of biological, biographical time. An authorial decision of an inexpressibly simple and drastic nature is made: at an incalculable remove from the close to which the remorseless logic of his *récit* has committed the writing, the author ceases, he literally can't go on. In breaking off, or in artfully constructing the endless, unpunctuated gap that succeeds the affirmation 'I'll go on', Beckett manufactures the silence onto which the inconceivable speech act of a Monsieur Valdemar would open. '[B]etween the metonymic eloquence of the "I am dead", and the instant when death ushers in absolute silence, allowing nothing more to be said', the purely autobiographical reveals itself as an impossible writing-towards-death which the authorial name alone survives.[40] What remains of the 'author as reader', as of the textual traces left behind by a proper name, can only be the author that remains to be read.

Notes

PREFACE: THE 'LIFE DEATH' OF THE AUTHOR

1. Hence Barthes's autobiographical experiments, his joy in the the idea of the body being read through the corpus, make his oeuvre hospitable to such reading in principle as well as practice (cf. the section entitled 'Autobiographies' in Chapter 1 below). Contrariwise, though Foucault wrote as insightfully on the body as any other theorist, the greatest impertinence would lie in seeking to superimpose connections between *The History of Sexuality*, and the death of its author from what was, in this case, a sexually transmitted disease.

2. Jacques Derrida, *The Work of Mourning*, ed. Pascale-Anne Brault and Michael Nass (Chicago and London: University of Chicago Press, 2001). All page references will be given parenthetically in the main text and the collection will be referenced in subsequent footnotes by the abbreviation WM.

3. In what is only a selection of such thanatographical texts, see 'Circumfession' in *Jacques Derrida*, trans. Geoffrey Bennington (Chicago: University of Chicago Press, 1993); *Memoirs of the Blind: The Self-Portrait and Other Ruins*, trans. Pascale-Anne Brault and Michael Nass (Chicago: University of Chicago Press, 1993); *Aporias: Dying – awaiting one another at the 'limits of truth'*, trans. Thomas Dutoit (Stanford: Stanford University Press, 1994); *The Gift of Death*, trans. David Willis (Chicago: Chicago University Press, 1995); Jacques Derrida, *Learning to Live Finally: An Interview with Jean Birnbaum*, trans. Pascale-Anne Brault and Michael Nass (Hoboken, NJ: Melville House Publishing, 2007).

4. To which Jean-Luc Nancy adds chiasmic balance (if not dialectical symmetry) when he writes of 'the impossibility of reliving [my birth], as well as the impossibility of crossing over into my death'. Jean-Luc Nancy, *The Inoperative Community* (Minneapolis: University of Minnesota Press, 1991), pp. 14–15.

5. Jason Powell, *Jacques Derrida: A Biography* (London and New York: Continuum, 2006), p. 95.

6. 'The Deaths of Roland Barthes' (WM, 31–67) was originally published as Jacques Derrida, 'Les morts de Roland Barthes', *Poétique* 47 (September 1981), pp. 269–92.

7. Jacques Derrida, *Learning to Live Finally*, op. cit., pp. 33–4. This interview originally appeared in *Le Monde* on 19 August 2004 and was published in France as Jacques Derrida, *Apprendre à Vivre Enfin; Entretien avec Jean Birnbaum* (Paris: Éditions Galilée/Le Monde, 2005).

8. Ibid., p. 33.

9. Here I am indebtedly in dialogue with Sean Gaston's impressive *The Impossible Mourning of Jacques Derrida* (London and New York: Continuum, 2006). Contra Gaston, it is argued here that mourning Derrida is made possible through a construal of canonisation which resists 'monumemorialisation' by emphasising a positive, dialogic iterability as the foremost 'quality' of the work which endures.

10. Ibid., p. 1.

11. Such recursion is a structural inevitability, let us be clear, rather than narcissistic reappropriation. See Jacques Derrida, 'Signature, Event, Context', in *Margins of Philosophy*, trans. Alan Bass (Brighton: Harvester, 1982), pp. 309–30.

12. Costas Douzinas (ed.), *Adieu Derrida* (Basingstoke: Palgrave Macmillan, 2007), p. 5. Douzinas,

in his introduction, describes a feeling shared by thousands (mainly theorists) who attended The Birkbeck Instutitute for the Humanities Lectures series that bade 'Adieu' to Derrida. Given the proximity of the terms 'haunting' and 'exorcise' to 'presence' in the closing sentence of *DRA*, there seemed no need at the time to underscore the amphibology of 'presence', but certain misconstruals in humanist and antihumanist responses to the return of the author suggest that I do so now.

13. I have made the argument for reading Barthes's 'The Death of the Author' as the implosive crisis statement of the impersonalist credo in 'Reconstructing the Author' in Seán Burke, *Authorship: From Plato to the Postmodern: A Reader* (Edinburgh: Edinburgh University Press, 1995), pp. xv–xxx: xix–xxv.

14. Indeed, as I only discovered in preparing this third edition, it was indeed underway beyond France (if not beyond French theory) in the work of the Romanian critic Eugen Simion as early as 1981. See Eugen Simion, *The Return of the Author*, ed. James W. Newcomb, trans. James W. Newcomb and Lidia Vianu (Evanston, IL: Northwestern University Press, 1996). This admirable and coherent collection of essays was originally published in Romanian as Eugen Simion, *Întoarcerea Autorului: Eseuri despre relatia creator-opera* (Bucharest: Cartea Romaneasca, 1981).

15. The relationship between logocentrism and theology is a central theme of my forthcoming work on discursive ethics in Levinas and Derrida.

16. See Andrew Bennett's lucid work, *The Author* (Abingdon and New York: Routledge, 2005), p. 127. *DRA* did, however, set itself assiduously against the facile association of Derrida's work with an anti-authorial nihilism (as lauded and bemoaned) during the 1980s in Anglo-American literature departments.

17. Cf. Chapter 2, 'Subjectivities' below.

18. In 'The Author as Reader', the autobiographical is re-opened in the familiar milieu of the relationship between the impersonalist credo and a certain strain of 'high modernist' literature. I am not a scholar of the authors considered, and some of the assumptions it makes may strike experts in the field as historically naïve. Nevertheless, the re-opening of this issue marks one move toward revisioning the question of the author as much from the point of view of literary artists as that of critics and theorists.

19. See George P. Landow, *Hypertext 3.0: Critical Theory and New Media in an Era of Globalisation* (Baltimore: Johns Hopkins University Press, 2006). I have made a preliminary attempt to open the issue of responsible legacy in Seán Burke, *The Ethics of Writing: Authorship and Legacy in Plato and Nietzsche* (Edinburgh: Edinburgh University Press, 2008). On proprietary rights, see Lise Buranen and Alice Myers Roy, *Perspectives on Plagiarism in a Postmodern World* (Albany: SUNY Press, 1999); Joseph Lowenstein, *The Author's Due: Printing and the Prehistory of Copyright* (Chicago: University of Chicago Press, 2002); Jody Greene, *Trouble With Ownership: Literary Property and Authorial Liability in England, 1660–1730* (Philadelphia: University of Pennsylvania Press, 2005).

20. See F.E. Manuel, *The Religion of Isaac Newton* (London: Oxford University Press, 1974) and B.J.T. Dobbs, *The Foundations of Newton's Alchemy* (Cambridge: Cambridge University Press, 1984).

21. Derrida wrote of the Marxist legacy and the Marxism that is 'still to come': 'deconstruction … has remained faithful to a certain spirit of Marxism, to at least one of its spirits for … there is *more than one of them* and they are heterogeneous' – Jacques Derrida, *Specters of Marx*, trans. Peggy Kamuf (London: Routledge, 1994), p. 75.

22. The initial touchstones for such projects would be Derrida's work on the signature and the proper name along with the wealth of unexploited questions raised in the first half of Foucault's 1969 essay – see Michel Foucault, 'What is an Author?' in *Language, Counter-Memory, Practice: Selected Essays and Interviews*, ed. Donald Bouchard, trans. Donald Bouchard and Sherry Simon (Ithaca: Cornell University Press, 1977), pp. 113–38.

23. See Jacques Derrida, *Geneses, Genealogies, Genres, & Genius: The Secrets of the Archive*, trans. Beverley Bie Brahic (Edinburgh: Edinburgh University Press, 2006). Appearing in the year prior to Derrida's death, this work was originally published as Jacques Derrida, *Genèse, généalogies, genres et le génie: Les secrets de l'archive* (Paris: Galilée, 2003).

24. These words are adapted from Maurice Blanchot, *The Infinite Conversation*, trans. Susan Hanson (Minneapolis: University of Minnesota Press), p. 52. The phrase 'critical thought' is substituted for 'philosophy' as the question of the author is not best opened by its embroilment in the issue as to what questions belong to 'philosophy proper'.

PROLOGUE: THE DEATHS OF PAUL DE MAN

1. Paul de Man, *Blindness and Insight: Essays in the Rhetoric of Contemporary Criticism*, second edition, revised and enlarged, ed. Wlad Godzich (London: Methuen, 1983), p. xii.
2. De Man's writings of this period – including also articles written in Flemish for *Het Vlaamsche Land* – have been collected as Paul de Man, *Wartime Journalism 1939–1943*, ed. Werner Hamacher, Neil Hertz and Thomas Keenan (Lincoln, NE: University of Nebraska Press, 1988).
3. See David Lehman, *Signs of the Times: Deconstruction and the Fall of Paul de Man* (London: André Deutsch, 1991) which, whilst not the most reliable guide to deconstruction, provides the fullest biographical account of de Man to date.
4. Paul de Man, *Blindness and Insight: Essays in the Rhetoric of Contemporary Criticism*, op. cit., p. 165.
5. For views of this kind, as well as vigorous defences of the integrity of deconstruction see Werner Hamacher, Neil Hertz and Thomas Keenan, eds, *Responses: On Paul de Man's Wartime Journalism* (Lincoln, NE: University of Nebraska Press, 1989).
6. Frank Kermode presents such a median position in *The Uses of Error* (London: Collins, 1990), pp. 102–18.
7. Paul de Man, cited in Jacques Derrida, 'Like the Sound of the Sea Deep within a Shell: Paul de Man's War', *Critical Inquiry*, vol. 12, no. 3 (Spring 1988), pp. 590–652: p. 623.
8. These categories characterise the debate in general. As Christopher Norris says: 'There are three possible lines of response to the discovery of these wartime writings. The first ... would take the worst possible view of their content, and would hold furthermore that everything de Man went on to write must (so to speak) carry guilt by association, and therefore be deeply suspect on ideological grounds. The second would hold, on the contrary, that de Man's later texts have absolutely nothing in common with his early writings, that in fact they exhibit an extreme resistance to precisely that form of dangerously mystified thinking, and should therefore be treated as belonging to a different order of discourse. The third ... is that de Man's later work grew out of an agonized reflection on his wartime experience, and can best be read as a protracted attempt to make amends (albeit indirectly) in the form of an ideological auto-critique.' – Christopher Norris, *Paul de Man: Deconstruction and the Critique of Aesthetic Ideology*, (London: Routledge, 1988), pp. 189–90. There is at least one more form of possible response, that of a radical anti-authorialism which would affirm that 'Paul de Man' signifies nothing, and that consequently there is no oeuvre. To the best of my knowledge, however – and for all the theoretical insistence on the death of the author – no-one has risked this particular line of argument.
9. One reviewer of the first edition of this book has noted: 'Such an emotive and controversial issue forestalls thinking' – Julian Wolfreys, 'Premature Obituaries', *Radical Philosophy* 67 (Summer 1994), pp. 57–8: p. 58. This may well be the case, but the fact of controversy itself opens attention to the *procedures by which* thought (good or bad) about the affair of de Man could occur. A signatory contract has always been in place, one which is raised to extreme visibility by the moment of controversy. As the very different cases of Heidegger and Rushdie also attest, questions of authorship are the first to be raised when a text finds itself at the centre of a cultural crisis. Tribunals are constituted with the primary mission of evaluating the discursive act in terms of its *res gestae*: close attention is given to the circumstances of writing, the placement of the writer relative to the historical moment, the contextualising effect of other writings within the oeuvre, local pressures to which the writing was subjected, the grounds for attributing a clear intention from text to writer, and so on. The necessity of holding an author to account is asserted in direct proportion to the perceived gravity of the issues raised by the text, but the signature has already preprogrammed channels of ethical recall to the still-living author, the heirs of the dead author (in the form of family, institutions associated

with the author's name), the field described by an author's life and work. A signature or act of authorship is thus addressed to an ethical future in which the still-living, dead or departed subject may be recalled to his or her text. This threadwork is woven in the gap between subject and sign, the space of formerly present absence which a signature marks; it describes nothing more and nothing less that the ethical contract on whose basis the institution of authorship is established. To sign is to accept, even to anticipate the possibility of resummons. What judgements are subsequently made between text, author and history are made independently of the act of signing but can only take place on its basis. In this sense, the authorial signature functions both as ethical prospect and as an ethical supplement of mortality. For a full elaboration of this argument see Seán Burke, 'The Textual Estate: Plato and the Ethics of Signature', *History of the Human Sciences*, vol. 9, no. 1 (February 1996), pp. 59–72.

10. De Man's theme of autobiography as a form of self-cancellation rather than self-expression is clearly stated in Paul de Man, *The Rhetoric of Romanticism* (New York: Columbia University Press, 1984), pp. 67–81.

11. Paul de Man, *Blindness and Insight: Essays in the Rhetoric of Contemporary Criticism*, *op. cit.*, p. 49.

12. Jacques Derrida, 'Like the Sound of the Sea Deep within a Shell: Paul de Man's War', *op. cit.*, p. 593.

13. It may be objected that the case of de Man is unrepresentative, that one could scarcely expect theorists to maintain their belief in the absence of the author when confronted with so grievous a situation; but my point is that it required such a grotesque scenario to force theory to recognise that the principle of the author has always been operative, that the author had never disappeared. The concept of the author could not have forced itself upon critical attention in this situation had it not always and everywhere – *de facto* and *de jure* – been active and resistant to theoretical repression.

INTRODUCTION: A PREHISTORY OF THE DEATH OF THE AUTHOR

1. 'In France, Mallarmé was doubtless the first to see and foresee in its full extent the necessity to substitute language itself for the person who until then had been supposed to be its owner. For him, for us too, it is language which speaks, not the author; to write is, through a prerequisite impersonality ... to reach that point where only language acts, "performs", and not "me"... Valéry ... never stopped calling into question and deriding the Author; he stressed the linguistic and, as it were, 'hazardous' nature of his activity, and throughout his prose works he militated in favour of the essentially verbal condition of literature, in the face of which all recourse to the interiority of the writer seemed to him pure superstition. Proust ... was visibly concerned with the task of inexorably blurring, by an extreme subtilisation, the relation between the writer and his characters ... Lastly, to go no further than this prehistory of modernity, Surrealism ... contributed to the desacralisation of the image of the Author by ceaselessly recommending the abrupt disappointment of expectations of meaning ... by entrusting the hand with the task of writing as quickly as possible what the head itself is unaware of (automatic writing), by accepting the principle and the experience of several people writing together.' – Roland Barthes, 'The Death of the Author' in Roland Barthes, *Image-Music-Text*, trans. and ed. Stephen Heath (London: Fontana, 1977), pp. 142–8: pp. 143–4.

2. As one counter example to Barthes's depiction of Valéry: 'The object of art and the principle of its artifice is precisely to communicate the impression of an ideal state in which the man who should possess it will be able to produce spontaneously, effortlessly and indefatigably a magnificent and marvellously ordered expression of his nature and of our destinies.' – Paul Valéry, 'Remarks on Poetry' in T. G. West trans. and ed., *Symbolism: An Anthology* (London: Methuen, 1980), pp. 43–60: pp. 59–60.

3. See 'Kafka and his Precursors' in Jorge Luis Borges, *Labyrinths* (Harmondsworth: Penguin Books, 1970), pp. 234–6.

4. Stephane Mallarmé, 'Crisis in Verse' in T. G. West trans. and ed., *Symbolism: An Anthology, op. cit.*, pp. 1–12: pp. 8–9.

5. Michel Foucault, *The Order of Things: An Archaeology of the Human Sciences*, trans. Alan Sheridan (London: Tavistock, 1970), pp. 305–6.

6. The differences between impersonalist and modern anti-authorial positions will be developed at various points throughout this work. For the moment it is sufficient to remark that, firstly, impersonalist ideas have been generally mooted by artists as aesthetic rather than theoretical statements; and secondly, the impersonalist aesthetic itself – as worked through by Flaubert, Eliot and Joyce amongst others – has usually assigned the highest degree of control to the writer, that of a creator presiding over the whole of his creation whilst not appearing anywhere within it.

7. Jacques Derrida, quoted in Christopher Norris, *Derrida* (London: Fontana, 1987), p. 240.

8. Roland Barthes, *Critical Essays*, trans. Richard Howard (Evanston: Northwestern University Press, 1972), p. 24. This quotation comes from one of Barthes's early essays 'Littérature objective' (Paris, 1954).

9. See Jacques Derrida, *'Speech and Phenomena' and Other Essays on Husserl's Theory of Signs* [1967], trans. David B. Allison (Evanston: Northwestern University Press, 1973).

10. See Claude Lévi-Strauss, *Tristes Tropiques* [1955], trans. John Russell (London: Hutchinson, 1966); Jacques Lacan, *Écrits: A Selection* [1966], trans. Alan Sheridan (London: Tavistock, 1977), pp. 146–78.

11. See Ferdinand de Saussure, *A Course in General Linguistics* [1915], trans. W. Baskin (London: Fontana, 1974).

12. The linguist Roman Jakobson provides the link here in that his work carries through from his early association with the Moscow Linguistic Circle (he was amongst its co-founders in 1915) to Prague Structuralism, and was later a seminal influence on Lévi-Strauss and Lacan. In fact, had Lévi-Strauss not become Visiting Professor at the New School for Social Research in New York (1941–5), where he worked with Jakobson, the development of critical theory may have taken significantly different routes. Jakobson's ideas on metaphor and metonymy – which form the cornerstone of Lacan's rereading of Freud – are perhaps best accessible in Roman Jakobson, 'Closing Statement: Linguistics and Poetics' in Thomas A. Sebeok, ed., *Style in Language* (Cambridge, MA: MIT Press, 1960).

13. See Claude Lévi-Strauss, *The Elementary Structures of Kinship*, trans. James Harle Bell, John Richard von Sturmer and Rodney Needham (Boston: Beacon Press, 1969); Claude Lévi-Strauss, *Structural Anthropology*, trans. Claire Jacobson and Brooke Grundfest Schoept (London: Allen Lane, 1967), pp. 33–99.

14. For Lacan's continual unfolding of the linguisticality of the unconscious, see *Écrits, op. cit.*

15. See Claude Lévi-Strauss, *Structural Anthropology, op. cit.*, p. 33. Lévi-Strauss is here taking his lead from Nikolai Troubetzkoy whose paper 'La phonologie actuèlle' (Paris, 1933), along with Saussure's *Cours* and the texts of Lévi-Strauss, belongs to the classic and inceptionary phase of structuralist analysis. Troubetzkoy's work in phonology is most readily accessible in Nikolai Troubetzkoy, *Principles of Phonology*, trans. Christiane A.M. Baltaxe (Berkeley and Los Angeles: University of California Press, 1969).

16. The concept of the dissolution of man is promulgated in direct opposition to the Sartrian notions of individuality and dialectical history by Lévi-Strauss in Claude Lévi-Strauss, *The Savage Mind* (London: Weidenfeld and Nicolson, 1966).

17. For perhaps the first statement of poststructural intent, and a vigorous testament to this historical turning-point, see Jacques Derrida, 'Structure, Sign, and Play in the Discourse of the Human Sciences' in Jacques Derrida, *Writing and Difference*, trans. Alan Bass (London: Routledge and Kegan Paul, 1981), pp. 278–93.

18. Roland Barthes, *Sade Fourier Loyola*, trans. Richard Miller (London: Cape, 1977), p. 8.

19. Michel Foucault, *The Order of Things: An Archaeology of the Human Sciences, op. cit.*, p. 386.

20. This early twentieth-century exclusion of the author was certainly a gesture no more drastic than the critical circumstances by which it was provoked. As the Russian Formalist Osip Brik lamented, Russian literary criticism of the time was riddled with 'maniacs … passionately seeking the answer to the question "did Pushkin smoke?"' Osip Brik, 'The so-called formal method' in L.M. O'Toole and Ann Shukman, eds, *Russian Poetics in Translation, 4* (Colchester: University of Essex Press, 1977), pp. 90–1: p. 90.

21. Roland Barthes, 'The Death of the Author', *op. cit.*, p. 142.

22. Michel Foucault, 'What is an Author?', trans. Josué V. Harari, in Josué V. Harari, ed., *Textual*

Strategies: Perspectives in Post-Structuralist Criticism (Ithaca: Cornell University Press, 1979), pp. 141–60: p. 143.

23. Roland Barthes, S/Z, trans. Richard Miller (London: Cape, 1975), p. 140.

24. Roland Barthes, 'The Death of the Author', op. cit., pp. 144–5.

25. Alice A. Jardine, Gynesis: Configurations of Woman and Modernity (Ithaca: Cornell University Press, 1985), p. 58.

26. In its more radical forms, this resistance produces statements of the order that anti-authorial discourse is 'a confused and entangled body of material which, at its most extreme, enters the realm of dementia...' Cedric Watts, 'Bottom's Children: The Fallacies of Structuralist, Post-structuralist and Deconstructionist Literary Theory' in Lawrence Lerner, ed., Reconstructing Literature (Oxford: Basil Blackwell, 1983), pp. 20–35: p. 22. Naturally, there are exceptions to this pattern of resistance, particularly in the phenomenological movement within which the conception of the subject differs significantly from traditional humanist conceptions of author-ship. Phenomenological positions will be discussed below in the second chapter and conclusion.

27. See Steven Knapp and Walter Benn Michaels, 'Against Theory', in W.J.T. Mitchell, ed., Against Theory: Literary Studies and the New Pragmatism (Chicago: University of Chicago Press, 1985), pp. 11–30. Knapp and Michaels' article was originally published in Critical Inquiry vol. 8 no. 4 (Summer 1982), pp. 732–42, and the long-running debate it prompted is collected in W.J.T. Mitchell, ed., Against Theory, op. cit. Knapp and Michaels' ideas on intention will be discussed below in the sections 'Doubling the Text' and 'Misreceptions'.

28. Despite many divergences of opinion on other matters, all pragmatists characterise themselves as opposed to theory in one way or another.

29. As it is, the refusal to debate or contest the arguments of theory is upheld as a point of principle by many pragmatists. Stanley Fish, for example, writes that: 'Arguments against theory will only keep it alive, by marking it as a sight of general concern ... theory's day is dying ... and, I think, not a moment too soon.' Stanley Fish, 'Consequences', in W.J.T. Mitchell, ed., Against Theory, op. cit., pp. 106–31: p. 128. Fish doubtless has in mind here Paul de Man's statement of the inescapably theoretical nature of pragmatist opposition to critical theory – see Paul de Man, The Resistance to Theory (Minneapolis: University of Minnesota Press, 1986). Such a non-combatant position avoids the de Manian counter-argument that theory is itself its own resistance, but only at the potential cost of implicating pragmatism in a Wittgensteinian silence on the texts and methods of theory.

30. It may seem, at a certain level, that the arrangement of these discourses in chapters which deal with individual theorists begs the question somewhat. However, virtually all theorists follow this convention and often in texts which uphold the disappearance of the author. Hopefully, in an argument which seeks to argue for rather than against the author, this procedure will at least attain a greater consistency. The relationship of author and oeuvre will be discussed passim, as well as that of author and critic/theorist.

CHAPTER ONE: THE BIRTH OF THE READER

1. William Shakespeare, Julius Caesar in Shakespeare: Complete Works (Oxford: Oxford University Press, 1905), pp. 820–45: p. 822.

2. 'The Death of the Author' was in fact written for publication in an American magazine, Aspen, nos. 5 and 6 whose editor Brian Doherty was inviting contributions from various distinguished names drawn from the French and American avant-gardes (for example Marcel Duchamp, Alain Robbe-Grillet, John Cage, Merce Cunningham) on the theme of closing the gap between art and low culture. Barthes's essay thus fitted into this general format in announcing the end of the elite figure of the author and proposing in its stead a textually anonymity free from tradi-tional hierarchies. The Aspen issues passed by with very little notice, but a year later Barthes republished the essay in France as 'La mort de l'auteur', in Mantéia V (1968) from whence it became one of the classic texts of poststructuralism. On the unusual and little-known origins of Barthes's text, see Molly Nesbit, 'What Was An Author?', Yale French Studies, 73 (1987), pp. 229–57. All references to the essay will here be made to Roland Barthes, 'The Death of the Author', Image-Music-Text, and trans. ed. Stephen Heath (London: Fontana, 1977), pp. 42–8,

and page references are provided parenthetically in the text.

3. See Roland Barthes, *On Racine*, trans. Richard Howard (New York: Octagon Books, 1977); *Criticism and Truth*, trans. K.P. Keuneman (London: Athlone Press, 1987). The terms *auteurist* and *auteurism* derive from the French for author (*auteur*) and are widely used in cinema criticism in the context of the *auteur* theory which asserts that the director, not the screenwriter, is the true author of any given film. As I will use the term, *auteurism* denotes any theory or critiism which centres on the author to the exclusion of other textual forces.

4. See Roland Barthes, *S/Z*, trans. Richard Miller (London: Cape, 1975), pp. 211–12. Originally published as Roland Barthes, *S/Z* (Paris: Seuil, 1970).

5. For instance, without any prior or further argumentation, Toril Moi writes: 'if we are truly to reject the model of the author as God the Father of the text, it is surely not enough to reject the patriarchal ideology implicit in the paternal metaphor. It is equally necessary to reject the *critical practice* it leads to, a critical practice that relies on the author as the transcendental signified of his or her text. For the patriarchal critic, the author is the source, origin and meaning of the text. If we are to undo this patriarchal practice of *authority* we must take one step further and proclaim with Roland Barthes the death of the author.' Toril Moi, *Sexual/Textual Politics: Feminist Literary Theory* (London: Methuen, 1985), pp. 62–3.

6. Cedric Watts, 'Bottom's Children: The Fallacies of Structuralist, Post-structuralist and Deconstructionist Literary Theory' in Lawrence Lerner, ed., *Reconstructing Literature* (Oxford: Basil Blackwell, 1983), pp. 20–35: p. 28.

7. Paul Taylor, 'Men on the Run and on the Make/Review of *Mensonge* by Malcolm Bradbury and *Saints and Sinners* by Terry Eagleton', *The Sunday Times*, 13 September 1987, p. 59.

8. William Gass, 'The Death of the Author' in *Habitations of the Word* (New York: Simon and Schuster, 1985), pp. 265–88.

9. See Friedrich Nietzsche, *The Joyful Wisdom*, trans. Thomas Common (Edinburgh: Foulis, 1910), especially pp. 167–9.

10. For Derrida's ideas on the transcendental signified, see Jacques Derrida, *Of Grammatology*, trans. Gayatri Chakravorty Spivak (Baltimore: Johns Hopkins University Press, 1976), *passim*.

11. Roland Barthes, *On Racine*, *op. cit.*, p. 168.

12. Friedrich Nietzsche, *The Joyful Wisdom*, *op. cit.*, p. 276.

13. Roland Barthes, *On Racine*, *op. cit.*, p. 170.

14. See Roland Barthes, *Image-Music-Text*, *op. cit.*, p. 156.

15. See Mikhail Bakhtin, *Problems of Dostoyevsky's Poetics*, trans. R.W. Rotsel (Ann Arbor, MI: University of Michigan Press, 1973) for this conception of the dialogic author of the modern polyphonic novel. Some of the implications of Bakhtin's work for author-theory will be considered below.

16. Osip Brik, 'The so-called formal method' in L.M. O'Toole and Ann Shukman, eds, *Russian Poetics in Translation 4* (Colchester: University of Essex Press, 1977), pp. 90–1: p. 90. For a Marxist extension of this artisanal picture of authorship see Walter Benjamin, 'The Author as Producer' in Walter Benjamin, *Understanding Brecht*, trans. Anna Bostock (London: NBL, 1973), pp. 85–101.

17. The phenomenological *auteurism* of Georges Poulet might be such a case in point. However, Barthes is not here concerned with specific instances, but rather with critical attitudes generally. The phenomenological position on the author will be discussed at some length below in the second chapter and conclusion, where it will be argued that whilst the the transcendental subject of phenomenology is undoubtedly deist, it is more so in the manner of the *deus absconditus* than that of the omnipresent author.

18. 'The Author, when believed in, is always conceived of as the past of his own book: book and author stand automatically on a single line divided into a *before* and an *after*. The Author is thought to *nourish* the book, which is to say that he exists before it, thinks, suffers, lives for it, is in the same relation of antecedence to his work as a father is to his child.' Roland Barthes, *Image-Music-Text*, *op. cit.*, p. 145.

19. Gayatri Chakravorty Spivak, 'Translator's Preface to *Of Grammatology*' in Jacques Derrida, *Of Grammatology*, *op. cit.*, pp. ix–lxxxvii: p. lxxiv.

20. The phrase 'monster of totality' is taken from Barthes. See Roland Barthes, *Roland Barthes by*

Roland Barthes, trans. Richard Howard (London: Macmillan, 1977), p. 179.

21. William Gass, *The World Within the Word* (New York: Alfred A. Knopf Inc., 1979), p. 36.

22. See Roland Barthes, 'The Death of the Author', *op. cit.*, p. 144.

23. Roland Barthes, *S/Z, op. cit.*, pp. 211–12.

24. See ibid., pp. 210–11.

25. Roland Barthes, *The Pleasure of the Text*, trans. Richard Howard (London: Cape, 1976), p. 27.

26. Ibid.

27. Roland Barthes, *Sade Fourier Loyola*, trans. Richard Miller (London: Cape, 1977), pp. 8–9. Originally published as *Sade, Fourier, Loyola* (Paris: Éditions de Seuil, 1971).

28. Roland Barthes, *Image-Music-Text, op. cit.*, p. 161.

29. Boris Tomaschevsky, 'Literature and Biography' in Ladislav Matejka and Krystyna Pomorska, eds, *Readings in Russian Poetics: Formalist and Structuralist Views* (Cambridge, MA: MIT Press, 1971), pp. 47–55: p. 50.

30. Michel Foucault, in Michel Foucault, ed., *I Pierre Rivière, having slaughtered my mother, my sister and my brother…: A Case of Parricide in the 19th Century*, trans. Frank Jellinek (New York: Pantheon Books, 1975), p. 209.

31. Tzvetan Todorov, quoted in Ann Jefferson and David Robey, *Modern Literary Theory: A Comparative Introduction* (London: Batsford, 1984), pp. 98–9.

32. Paul de Man, *The Rhetoric of Romanticism* (New York: Columbia University Press, 1984), p. 69.

33. On the theme of the 'hospitality' of the critic see J. Hillis Miller, 'The Critic as Host' in Harold Bloom et al., *Deconstruction and Criticism* (New York: Seabury Press, 1979), pp. 217–53.

34. See Roland Barthes, 'The Death of the Author', *op. cit.*, p. 146.

35. Roland Barthes, *Sade Fourier Loyola, op. cit.* p. 3. All subsequent page references for citation are given parenthetically within the text.

36. See ibid., pp. 87–8.

37. Roland Barthes, 'The Death of the Author', *op. cit.*, p. 146.

38. In a way, *Sade Fourier Loyola* can be seen to continue the project of *écriture blanche* so hauntingly proposed in *Writing Degree Zero* – see Roland Barthes, *Writing Degree Zero*, trans. Annette Lavers and Colin Smith (London: Cape, 1967). Barthes had here argued – pace Lukács and Sartre – that writing realises its true political status through its formal and stylistic structures: the manner rather than the content of what is written constitutes its praxis. The dream of the *écrivain* is to break with the language of his time, to evolve a colourless writing devolved of ideology, cleansed of institutional traces. Such a quest involves an absolute purgation of the encratic bourgeois language, since to break with the values of a society is most importantly to break with its modes of expression. However, *Writing Degree Zero*, so full of promise and prospect for the future of writing finally presents the *écrivain* as the unhappiest of consciousnesses, and the dream of *écriture blanche* as condemned in advance. Every assertion of freedom invariably falls prey to the snares of recuperation. Impelled by History to a commitment he cannot make, forced to choose between modes of writing that are destined to be classicised, the modern writer is forever caught on the wrong side of both freedom and necessity. What *Sade Fourier Loyola* presents, by contrast, are writers who have indeed succeeded in stepping out of the languages of their times, anchorite figures who have defended their texts against the incursion of the language of the other. Unlike *écriture* (as understood by *Writing Degree Zero*) logothesis is not obliged to use the language of social reality against society; rather, like the language of madness, it rejects the sociolect, it becomes *sui generis*.

39. It might be maintained that the logothete stays within language, and that it is only the transgressive power of his reconfigurations and 'theatricalising' of the pre-existent system that gives to his text the appearance of a new language. But *Sade Fourier Loyola* does not say this: nothing of the earlier position can be recuperated from this depiction. If Sade, Fourier and Loyola remain within language as inscribed subjects then they do so at its outermost limit: the logothete will not deign to speak any language not uniquely his own. He does what 'The Death of the Author' claimed no writer could do – that is, to exorcise the anterior language and stage an entirely hermetic and idiorhythmic scene of writing.

40. Roland Barthes, *Writing Degree Zero, op. cit.*, p. 25.

41. Ibid., p. 16. Also in 'From Work to Text' Barthes wrote: 'How do you classify a writer like

Georges Bataille? Novelist, poet, essayist, economist, philosopher, mystic? The answer is so difficult that the literary manuals generally prefer to forget about Bataille who, in fact, wrote texts, perhaps continuously one single text.' – Roland Barthes, *Image-Music-Text*, *op. cit.*, p. 157. Barthes himself, like Bataille, like Kierkegaard and Nietzsche, is the most protean of writers, yet nevertheless – or perhaps because of this – he attracts more oeuvre-centred readings than any other post-war European writer. Steven Ungar in *Roland Barthes: the Professor of Desire* (Lincoln, NE: University of Nebraska Press, 1983) introduces Barthes's adolescent pastiche on Socrates to the canon, and sees in it the first step on the long road to Barthes's last works. Roland Champagne too will utilise this piece of juvenilia, and argue that the 'new humanism' outlined in *Writing Degree Zero* is the ground traversed in the quarter-century that separates it from Barthes's inaugural address to the College of France in 1977 – see Roland Champagne, *Literary History in the Wake of Roland Barthes: Re-defining the Myths of Reality* (Alabama: Summa Publications Inc., 1984). For Annette Lavers there is a Barthesian 'voyage' – see Annette Lavers, *Roland Barthes: Structuralism and After* (London: Methuen, 1982). Tim Clark, reviewing Lavers's book in an article called 'Roland Barthes: Dead and Alive', challenges the notion of the Barthesian oeuvre. Unfortunately, as with most (perhaps all) responses of this sort, he flits about between Barthes's texts establishing what amounts to the oeuvre's objection to the notion of the oeuvre, a procedure in which the greater consistency remains on Lavers's side. See Tim Clark, 'Roland Barthes: Dead and Alive', *Oxford Literary Review*, vol. 6, no. 1 (1983), pp. 97–107.

42. Roland Barthes, *Michelet*, trans. Richard Howard (Oxford: Basil Blackwell, 1987), p. 3.
43. See Boris Tomaschevsky, 'Literature and Biography', *op. cit.*, p. 55.
44. Friedrich Nietzsche, *The Philosophy of Nietzsche*, ed. John Clive (New York: Mentor, 1965), p. 142.
45. Roland Barthes, *Camera Lucida: Reflections on Photography*, trans. Richard Howard (London: Cape, 1982), p. 30.
46. *S/Z*, though it certainly marks the movement toward a poststructuralist or deconstructive approach, is still caught within certain structuralist presuppositions, *viz* its insistence that the literary text can be exhaustively reconstituted via the five organising codes.
47. 'Sade I' was in fact published in the same year that 'The Death of the Author' was written. It appeared in *Tel Quel,* 28 (Winter 1967) under the title 'L'Arbre du crime'.
48. Those who do alight here do so only briefly, and often pass over the idea of the logothete completely. And when the idea of the logothete is addressed (as here under the imperatives of a review article) a distinguished theorist can proclaim, in the face of all that *Sade Fourier Loyola* says and does: 'The author is no more than a mythic narrator to whom we attribute the meanings that successive generations have found in his text.' Michael Riffaterre, 'Sade or Text as Fantasy?', *Diacritics,* vol. 2, no. 3 (1971), pp. 2–9: p. 3. And the sole basis for this in the text? A footnote in which Barthes makes the commonplace observation that Sade cannot be held responsible for the effects his texts have had since he could not divine their destiny.(34, n.21) Contrariwise, on the few occasions when logothesis is given a fair hearing, 'The Death of the Author' is nowhere to be found. Roland Champagne gives some space to the logothete, but only at the price of utterly suppressing 'The Death of the Author'. Roland Champagne, *Literary History in the Wake of Roland Barthes*, *op. cit.* The same refusal to countenance this contradiction between 'The Death of the Author' and *Sade Fourier Loyola* is to be found throughout the secondary literature that has developed around Barthes in Anglo-American criticism.
49. André Gide, quoted in Roland Barthes, *Roland Barthes by Roland Barthes, op. cit.* p. 93.
50. Roland Barthes, 'The Death of the Author', *op. cit.*, p. 143.
51. Roland Barthes, *The Grain of the Voice: Interviews 1962–1980*, trans. Linda Coverdale (London: Cape, 1980), p. 348.
52. Toril Moi, *Sexual/Textual Politics, op. cit.*, p. 8.
53. Ibid., p. 63.
54. On changing historical attitudes to authorship, see A.J. Minnis, *Medieval Theory of Authorship: Scholastic Literary Attitudes in the Later Middle Ages* (London: Scolar Press, 1984).
55. Roland Barthes, *S/Z, op. cit.*, p. 174.
56. Emile Zola, quoted in John Hospers, *Meaning and Truth in the Arts* (Chapel Hill: University of

North Carolina Press, 1946), p. 146.

57. As indeed Barthes had done in his study of Michelet's history-writing, preferring to see it as 'an organised network of obsessions' rather than as the depiction of any historical reality – Roland Barthes, *Michelet, op. cit.*, p. 3.

58. See Jacques Lacan, 'Seminar on "The Purloined Letter"', trans. Jeffrey Mehlman, *Yale French, Studies* no. 48 (1972), pp. 38–72; Jacques Derrida, 'Le Facteur de Verité', *The Post Card: From Socrates to Freud and Beyond*, trans. Alan Bass (Chicago and London: University of Chicago Press, 1987), pp. 411–96; and Barbara Johnson 'The Frame of Reference' in Geoffrey Hartman, ed., *Psychoanalysis and the Question of the Text* (Baltimore: Johns Hopkins University Press, 1978), pp. 149–71.

59. Roland Barthes, *S/Z, op. cit.*, p. 13.

60. The phrase, 'adding pitiful graffiti to an immense poem' is one Jacques Derrida uses to describe his own reading of Edmund Jabès. See Jacques Derrida, *Writing and Difference*, trans. Alan Bass (London: Routledge and Kegan Paul, 1981), p. 74.

61. Roland Barthes, *S/Z, op. cit.*, p. 216.

62. Ibid., p. 211.

63. Ibid., p. vii.

64. Mikhail Bakhtin, quoted in Julia Kristeva, *Desire in Language: A Semiotic Approach to Literature and Art*, ed. L.S. Roudiez (Oxford: Basil Blackwell, 1984).

65. Mikhail Bakhtin, quoted in Tzvetan Todorov, *Mikhail Bakhtin: The Dialogic Principle*, trans. Wlad Godzich (Manchester: Manchester University Press, 1984), p. 106.

66. Mikhail Bakhtin, *Problems of Dostoyevsky's Poetics, op. cit.*, p. 4.

67. Kristeva's conception of the semiotic and the symbolic owes much to Lacan's distinction between the imaginary and symbolic registers which is discussed in the second chapter below. For Kristeva's revision of Bakhtin's work see Julia Kristeva, *Desire in Language: A Semiotic Approach to Literature and Art, op. cit.* (Oxford: Basil Blackwell, 1980), pp. 64–89.

68. Naturally, many invaluable readings, and fine cultural and ideological insights were arrived at in this manner, but the justification for the structuralist interpretation lay in the power and originality of these readings not in the 'truth' of the death of the subject.

69. As Umberto Eco says of the related science of semiotics: 'Semiosis is the process by which empirical subjects communicate, communication processes being made possible by the organisation of signification systems. Empirical subjects, from a semiotic point of view, can only be defined and isolated as manifestations of this double (systematic and processual) aspect of semiosis. This is not a metaphysical statement, but a methodological one; physics knows Caesar and Brutus as spatio-temporal events defined by an interrelationship of elementary particles and must not be concerned with the motivation of their acts, nor with ethical evaluation of the result of these acts. Semiosis treats subjects of semiosic acts in the same way: either they can be defined in terms of semiotic structures or – from this point of view – they do not exist at all.' Umberto Eco, *A Theory of Semiotics* (Bloomington and London: Indiana University Press, 1976), p. 315. Semiotic theory has thus shown itself more willing than structuralism to accept that it operates only within a certain area which it has itself demarcated and defined. The exclusion of the speaking subject operates much like the exclusion of author and human subject in (post) structuralist theories, but with the difference that for the semiotician it is openly acknowledged as a point of method rather than disguised as a description of the entire discursive field. The absence of the subject, as Eco suggests, is true only to the extent that it is required in order that the semiotic science may be founded and elaborated. And as Eco is well aware, the problem of the speaking subject is not abolished by semiotic theory, but – quite to the contrary – one whose confrontation is beyond the reach of any extant semiotic inquiry.

70. The influential fictions of the South American magical realists may seem to prima facie contradict this general trend, but only on the basis of a concept of representation which has little if anything in common with the ethos of traditional realism. Indeed, here and in many other literary, artistic and cultural contexts, the current trend seems to be to attempt to create rather than represent 'realities'.

71. See John Hospers, *Meaning and Truth in the Arts, op. cit.*

72. Roland Barthes, *On Racine, op. cit.*, p. 171.

73. *Roland Barthes by Roland Barthes, op. cit.*, p. 168. Originally published as *Roland Barthes par Roland Barthes* (Paris: Éditions du Seuil, 1975). All subsequent page references are given parenthetically in the text.

74. Jorge Luis Borges, 'Borges and I', *Labyrinths* (Harmondsworth: Penguin Books, 1970), pp. 282–3: p. 282.

75. Ibid.

76. Ibid.

77. Ibid., pp. 282–3.

78. Mikhail Bakhtin, quoted in Tzvetan Todorov, *Mikhail Bakhtin, op. cit.*, p. 52.

79. Michel de Montaigne, *Essays,* trans. J.M. Cohen (Harmondsworth: Penguin Books, 1958), p. 235. For a peerless analysis of Montaigne and the autobiographical, see Erich Auerbach, *Mimesis: The Representation of Reality in Western Literature*, trans. William R. Trask (Princeton: Princeton University Press, 1953), pp. 285–310.

80. See Saint Augustine, *Confessions*, trans. Henry Chadwick (Oxford: Oxford University Press, 1991).

81. See James Joyce, *A Portrait of the Artist as a Young Man,* in Harry Levin, ed., *The Essential James Joyce* (Harmondsworth: Penguin Books, 1963).

82. On the role of time and memory in the autobiographical act, see James Olney, 'Some Versions of Memory/Some Versions of Bios: The Ontology of Autobiography', in James Olney, ed., *Autobiography: Essays Theoretical and Critical* (Princeton: Princeton University Press, 1980), pp. 236–67. As Olney well argues, the situation of the subject within a timeless present serves to close any gap between the autobiographical subject of the utterance and the subject of the enunciation.

83. Victor Shklovsky, 'Sterne's *Tristam Shandy*: Stylistic Commentary' in Lee T. Lemon and Marion J. Reis, eds, *Russian Formalist Criticism: Four Essays*, pp. 25–57: p. 57.

84. Jacques Derrida, *The Ear of the Other: Otobiography, Transference, Translation: Texts and Discussions with Jacques Derrida*, trans. Peggy Kamuf and Avital Ronell (New York: Schoken Books, 1986), pp. 44–5.

85. Ibid., pp. 5–6.

86. 'Style is always a secret; but the occult aspect of its implications does not arise from the mobile and ever-provisional nature of language; its secret is recollection locked in the body of the writer ... a kind of supra-literary operation which carries man to the threshold of power and magic. By reason of its biological origin, style resides outside art, outside the pact which binds the writer to society.' Roland Barthes, *Writing Degree Zero, op. cit.*, p. 18.

87. Friedrich Nietzsche, *Ecce Homo: How One Becomes What One Is*, trans. R.J. Hollingdale (Harmondsworth: Penguin Books, 1979). On the Nietzschean philosophy of the body, see also *Thus Spoke Zarathustra: A Book for Everyone and No One*, trans. R.J. Hollingdale (Harmondsworth: Penguin Books, 1961), pp. 61–3. For Barthes's declaration of the Nietzschean influence, see *Roland Barthes by Roland Barthes, op. cit.* p. 145.

88. Roland Barthes, *The Pleasure of the Text, op. cit.*, p. 17.

89. See Roland Champagne, *Literary History in the Wake of Roland Barthes, op. cit.*, pp. 79–101.

90. Ibid., p. 97; Roland Barthes, *Sade Fourier Loyola, op. cit.*, p. 9.

91. Gabriel Josipovici develops the elegant thesis that Barthes sought to create a Proustian work of art in later years, but was frustrated by his essential distrust of the world of signs. See Gabriel Josipovici, 'The Balzac of M. Barthes and the Balzac of M. de Guermantes' in Lawrence Lerner, ed., *Reconstructing Literature* (Oxford: Basil Blackwell, 1983), pp. 81–105.

92. Susan Sontag, in her introduction to Roland Barthes, *A Barthes Reader*, ed. Susan Sontag (London: Cape, 1982), p. xxxviii. See also, Susan Sontag, 'Remembering Barthes', in *Under the Sign of Saturn* (New York: Farrar Straus Giroux, 1980), pp. 169–77.

93. Susan Sontag, quoted in Philip Thody, *Roland Barthes: A Conservative Estimate* (London: Macmillan, 1977), p. 142.

94. Harold Bloom, *Agon: Toward a Theory of Revisionism* (New York and London: Oxford University Press, 1982), p. 48.

95. See Oscar Wilde, 'The Critic as Artist', *Complete Works of Oscar Wilde* (London and Glasgow: Collins, 1948), pp. 1009–59.

CHAPTER TWO: THE AUTHOR AND THE DEATH OF MAN

1. Michel Foucault, *The Order of Things: An Archaeology of the Human Sciences*, trans. Alan Sheridan (London: Tavistock, 1970). Originally published as *Les mots et les choses: un archéologie des sciences humaines* (Paris: Gallimard, 1966). Page references are made parenthetically within the text.

2. See Michel Foucault, *Madness and Civilization: A History of Insanity in the Age of Reason*, trans. Richard Howard (London: Tavistock, 1967).

3. 'Thought' here is used – as it is Foucault's text – to denote the thought of the human sciences, and of the humanities in general. Foucault occasionally draws the science of mathematics and physics into his discussion of the Classical era, though, within his account of modernity, he is obviously not suggesting that the hard sciences partake of the epistemic (i.e. anthropomorphic) configuration.

4. See Michel Foucault, *The Order of Things*, *op. cit.*, pp. 340–1. *The Order of Things* began as an introduction to Kant's *Anthropology*, and this might explain in part why Foucault puts such undue emphasis on the anthropological in Kant's work. The anthropological concern is not to be found elsewhere in the Kantian philosophy. Indeed Kant is concerned to stress that this, his last work, is of a marginal and occasional nature, and to be regarded as quite distinct from transcendental idealism. See Immanuel Kant, *Anthropology From A Pragmatic Point of View*, trans. Mary J. Gregor (The Hague: Martinus Nijhoff, 1974).

5. See Michel Foucault, *The Order of Things*, *op. cit.*, pp. 318–35.For a clear account of the anthropological doubles see Hubert L. Dreyfus and Paul Rabinow, *Michel Foucault: Beyond Structuralism and Hermeneutics* (Brighton: Harvester Press, 1982), pp. 34–43

6. James M. Edie, 'Sartre as Phenomenologist and as Existentialist Psychoanalyst', in Edward N. Lee and Maurice Mandelbaum, eds, *Phenomenology and Existentialism* (Baltimore: Johns Hopkins University Press, 1967), pp. 139–78: p. 142.

7. Michel Foucault, *The Order of Things*, *op. cit.*, p. xiv.

8. See Michel Foucault, *The Order of Things*, *op. cit.*, pp. 52–6.

9. 'The relation of all knowledge to the mathesis is posited as the possibility of establishing an ordered succession between things, even non-measurable ones. In this sense, *analysis* was very quickly to acquire the value of a universal method; and the Leibnizian project of establishing a mathematics of qualitative orders is situated at the very heart of Classical thought; its gravitational centre. But, on the other hand, this relation to the mathesis as a general science of order does not signify that knowledge is absorbed into mathematics, or that the latter becomes the foundation for all possible knowledge; on the contrary, in correlation with the quest for a mathesis, we perceive the appearance of a certain number of empirical fields now being formed and defined for the very first time. In none of these, or almost none, is it possible to find any trace of mechanism or mathematicisation; and yet they all rely for their foundation upon a possible science of order. Although they were all dependent upon *analysis* in general, their particular instrument was not the *algebraic method* but the *system of signs*.' Michel Foucault, *The Order of Things*, *op. cit.*, p. 57.

10. No account is taken of the consideration that the formularies – Cartesian or Newtonian – for a science of order might be transposed onto the planes of general grammar, natural history, and the analysis of wealth, or at least, that the promptings toward such an order might derive in part from the Cartesian rationalism. While Foucault is unquestionably correct in saying that 'this relation to the mathesis in general does not signify that knowledge is absorbed into mathematics' (*The Order of Things*, p. 57), the relation itself – potent and hierarchicalised – remains between a primary mathematical model and a derived analysis within Foucault's very account itself. Nor is there any reason why the Cartesian mathematics and Newtonian mechanics should not have played a dominant part in the constitution of the classical science of order even if the subsequent empirical sciences are irreducible to mathematics and mechanism. Foucault seems here to be erecting a forcefield between mathematical and verbal discourses which would seem to contradict the cross-disciplinary coherencies of the epistemic continuum.

11. See René Descartes, *The Discourse on Method and the Meditations*, trans. F.E. Sutcliffe (Harmondsworth: Penguin Books, 1968), p. 96.

12. Ibid., p. 103.

13. Ibid., pp. 113–31. For a brief and clear account of this argument, see J.H. Hick *Arguments for the Existence of God* (London: Macmillan, 1970), pp. 79–83.

14. Ibid., p. 162.

15. No adherence to the representational theory of ideas is to be found in the *Meditations*. It is speculated that Descartes might elsewhere have subscribed to this theory, but no decisive evidence exists in support of this claim. For a statement of this contention, see Richard E. Aquila's introduction to his *Representational Mind* (Bloomington: Indiana University Press, 1983). It may of course be countered that language is the one representation that Descartes does not seem to doubt, but the entire representational function of language is suspended within hyperbolic doubt. Only the performative (that is non-constative, non-representational) aspect of the *cogito* proposition – '*I am, I exist*, is necessarily true, every time I express it or conceive of it in my mind' – guarantees the existence of the meditating subject.

16. The ontological argument, which states, at its baldest – God is a perfect being, existence is a perfection, therefore God exists – makes no recourse to a posteriori judgements. Descartes also forwards other non-empirical proofs in the 'Third Meditation', again refusing the Thomistic arguments that God represents himself to us in the world of appearances. See René Descartes, *The Discourse on Method and the Meditations, op. cit.,* pp. 113–31.

17. Edmund Husserl, *Cartesian Meditations: An Introduction to Phenomenology*, trans. D. Cairns (The Hague: Martinus Nijhoff, 1960), p. 1.

18. And, naturally, Foucault nowhere doubts that the thought of Descartes belongs to the Classical *episteme*. See Michel Foucault, *The Order of Things, op. cit.,* pp. 51–6.

19. Jacques Derrida, *The Post Card: From Socrates to Freud and Beyond*, trans. Alan Bass (Chicago and London: University of Chicago Press, 1987), p. 305.

20. For a challenge to Foucault's presentation of the Renaissance, see George Huppert, '*Divinatio et Eruditio*: Thoughts on Foucault', *History and Theory,* 13 (1974), pp. 191–207.

21. See David Hume, *A Treatise of Human Nature* (Oxford: Clarendon Press, 1978), Book 1, Pt. IV, pp. 251–63. Hume concludes: 'all the nice and subtile questions concerning personal identity can never possibly be decided, and are to be regarded rather as grammatical rather than philosophical difficulties. Identity depends upon the relation of ideas; and these relations produce identity, by means of that easy transition they occasion. But as the relations, and the easiness of the transition may diminish by insensible degrees, we can have no just standard by which we can decide any dispute concerning the time when they acquire or lose a title to the name of identity. All the disputes concerning the identity of connected objects are merely verbal, except so far as the relation of parts gives me to some fiction or imaginary principle of union, as wee have already observ'd.' (262) Herein Hume demonstrates that not only was the question of man at issue prior to Kant, but that it also admitted of severe scepticism long before Nietzsche, or Foucault, took arms against anthropologism.

22. Ralph Waldo Emerson, *Selections from Ralph Waldo Emerson*, ed. Stephen E. Whicher (Cambridge, MA: Riverside Press, 1957), p. 172.

23. Friedrich Nietzsche, *The Joyful Wisdom*, trans. Thomas Common (Edinburgh: Foulis, 1910), pp. 168–9.

24. David Carroll, 'The Subject of Archaeology or the Sovereignty of the *Episteme*', *Modern Language Notes* 93, no. 4 (May 1978), pp. 695–722.

25. See G.W.F. Hegel, *The Philosophy of World History*, trans. H.B. Nisbet (Cambridge: Cambridge University Press, 1975). For Hegel, the four ages of world history are: the Oriental, the Greek, the Roman and the Germanic eras. Interestingly, this last and final era is that of subjectivity. Foucault is always concerned to deny the existence of any Hegelian residues in his work, even going so far as to make the unconvincing claim that he has learned more about the nature of modern discourse from Cuvier, Bopp, and Ricardo than from Kant or Hegel – see Michel Foucault, *The Order of Things, op. cit.,* p. 307. Attentive readers of this text will note the recurrence of Hegelian (and Kantian) motifs, even if unaware that Foucault's great mentor was none other than the French Hegelian, Jean Hyppolite.

26. For Foucault, dialectic and anthropology are always 'intermingled', arising together at the beginning of the nineteenth century and destined to disappear together at the close of the modern *episteme*. Consequently, the end of anthropology will be coincident with the end of

dialectic. See Michel Foucault, *The Order of Things, op. cit.,* pp. 262–3.

27. For example, the Kantian transcendental subject met with strenuous opposition from both
    Schopenhauer and Nietzsche. See Arthur Schopenhauer, *The World as Will and Representation,*
    vol. 1, trans. E.J.F. Payne (New York: Dover Publications, 1969), pp. 413–534; Friedrich
    Nietzsche, *The Will to Power,* trans. Walter Kaufmann and R.J. Hollingdale (New York: Vintage
    Books, 1968), pp. 267–71.

28. Friedrich Nietzsche, *Thus Spoke Zarathustra: A Book for Everyone and No One,* trans. R.J.
    Hollingdale (Harmondsworth: Penguin Books, 1969), p. 41.

29. Friedrich Nietzsche, *The Birth of Tragedy and the Genealogy of Morals,* trans. Francis Golffing (New
    York: Doubleday, 1956), p. 177.

30. Friedrich Nietzsche, *Thus Spoke Zarathustra, op. cit.,* p. 236.

31. 'Let me speak to them of what is most contemptible: but that is the *last man* … The earth has
    become small, and on it hops the last man who makes everything small. His race is as ineradi-
    cable as the flea-beetle; the last man lives longest.' Friedrich Nietzsche, *Thus Spoke Zarathustra,*
    trans. Walter Kaufmann (New York: Viking Books, 1966), p. 23. I use Kaufmann's translation
    here in fidelity to *The Order of Things*' use of the phrase 'last man'. Hollingdale's translation is
    still less propitious to Foucault's purposes: 'Behold! I shall show you the *Ultimate Man* … The
    earth has become small, and on it hops the Ultimate Man, who makes everything small. His
    race is as inexterminable as the flea; the Ultimate Man lives longest.' (46)

32. For example, see David B. Alison, ed., *The New Nietzsche* (New York: Dell, 1977); Daniel O'Hara,
    ed. *Why Nietzsche Now?* (Bloomington: Indiana University Press, 1985); Stanley Corngold, *The
    Fate of the Self: German Writers and French Theory* (New York: Columbia University Press, 1986).

33. In the earliest days of the anthropological era Marx was still able to declare that the subject is
    'the merest vapourings of idealism': 'The individuals, who are no longer subject to the division
    of labour, have been conceived by philosophers as an ideal, under the name "Man". They have
    conceived the whole process, which we have outlined as the evolutionary process of "Man",
    so that at every historical stage "Man" was substituted for the individuals and shown as the
    motive force of history … Through this inversion, which from the first is an abstract image of
    the actual conditions, it was possible to transform the whole of history into an evolutionary
    process of consciousness.' Karl Marx, *The German Ideology* I (London: Lawrence and Wishart,
    1970), pp. 84–5. Marxism, we recall, is said to have introduced 'no real discontinuity', yet
    here, over a century earlier, Marx announces the radical archaeological thesis that man is not an
    aeterna veritas, that he arose as the result of certain historical pressures. Such statements, and this
    aspect of Marxism, should prove invaluable to a work concerned with the emergence and the
    disappearance of man but for the fact that they entirely contradict the archaeological theses that
    man was born at the end of the eighteenth century, and that it was not possible to think beyond
    man in the nineteenth century. We might find some explanation here of why Marx is so rigor-
    ously excluded from *The Order of Things,* when in so many other of the Foucauldian texts he
    is presented as a great precursor of modern discourse. The concept of *episteme* might withstand
    the introduction of one meta-epistemic author, but the introduction of two nineteenth-century
    thinkers who think beyond the universal conditions of discourse can only have the effect of
    critically undermining the integrity of these epistemological fields.

34. Michel Foucault, *Madness and Civilization, op. cit.,* p. 278.

35. See Michel Foucault, *The Birth of the Clinic,* trans. Alan Sheridan (London: Tavistock, 1973),
    p. 197. Even Foucault's later work on carceral and punitive institutions would seem to take its
    directions from the analysis in Nietzsche's *Genealogy* of the origins of morality in torture and
    punishment. See Friedrich Nietzsche, *The Birth of Tragedy and The Genealogy of Morals, op. cit.,*
    pp. 189–230.

36. Michel Foucault, *Language, Counter-Memory, Practice: Selected Essays and Interviews,* ed. Donald F.
    Bouchard, trans. Donald F. Bouchard and Sherry Simon (Oxford: Basil Blackwell, 1977), p. 33.

37. Ibid., p. 38.

38. Ibid., p. 165; p. 196.

39. *The Archaeology of Knowledge,* trans. A. M. Sheridan Smith (London: Tavistock, 1972), p. 209.

40. For Deleuze's interpretation of Foucault, see Giles Deleuze, *Foucault,* trans. Sean Hand
    (London: Athlone Press, 1988).

41. See Michel Foucault, 'A Preface to Transgression', in *Language, Counter-Memory, Practice, op. cit.*, pp. 29–52; 'Of Other Spaces', *Diacritics*, vol 16, no. 1 (Spring 1986), pp. 22–7.

42. This paper was originally delivered to the *Société française de Philosophie* in February 1969 – see Michel Foucault, 'Qu'est-ce qu'un auteur?', *Bulletin de la Société française de Philosophie*, 63 (1969), pp. 73–104 – a translation of which, by Donald Bouchard, is included in *Language, Counter-Memory, Practice, op. cit.*, pp. 113–38. A revised version of this paper was presented by Foucault at a conference at SUNY-Buffalo, and as since been translated by Josué V. Harari as 'What is an Author' in Josué V. Harari, ed., *Textual Strategies: Perspectives in Post-Structuralist Criticism* (Ithaca: Cornell University Press, 1979), pp. 141–60. As Harari emphasises, the difference between the two versions is important – see *Textual Strategies, op. cit.*, p. 43 – and all page references made parenthetically within the text will be to Harari's translation of this subsequent version. Recourse to the *Language, Counter-Memory, Practice* version will be signalled in the notes.

43. Michel Foucault, 'What is an Author?', *Language, Counter-Memory, Practice, op. cit.*, pp. 113–14. These remarks, which belong to Foucault's preamble to 'Qu'est-ce qu'un auteur?' before the *Société française de Philosophie* are omitted in the later version of the paper, and therefore do not appear in Harari's translation.

44. See Michel Foucault, 'What is an Author?' in *Textual Strategies, op. cit.*, pp. 159–60.

45. In locating the emergence of the founder of discursivity in the nineteenth century, however, we cannot but suspect that insufficient time has elapsed for powerful modifications or transformations to have occured. Time may still surrender a dialectical materialism or psychoanalysis which encompasses and transcends the inaugural texts.

46. A certain local displacement of the author may well be at work here, for this paragraph – which forms part of the main text of 'Qu'est-ce qu'un auteur?' as presented to the *Société française de Philosophie* – appears in *Textual Strategies* as a particularly astute and intrusive editor's footnote! To compare with Bouchard's translation of the paper delivered to the *Société française de Philosophie*, see Michel Foucault, *Language, Counter-Memory, Practice, op. cit.*, p. 136. Given its appearance in the original French text and in Bouchard's translation, it seems justifiable to treat the passage as though it belongs to the body proper of 'What is an Author?'.

47. Correspondingly, Foucault's exegetes have steered well away from this essay, just as they have passed over the presentation of a Delphic Nietzsche as though it were of no consequence for a transindividual theory of discursive practices. Alan Sheridan makes no mention of 'What is an Author?'; Pamela Major-Poetzl makes the solitary observation that it attests to the 'effacement, even the destruction of the subject' – *Michel Foucault's Archaeology of Western Culture: Towards a New Science of History* (Brighton: Harvester Press, 1983) p. 103; Karlis Racevskis claims that the essay has shown 'that the author is a convenient explanatory device, an a priori principle with which we are able to domesticate a text for our own specific purposes', *Michel Foucault and the Subversion of Intellect* (Ithaca: Cornell University Press, 1983), p. 39. Not surprisingly either, when the idea of the founder of discursivity is raised, it is in the context of Foucault himself. See Paul Rabinow's introduction to *The Foucault Reader*, ed. Paul Rabinow (Harmondsworth: Penguin Books, 1984), p. 26; and Edward Said, who prophesies: 'it is as the founder of a new field of research (or a new way of knowing and doing research) that he will continue to be known and regarded. The virtual representation and reperception of documentary and historical evidence is done by Foucault in such an unusual way as to have *created* for his evidence a new mental domain.' Edward Said, *Beginnings: Intention and Method* (Baltimore: Johns Hopkins University Press, 1975), p. 191.

48. See Michel Foucault, 'What is an Author', *Textual Strategies, op. cit.*, p. 145.

49. See Michel Foucault, 'Nietzsche, Marx, Freud' in *Nietzsche*, Proceedings of the Seventh International Philosophical Colloquium of the Cahièrs de Royaumont, 4–8 July, 1964 (Paris: Éditions de Minuit, 1967), pp. 183–200.

50. See *Bulletin de la Société française de philosophie*, 1969, p. 101.

51. Of course, it is of not of any material significance, in this context, whether or not Nietzsche is strictly speaking a founder of discursivity or a transdiscursive author, or whether he is to be located somewhere between the two – the fact remains that he will be there or thereabouts and consequently has every place within a discussion of this sort. Indeed, given Foucault's period of withdrawl from discourse at this time and his reemergence as a Nietzschean *revisionist* in

his genealogical period, the relationship between Foucault and Nietzsche conforms neatly to Harold Bloom's figure of affirmation-negation in the ephebe's anxious history of influence.

52. Friedrich Nietzsche, *Ecce Homo: How One Becomes What One Is*, trans. R.J. Hollingdale (Harmondsworth: Penguin Books, 1979), p. 88.

53. Michel Foucault, 'Postscript: An Interview with Michel Foucault by Charles Raus', *Death and the Labyrinth: The World of Raymond Roussel*, trans. Charles Raus (London: Athlone Press, 1987), p. 184.

54. Jorge Luis Borges, *The Aleph and Other Stories: 1933–1969*, trans. N. Di Giovanni (New York: Bantam Books, 1971), p. 180.

55. Michel Foucault, 'Prison Talk', *Radical Philosophy*, no. 16 (Spring, 1977), p. 33.

56. Michel Foucault, *The Foucault Reader, op. cit.*, pp. 76–100.

57. 'Truly I advise you: go away from me and guard yourselves against Zarathustra! ... One repays a teacher badly if one remains only a pupil. And why, then, should you not pluck at my laurels?' – Friedrich Nietzsche, *Thus Spoke Zarathustra, op. cit.*, p. 103. Nietzsche will say this many times, and in many different ways: 'The philosopher believes that the value of his philosophy lies in the whole, in the building: posterity discovers it in the bricks with which he built, and which are then often used for better building...' Friedrich Nietzsche, *A Nietzsche Reader*, selected and trans. R.J. Hollingdale (Harmondsworth: Penguin Books, 1977), p. 33.

58. 'We have to remember ... that the ancient conception of authorship was widely different from our own ... A writer might even go so far as to assume the name of a great teacher in order to gain a reading for his book ...'. Arthur S. Peake, *Peake's Commentary on the Bible* (London: Nelson, 1919), p. 902.

59. As Jacques Derrida says: '*The thinking of the end of man ... is always already prescribed in metaphysics, in the thinking of the truth of man.*' Jacques Derrida, 'The Ends of Man', *Margins – of Philosophy*, trans. Alan Bass (Brighton: Harvester Press, 1982), pp. 109–36: p. 121.

60. It is perhaps partly for this reason that Foucault maintains a scrupulous uncertainty as to whether we are still (at the time of writing) within the Age of Man, or are instead dazzled by the unaccustomed light of the coming *episteme*. This space between *epistemi* is the ideal point from which the archaeologist might speak for it frees him from the specific determinations of any particular configuration of knowledge and forms so to speak, a lyrical *intermezzo* between rigid, prescriptive systems. Foucault's elusiveness on the epistemic stationing of the archaeo-logical discourse has led Pamela Major-Poetzl to postulate a fourth and contemporary *episteme* commencing in 1950, though she does so with no direct authorisation from the text. See Pamela Major-Poetzl, *Michel Foucault's Archaeology of Western Culture, op. cit.*, pp. 158–9; 191–5.

61. And Foucault's style does everything to confirm the transcendental status of the archaeological author. He writes with an omniscient assurance, in tones peremptory and portentous; with what Roland Barthes would call the voice of God. Indeed, Edward Said makes the point that Foucault's voice is undoubtedly the 'voice of an Author', though he sees no particular contradiction in an authorful and authoritarian discourse which recommends the anonymity of discourse. See Edward Said, 'An Ethics of Language', *Diacritics*, vol. 4, no. 2 (Summer 1974), pp. 28–37: p. 28.

62. On Nietzsche's perspectivism see Arthur C. Danto, *Nietzsche as Philosopher* (New York: Columbia University Press, 1980), pp. 68–99.

63. And it is surely due in large measure to the Cartesian tradition that phenomenology should have exerted its greatest influence not in its native Germany but in France.

64. Michel Foucault, quoted in Pamela Major-Poetzl, *Michel Foucault's Archaeology of Western Culture, op. cit.*, p. 9.

65. Indeed Dreyfus and Rabinow say that Foucault told them that this was its 'real subtitle' – Hubert L. Dreyfus and Paul Rabinow, *Michel Foucault: Beyond Structuralism and Hermeneutics, op. cit.*, p. vii. This view of *The Order of Things* as an allegory of the present told through the past receives a certain confirmation from Foucault himself. He later said: 'my book is a pure and simple fiction: it is a novel, but it is not I who invented it; it is the relation of our epoch and its epistemological configuration to a whole mass of statements.' Michel Foucault, quoted in Pamela Major-Poetzl, *Michel Foucault's Archaeology of Western Culture, op. cit.*, p. 19.

66. Also, following Dreyfus and Rabinow, we might read, for 'Husserl', Merleau-Ponty: 'Foucault's account of Husserl is similar to that found in Merleau-Ponty's Sorbonne lectures,

"Phenomenolology and the Sciences of Man" ... Foucault's mischaracterisation of Husserl's account of the cogito is, in fact, an accurate characterisation of the thought of Merleau-Ponty.' Hubert L. Dreyfus and Paul Rabinow, *Michel Foucault: Beyond Structuralism and Hermeneutics*, *op. cit.*, pp. 36–7. Dreyfus and Rabinow suggest that Foucault 'accepts' this reading, but it is doubtful that Foucault's misreading is quite as naive as they imply. They also say: 'Husserl, in fact, holds to the end the view that Foucault succinctly characterizes and then implies he rejects, viz. that he "revived the deepest vocation of the Western *ratio*, bending it back upon itself in a reflection which is a radicalisation of pure philosophy and a basis for the possibility of its own history"'. *Ibid.*, p. 37. With both readings available to Foucault, it is surely no accident that he decided upon the one which serves to distance Husserlian phenomenology from the Cartesian *cogito*.

67. For an account of this controversy see Pamela Major-Poetzl, *Michel Foucault's Archaeology of Western Culture*, *op. cit.*, pp. 8–11.

68. Jorge Luis Borges, *Labyrinths* (Harmondsworth: Penguin Books, 1970), p. 53. The word, naturally, is 'chess'.

69. See, as two examples among many of Foucault's resistance to being categorised as a structuralist, *The Order of Things*, *op. cit.*, p. xiv, and *The Archaeology of Knowledge*, *op. cit.*, pp. 199–205. Foucault's statement that he did not once use the word 'structure' in *The Order of Things* is to be found in the discussion following 'Qu'est-ce qu'un auteur?': 'I have never, for my part, used the word "structure". Seek it in *The Order of Things*, you will not find it there.' Michel Foucault, 'Qu'est-ce qu'un auteur?', *op. cit.*, p. 100.

70. Michel Foucault, quoted in John Rajchman, *Michel Foucault: The Freedom of Philosophy* (New York: Columbia University Press, 1985), pp. 35–6.

71. René Descartes, *Discourse on Method and the Meditations*, *op. cit.*, p. 54.

72. See Jacques Lacan, *Écrits: A Selection*, trans. Alan Sheridan (London: Tavistock, 1977), pp. 164–5 for the clearest of Lacan's many accounts of this modern anti-*cogito*. This selection was based on the original French text *Écrits* (Paris: Seuil, 1966).

73. Jacques Lacan in Jeffrey Mehlman, ed., *French Freud: Structural Studies in Psychoanalysis*, Yale French Studies 48 (1972), p. 50 and p. 70.

74. *Ibid.*, p. 60.

75. Lacan's responses to these problems, such as they can be termed 'responses', are strategic rather than philosophical. Firstly, by reserving space in his texts and seminars wherein he mimics the dissonance and poetry of psychotic speech, indulges in puns, paradoxes, solecisms, ellipses, glossolalia and echolalia, he attempts to exhibit the play of unconscious signification within his discourse of the unconscious. But *exhibit* is precisely what those occasional performances do with the unconscious, in that they function as demonstrations or examples much as the dream-text does within the Freudian discursus. Were Lacan's texts manifestations of the unconscious rather than its description, then the very claims he makes about the unconscious would be rendered irremediably illogical and incommunicable. In a word, such claims would not exist. No constative thread could be told apart from the unconscious of his text, for the unconscious – in accordance with the universal progeniture it acquires in Lacanianism – would play itself out to the engulfment of all besides. The dynamics of this aporetic situation seem to have misunderstood in an otherwise most perceptive review of the first edition of my book: 'Burke's argument concerning the paradox in the Lacanian theory of subjectivity does not convince. Lacan, he argues, positions a fundamental paradox in his theory, in that his own mastery of Freudian discourse is implicitly at odds with his insistence that our unconscious determines everything we do, and that we cannot master our own discourses. Lacan's mastery of Freud is merely local, however, revealing the work of the unconscious.' – Julian Wolfreys, 'Premature Obituaries', *Radical Philosophy* 67 (Summer 1994), pp. 57–8: p. 57. However, as I trust my argument makes clear, Lacan's recourse to Freud takes the form of deference to, rather than mastery of, the founder of psychoanalysis. Lacan would sooner be mastered by Freud than confront the authority implicit in his own theoretical stance. The problems raised by the claim that Lacan is merely 'revealing the work of the unconscious' are dealt with below.

76. Jean Michel Palmier, quoted in Jane Gallop, *Reading Lacan* (Ithaca: Cornell University Press, 1985), p. 40. Gallop forwards an interesting discussion of Lacan's implicit mastery of language,

but admits a similar susceptibility to the *auctoritas* of his text.

77. Catherine Clément, *The Lives and Legends of Jacques Lacan*, trans. Arthur Goldhammer (New York: Columbia University Press, 1983), p. 31.

78. Ibid., p. 201.

79. This is not to suggest that Lacan is free of any defensive anxieties of influence but that such anxieties do not take Freud as their object. For a glimpse of Lacan *agonistes* concerning Hegel see Jacques Lacan, *The Four Fundamental Concepts of Psycho-analysis*, trans. Alan Sheridan (Harmondsworth: Penguin Books, 1977), p. 215.

80. Ibid., p. 232.

81. Jacques Lacan, quoted in Karlis Racevskis, *Michel Foucault and the Subversion of Intellect*, *op. cit.*, pp. 34–5.

82. Julia Kristeva, 'The System and the Speaking Subject', *The Times Literary Supplement*, 12 October 1973, pp. 1249–50: p. 1249.

83. Ludwig Wittgenstein, *Tractatus Logico-Philosophicus*, trans. D.F. Pears and B.F. McGuinness (London: Routledge and Kegan Paul, 1962), 5.641, p. 58.

84. Indeed when Foucault was pressed on this issue he replied by saying that the death of man and the question of the author are not to be hastily consociated. See Michel Foucault, 'Qu'est-ce qu'un auteur?', *op. cit.*, p. 102.

85. There are of course strategic reasons why Foucault should wish to keep the issues of author and man at a certain distance. Not least among these is the fact that Foucault had said that the author was constituted in the era of representation: 'The artist was able to emerge from the age-old anonymity of epic singers only by usurping the power and the meaning of the same epic values. The heroic dimension passed from the hero to the one whose task it had been to represent him at a time when Western culture itself became a world of representations.' – Michel Foucault, *Language, Counter-Memory, Practice*, *op. cit.*, p. 73. There could then be no question of associating the deaths of author and man on the basis of the epistemic economy of *The Order of Things*.

86. Jean-Marie Benoist, *The Structural Revolution* (London: Weidenfeld and Nicolson, 1978), p. 13.

87. Stephen Heath, 'Comment on "The idea of authorship"', in John Caughie, ed., *Theories of Authorship: A Reader* (London: Routledge and Kegan Paul, 1981), pp. 214–20: p. 216.

88. Martin Jay, 'Should Intellectual History Take a Linguistic Turn'?, in Dominick LaCapra and Steven L. Caplan, eds, *Modern European Intellectual History: Reappraisals and New Perspectives* (Ithaca: Cornell University Press, 1982), pp. 86–110: p. 89.

89. Charles C. Lemert, and Garth Gillan, *Michel Foucault: Social Theory and Transgression* (New York: Columbia University Press, 1982), p. 136. For another example of the over-hasty identification of authorial, transcendental and divine subjects see Pierre Macherey, *A Theory of Literary Production*, trans. Geoffrey Wall (London: Routledge and Kegan Paul, 1978), especially pp. 66–8.

90. Immanuel Kant, *A Critique of Pure Reason*, *op. cit.*, B 404, p. 331.

91. Edmund Husserl, *The Idea of Phenomenology*, trans. William P. Alston and George Nakhnikian (Hague: Martinus Nijhoff, 1964), pp. xviii–xix.

92. Edmund Husserl, *Cartesian Meditations*, *op. cit.*, pp. 31–2.

93. Paul de Man, *Blindness and Insight: Essays in the Rhetoric of Contemporary Criticism*, second edition, revised and enlarged, ed. Wlad Godzich (London: Methuen, 1983), p. 49.

94. Ibid., p. 38.

95. E.D. Hirsch Jr, *Validity in Interpretation* (New Haven: Yale University Press, 1967), p. 32.

96. Ibid., p. 23; p. 51.

97. Ibid., p. 51.

98. Roland Barthes, *Image-Music-Text*, trans. and ed. Stephen Heath (London: Fontana, 1977), p. 147.

99. Michel Foucault, 'What is an Author?', *Textual Strategies*, p. 159.

100. James Joyce, *A Portrait of the Artist as a Young Man*, in Harry Levin, ed., *The Essential James Joyce* (Harmondsworth: Penguin Books, 1963), pp. 52–252: p. 221.

101. Michel Foucault, 'What is an Author?', *Textual Strategies*, *op. cit.*, p. 144.

102. Georges Poulet, in Richard Macksey and Eugenio Donato, eds, *The Structuralist Controversy: The Languages of Criticism and the Sciences of Man* (Baltimore: Johns Hopkins University Press, 1972), p. 145.

103. This autobiographical emphasis is to be found not only in the later work, but virtually right across the Nietzschean corpus. In the earlier period, for example, Nietzsche went so far as to ask: 'Whither does this whole philosophy, with all its circuitous paths, want to go? Does it do more than translate, as it were, a strong and constant drive, a drive for … all those things which … are most endurable precisely for me? A philosophy which is at bottom the instinct for personal diet? An instinct which seeks my own air, my own heights, my own kind of health and weather, by the circuitous paths of my head?' Friedrich Nietzsche, *Daybreak: Thoughts on the Prejudices of Morality*, trans. R.J. Hollingdale (Cambridge: Cambridge University Press, 1982), p. 223.

104. Friedrich Nietzsche, *Beyond Good and Evil: Prelude to a Philosophy of the Future*, trans. R.J. Hollingdale (Harmondsworth: Penguin Books, 1973), p. 18.

105. Ibid., pp. 19–20.

106. Friedrich Nietzsche, *The Joyful Wisdom*, *op. cit.*, pp. 333–4.

107. See Friedrich Nietzsche, *The Will to Power*, *op. cit.*, pp. 267–72.

108. Friedrich Nietzsche, *The Joyful Wisdom*, *op. cit.*, p. 280.

109. Martin Heidegger, 'Letter on Humanism', in *Basic Writings*, ed. David Farrell Krell (London: Routledge and Kegan Paul, 1978), pp. 193–42: p. 225.

110. Ibid., p. 221.

111. Ibid., p. 208.

112. See Michel Foucault, *The History of Sexuality*, 3 vols, trans. Robert Hurley (New York: Viking Press, 1986).

113. Michel Foucault, 'Afterword: The Subject and Power' in Hubert L. Dreyfus and Paul Rabinow, *Michel Foucault: Beyond Structuralism and Hermeneutics*, *op. cit.*, pp. 208–26: p. 208.

114. Michel Foucault, *The Order of Things*, *op. cit.*, p. 328.

CHAPTER THREE: MISREAD INTENTIONS

1. Jacques Derrida, *Of Grammatology*, trans. Gayatri Chakravorty Spivak (Baltimore: Johns Hopkins University Press, 1976). Originally published as *De la Grammatologie* (Paris: Éditions de Minuit, 1967). All page references are given parenthetically in the text.

2. In the course of this chapter, unless otherwise indicated, the word 'deconstruction' is only used to designate Derrida's work, and is not meant to extend to the movement in general. The Anglo-American varieties of deconstruction are discussed in the concluding chapter.

3. For Heidegger the work of the pre-Socratics is irreducible to the frameworks of Western metaphysics, or as he calls it, the epoch of onto-theology. See, for example, Martin Heidegger, *Early Greek Thinking*, trans. David Farrell Krell and Frank A. Capuzzi (New York: Harper and Row, 1975), *passim*. Derrida would appear to disagree with Heidegger here. Early in the *Grammatology* he declares that Western thought has 'from the pre-Socratics to Heidegger, always assigned the origin of truth in general to the logos'. Jacques Derrida, *Of Grammatology*, *op. cit.*, p. 4. However, Derrida does not, here or elsewhere, convincingly explain why we should regard the pre-Socratic philosophy as necessarily logocentric.

4. On this difficult aspect of Heidegger's thought, see L.M. Vail, *Heidegger and Ontological Difference* (London: Pennsylvania State University Press, 1972).

5. Martin Heidegger, *Early Greek Thinking*, *op. cit.*, p. 50. Derrida quotes these sentences during the essay 'Différance', in *Margins – of Philosophy*, trans. Alan Bass (Brighton: Harvester Press, 1982), pp. 1–27: p. 23.

6. Though *différance* is held to exceed ontological difference it can only do so through passing by way of the difference between being and beings. The ontological difference cannot, therefore, be circumvented. Rather it opens the way for the thought of *différance*. As Derrida says: 'to prepare, beyond our *logos*, for a *différance* so violent that it can be interpellated neither as the epochality of Being nor as ontological difference, is not in any way to dispense with the passage through the truth of Being, or to "criticise", "contest" or misconstrue its incessant necessity. On the contrary, we must stay within the difficulty of this passage, and repeat it in the rigorous reading of metaphysics, wherever metaphysics normalises Western discourse', Jacques Derrida, *Margins – of Philosophy*, *op. cit.*, pp. 22–3.

7. Ibid., p. 22.

8. Ibid., pp. 66–7. Derrida had said much the same in *Of Grammatology*, pp. 20–4.

9. 'We must begin *wherever we are* and the thought of the trace, which cannot take the scent into account, has already taught us that it was impossible to justify a point of departure absolutely.' Jacques Derrida, *Of Grammatology, op. cit.*, p. 162.

10. 'If I have chosen the texts of Claude Lévi-Strauss, as points of departure and as a springboard for a reading of Rousseau, it is for more than one reason; for the theoretical wealth and interest of these texts, for the animating role that they currently play, but also for the place played in them by the theory of writing and the theme of fidelity to Rousseau.' Jacques Derrida, *Of Grammatology, op. cit.*, pp. 99–100.

11. Jacques Derrida, quoted in Christopher Norris, *Derrida* (London: Fontana, 1987), p. 144.

12. See Jean-Jacques Rousseau, *The Confessions of Jean-Jacques Rousseau*, trans. J.M. Cohen (Harmondsworth: Penguin Books, 1953).

13. Jacques Derrida, 'Cogito and the History of Madness', in Jacques Derrida, *Writing and Difference*, trans. Alan Bass (London: Routledge and Kegan Paul, 1981), pp. 31–63: p. 35. The impossibility of writing 'a history of silence' is one of the criticisms Derrida makes of Foucault's history of madness. See Michel Foucault, *Madness and Civilization: A History of Insanity in the Age of Reason*, trans. Richard Howard (London: Tavistock, 1967).

14. See Jean-Jacques Rousseau, *Essay on the Origin of Languages*, trans. J.H. Moran and Alexander Gode (New York: Fredric Ungar, 1966).

15. See Jean-Jacques Rousseau, *Discourse on Inequality*, trans. Maurice Cranston (Harmondsworth: Penguin Books, 1984).

16. See Jacques Derrida, *Of Grammatology, op. cit.*, p. 194.

17. Ibid., pp. 193–4.

18. Gayatri Chakravorty Spivak, 'Translator's Preface', *Of Grammatology, op. cit.*, p. lxxxv.

19. Ibid.

20. See Jacques Derrida, 'Plato's Pharmacy', *Dissemination*, trans. Barbara Johnson (London: Athlone Press, 1981), pp. 61–171.

21. See Plato, *Phaedrus* in *The Collected Dialogues of Plato, Including the Letters*, ed. Edith Hamilton and Huntington Cairns, Bollingen Series LXXI (Princeton: Princeton University Press, 1961).

22. Jacques Derrida, *Dissemination, op. cit.*, pp. 66–7.

23. Full references to the pretexts and contexts of Derrida's reading of Plato will be made to the section 'The Myth of Writing' below.

24. See Plato, *Phaedrus, op. cit.*, pp. 95–9.

25. Jacques Derrida, 'Plato's Pharmacy', *op. cit.*, p. 67.

26. Irene E. Harvey highlights the problem of Rousseau's exemplarity in an article entitled 'Doubling the Space of Existence: Exemplarity in Derrida – the Case of Rousseau' in John Sallis, ed., *Deconstruction and Philosophy: The Texts of Jacques Derrida* (Chicago and London: University of Chicago Press, 1987), pp. 60–70. She argues that 'Rousseau is a *mere example* on the one hand, a *superfluous addition* and in principle could have been replaced or substituted by anyone else in such a demonstration, yet on the other hand is a particularly *good example* – a crucial and critical choice, a unique individual, non-substitutable, and offering an *essential addition* in order to fill a void'. (62) Harvey does not, however, argue a paucity of logocentric texts from this, nor does she connect the question of exemplarity to the question of the author, contending rather that the notion of exemplarity itself should be deconstructed.

27. These problems are still further compounded when we consider that the full title of the *Essay* is the *Essay on the Origin of Languages, which Treats of Melody and Musical Imitation*, and that since it gives over a good part of its labour to discoursing on music, many scholars have concluded that this is its proper subject. As is to be expected, Derrida challenges this position, and spends a full twenty pages arguing that, in any case, Rousseau's thought on the origin of music is simply another expression of his thought on the origin of languages. (See Jacques Derrida, *Of Grammatology, op. cit.*, pp. 195–216.) That Derrida might be utterly persuasive here is irrelevant to our concern, which is simply to note the complications involved in using one problematical text and one problematical author to exemplify an entire epoch.

28. For example: 'from the *Discourse* to the *Essay* the sliding movement is toward continuity. The

Discourse wants to *mark the beginning* ... The *Essay* would make us *sense the beginnings* by which "men sparsely placed on the face of the earth" continuously wrench themselves away, within a society *being born*, from the pure state of nature. It captures man as he *passes* into birth, in that subtle transition from origin to genesis.' Jacques Derrida, *Of Grammatology*, *op. cit.*, p. 253.

29. From Derrida's footnote to this claim, it would not appear 'easy' at all: 'It is beside the point both of our projects and of the possibility of our demonstrating from internal evidence the link between the characteristic and Leibniz's infinitist theology. For that it would be necessary to go through and exhaust the entire content of the project.' Jacques Derrida, *Of Grammatology*, *op. cit.*, p. 331, n.14.

30. Once again, whatever novelty and impact we ascribe to Derrida's thinking on metaphysics is only to be determined via the extent to which he can be said to move beyond the Heideggerian critique.

31. For instance, in an interview with Guy Scarpetta, Derrida responds to the imputation that he has denied the subject, by saying: 'As you recall, I have never said that *there is not* a subject of writing ... It is solely necessary to reconsider the problem of the effect of subjectivity such as it is produced by the structure of the text ... Doubtless this effect is inseparable from a certain relationship between sublimation and the death instinct, from a movement of interiorisation-idealisation-*relève*-sublimation, etc., and therefore from a certain repression. And it would be ridiculous to overlook the necessity of this chain, and even more so to raise some moral or political "objection" to it.' Jacques Derrida, *Positions*, trans. Alan Bass (London: Athlone Press, 1981), p. 88.

32. Harold Bloom, 'Auras: The Sublime Crossing and the Death of Love', *Oxford Literary Review*, vol. 4, no. 3 (1981), pp. 3–19: pp. 18–19.

33. Jacques Derrida, *Of Grammatology*, *op. cit.*, p. 160.

34. W.K. Wimsatt Jr and Monroe C. Beardsley, 'The Intentional Fallacy', *Sewanee Review*, vol. 54, no. 3 (1946), pp. 468–88. Revised version in W.K. Wimsatt Jr, *The Verbal Icon: Studies in the Meaning of Poetry* (Lexington: University of Kentucky Press, 1954), pp. 3–18. Steven Knapp and Walter Benn Michaels, 'Against Theory', in W.J.T. Mitchell, ed., *Against Theory: Literary Studies and the New Pragmatism* (Chicago: University of Chicago Press, 1985), pp. 11–30. 'Against Theory' was originally published in *Critical Inquiry*, vol. 8, no. 4 (Summer 1982), pp. 732–42.

35. See J.L. Austin, *How to Do Things with Words* (Oxford: Clarendon Press, 1962); John R. Searle, *Speech Acts: An Essay in the Philosophy of Language* (Cambridge: Cambridge University Press, 1969); H.P. Grice 'Intention and Uncertainty', *Proceedings of the British Academy*, 57 (1971), pp. 263–79. It is too early at this stage to foresee the impact which Grice's impressive, long-evolving and largely unpublished work will have upon literary theory. A detailed introduction to his thought is provided in Richard E. Grandy and Richard Warner, eds, *Philosophical Grounds of Rationality: Intentions, Categories, Ends* (Oxford: Clarendon Press, 1986).

36. John R. Searle, 'Reiterating the Differences: A Reply to Derrida' in *Glyph I* (1977), pp. 198–208: p. 201.

37. Jacques Derrida, 'Signature Event Context', trans. Samuel Weber and Jeffrey Mehlman in *Glyph I* (1977), pp. 172–97: p. 192. This essay also appears in *Margins – of Philosophy*, *op. cit.*, pp. 307–30, but the *Glyph* translation is preferred in the interests of the continuity of the exchange. For Derrida's reply to Searle's reply see 'Limited Inc', trans. Samuel Weber in *Glyph II* (1977), pp. 162–51. For Derrida's defence of his own position on intention see ibid., pp. 191–218.

38. The models of intention Derrida deploys are not to be seen as purely intratextual reconstructions. Not only the *Grammatology*, but the vast majority of Derrida's readings patiently develop the pattern of an author's determinate meaning through full, unimpeded access to the oeuvre. In accordance with deconstructive insistence that no one mode of writing has any necessary privilege over another, the oeuvre is extended to include letters, early manuscripts, notebook entries, 'immature' works, all of which inhabit the textual space on an equal footing. Indeed, quite against intratextualism, Derrida is to be found most often arguing for the continuity and inseparability of an author's various writings. For example, he resolutely resists the idea that there is any 'turn' in Heidegger's philosophy. See, Jacques Derrida, 'The Ends of Man', *Margins – of Philosophy*, *op. cit.*, pp. 109–36; as too the clearing of a continuous pathway between the

two Freudian topologies in 'Freud and the Scene of Writing', *Writing and Difference, op. cit.*,
pp. 196–231. The case could even be made that the ascription of continuous intentions to the
authors he reads is a general characteristic of Derrida's work. The reconciliation of marginal
texts to the body proper is also, of course, the operation performed upon the *Phaedrus* and the
Essay.

39.   See Michael Hancher, 'Three Kinds of Intention', *Modern Language Notes*, 87 (1972), pp.
      827–51. On Hancher's classification of intent, see J. Timothy Bagwell, *American Formalism and
      the Problem of Interpretation* (Houston, TX: Rice University Press, 1986), pp. 119–21. Bagwell's
      book is very useful on the history of critical attitudes to intention, and offers an interesting
      modern pro-intentionalist argument. Another significant challenge to New Critical pictures
      of intention is provided by Stein Olsen in his book *The End of Literary Theory* (Cambridge:
      Cambridge University Press, 1987). See, in particular, pp. 29–52.

40.   Given the density, and the mimicry of Derrida's prose, it is often necessary, however, to read
      very attentively in order to separate what is explicative and what is deconstructive in his
      readings. Occasionally, too, the deconstructive and the explicative phases of his critiques will
      be confused, as, for example, when one of his commentators says: 'Writing asserts itself despite
      Freud's will to restrict it to a figural and secondary status. As Derrida predicts, "it is with a
      graphematics still to come, rather than with a linguistics dominated by an ancient phonologism
      that psychoanalysis sees itself as destined to collaborate".' Christopher Norris, *Deconstruction:
      Theory and Practice* (London: Methuen, 1982). This is not, however, what Derrida predicts, but
      what Freud predicts. As Derrida makes clear in the succeeding sentence: 'Freud recommends
      this *literally* in a text from 1913, and in this case we have nothing to add, interpret, alter.'
      Jacques Derrida, 'Freud and the Scene of Writing', *Writing and Difference, op. cit.*, p. 220.

41.   This is the format of Derrida's arguments that Heidegger's reading of Nietzsche betrays the
      seminally counter-metaphysical directions of the Nietzschean project. See Jacques Derrida,
      Spurs/Éperons, trans. Barbara Harlow (London: University of Chicago Press, 1979). Curiously,
      but according to the same principle, Derrida also argues that Emmanuel Levinas's reading of
      Heidegger falsifies the original Heideggerian intent even, and especially as it feigns to move
      beyond the Heideggerian deconstruction. See Jacques Derrida, 'Violence and Metaphysics:
      An Essay on the Thought of Emmanuel Levinas', *Writing and Difference, op. cit.*, pp. 79–153.
      Similarly, Derrida's paper, 'The Ends of Man' finds itself by no means in opposition to the
      thought of Hegel, Husserl and Heidegger, but is rather a carefully steered liberation of their
      thought from both the overly anthropological readings of both humanists like Sartre who
      sought therein justification for his own existential humanism, and anti-humanists whose naively
      humanist interpretations of their work made it all the easier to dismiss the phenomenological
      project. See Jacques Derrida, 'The Ends of Man', *Margins – of Philosophy*, pp. 109–36.

42.   As one example amongst so many, Derrida writes of Freud's notion of the unconscious trace:
      'Freud's notion of the trace must be radicalized and extracted from the metaphysics which still
      retains it ... Such a radicalization of the *thought of the trace* ... would be fruitful not only in the
      deconstruction of logocentrism, but in a kind of reflection exercised more positively at different
      levels of writing in general.' Jacques Derrida, 'Freud and the Scene of Writing', *op. cit.*, pp.
      229–30.

43.   In a classic, point-for-point statement of revisionist influence, Derrida explains to Henri Ronse:
      'What I have attempted would not have been possible without the opening of Heidegger's
      questions. And first ... would not have been possible without the attention to what Heidegger
      calls the difference between Being and beings, the ontico-ontological difference such as, in a
      way, it remains unthought by philosophy. But despite this debt to Heidegger, or rather because
      of it, I attempt to locate in Heidegger's text ... the signs of a belonging to metaphysics, or to
      what he calls onto-theology.' Jacques Derrida, *Positions, op. cit.*, pp. 9–10. Doubtless we should
      read Derrida as Derrida read Heidegger, for the 'signs of a belonging to metaphysics'. No
      activity, at base, could be more faithful.

44.   I adapt this formulation from the text: 'What does Rousseau say without saying, see without
      seeing?' Jacques Derrida, *Of Grammatology, op. cit.*, p. 215.

45.   On the dual meaning of *pharmakon* as both poison and remedy, see Jacques Derrida, 'Plato's
      Pharmacy', *op. cit.*

46. To reverse the priority of speech over writing is simply to reconfirm their opposition and to remain 'irreducibly rooted in that metaphysics'. See Jacques Derrida, *Of Grammatology, op. cit.*, p. 314.

47. J. Hillis Miller, 'Deconstructing the Deconstructers', *Diacritics*, vol. 5, no. 2 (1975), pp. 24–31: p. 31. Derrida, too, raises the possibility of a text that everywhere exceeds and incorporates any interpretation that might be made of it, but he does so in the context of his polemic with Lacan: 'what happens in the psychoanalytic deciphering of a text when the latter, the deciphered itself, already explicates itself? When it says more about itself than the deciphering (a debt acknowledged by Freud more than once)? And especially when the deciphered text inscribes in itself *additionally* the scene of the deciphering?' Jacques Derrida, 'Le facteur de la vérité', *The Post Card: From Socrates to Freud and Beyond*, trans. Alan Bass (Chicago and London: University of Chicago Press, 1987), pp. 411–96: p. 414.

48. Which again reflects the convergence – noted in the previous chapter – of transcendentally *auteurist* and transcendentally anti-*auteurist* theories in a similarly idealised notion of the text.

49. As Paul de Man does in an otherwise superb essay, 'The Rhetoric of Blindness' in *Blindness and Insight: Essays in the Rhetoric of Contemporary Criticism*, second edition, revised and enlarged, ed. Wlad Godzich (London: Methuen, 1983), pp. 102–41. Intention does not appear by name in the essay, but that is plainly its subject. De Man claims: 'Rousseau's text has no blind-spots ... There is no need to deconstruct Rousseau; the established tradition of Rousseau interpretation, however, stands in dire need of deconstruction ... instead of having Rousseau deconstruct his critics, we have Derrida deconstructing a pseudo-Rousseau by means of insights that could have been gained from the 'real' Rousseau'. (141–2) We do not need to be constrained by the terms of de Man's argument here. Nothing obliges us to decide between the absolute deconstruction of Rousseauian intention and its absolute recuperation; a thoroughgoing comparison of the *Essay* and the *Grammatology* would doubtless reveal a pattern of partial deconstruction and partial appropriation. In a sense, we are again presented with the same absolute divide on intention that we sketched at the opening of this section. One which is further confirmed when we consider that a few years later de Man ventured an interpretation of Rousseau – written very much under the influence of Derrida – which took up a rigidly anti-intentionalist standpoint. See Paul de Man, *Allegories of Reading: Figural Language in Rousseau, Nietzsche, Rilke and Proust* (New Haven: Yale University Press, 1979), especially pp. 278–301. De Man's changing positions on intention and the author will be discussed in the conclusion.

50. Gayatri Chakravorty Spivak, *The Post-Colonial Critic: Interviews, Strategies, Dialogues*, ed. Sarah Harasym (New York and London: Routledge, 1990), p. 136.

51. References will be made parenthetically in the text to Jacques Derrida, 'Plato's Pharmacy' in Jacques Derrida, *Dissemination*, trans. Barbara Johnson, (London: Athlone Press, 1981), pp. 61–171. An early version was published as 'La Pharmacie de Platon' in *Tel Quel*, nos. 32 and 33 (1968); the later French version is collected in Jacques Derrida, *La Dissémination* (Paris: Editions du Seuil, 1972), pp. 71–197.

52. All references to Plato will be made to Plato, *The Collected Dialogues of Plato, Including the Letters*, ed. Edith Hamilton and Huntington Cairns, Bollingen Series LXXI (Princeton: Princeton University Press, 1961). Page numbers and letters given parenthetically within the text refer to Stephanus's Renaissance edition. The translation of the *Phaedrus* in the Princeton edition is by R. Hackforth and may also be consulted in R. Hackforth, *Plato's Phaedrus, translated with an introduction and commentary* (Cambridge: Cambridge University Press, 1952). For an alternative to Hackforth's translation as well as suggestive commentary, the reader would do well to consult C.J. Rowe, *Plato: Phaedrus, with Translation and Commentary* (Warminster: Aris and Phillips, 1986). For those who wish to read in French, 'La Pharmacie de Platon' should be read alongside Léon Robin, *Platon, Oeuvres Complêtes IV. 3: Phèdre*, 2nd edition (Paris, 1950).

53. Derrida clearly wishes us to read 'Plato's Pharmacy' with *Of Grammatology* in terms of the latter's work on intention and supplementarity: 'I take the liberty of referring the reader, in order to give him a preliminary, indicative direction, to the 'Question of Method' proposed in *De la grammatologie* ... With a few precautions, one could say that the *pharmakon* plays a role analogous, in this reading of Plato, to that of *supplément* in the reading of Rousseau.' (96, n. 43)

54. These protocols are persuasive in their own terms and have certain points of specific relevance

to the section of the *Phaedrus* concerned with speech and writing. Indeed, Derrida might have consolidated his position here with an eye to the Socratic problem, to the play of 'voices' and signatures which take place in a scene of writing which purports to be a scene of dialogic voicing, to the potentially ironic contests between a Socrates who 'speaks' against writing in a text which is written by Plato. That he does not do so is a matter we shall address a little later.

55. In fact, the path of Derrida's reading does not disallow Platonic intention but sets it off against the supplementary play of the *pharmakon*. To this extent, 'Plato's Pharmacy' conforms to the pattern of early Derridean reading outlined in the section 'Doubling the Text' above.

56. Literature on the authenticity of the Platonic letters is extensive and finds recommendation here only to illustrate the difficulties facing Derrida in constructing a Platonic privileging of speech, let alone an 'epoch of logocentrism'. Nineteenth-century scholarship simply assumed the letters to be forgeries. Wilamowitz-Moellendorff upset this consensus by declaring the *Seventh* and *Eighth* Letters to be genuine; and early in this century, Hackforth's discriminations served to orient the debate in the English-speaking world as follows: 'we may hold five of the Platonic Epistles genuine, *viz.*, iii, iv, vii, viii, xiii ... we must reject five, *viz.*, i, ii, v, vi, xii ... the remaining three, ix, x and xi, must be left doubtful.' – R. Hackforth, *The Authorship of the Platonic Epistles* (Manchester: Manchester University Press, 1913), p. 188. For a relatively recent formulation of the case against the *Seventh Letter*'s authenticity, see Ludwig Edelstein, *Plato's Seventh Letter, Philosophia Antiqua* vol. XIV (Leiden: E.J. Brill, 1966), especially pp. 76–85 where the argument against authenticity is pursued in the specific context of the repudiation of writing. Quite the contrary argument can be found in Paul Friedländer, *Plato I: An Introduction*, 3 vols., trans. Hans Meyerhoff (London: Routledge & Kegan Paul, 1958), pp. 236–45.

57. The dividend of the mythological excursus is that 'Plato's Pharmacy' will then talk about the 'hierarchical opposition between son and father, subject and king, death and life, writing and speech, etc.'. (92) as though it were structured into the very warp and woof of the *Phaedrus*. One will also notice that when the life/death opposition appears in Derrida's text, it invariably does so adjacent to 'speech/writing'.

58. 'If *logos* has a father, if it is a *logos* only when attended by its father, this is because it is always a being (*on*) and even a certain species of being (the *Sophist*, 260a), more precisely a *living* being. *Logos* is a *zōon*. An animal that is born, grows, belongs to the *phusis*. Linguistics, logic, dialectics, and zoology are all in the same camp.' (79)

59. 'The inventor of writing in Greek legend was Prometheus; but he was unsuitable for Plato's purpose, since it would have been difficult to make anyone play against him the part that Thamus plays against Theuth. And in any case it was natural enough for Plato to go to Egypt for a tale of pre-history, just as in a later dialogue he goes to an Egyptian priest for his story of Atlantis.' – R. Hackforth, *Plato's Phaedrus, op. cit.*, p. 157, n. 2. Hackforth's judgement is corroborated by G.J. De Vries, *A Commentary on the Phaedrus of Plato, op. cit.* (Amsterdam: Adolf M. Hakkert, 1969), p. 248.

60. Exploratory rather than thetic, the section on the inferiority of the written word is also exceedingly brief in its attention to speech and writing – just under four pages (274b–277a) in Stephanus's Renaissance edition.

61. The comparison of writing to painting will be considered below. Socrates might seem to provide some encouragement to the life/death opposition by saying that written words speak to you as though they were alive. (*Phaedrus*, 275d) However, it is not the deceptive appearance of 'life' in paintings but their property of muteness before questioning which transfers to the graphic.

62. Cf. also *Apology* 29b–c; *Protagoras*, 239a; *Phaedrus*, 277d–e.

63. For a variety of perspectives on the Socratic problem see A.E. Taylor, *Socrates* (Edinburgh: Edinburgh University Press, 1933), pp. 131–74; Paul Friedländer, *Plato I, op. cit.*, pp. 126–36; Gregory Vlastos, *Socratic Studies* (Cambridge and New York: Cambridge University Press, 1994), pp. 1–37.

64. Derrida talks of 'the permanence of a Platonic schema that assigns the origin and power of speech, precisely of *logos*, to the paternal position.' (76)

65. G.R.F. Ferrari almost goes so far as to endorse this reversal of the conventional association of King Thamus with the Platonic viewpoint: 'If anything, the philosopher is a combination of Thoth, the inventor, and Ammon, the judge of arts ... for by attempting to judge the good life,

the philosopher brings it into being.' – G.R.F. Ferrari, *Listening to the Cicadas: A Study of Plato's 'Phaedrus'* (Cambridge: Cambridge University Press, 1987), p. 281, n. 25.

66. This position is articulated in Ronna Burger, *Plato's Phaedrus: A Defence of a Philosophic Art of Writing* (Alabama: University of Alabama Press, 1980). Neoplatonic thinkers also proposed that the *Phaedrus* ultimately defends the Platonic writing: 'A Neoplatonic treatise refers to the aporetic dilemma presented by the fact that while the master in the *Phaedrus* spoke so disparagingly about writing, he still considered his own works as worthy of being written down. As a solution, it is proposed that he also tried to follow the deity in this respect. Just as the deity created both the invisible and what is visible to our senses, so he, too, wrote down many things and transmitted others unwritten.' – Paul Friedländer, *Plato I, op. cit.*, p. 124.

67. 'The authority of truth, of dialectics, of seriousness, of presence, will not be gainsaid at the close of this admirable movement, when Plato, after having in a sense reappropriated writing, pushes his irony – and his seriousness – to the point of rehabilitating a certain form of play.' (154) This admirable movement, though, is countenanced by 'Plato's Pharmacy' only insofar as it avoids the Socratic recapitulation (*Phaedrus*, 278b–d).

68. Derrida is aware that the issue is also one of social ordering, of morality and the city. Indeed, near the start he draws attention to precisely what his reading will bypass in favour of a reflection on the metaphysical dynamics of the speech/writing issue: 'the question of writing opens as a question of *morality*. It is truly morality that is at stake, both in the sense of the opposition between good and evil, or good and bad, and in the sense of mores, public morals and social conventions. It is a question of knowing what is done and what is not done. This moral disquiet is in no way to be distinguished from questions of truth, memory and dialectics. This latter question, which will quickly be engaged as *the* question of writing, is closely associated with the morality theme, and indeed develops it by affinity of essence and not by superimposition.' (74) Henceforth, however, the metaphysical theme will everywhere subordinate the ethical concerns of the *Phaedrus*.

69. Having questioned the epic, lyric and dramatic poets as to the meaning of their work, Socrates lamented: 'It is hardly an exaggeration to say that any of the bystanders could have explained those poems better than their actual authors … I decided that it was not wisdom that enabled them to write their poetry, but a kind of instinct or inspiration, such as you find in seers and prophets who deliver all their sublime messages without knowing in the least what they mean. It seemed clear to me that the poets were in much the same case, and I also observed that the very fact that they were poets made them think that they had a perfect understanding of all other subjects, of which they were totally ignorant.' (*Apology* 22b–c) This anxiety is comparable to the *Phaedrus*'s concerns that writing will allow men of opinion (*doxa*) to be taken as authorities (275a–b). What Socrates encounters in the case of a poetic text is a structure of words which is quite unresponsive in spite of its having been spoken, one which cannot explain itself and if questioned keeps repeating the same answer over and over again, much as written words 'go on telling you just the same thing forever'. (*Phaedrus*, 275d)

70. On Socrates as critic of poetry, see Nickolas Pappas, 'Socrates' Charitable Treatment of Poetry', *Philosophy and Literature*, vol. 13, no. 2 (1989), pp. 248–61.

71. 'One of the main effects of this transitional section is to widen the area of discussion: not just speech-writing as defined by Lysias' activity, but speaking and writing of all kinds.' – C.J. Rowe, *Plato: Phaedrus, with Translation and Commentary, op. cit.*, p. 192. Rowe also adds: 'If the ensuing discussion begins with Lysias, it ends by being wholly general' (ibid., p. 193).

72. Ferrari also confirms this general observation, noting that 'speech' is often 'shorthand for "speaking and writing"; for [Socrates] shifts between labels without making a point of the difference.' – G.R.F. Ferrari, *Listening to the Cicadas, op. cit.*, p. 277, n. 1.

73. C.J. Rowe comments on 259e1–274b5: 'Throughout this section, speaking and writing are taken together; "rhetoric" is to be understood as including both … In Greek as in English, what is written, as well as what is actually spoken, can be described as "said" (*legomenon*): so, e.g., in 259e4–5 "things that are going to be said" should be read as "things that are going to be written and/or said".' – C.J. Rowe, *Plato: Phaedrus, with Translation and Commentary, op. cit.*, pp. 194–5. Cf. also p. 208; p. 211; p. 214.

74. Derrida passes over this section without citation. He concedes that Socrates is not overtly

hostile to writing at this moment, but neglects to mention that speech and writing are considered under the same heading: 'Socrates still has a neutral attitude: writing is not in itself a shameful, indecent, infamous (*aiskhron*) activity. One is dishonoured only if one writes in a dishonourable manner. But what does it mean to write in a dishonourable manner?' (68) Rather than wait around to answer its own question, 'Plato's Pharmacy' then proceeds to a discussion of the myth of the cicadas.

75. In this closing section (156–71), Derrida quotes at considerable length from the *Laws*, *Republic*, *Timaeus*, and *Sophist* but does not see fit to return to the *Phaedrus*, least of to give notice of the qualified rehabilitation of writing at 278b–d.

76. 'The best sense of play is play that is supervised and contained within the safeguards of ethics and politics. This is play comprehended under the innocent, innocuous category of "fun". Amusement: however far off it may be, the common translation of *paidia* by *pastime* ... no doubt only helps consolidate the Platonic repression of play.' (156) Robin renders '*divertisse-ment*'; in Hackforth *paidia* is here given as 'pastime'; Rowe translates as 'amusement'; Hamilton translates the remark as 'the literary discussion with which we have been amusing ourselves.' See Léon Robin, *Platon, Oeuvres Complètes IV. 3: Phèdre, op. cit.*; C.J. Rowe, *Plato: Phaedrus, with Translation and Commentary, op. cit.*; Plato, *Phaedrus and Seventh and Eighth Letters*, trans. Walter Hamilton (Harmondsworth: Penguin, 1973).

77. Jacques Derrida, *Margins – of Philosophy*, trans. Alan Bass (Brighton: Harvester, 1982), p. 316.

78. In the *Euthyphro* Socrates laments the fact that his *logoi* are mobile rather than static: 'the rarest thing about my talent is that I am an unwilling artist, since I would rather see our arguments stand fast and hold their ground than have the art of Daedalus plus all the wealth of Tantalus to boot.' (*Euthyphro*, 11d–e)

79. One might even suspect that a forcefield has build up around these words. Not only Derrida but critics such as Ferrari and Burger – who present their theses in the form of running commentaries – do not register the immense significance of this passage. Despite arguing for the strongest ironic reading – one which sees Plato as consciously and deliberately defending his practice of philosophical writing – Burger applies these words self-reflexively and thus does not register their import for the practice of writing in general (Ronna Burger, *Plato's Phaedrus*, pp.105–6). Even Ferrari says little more of it beyond (rightly) noting: 'the dangers of the written word are defused. One who is not reliant on the written word for understanding, who has no false expectations of it, and who is able to supplement its inadequacies in speech may write about what matters to him ... and yet merit the title "philosopher" ' – G.R.F. Ferrari, *Listening to the Cicadas, op. cit.*, pp. 205–6.

80. Aristotle, *De Sophisticis Elenchis*, trans. W.A. Pickard-Cambridge in W.D. Ross, ed., *The Works of Aristotle*, vol. 1 (Oxford: Clarendon, 1928), 171b35–172a2; 172a23–33.

81. See Martin Elsky, *Authorising Words: Speech, Writing, and Print in the English Renaissance* (Ithaca and London: Cornell University Press, 1989), pp. 8–34. Elsky's landmark study exhibits deep scepticism toward Derrida's deconstruction of logocentrism: 'the deconstructive certification that Renaissance language theory is incoherent and its attendant claim that speech is reducible to writing and writing to speech glosses over phenomena of major importance in the history of language and literature ... The deconstructive attempt to bury these distinctions beneath assertions of incoherence would render invisible concepts of great historical – and current – interest.' (ibid., p. 3)

82. Ibid., p. 33. Elsky also highlights those moments in the Renaissance when writing is elevated above speech, as in the (heterogeneous) instances of Francis Bacon and George Herbert (ibid., pp. 110–208).

83. William of Ockham, *Ockham's Theory of Terms: Part I of the Summa Logicae*, trans. Michael J. Loux (Notre Dame: University of Notre Dame Press, 1974), p. 9.

84. Derrida even cites the relevant lines of the discredited *Second Letter*, although he does so only under the shelter of a closing fantasy (170–1) which (presumably) does not wish to be judged on scholarly terms. He dramatises the citation thus: 'I hope this one won't get lost. Quick, a duplicate ... graphite ... carbon ... reread this letter ... burn it.' (171)

85. On one of the occasions when 'Plato's Pharmacy' cites the *Laws*, an effect of multiple transla-tion/citation is produced. On page 121 of the essay, the following passage from the *Laws* is

cited from the Princeton edition in A.E. Taylor's translation: 'consider all other discourse, poesy with its eulogies and its satires, or utterances in prose, whether in literature or in the common converse of daily life, with their contentious disagreements and their too often unmeaning admissions. The one certain touchstone of all is the writings of the legislator (*ta tou nomothetou grammata*). *The good judge will possess those writings within his own soul (ha dei ketēmenon en hautōi) as antidotes (alexipharmaka) against other discourse*, and thus he will be the state's preserver as well as his own.' (*Laws*, 957d) The emphases are Derrida/Johnson's but they also mark a departure from Taylor's translation. Were the cited passage to remain in Taylor's rendering, then the emphasised text would read: 'The good judge will possess the text within his own breast as an antidote against other discourse ' (*Laws*, 957d4–5). Once again, the pharmaceutical reading wills 'writing' in Plato to denote the metaphysical notion of 'writing in the soul'.

86. Derek Attridge, 'Introduction' in Jacques Derrida, *Acts of Literature*, ed. Derek Attridge (New York and London: Routledge, 1992), pp. 1–29: p. 15.

87. Christopher Norris, *Reclaiming Truth: Contribution to a Critique of Cultural Relativism* (London: Lawrence & Wishart, 1996), p. 235. It must be said, however, that Norris would see the value of Derrida's intervention in terms of philosophic rigour rather than poetic performativity.

88. Jacques Derrida, 'This Strange Institution Called Literature' in Jacques Derrida, *Acts of Literature*, *op. cit.*, pp. 33–75: p. 68.

89. Derrida talks on numerous occasions of 'the affinity between writing and *mythos* created by their common opposition to *logos*' (145, n.69), but he does so in order to see writing rather than myth as the primary focus of Plato's anxieties. Myth can be a form of writing, of course, but it as *muthos* rather than as writing that it encounters Plato's condemnation.

90. On Plato's critique of the tendency of oral poetry to propagate unexamined dogmas see Eric A. Havelock, *Preface to Plato* (Cambridge, MA and London: Belknap Press of Harvard University Press, 1963).

91. Jacques Derrida, *Points ... : Interviews, 1974–1994*, ed. Elisabeth Weber, trans. Peggy Kamuf and Others (Stanford: Stanford University Press, 1995), p. 198. The above emphasis is mine.

92. Harold Bloom, *Kabbalah and Criticism* (New York: Seabury Press, 1985), p. 104.

93. Jacques Derrida, *Margins of Philosophy*, *op. cit.*, p. 14.

94. On the relationship between the Levinasian and Derridean notions of the trace, see Robert Bernasconi, 'The Trace of Levinas in Derrida' in David Wood and Robert Bernasconi, eds, *Derrida and Différance* (Warwick: Parousia Press, 1985), pp. 122–39.

95. Derrida uses this phrase in describing the 'subtle nuances' by which *différance* differs from Hegelian difference. See Jacques Derrida, *Positions*, *op. cit.*, p. 44.

96. After Derrida's opening remarks, the essay 'Différance' proceeds as a sequence of short readings of Saussure, Hegel, Nietzsche, Freud and Heidegger, with an important glance at Levinas. The essay itself, amongst other things, serves as the clearest testament of Derrida's influences, or borrowings. See Jacques Derrida, 'Différance', *op. cit.*

97. Jacques Derrida, *Writing and Difference*, *op. cit.*, p. xiii.

98. Jacques Derrida, *Positions*, p. 6.

99. Jacques Derrida, *Writing and Difference*, *op. cit.*, p. 32.

100. See Jacques Derrida, *Dissemination*, *op. cit.*, pp. 169–71 for the theatrical finale of 'Plato's Pharmacy'. For the intensely curious repertoire of refractions, and intertextual displacements whereby Derrida 'begins to speak' of the mother, and the imminence of her demise – in the form of a vast 'footnote' running under a commentary on his work – see 'Circumfession' in *Jacques Derrida*, trans. Geoffrey Bennington (Chicago: University of Chicago Press, 1993). Here, composing from Santa Monica in the US, Derrida is unremittingly in dialogue with the *Confessions*, particularly as the text speaks of the life and passing of Augustine's mother, Monica – even to the extent of attaching significance in the coincidence between the ancient maternal name and that of the contemporary scene of writing.

101. On the nomocentricity of Derrida's later work, see Gregory L. Ulmer, *Applied Grammatology: Post(e)-pedagogy from Jacques Derrida to Joseph Beuys* (Baltimore: Johns Hopkins University Press, 1985), pp. 125–41.

102. Jacques Derrida, *Specters of Marx*, trans. Peggy Kamuf (New York and London: Routledge, 1994), p. xv.

103. See Jacques Derrida, *Signéponge/Signsponge*, trans. Richard Rand (New York: Columbia University Press, 1984); and *Dissemination*, *op. cit.*, pp. 287–366.

104. See Jacques Derrida, 'Otobiographies: Nietzsche and the Politics of the Proper Name' in Jacques Derrida, *The Ear of the Other: Otobiography, Transference, Translation: Texts and Discussions with Jacques Derrida* trans. Peggy Kamuf and Avital Ronell (New York: Schocken Books, 1986) pp. 1–38. See also Jacques Derrida, *The Post Card*, *op. cit.*, pp. 257–409, for Derrida's interpretation of Freud. One of the main concerns in this latter work is to address the following question: 'how can an autobiographical writing, in the abyss of an unterminated self-analysis, give to a worldwide institution *its* birth?' Jacques Derrida, *The Post Card*, *op. cit.*, p. 305. On the significance of Freud's proper name see 'Freud's Legacy', ibid., pp. 292–37. Elucidating his nomocentric interpretation, Derrida later said: 'In writing *Beyond the Pleasure Principle*, Freud is writing a textual testament not only as regards his own name and his own family, but as regards the analytic movement which he also constructed in a certain fashion, that is, as a great inheritance, a great institution bearing his name. The history of the analytic movement has to deal with that. It is an institution that can't get along without Freud's name, a practical and theoretical science which must for once come to terms and explain itself with its founder's name. Mathematics, physics, et cetera, might on occasion celebrate the name of a great physicist or a great mathematician, but the proper name is not a structural part of the corpus of the science or the scientific institution. Psychoanalysis, on the other hand, has been inherited from Freud and accounts for itself with the structure of this inheritance. I think that one must finally decipher his text by means of these questions: the questions of the inheritance, of the proper name, of the *fort/da* infinitely exceeding the limits of the text.' Jacques Derrida, *The Ear of the Other*, *op. cit.*, p. 71. Derrida's rereading of Freud will be discussed in the conclusion.

105. See Jacques Derrida, *The Ear of the Other*, *op. cit.*, especially pp. 4–19.

106. Jacques Derrida, *The Ear of the Other*, *op. cit.*, p. 30.

107. Indeed, the worst dreams of Platonism are recurring in this context of the ethically overdetermined scene of Nietzsche's reception history. We witness here writing's inability to sow its 'seeds in suitable soil', (*Phaedrus*, 276b) its failure to 'address the right people, and not address the wrong', (275e) its proclivity for being 'ill-treated and unfairly abused' (275e) its availability to 'those who have no business with it'. (275e)

108. Jacques Derrida, *The Post Card*, *op. cit.*, back cover.

109. Christopher Norris, for instance, writes: 'it is pointless to ask who is *speaking* in any given part of this text, whether Hegel, Genet, Derrida *ipse* or some other ghostly intertextual 'presence'. For there is no last word, no metalanguage, or voice of authorial control that would ultimately serve to adjudicate the matter.' Christopher Norris, *Derrida*, *op. cit.*, p. 64.

110. Jacques Derrida, in an interview with Irme Salusinszky, in Irme Salusinszky, ed., *Criticism in Society* (London: Methuen, 1987), pp. 7–24: pp. 22–3.

111. Michel Foucault, 'Postscript: an Interview with Michel Foucault by Charles Raus', in Michel Foucault, *Death and the Labyrinth: The World of Raymond Roussel*, trans. Charles Raus (London: Athlone Press, 1987), p. 186.

112. Jacques Derrida, *The Post Card*, *op. cit.*, p. 194.

113. Jacques Derrida, *Mémoires: For Paul de Man*, trans. Cecile Lindsay, Jonathan Culler and Eduardo Cadava (New York: Columbia University Press, 1986), p. 3.

CONCLUSION: CRITIC AND AUTHOR

1. Sigmund Freud, *Art and Literature*, vol. 14 of the Pelican Freud Library, ed. Albert Dickson (Harmondsworth: Penguin Books, 1985), p. 60.

2. See Plato, *The Republic*, trans. H.P. D. Lee (Harmondsworth: Penguin, 1955), pp. 370–86. A similar contradiction is also encountered in the Platonic repudiation of the poets and the discourses of the death of the author since, just as Plato was himself obliged to use poetic devices in the elaboration of a pure philosophy, so too have theorists fallen back into subjective categories even and especially as they pronounce subjectivity dead.

3. For de Man's reading of Rousseau, see Paul de Man, *Allegories of Reading: Figural Language in Rousseau, Nietzsche, Rilke and Proust* (New Haven: Yale University Press, 1979), pp. 133–301.

4. As Paul de Man argues in his work during the 1960s. See Paul de Man, *Blindness and Insight*: *Essays in the Rhetoric of Contemporary Criticism*, second edition, revised and enlarged, ed. Wlad Godzich (London: Methuen, 1983), *passim*.

5. Roland Barthes, *Criticism and Truth*, trans. K.P. Keuneman (London: Athlone Press, 1987), p. 77.

6. Roland Barthes, *S/Z*, trans. Richard Miller (London: Jonathan Cape, 1970), p. 140.

7. Roland Barthes, *Image-Music-Text*, trans. and ed. Stephen Heath (London: Fontana, 1977), p. 142.

8. See Harold Bloom, *The Anxiety of Influence: A Theory of Poetry* (New York and London: Oxford University Press, 1973); *Kabbalah and Criticism* (New York: Seabury Press, 1975); *A Map of Misreading* (New York and London: Oxford University Press, 1975); *Poetry and Repression: Revisionism from Blake to Stevens* (New Haven: Yale University Press, 1976). Perhaps unironically, Bloom's theory has thus far been without influence.

9. Wilde's dialogic essay 'The Critic as Artist' remains the most elegant statement of the creativity of critical prose, as well as one of its finest examples. See Oscar Wilde, 'The Critic as Artist', *Complete Works of Oscar Wilde* (London and Glasgow: Collins, 1948), pp. 1009–59.

10. This applies not only to introductory works, but to more advanced criticisms also. See, for example, Annette Lavers, *Roland Barthes: Structuralism and After* (London: Methuen, 1982); Alan Sheridan, *Michel Foucault: The Will to Truth* (London: Tavistock, 1980); Irene E. Harvey, *Derrida and the Economy of Différance* (Bloomington: Indiana University Press, 1986).

11. See Geoffrey Hartman, *Criticism in the Wilderness: The Study of Literature Today* (New Haven: Yale University Press, 1980), pp. 189–213.

12. Ibid., p. 204.

13. Ibid., p. 206.

14. See Jacques Derrida, 'Edmund Jabès and the Question of the Book' in *Writing and Difference*, trans. Alan Bass (London: Routledge and Kegan Paul, 1981), pp. 64–78. Here Derrida describes his labour as that of 'adding pitiful graffiti to an immense poem'. (76)

15. Michel Foucault, *Death and the Labyrinth: The World of Raymond Roussel*, trans. Charles Raus (London: Athlone Press, 1987).

16. In what follows we shall be concerned mainly with the effect of the death of the author upon American criticism, and in its deconstructionist modes in particular. However, much of what has occurred in America has been paralleled by the English critical scene, in that the anti-autho-rialism of Barthes, Foucault and Derrida has been utilised to facilitate a return to methods of practical criticism which bypass the issue of authorial subjectivity. The phrase 'Anglo-American tradition' is not used here to designate a monolithic body of criticism, nor even a strictly geographic situation, but as a provisional shorthand for a particular reception-history.

17. Georges Poulet, 'Criticism and the Experience of Interiority' in Richard Macksey and Eugenio Donato, eds, *The Structuralist Controversy: The Languages of Criticism and the Sciences of Man* (Baltimore: Johns Hopkins University Press, 1972), pp. 56–72: p. 72.

18. Georges Poulet, *The Interior Distance*, trans. Elliott Coleman (Ann Arbor, MI: University of Michigan Press, 1964), p. viii.

19. Paul de Man, *Blindness and Insight*, *op. cit.*, p. 27.

20. Ibid., p. 25.

21. Ibid., p. 50.

22. See 'Impersonality in the Criticism of Maurice Blanchot', ibid., pp. 60–78.

23. J. Hillis Miller, *The Disappearance of God* (Cambridge, MA: Harvard University Press, 1963), p. vii.

24. J. Hillis Miller, 'The Geneva School', *Modern French Criticism: From Proust and Valéry to Structuralism*, ed. John K. Simon (Chicago: University of Chicago Press, 1972), pp. 277–310: p. 282.

25. J. Hillis Miller, 'The Literary Criticism of Georges Poulet', *Modern Language Notes* 78 (1963), pp. 471–88: pp. 480–1.

26. J. Hillis Miller, *Charles Dickens: The World of his Novels*, *op. cit.*, p. ix.

27. See J. Hillis Miller, 'The Geneva School', *op. cit.*

28. See Richard Macksey and Eugenio Donato, eds, *The Structuralist Controversy*, *op. cit.*, for the proceedings of this symposium.

29. See Jacques Derrida, 'Structure, Sign, and Play in the Discourse of the Human Sciences' in *The*

Structuralist Controversy, op. cit., pp. 247–65. Also collected in Jacques Derrida, *Writing and Difference*, trans. Alan Bass (London: Routledge & Kegan Paul, 1981), pp. 278–93.

30. See Paul de Man, 'The Literary Self as Origin: The Work of Georges Poulet', *Blindness and Insight, op. cit.*, pp. 79–101.

31. See Paul de Man, 'The Rhetoric of Blindness', ibid., pp. 102–41.

32. See Paul de Man, *Allegories of Reading, op. cit.*, pp. 133–301.

33. J. Hillis Miller, 'Ariachne's Broken Woof', *Georgia Review*, 31 (1977), pp. 44–60: p. 51.

34. Jacques Derrida, 'Discussion' in *The Structuralist Controversy, op. cit.*, pp. 265–72: p. 271.

35. Jacques Derrida, 'Structure, Sign and Play', ibid., p. 264.

36. Jacques Derrida, 'Freud and the Scene of Writing', *Writing and Difference, op. cit.*, pp. 196–231.

37. The phrase 'region of historicity' is the one which Derrida uses to describe the situation of the participants and colloquists at the Johns Hopkins conference. See 'Structure, Sign and Play', *The Structuralist Controversy, op. cit.*, p. 265. However, as has become apparent, the historicity of the French and Anglo-American traditions are by no means as convergent as Derrida presumes here.

38. Christopher Norris, *The Contest of Faculties: Philosophy and Theory After Deconstruction* (London: Methuen, 1985), p. 223.

39. In very different ways, naturally, but it is nonetheless plausible to see the freeplaying textualism of Hartman, and the austere, consequent textualism of de Man as divergent developments from a common basis in the New textual ethic of disengaging criticism from any direct social, historical and political issues in pursuit of the inherent ambiguities, and rhetorical features of literature.

40. I do not refer here to the work of H.P. Grice or that of discourse analysts such as Deirdre Wilson and Dan Sperber, whose painstaking researches have yet to be absorbed within critical theory.

41. 'What a text means and what its author intends it to mean are identical and … their identity robs intention of any theoretical interest.'; 'The idea of intention is useless as a guide to practice'; 'Since it provides no help in choosing among critical procedures, the idea of intention is methodologically useless.' Steven Knapp and Walter Benn Michaels, in W.J.T. Mitchell, ed., *Against Theory: Literary Studies and the New Pragmatism* (Chicago: University of Chicago Press, 1985), pp. 19, 101, 104.

42. Friedrich Nietzsche, *Ecce Homo: How One Becomes What One Is*, trans. R.J. Hollingdale (Harmondsworth: Penguin Books, 1979), p. 128.

43. 'The name Voltaire on a writing by me – that really was progress – *towards myself*' Friedrich Nietzsche, *Ecce Homo: How One Becomes What One Is, op. cit.*, p. 89. On the preceding page Nietzsche also claims that his writings on Schopenhauer are most fundamentally autobiographical, that the name 'Schopenhauer' had functioned as another mask of Nietzsche.

44. Ibid., p. 134. For interesting deconstructive readings of the inscription of the Nietzschean subject in *Ecce Homo*, see Jacques Derrida, *The Ear of the Other: Otobiography, Transference, Translation: Texts and Discussions with Jacques Derrida* [1984], trans. Peggy Kamuf and Avital Ronell (New York: Schoken Books, 1986), pp. 1–38; and Michael Ryan, 'The Act', *Glyph* II (1978), pp. 64–87.

45. See Jacques Derrida, *The Post Card: From Socrates to Freud and Beyond*, trans. Alan Bass (Chicago and London: University of Chicago Press, 1987), pp. 257–409.

46. See Sigmund Freud, *Beyond the Pleasure Principle* in *On Metapsychology: the Theory of Psychoanalysis*, vol. 11 of the Pelican Freud Library, ed. Angela Richards (Harmondsworth: Penguin Books, 1984), pp. 275–337. See pp. 283–7 for the recounting of the *fort/da* episode. In following Derrida's reading it is also very useful to consult Sigmund Freud, *An Autobiographical Study* in vol. XX of *The Standard Edition of the Complete Psychological Works of Sigmund Freud*, ed. James Strachey (London: Hogarth Press, 1959), pp. 4–74.

47. Jacques Derrida, *The Post Card, op. cit.*, p. 311.

48. Ibid., pp. 320–1.

49. Ibid., p. 322.

50. Naturally the question of gender is of the utmost importance here, and raises issues vastly beyond the scope of this particular work. As Barbara Johnson has observed, the very existence of two sexes is sufficient of itself to break up the idea of a unitary transcendental subjectivity.

See Barbara Johnson, *The Critical Difference* (Baltimore: Johns Hopkins University Press, 1980). The American theoretician, Nancy Miller, sees in women's historical exclusion from metaphysical determinations of subjectivity the possibility of a feminine rematerialisation of the subject: 'Because women have not had the same historical relation of identity to origin, institution, production that men have had they have not … felt burdened by too much Self, Ego, Cogito, etc. Because the female subject has juridically been excluded from the polis, hence decentred, 'disoriginated', deinstitutionalised, etc., her relation to integrity and textuality, desire and authority, displays structurally important differences from that universal position.' Nancy K. Miller, *Subject to Change: Reading Feminist Writing* (Ithaca: Cornell University Press, 1988). Though the relation of feminism to the issues of author and gen(d)eric subjectivity have been scarcely touched upon here, the bibliography cites many texts influential in formulating and debating the concepts of the deaths of woman-as-author and Woman-as-woman, the ideas of *écriture féminine*, the deconstruction of the binarism male-female and so on. In general, what is said in this work of the death of the author applies in general to feminist thanatography, but would need to be reformulated in accordance with ethico-political and ontological questions of inexhaustible complexity.

EPILOGUE

1. Régis Debray, 'The Book as Symbolic Object' in Geoffrey Nunberg, ed., *The Future of the Book* (Berkeley: University of California Press, 1996), pp. 139–51: pp. 145–6.
2. George P. Landow, *Hypertext: The Convergence of Contemporary Crticial Theory and Technology* (Baltimore: Johns Hopkins University Press, 1992). While more recent contributions have been made to this convergence theory, Landow's work continues to orient the debate. A more sceptical (and splendid) account of the relations between technology and authorship can be found in James Boyle, *Shamans, Software, and Spleens: Law and the Construction of the Information Society* (Harvard: Harvard University Press, 1997).
3. R. Lanham, *The Electronic Word: Democracy, Technology and the Arts* (Chicago: University of Chicago Press, 1994), p. 23.
4. Michel Foucault, *The Order of Things: An Archaeology of the Human Sciences*, trans. Alan Sheridan (London: Tavistock, 1970), p. xxiv. It should also be noted that digital arguments tend to draw upon the most vulgar and vulgarised tenets of 'poststructuralism'.
5. This rhetoric is finely critiqued in Paul Duguid, 'Material Matters: The Past and Futurology of the Book' in Geoffrey Nunberg, ed., *The Future of the Book*, *op. cit.*, pp. 63–101.
6. See Marshall McLuhan, *The Gutenberg Galaxy: The Making of Typographic Man* (Toronto: University of Toronto Press, 1962); Eric A. Havelock, *Preface to Plato* (Cambridge, MA: Belknap Press of Harvard University Press, 1963); Walter J. Ong, *Orality and Literacy: The Technologizing of the Word* (London: Methuen, 1982).
7. Raffaele Simone, 'The Body of the Text' in Geoffrey Nunberg, ed., *The Future of the Book*, *op. cit.*, pp. 239–51: p. 241; p. 251. Nicole Yankelovich, Norman Meyrowitz, and Andries van Dam, 'Reading and Writing the Electronic Book', *IEEE* Computer 18 (October 1985), pp. 15–30: p. 21.
8. Michael Heim, *Electronic Language: A Philosophical Study of Word Processing* (New Haven: Yale University Press, 1987), p. 215.
9. See Jorge Luis Borges, 'Pierre Menard: Author of the *Quixote*' in Borges, *Labyrinths*, edited by Donald A. Yates and James E. Irby (Harmondsworth: Penguin, 1970), pp. 62–71.
10. See Roman Ingarden, *The Literary Work of Art*, trans. George G. Grabowicz (Evanston: Northwestern University Press, 1973).
11. See Sadie Plant, *Zeros and Ones: Digital Women and the New Technoculture* (London: Fourth Estate, 1997), p. 194. Plant then bids us look at the *Mona Lisa* with eyes refocused by the technological revolution: 'The *Mona Lisa*'s appeal is precisely the fact that the image does more than passively hang on the gallery wall. As her spectators always say, Mona Lisa looks at them as much as, if not more than, they can look at her. To the extent that it works so well, Leonardo's picture is a piece of careful software engineering. An interactive machine has been camouflaged as a work of Western art' (ibid.).

12. Raffaele Simone, 'The Body of the Text' in Geoffrey Nunberg, ed., *The Future of the Book*, *op. cit.*, p. 240.

13. See Jack Stillinger, *Multiple Authorship and the Myth of Solitary Genius* (New York and Oxford: Oxford University Press, 1991). Stillinger's interesting book, however, must succumb to the myth of solitary genius in order to reject it.

14. George P. Landow, *Hypertext*, *op. cit.*, p. 96.

15. Luca Toshi, 'Hypertext and Authorship' in Geoffrey Nunberg, ed., *The Future of the Book*, *op. cit.*, pp. 169–207: p. 202.

16. Georges Poulet, 'Criticism and the Experience of Interiority' in Richard Macksey and Eugenio Donato, eds, *The Structuralist Controversy: The Languages of Criticism and the Sciences of Man* (Baltimore: Johns Hopkins University Press, 1972), pp. 56–72: p. 56.

17. Geoffrey Nunberg in Geoffrey Nunberg, ed. *The Future of the Book*, *op. cit.*, p. 18. Nunberg is here summarising Raffaele Simone's argument (ibid., pp. 239–51).

18. St Augustine, *Confessions*, trans. Henry Chadwick (Oxford: Oxford University Press, 1991), pp. 92–3.

19. See J. Hillis Miller, 'The Ethics of Hypertext', *Diacritics*, vol. 25, no. 3 (Fall 1995), pp. 27–39: p. 35; Georges Poulet, *Les Métamorphoses du Cercle* (Paris: Plon, 1961).

20. George P. Landow, *Hypertext*, *op. cit.*, p. 178.

21. Sadie Plant, *Zeros and Ones*, *op. cit.*, pp. 189–90. Of the connection between weaving and computing, she declares: 'On the computer monitor, any change to the image is also a change to the program; any change to the programming brings another image to the screen. There is a continuity of product and process at work in the textiles produced on the loom. The program, the image, the process, and the product: these are all the softwares of the loom. Digital fabrications can be endlessly copied without fading into inferiority; patterns can be pleated and repeat, replicated folds across a screen. Like all textiles, the new softwares have no essence, no authenticity' (ibid., p. 189). The metaphor (industrial art = technological freedom) no more promises feminist empowerment than the dependence of cyberspace on nautical images guarantees the enfranchisment of Third World fishermen.

22. Fredric Jameson, *The Political Unconscious: Narrative as a Socially Symbolic Act* (Ithaca: Cornell University Press, 1981), p. 20.

23. Gayatri Chakravorty Spivak, *The Post-Colonial Critic: Interviews, Strategies, Dialogues*, ed. Sarah Harasym (New York and London: Routledge, 1990), p. 153.

24. On the false opposition between 'a view from nowhere' and 'a view from everywhere', see Patricia Waugh, 'Feminism and Postmodernism' in Stevi Jackson and Jackie Jones, eds, *Contemporary Feminist Theories* (Edinburgh: Edinburgh University Press, 1998), pp. 177–93. In its movement from subjective to linguistic disembodiment, digital technology follows the trajectory of a vulgar poststructuralism (see also note 4 above). One might indeed wonder whether the academic version of hypertextual discourse is less the enthusiasm of digital technologists than the last stand of a 'weak' poststructuralism which sees its own (idealist) preoccupations mirrored in current material technology.

25. Seyla Benhabib, *Situating the Self: Gender, Community and Postmodernism in Contemporary Ethics* (Cambridge: Polity Press, 1992), p. 214.

26. Jerome J. McGann, *The Beauty of Inflections: Literary Investigations in Historical Method and Theory* (Oxford: Clarendon Press, 1988), p. 131.

27. See Stephen Greenblatt, *Shakespearean Negotiations: The Circulation of Social Energy in Renaissance England* (Oxford: Clarendon Press, 1988), p. 20. In less delicate hands, this sidestepping of authorial categories can seem like a reaction formation: 'The hollowness of the self that so enraged and demoralised ... now inspires respect and study, not recrimination and calls for revolution. N[ew] H[istoricism] intiates a truly radical change. It accepts the inevitability of emptiness.' – H. Aram Veeser 'The New Historicism' in H. Aram Veeser, ed., *The New Historicism Reader* (New York and London: Routledge, 1994), pp. 1–32: p. 19.

28. Jerome J. McGann, *The Beauty of Inflections*, *op. cit.*, p. 125.

29. Ibid., p. 118.

30. Stephen Greenblatt, 'Resonance and Wonder', in Peter Collier and Helga Geyer-Ryan, eds, *Literary Theory Today* (Cambridge: Polity Press, 1990), pp. 74–9: p. 74.

31. On modernity's tendency to depict authorship in terms of a false opposition between transcendence and impersonality, see Seán Burke, 'Reconstructing the Author' in Seán Burke, ed., *Authorship: From Plato to the Postmodern: A Reader* (Edinburgh: Edinburgh University Press, 1995), pp. xv–xxx.

32. Cf. Immanuel Kant, *A Critique of Pure Reason*, trans. Norman Kemp Smith (London: Macmillan, 1933). Marjorie Greene has some excellent pages – to which the above is indebted – on the hollowness of the transcendental subject postion. See Marjorie Greene, *The Knower and the Known* (London: Faber & Faber, 1966), pp. 120–56.

33. Martin Heidegger, *Kant and the Problem of Metaphysics*, trans. J.S. Churchill (Bloomington: Indiana University Press, 1962).

34. Harold Bloom, *The Breaking of the Vessels* (Chicago: University of Chicago Press, 1982), p. 82.

35. Michel de Montaigne, *Essays I:20, trans. J.M. Cohen* (Harmondsworth: Penguin Books, 1958).

APPENDIX I: THE BIOGRAPHICAL IMPERATIVE

1. Terry Eagleton, *Criticism and Ideology: A Study in Marxist Theory* (London: New Left Books, 1976), pp. 112–13. What Eagleton says here of ideological criticism is broadly the case for all theorised forms of contextual criticism. Aside from the pioneering work of Stephen Greenblatt in which the critic (like a latter-day Pierre Menard) rewrites the text in terms of information to which its actual author could not have had access, the creative conjunction of the factual and fictive has surreptitiously conformed to a positivist agenda.

2. Louis Montrose, 'Professing the Renaissance', in *Literary Theory: An Anthology*, ed. Julie Rivkin and Michael Ryan (Oxford: Basil Blackwell, 1998), pp. 777–85: p. 780

3. Paul de Man, *Blindness and Insight: Essays in the Rhetoric of Contemporary Criticism*, second edition, revised and enlarged, ed. Wlad Godzich (London: Methuen, 1983), p. 38.

4. Virginia Woolf, *A Room of One's Own* (Harmondsworth: Penguin Books, 1945), p. 43.

5. Jorge Luis Borges, *Labyrinths* (Harmondsworth: Penguin Books, 1970), p. 66.

6. On this issue, see Patricia Cox, *Biography in Late Antiquity: A Quest for the Holy Man* (Berkeley: University of California Press, 1983).

7. See Boris Tomasevskij, 'Literature and Biography' in Ladislav Matejka and Krystyna Pomoroska (eds), *Readings in Russian Poetics: Formalist and Structuralist Views* (Cambridge, MA: MIT Press, 1971); Roland Barthes, *Sade Fourier Loyola*, trans. Richard Miller (London: Cape, 1977). Later in his career, Barthes succinctly defined his notion of the biographeme as follows: 'Photography has the same relation to History that the biographeme has to biography' – *Camera Lucida: Reflections on Photography*, trans. Richard Howard (London: Cape, 1982), p. 30.

8. T.S. Eliot, in Frank Kermode (ed.), *Selected Prose of T.S. Eliot* (London: Faber & Faber, 1975), pp. 37–44: p. 43. These sentences, and the apparent paradox they encapsulate, serve as an aphoristic point of return for twentieth-century criticism much as has Heraclitus's apothegm "you shall not go down twice to the same river' for epistemology. These two appendices (or, more accurately, 'pieces') might be taken as complementary meditations on Eliot's words here, just as Socrates's single sentence on the absence of the author from the scene of reception motivates my work on textual ethics – see Seán Burke, *The Ethics of Writing: Authorship and Legacy in Plato and Nietzsche* (Edinburgh: Edinburgh University Press, 2008).

9. W.K. Wimsatt and Monroe C. Beardsley, *The Verbal Icon* (Lexington: University of Kentucky Press, 1954), p. 5.

10. Ibid., p. 18.

11. E.D. Hirsch, 'Three Dimensions of Hermeneutics', in David Newton-de Molina, *On Literary Intention* (Edinburgh: Edinburgh University Press, 1976), pp. 194–209: p. 203.

12. Ibid., p. 207.

13. Ibid., p. 209.

14. Tobin Siebers, *The Ethics of Criticism* (Ithaca: Cornell University Press, 1988).

15. Thomas Nagel, *The View from Nowhere* (New York: Oxford University Press, 1986), p. 3.

16. Paul de Man, *Blindness and Insight, op. cit.*, p. 50.

17. Ibid., p. 49.

18. Georg Lukács, cited in ibid., p. 42.

19. J.L. Mackie, *Ethics* (Harmondsworth: Penguin Books, 1977), p. 38.
20. Friedrich Nietzsche, *Beyond Good and Evil: Prelude to a Philosophy of the Future*, trans. R.J. Hollingdale (Harmondsworth: Penguin Books, 1973), p. 17. One cannot now know what role this critique might have played in the promised 'transvaluation', particularly given the centrality of will-to-power and a biologistic theory of knowledge to the *Nachlass*. Certainly, Nietzsche had already hoped to instantiate the individuated self of ethics into the impersonal subject of epistemology ('Know what is good for you!'), just as he had constructed his own personal canon of savants on the grounds that their works constitute 'the instinctive biography of a soul'.
21. Thomas Nagel, *op. cit.*, p. 10.
22. Ibid., p. 9.
23. Ibid., pp. 5–6.
24. Ibid., p. 6.
25. Immanuel Kant, *Critique of Pure Reason*, trans. Norman Kemp Smith (London: Macmillan, 1933), A 111.
26. Ibid., A 112.
27. Marjorie Greene, *The Knower and the Known* (London: Faber & Faber, 1966), p. 143.

APPENDIX 2: THE AUTHOR AS READER

1. Paul de Man, *Blindness and Insight: Essays in the Rhetoric of Contemporary Criticism*, second edition, revised and enlarged, ed. Wlad Godzich (London: Methuen, 1983), p. 39.
2. Augustine's *Confessions* remains the model of autobiographical sophistication in terms of negotiating the split in the subject. Enacting the death of the (sinful) self as character, the text impersonalises the converted self and steps out of narrative time in Books X–XIII.
3. W.B. Yeats, *Essays and Introductions* (London: Macmillan, 1969), p. 509.
4. William Wordsworth, *The Prelude*, ed. E. de Selincourt (Oxford: Clarendon Press, 1926), III, ll. 645–8.
5. This illumination in the moment of dialectical understanding is evoked in the *Phaedrus* (276a) as also in the disputed *Seventh Letter* (344b).
6. Jorge Luis Borges astutely notes that this ninety-first fragment of Heraclitus possesses 'dialectical dexterity, because the ease with which we accept the first meaning ("The river is different") clandestinely imposes upon us the second ("I am different") and grants us the illusion of having invented it ...' - Jorge Luis Borges, *Labyrinths* (Harmondsworth: Penguin Books, 1970), p. 259.
7. Paul De Man, *The Rhetoric of Romanticism* (New York: Columbia University Press, 1984), p. 81.
8. Samuel Beckett, *Molloy, Malone Dies, The Unnamable* (London: Calder, 1959), p. 305.
9. T.S. Eliot characterised Pound's *Cantos* as 'an objective and reticent autobiography'. See Ronald Bush, *The Genesis of Ezra Pound's Cantos* (Princeton: Princeton University Press, 1976), p. 5.
10. T.S. Eliot, 'Tradition and the Individual Talent' in Frank Kermode (ed.), *Selected Prose of T.S. Eliot* (London: Faber & Faber, 1975), pp. 37–44: p. 41.
11. T.S. Eliot, *The Complete Poems and Plays of T.S. Eliot* (London: Faber & Faber, 1969), p. 62.
12. F.H. Bradley, *Collected Essays* (Oxford: Clarendon Press, 1935), p. 216.
13. '[T]he Absolute, a notion which Bradley hesitates to define but one which, in spite of his anti-Hegelianism, is close enough to the idealist tradition to prevent Eliot (in the 1910s) from uncritically accepting it' – Douwe Fokkema and Elrud Ibsch, *Modernist Conjectures: A Mainstream in European Literature, 1910–1940* (London: C. Hurst & Co., 1987), p. 97.
14. T.S. Eliot, *The Complete Poems and Plays of T.S. Eliot, op. cit.*, p. 188.
15. William Faulkner, *The Sound and the Fury* (London: Picador, 1993), p. 73.
16. Virginia Woolf, *To the Lighthouse* (London: Penguin Books, 1992), p. 28.
17. Ibid., p. 69.
18. Ibid.
19. Ibid.
20. See Maud Ellmann's splendid discussion in *The Poetics of Impersonality: T.S.Eliot and Ezra Pound* (Brighton: Harvester Press, 1987), pp. 23–57. For a contemporary demonstration of the continuing relevance of this issue (and its dynamic bearing on the work of canonical American

authors), see Sharon Cameron, *Impersonality: Seven Essays* (Chicago: University of Chicago Press, 2007).

21. Interviewed by Elie-Joseph Bois in 1913, Proust declared that the application of the term 'Bergsonian' to his work 'would be inaccurate, for my work is based on the distinction between involuntary and voluntary memory, a distinction which not only does not appear in Mr Bergson's philosophy but is even contradicted by it' – Roger Shattuck, *Proust* (London: Fontana, 1974), p. 169.

22. Marcel Proust, *Remembrance of Things Past*, 3 vols, trans. C.K. Scott Moncrieff and Terence Kilmartin (Harmondsworth: Penguin Books, 1983), 1:47. Subsequent volume and page references will be made parenthetically within the text.

23. Julia Kristeva, *Proust and the Sense of Time* (London: Faber & Faber, 1993), p. 44.

24. Ibid., pp. 48–9. Without disputing Kristeva's brilliant reading of this episode in terms of displacements from mother to madeleine and so on, I have chosen to interpret this image in terms of cognitive rather than maternal distance.

25. The hypothesis of an *a posteriori* unity achieved by Proust's novel is discussed in Douwe Fokkema and Elrud Ibsch, *Modernist Conjectures, op. cit.*, pp. 141–71.

26. Roger Shattuck, *Proust, op. cit.*, pp. 43–5.

27. Paul de Man, *Allegories of Reading: Figural Language in Rousseau, Nietzsche, Rilke and Proust* (New Haven: Yale University Press, 1979), p. 78.

28. Gerard Genette, *Figures III* (Paris: Seuil, 1972), p. 136. The translation is cited in Douwe Fokkema and Elrud Ibsch, *Modernist Conjectures, op. cit.*, p. 144. A considerably reduced text of *Figures* is available in translation – cf. Gerard Genette, *Narrative Discourse: An Essay in Method*, trans. Jane E. Lewin (Oxford: Blackwell, 1980).

29. Jacques Derrida, *Of Grammatology*, trans. Gayatri Chakravorty Spivak (Baltimore: Johns Hopkins University Press, 1976), p. 153.

30. Cf. T.S. Eliot, 'Tradition and the Individual Talent', *op. cit.*, p. 43.

31. Marcel Proust, *Remembrance of Things Past, op. cit.*, 1:1010.

32. Samuel Beckett, *Molloy, Malone Dies, The Unnamable* (London: Calder, 1959), p. 305. All subsequent page references will be made parenthetically to this edition within the text. *The Unnamable* (the English translation is the author's own) was originally published as Samuel Beckett, *L'Innommable* (Paris: Éditions de Minuit, 1953).

33. Samuel Beckett, *Proust and Three Dialogues with Georges Duthuit* (London: Calder, 1965), p. 13.

34. Interestingly, the movement from natural memory (the sensation of taste) to the artificiality of mnemotechnics (Krapp's tape recorder) is precisely the one denounced by King Thamus in Plato's *Phaedrus* (275a).

35. The phrase 'phalanstery of selves' is that of Wyndam Lewis in his *Time and Western Man* (London: Chatto and Windus, 1927), p. 175

36. The Beckett of *The Unnamable* moves between the infintesimal and infinite, the instant of inscription and the 'eternal now' of writerly enunciation. As with Augustine's *Confessions*, the achievement of pure enunciation involves the usurpation of the narrator as character or focaliser by the extradiegetic narrator. Augustine moves from sin to conversion by way of antithetical episodes of mourning in the first nine books so to step out of diagetic time and articulate books X–XIII from 'a place beyond place' (which the *Confessions* would identify with the standing present of eternity). Taken in theological or narratological terms, the complete abnegation of the experiencing self allows for the indefinite expansion of the space of authorship into the narrative present of the enunciation.

37. Simon Critchley, *Very Little ... Almost Nothing: Death, Philosophy, Literature* (London: Routledge, 1997), pp. 167–76.

38. Yet to see an end of literature in this novel which refuses the consolations of synthesis, reconciliation or metaphor is no more useful or coherent than the primitive reading which saw it as a nihilistic endorsement of existential futility. The imposition of such ends, perhaps characteristic of the immense Hegelian self-regard of modernity, is even more absurd when applied to literature than to the philosophical dream of gathering all experience and images under concepts. Surrendering no 'essence', literature can know no ends as such, whether registered as *telos* or *eschaton*. It continues in the absence of goals (or even with its own demise as goal) as it did in

the work of Beckett himself for whom the exertion of *The Unnamable* was to be succeeded by numerous arresting – if minimalist – literary productions.

39.   The above citations are from Roland Barthes, 'The Death of the Author' in Roland Barthes, *Image-Music-Text*, trans. Stephen Heath (London: Fontana, 1977), pp. 142–8: pp. 145–6. Given that the modern scriptor has turned out to be no less of a myth than the now-ironic notion of the *nouveau roman*, it is quite conceivable that Barthes extrapolated a new discursive figure from a handful of highly idiosyncratic, idiomatic and singular acts of literature, of which *L'Innommable* will remain the most distinctive and hence the most irreducible.

40.   These words were used by Derrida in his meditation on the 'last words' of Poe's M. Valdemar and the fascination they likewise held for the mourned Roland Barthes – Jacques Derrida, *The Work of Mourning*, ed. Pascale-Anne Brault and Michael Nass (Chicago and London: The University of Chicago Press, 2001), p. 66. See also Jacques Derrida, 'Les morts de Roland Barthes', *Poétique* 47 (September 1981), pp. 269–92.

Bibliography

Note: A small number of works cited in the text do not appear here since they have no direct bearing on either the author-question or literary studies. According to the same principle, many works which have not been cited in the text are included below as suggestions for further reading.

Althusser, Louis, *For Marx*, trans. Ben Brewster (London: Allen Lane, 1969).

Aristotle, *De Sophisticis Elenchis*, trans. W.A. Pickard-Cambridge in W.D. Ross, ed., *The Works of Aristotle*, vol. 1 (Oxford: Clarendon, 1928).

Auerbach, Erich, *Mimesis: The Representation of Reality in Western Literature*, trans. William R. Trask (Princeton: Princeton University Press, 1953).

Austin, J.L., *How to Do Things with Words* (Oxford: Clarendon Press, 1962).

Augustine, St, *Confessions*, trans. Henry Chadwick (Oxford: Oxford University Press, 1991).

Bagwell, J. Timothy, *American Formalism and the Problem of Interpretation* (Houston, TX: Rice University Press, 1986).

Bakhtin, Mikhail, *Problems of Dostoyevsky's Poetics*, trans. R.W. Rotsel (Ann Arbor, MI: University of Michigan Press, 1973).

Bann, Stephen and John E. Bowlt, *Russian Formalism: A Collection of Articles and Texts in Translation* (Edinburgh: Scottish Academic Press, 1973).

Bannet, Eve Tavor, *Structuralism and the Logic of Dissent: Barthes, Derrida, Foucault, Lacan* (London and Basingstoke: Macmillan, 1989).

Barthes, Roland, *Writing Degree Zero* [1953], trans. Annette Lavers and Colin Smith (London: Cape, 1967).

Barthes, Roland, *On Racine* [1963], trans. Richard Howard (New York: Octagon Books, 1977).

Barthes, Roland, *Critical Essays* [1964], trans. Richard Howard (Evanston: Northwestern University Press, 1972).

Barthes, Roland, *Criticism and Truth* [1966], trans. K.P. Keuneman (London: Athlone Press, 1987).

Barthes, Roland, 'To Write: An Intransitive Verb?' [1966], in Richard Macksey and Eugenio Donato, eds, *The Structuralist Controversy: The Languages of Criticism and the Sciences of Man* (Baltimore: Johns Hopkins University Press, 1972), pp. 134–45.

Barthes, Roland, *S/Z* [1970], trans. Richard Miller (London: Cape, 1975).

Barthes, Roland, *Sade Fourier Loyola* [1971], trans. Richard Miller (London: Cape, 1977).

Barthes, Roland, *New Critical Essays* [1972], trans. Richard Howard (New York: Hill and Wang, 1980).

Barthes, Roland, *The Pleasure of the Text* [1973], trans. Richard Howard (London: Cape, 1976).

Barthes, Roland, *Roland Barthes by Roland Barthes* [1975], trans. Richard Howard (London: Macmillan, 1977).

Barthes, Roland, *A Lover's Discourse*: *Fragments* [1977], trans. Richard Howard (London: Cape, 1979).

Barthes, Roland, *Image-Music-Text*, trans. and ed. Stephen Heath (London: Fontana, 1977).

Barthes, Roland, 'Lecture' [1978], trans. Richard Howard, *Oxford Literary Review*, vol. 4, no. 2 (1979), pp. 31–44.

Barthes, Roland, *Camera Lucida*: *Reflections on Photography* [1980], trans. Richard Howard (London: Cape, 1982).

Barthes, Roland, *The Grain of the Voice*: *Interviews 1962–1980* [1982], trans. Linda Coverdale (London: Cape, 1985).

Barthes, Roland, *A Barthes Reader*, ed. Susan Sontag (London: Cape, 1982).

Barthes, Roland, *The Semiotic Challenge*, trans. Richard Howard (Oxford: Basil Blackwell, 1988).

Battersby, Christine, *Gender and Genius: Towards a Feminist Aesthetics* (London: The Women's Press, 1989).

Beardsley, Monroe C., 'Intentions and Interpretations', in Beardsley, *The Aesthetic Point of View* (Ithaca: Cornell University Press, 1982).

Beckett, Samuel, *L'Innommable* (Paris: Éditions de Minuit, 1953).

Beckett, Samuel, *Molloy, Malone Dies, The Unnamable* (London: Calder, 1959).

Beckett, Samuel, *Proust and Three Dialogues with Georges Duthuit* (London: Calder, 1965).

Belsey, Catherine, *Critical Practice* (London: Methuen, 1980).

Benhabib, Seyla, *Situating the Self: Gender, Community and Postmodernism in Contemporary Ethics* (Cambridge: Polity Press, 1992).

Benjamin, Walter, *Understanding Brecht*, trans. Anna Bostock (London: NLB, 1973).

Bennett, Andrew, *The Author* (Abingdon and New York: Routledge, 2005).

Benoist, Jean-Marie, *The Structural Revolution* (London: Weidenfeld and Nicolson, 1978).

Berger, Gaston, *The Cogito in Husserl's Philosophy*, trans. Kathleen McLaughlin (Evanston: Northwestern University Press, 1972).

Bettig, Ronald V., *Copyrighting Culture: The Political Economy of Intellectual Property* (Westview: Oxford, 1997).

Bhabha, Homi K., *The Location of Culture* (London: Routledge, 1994).

Biriotti, Maurice and Nicola Miller, eds, *What is an Author?* (Manchester: Manchester University Press, 1993).

Blanchot, Maurice, *The Infinite Conversation*, trans. Susan Hanson (Minneapolis: University of Minnesota Press).

Bloom, Harold, *The Anxiety of Influence: A Theory of Poetry* (New York and London: Oxford University Press, 1973).

Bloom, Harold, *Kabbalah and Criticism* (New York: Seabury Press, 1975).

Bloom, Harold, *A Map of Misreading* (New York and London: Oxford University Press, 1975).

Bloom, Harold, *Poetry and Repression: Revisionism from Blake to Stevens* (New Haven: Yale University Press, 1976).

Bloom, Harold, *Agon: Toward a Theory of Revisionism* (New York and London: Oxford University Press, 1982).

Bloom, Harold, *The Breaking of the Vessels* (Chicago: University of Chicago Press, 1982).

Bolter, Jay David, 'Virtual Reality and the Redefinition of Self', in R. Jackson and S. Gibson, eds, *Communication and Cyberspace: Social Interaction in an Electronic Environment* (New York: Hampton Press, 1996).

Booth, Wayne C., *The Rhetoric of Fiction* (Chicago: University of Chicago Press, 1962).

Borges, Jorge Luis, *Labyrinths*, ed. Donald A. Yates and James E. Irby (Harmondsworth: Penguin Books, 1970).

Boyle, James, *Shamans, Software, and Spleens: Law and the Construction of the Information Society* (Cambridge, MA: Harvard University Press, 1997).

Boyne, Roy, *Foucault and Derrida: The Other Side of Reason* (London: Unwin Hyman, 1990).

Bradley, F. H., *Collected Essays* (Oxford: Clarendon Press, 1935).

Brik, Osip, 'The so-called formal method', in L.M. O'Toole and Ann Shukman, eds, *Russian Poetics in Translation 4* (Colchester: University of Essex Press, 1977), pp. 90–1.

Bruss, Elizabeth W., *Autobiographical Acts: The Changing Situation of a Literary Genre* (Baltimore: Johns Hopkins University Press, 1976).

Buranen, Lise and Alice Myers Roy, *Perspectives on Plagiarism in a Postmodern World* (Albany: SUNY Press, 1999).

Burke, Seán, *Authorship: From Plato to the Postmodern: A Reader* (Edinburgh: Edinburgh University Press, 1995).

Burke, Seán, *The Ethics of Writing: Authorship and Legacy in Plato and Nietzsche* (Edinburgh: Edinburgh University Press, 2008).

Bush, Ronald, *The Genesis of Ezra Pound's Cantos* (Princeton: Princeton University Press, 1976).

Butler, Christopher, *Interpretation, Deconstruction and Ideology: An Introduction to Some Current Issues in Literary Theory* (Oxford: Clarendon Press, 1984).

Cain, William E., *The Crisis in Criticism: Theory, Literature and Reform in English Studies* (Baltimore: Johns Hopkins University Press, 1984).

Cameron, Sharon, *Impersonality: Seven Essays* (Chicago: University of Chicago Press, 2007).

Carroll, David, 'The Subject of Archaeology or the Sovereignty of the *Episteme*', *Modern Language Notes,* 93, no. 4 (1978), pp. 695–722.

Carroll, David, *The Subject in Question: The Languages of Theory and the Strategies of Fiction* (Chicago: University of Chicago Press, 1982).

Caughie, John, ed., *Theories of Authorship: A Reader* (London: Routledge and Kegan Paul, 1981).

Champagne, Roland, *Beyond the Structuralist Myth of Écriture* (The Hague: Mouton, 1977).

Champagne, Roland, *Literary History in the Wake of Roland Barthes: Re-defining the Myths of Reality* (Alabama: Summa Publications Inc., 1984).

Cixous, Hélène, 'The Laugh of the Medusa', trans. Keith Cohen and Paula Cohen, *Signs*, vol. 1, no. 4 (1976) pp. 875–94.

Cixous, Hélène, *Portrait of Jacques Derrida as a Young Jewish Saint*, trans. Beverley Bie Brahic (New York: Columbia University Press, 2004).

Cixous, Hélène, *Insister of Derrida*, trans. Peggy Kamuf (Edinburgh: Edinburgh University Press, 2008).

Clark, Tim, 'Roland Barthes, Dead and Alive', *Oxford Literary Review*, vol. 6, no. 1 (1983), pp. 97–107.

Clément, Catherine, *The Lives and Legends of Jacques Lacan*, trans. Arthur Goldhammer (New York: Columbia University Press, 1983).

Clery, E.J., Caroline Franklin and Peter Garside (eds), *Authorship, Commerce and the Public: Scenes of Writing 1750–1850* (Basingstoke: Palgrave Macmillan, 2002).

Close, Anthony, 'The Empirical Author: Salman Rushdie's *The Satanic Verses*', *Philosophy and Literature*, vol. 14, no. 2 (1990).

Coleridge, Samuel Taylor, *Biographia Literaria*, ed. G. Watson (London: Dent, 1965).

Collins, A.S., *Authorship in the Days of Johnson* (New York: Dutton, 1929).

Coomaraswamy, Ananda K., 'Intention', *American Bookman*, vol. 1, no. 1 (1944), pp. 41–8.

Coombe, Rosemary J., *The Cultural Life of Intellectual Properties: Authorship, Appropriation, and the Law* (Durham, NC: Duke University Press, 1998).

Corngold, Stanley, *The Fate of the Self: German Writers and French Theory* (New York: Columbia University Press, 1986).

Corngold, Stanley, 'Paul de Man on the Contingencies of Intention' in Luc Herman, Kris Humbeeck and Geert Lernout, eds, *(Dis)continuities: Essays on Paul de Man* (Amsterdam: Rodopi, 1989).

Couturier, Maurice, *La Figure de l'auteur* (Paris: Editions de Seuil, 1995).

Cox, Patricia, *Biography in Late Antiquity: A Quest for the Holy Man* (Berkeley: University of California Press, 1983).

Crewe, Jonathan, *Trials of Authorship: Anterior Forms and Poetic Reconstruction from Wyatt to Shakespeare* (Berkeley: University of California Press, 1990).

Critchley, Simon, *Very Little … Almost Nothing: Death, Philosophy, Literature* (London and New York: Routledge, 1997).

Culler, Jonathan, *Structuralist Poetics* (London: Routledge and Kegan Paul, 1975).

Culler, Jonathan, *Barthes* (Fontana: London, 1982).

Culler, Jonathan, *On Deconstruction* (London: Routledge and Kegan Paul, 1982).

Davis, Oliver, 'The Author at Work in Genetic Criticism', *Paragraph*, 25 (2002), pp. 92–106.

Delany, Paul and George P. Landow, ed., *Hypermedia and Literary Studies* (Cambrige, MA: MIT Press, 1991).

Dennett, Daniel C., 'Self-Invention', *Times Literary Supplement*, 16–22, September 1988, pp. 1,016; 1,028–9.

Derrida, Jacques, *'Speech and Phenomena' and Other Essays on Husserl's Theory of Signs* [1967], trans. David B. Allison (Evanston: Northwestern University Press, 1973).

Derrida, Jacques, *Of Grammatology* [1967], trans. Gayatri Chakravorty Spivak (Baltimore: Johns Hopkins University Press, 1976).

Derrida, Jacques, *Writing and Difference* [1967], trans. Alan Bass (London: Routledge and Kegan Paul, 1981).

Derrida, Jacques, *Dissemination* [1972], trans. Barbara Johnson (London: Athlone Press, 1981).

Derrida, Jacques, *Margins – of Philosophy* [1972], trans. Alan Bass (Brighton: Harvester Press, 1982).

Derrida, Jacques, *Positions* [1972], trans. Alan Bass (London: Athlone Press, 1981).

Derrida, Jacques, *Spurs/Éperons* [1972], trans. Barbara Harlow (Chicago: University of Chicago Press, 1979).

Derrida, Jacques, *Glas* [1974], trans. John P. Leavey and Richard Rand (Lincoln, Nebraska: University of Nebraska Press, 1986).

Derrida, Jacques, *Signéponge/Signsponge* [1975], trans. Richard Rand (New York: Columbia University Press, 1984).

Derrida, Jacques, 'Signature Event Context', trans. Samuel Weber and Jeffrey Mehlman, *Glyph* I (1977), pp. 172–97.

Derrida, Jacques, 'Limited Inc', *Glyph* II (1977), pp. 162–251.

Derrida, Jacques, *The Post Card: From Socrates to Freud and Beyond* [1980], trans. Alan Bass (Chicago and London: University of Chicago Press, 1987).

Derrida, Jacques, *The Ear of the Other: Otobiography, Transference, Translation: Texts and Discussions with Jacques Derrida* [1984], trans. Peggy Kamuf and Avital Ronell (New York: Schoken Books, 1986).

Derrida, Jacques, *Of Spirit: Heidegger and the Question* [1987], trans. Geoff Bennington and Rachel Bowlby (Chicago: University of Chicago Press, 1989).

Derrida, Jacques, 'Like the Sound of the Sea Deep within a Shell: Paul de Man's War', *Critical Inquiry*, vol. 12, no. 3 (Spring 1988), pp. 590–652.

Derrida, Jacques, '"Eating Well": An Interview' in *Who Comes after the Subject?*, ed. Eduardo Cadava, Peter Connor and Jean-Luc Nancy (New York and London: Routledge, 1991).

Derrida, Jacques, 'Circumfession' in *Jacques Derrida*, trans. Geoffrey Bennington (Chicago: University of Chicago Press, 1993).

Derrida, Jacques, *Memoirs of the Blind: The Self-Portrait and Other Ruins*, trans. Pascale-Anne Brault and Michael Nass (Chicago: University of Chicago Press, 1993).

Derrida, Jacques, *Aporias: Dying – awaiting one another at the 'limits of truth'*, trans. Thomas Dutoit (Stanford: Stanford University Press, 1994).

Derrida, Jacques, *Specters of Marx: The State of the Debt, the Work of Mourning and the New International*, trans. Peggy Kamuf (New York and London: Routledge, 1994).

Derrida, Jacques, *Points ...: Interviews, 1974–1994*, ed. Elisabeth Weber, trans. Peggy Kamuf and Others (Stanford: Stanford University Press, 1995).

Derrida, Jacques, *The Gift of Death*, trans. David Willis (Chicago: Chicago University Press, 1995).

Derrida, Jacques, *On the Name*, ed. Thomas Dutoit (Stanford: Stanford University Press, 1995).

Derrida, Jacques, *The Work of Mourning*, ed. Pascale-Anne Brault and Michael Nass (Chicago and London: The University of Chicago Press, 2001).

Derrida, Jacques, *Geneses, Genealogies, Genres, & Genius*, trans. Beverley Bie Brahic (Edinburgh: Edinburgh University Press, 2006).

Derrida, Jacques, *Learning to Live Finally: An Interview with Jean Birnbaum*, trans. Pascale-Anne Brault and Michael Nass (Hoboken, NJ: Melville House Publishing, 2007).

Dery, Mark (ed.), *Flame Wars; The Discourse of Cyberculture* (Durham, NC: Duke University Press, 1994).

Descartes, René, *Discourse on Method and the Meditations*, trans. F.E. Sutcliffe (Harmondsworth: Penguin Books, 1968).

Descombes, Vincent, *Modern French Philosophy*, trans. L. Scott-Fox and J.M. Harding (Cambridge: Cambridge University Press, 1980).

Douzinas, Costas (ed.), *Adieu Derrida* (Basingstoke: Palgrave Macmillan, 2007).

Dreyfus, Hubert L. and Paul Rabinow, *Michel Foucault: Beyond Structuralism and Hermeneutics* (Brighton: Harvester Press, 1982).

Duff, William, *An Essay on Original Genius* (Gainsville, FL: Scholars' Facsimiles, 1964).

Dunn, Kevin, *Pretexts of Authority: The Rhetoric of Authorship in the Renaissance Preface* (Stanford: University of California Press, 1994).

Eagleton, Terry, *Criticism and Ideology: A Study in Marxist Theory* (London: New Left Books, 1976).

Eakin, Paul John, *Fictions in Autobiography: Studies in the Art of Self-Invention* (Princeton: Princeton University Press, 1985).

Eco, Umberto, *A Theory of Semiotics* (Bloomington and London: Indiana University Press, 1976).

Ede, Lisa and Andrea Lunsford, *Singular Texts/Plural Authors: Perspectives on Collaborative Writing* (Carbondale: Southern Illinois University Press, 1990).

Eisenstein, Elizabeth L., *The Printing Press as an Agent of Change: Communications and Cultural Transformations in Early-Modern Europe* (Cambridge: Cambridge University Press, 1980).

Eliot, T. S., *The Complete Poems and Plays of T.S. Eliot* (London: Faber & Faber, 1969).

Eliot, T. S., *Selected Prose of T.S. Eliot*, ed. Frank Kermode (London: Faber & Faber, 1975).

Ellmann, Maud, *The Poetics of Impersonality: T.S. Eliot and Ezra Pound* (Brighton: Harvester, 1987).

Elsky, Martin, *Authorizing Words: Speech, Writing, and Print in the English Renaissance* (Ithaca and London: Cornell University Press, 1989).

Erlich, Victor, *Russian Formalism: History-Doctrine* (The Hague: Mouton, 1980).

Farias, Victor, *Heidegger and Nazism* (Philadelphia: Temple University Press, 1989).

Felperin, Howard, *Beyond Deconstruction: The Uses and Abuses of Literary Theory* (New York: Oxford University Press, 1985).

Ferry, Anne, '*Anonymity*: The Literary History of a Word', *New Literary History*, 33 (2002), pp. 193–214.

Fish, Stanley, *Is There a Text in This Class?: The Authority of Interpretive Communities* (Cambridge, MA: Harvard University Press, 1980).

Fish, Stanley, *Doing What Comes Naturally: Rhetoric and the Practice of Theory in Literary and Legal Studies* (Oxford: Clarendon Press, 1989).

Fokkema, Douwe and Elrud Ibsch, *Modernist Conjectures: A Mainstream in European Literature, 1910–1940* (London: C. Hurst & Co., 1987).

Forrester, John, *The Seductions of Psychoanalysis: Freud, Lacan and Derrida* (Cambridge: Cambridge University Press, 1991).

Foster, Don, *Author Unknown: On the Trail of Anonymous* (London: Routledge, 2001).

Foucault, Michel, *Madness and Civilization: A History of Insanity in the Age of Reason* [1961], trans. Richard Howard (London: Tavistock, 1967).

Foucault, Michel, *The Order of Things: An Archaeology of the Human Sciences* [1966], trans. Alan Sheridan (London: Tavistock, 1970).

Foucault, Michel, *The Archaeology of Knowledge* [1969], trans. A.M. Sheridan Smith (London: Tavistock, 1972).

Foucault, Michel, 'What is an Author?' [1969], trans. Josué V. Harari, in Josué V. Harari, ed., *Textual Strategies: Perspectives in Post-Structuralist Criticism* (Ithaca: Cornell University Press, 1979), pp. 141–60.

Foucault, Michel, *Language, Counter-Memory, Practice: Selected Essays and Interviews*, ed. Donald F. Bouchard, trans. Donald F. Bouchard and Sherry Simon (Ithaca: Cornell University Press, 1977).

Foucault, Michel, *Power/Knowledge: Selected Interviews and Other Writings 1972–1977*, ed. Colin Gordon (Brighton: Harvester Press, 1980).

Foucault, Michel, 'Afterword: The Subject and Power', in Hubert L. Dreyfus and Paul Rabinow, *Michel Foucault: Beyond Structuralism and Hermeneutics* (Brighton: Harvester Press, 1982), pp. 208–26.

Foucault, Michel, *The Foucault Reader*, ed. Paul Rabinow (Harmondsworth: Penguin Books, 1986).

Foucault, Michel, *The History of Sexuality*, trans. Robert Hurley, 3 vols (New York: Viking Press, 1986).

Foucault, Michel, *Politics, Philosophy and Culture: Interviews and Other Writings 1977–1984*, trans. Alan Sheridan and others, ed. Laurence D. Kritzman (New York: Routledge, 1988).

Foucault, Michel, 'Technologies of the Self', in L.H. Martin, H. Gutman and P.H. Hutton, eds, *Technologies of the Self* (London: Tavistock, 1988), pp. 16–49.

Freud, Sigmund, *Art and Literature*, vol. 14 of the Pelican Freud Library, ed. Albert Dickson (Harmondsworth: Penguin Books, 1985).

Furman, Nelly, 'The Politics of Difference: Beyond the Gender Principle' in Sayle Greene and Kahn Coppelia, eds, *Making a Difference: Feminist Literary Criticism* (London: Methuen, 1985), pp. 59–79.

Gallop, Jane, *Reading Lacan* (Ithaca: Cornell University Press, 1985).

Gane, Mike, ed., *Towards a Critique of Foucault* (London: Routledge and Kegan Paul, 1986).

Gasché, Rodolphe, *The Tain of the Mirror: Derrida and the Philosophy of Reflection* (Cambridge, MA: Harvard University Press, 1986).

Gass, William, *The World Within the Word* (New York: Alfred A. Knopf Inc., 1979).

Gass, William, *Habitations of the Word* (New York: Simon and Schuster, 1985).

Gaston, Sean, *The Impossible Mourning of Jacques Derrida* (London and New York: Continuum, 2006).

Geertz, Clifford, *Works and Lives: The Anthropologist as Author* (Cambridge: Polity Press, 1988).

Genette, Gerard, *Figures III* (Paris: Seuil, 1972).

Genette, Gerard, *Narrative Discourse: An Essay in Method*, trans. Jane E. Lewin (Oxford: Basil Blackwell, 1980).

Gerstner, David A. and Janet Staiger (eds), *Authorship and Film* (New York: Routledge, 2003).

Gilbert, Sandra M. and Susan Gubar, *The Madwoman in the Attic: The Woman Writer and the Nineteenth-Century Literary Imagination* (New Haven: Yale University Press, 1979).

Gloversmith, Frank, ed., *The Theory of Reading* (Brighton: Harvester Press, 1984).

Goldstein, Paul, *Copyright's Highway: From Gutenberg to the Celestial Jukebox* (New York: Hill and Wang, 1997).

Grandy, Richard E. and Richard Warner, eds, *Philosophical Grounds of Rationality: Intentions, Categories, Ends* (Oxford: Clarendon Press, 1986).

Greenblatt, Stephen, *Shakespearean Negotiations: The Circulation of Social Energy in Renaissance England* (Berkeley and Los Angeles: University of California Press, 1988).

Greenblatt, Stephen, 'Resonance and Wonder', in Peter Collier and Helga Geyer-Ryan, eds, *Literary Theory Today* (Cambridge: Polity Press, 1990).

Greene, Jody, *Trouble With Ownership: Literary Property and Authorial Liability in England, 1660–1730* (Philadelphia: University of Pennsylvania Press, 2005).

Greene, Marjorie, *The Knower and the Known* (London: Faber & Faber, 1966).

Greene, Sayle and Kahn Coppelia, eds, *Making a Difference: Feminist Literary Criticism* (London: Methuen, 1985).

Grice, H.P., 'Intention and Uncertainty', *Proceedings of the British Academy*, 57 (1971), pp. 263–79.

Grice, H.P., 'Logic and Conversation', in P. Cole and J. Morgan, eds, *Syntax and Semantics 3: Speech Acts* (New York: Academic Press, 1975), pp. 41–58.

Grice, H.P., *Studies in the Way of Words* (Cambridge, MA: Harvard University Press, 1989).

Hackforth, R., *The Authorship of the Platonic Epistles* (Manchester: Manchester University Press, 1913).

Hackforth, R., *Plato's Phaedrus, translated with an introduction and commentary* (Cambridge: Cambridge University Press, 1952).

Harari, Josué V., ed., *Textual Strategies: Perspectives in Post-Structuralist Criticism* (Ithaca: Cornell University Press, 1979).

Hartman, Geoffrey, *Beyond Formalism: Literary Essays 1958–1970* (New Haven: Yale University Press, 1970).

Hartman, Geoffrey, *The Fate of Reading and Other Essays* (Chicago and London: University of Chicago Press, 1975).

Hartman, Geoffrey, *Criticism in the Wilderness: The Study of Literature Today* (New Haven: Yale University Press, 1980).

Hartman, Geoffrey, *Saving the Text: Literature/Derrida/Philosophy* (Baltimore: Johns Hopkins University Press, 1981).

Harvey, Irene, *Derrida and the Economy of Différance* (Bloomington: Indiana University Press, 1986).

Harvey, Irene, 'Doubling the Space of Existence: Exemplarity in Derrida – the Case of Rousseau', in John Sallis, ed., *Deconstruction and Philosophy: The Texts of Jacques Derrida* (Chicago and London: University of Chicago Press, 1987).

Havelock, Eric A., *Preface to Plato* (Cambridge, MA: Belknap Press of Harvard University Press, 1963).

Heidegger, Martin, *Being and Time*, trans. J. Macquarrie and E. Robinson (New York: Harper and Row, 1962).

Heidegger, Martin, *Kant and the Problem of Metaphysics*, trans. J.S. Churchill (Bloomington: Indiana University Press, 1962).

Heidegger, Martin, *Early Greek Thinking*, ed. David Farrell Krell and Frank A. Capuzzi (New York: Harper and Row, 1975).

Heidegger, Martin, *Basic Writings*, ed. David Farrell Krell (London: Routledge and Kegan Paul, 1978).

Heim, Michael, *Electronic Language: A Philosophical Study of Word Processing* (New Haven: Yale University Press, 1987).

Hirsch, E.D., Jr, *Validity in Interpretation* (New Haven: Yale University Press, 1967).

Hirsch, E.D., Jr, *The Aims of Interpretation* (New Haven: Yale University Press, 1976).

Hirsch, E.D., 'Three Dimensions of Hermeneutics' in David Newton-de Molina, *On Literary Intention* (Edinburgh: Edinburgh University Press, 1976), pp. 194–209.

Hospers, John, *Meaning and Truth in the Arts* (Chapel Hill: University of North Carolina Press, 1946).

Hoy, David Couzens, *Foucault: A Critical Reader* (Oxford: Basil Blackwell, 1986).

Husserl, Edmund, *Cartesian Meditations: An Introduction to Phenomenology*, trans. D. Cairns (Hague: Martinus Nijhoff, 1960).

Husserl, Edmund, *The Idea of Phenomenology*, trans. William P. Alston and George Nakhnikian (Hague: Martinus Nijhoff, 1964).

Ingarden, Roman, *The Literary Work of Art*, trans. George G. Grabowicz (Evanston: Northwestern University Press, 1973).

Inge, M. Thomas, 'Collaboration and Concepts of Authorship', *PMLA*, vol. 116, no. 3 (May 2001), pp. 609–22.

Irigaray, Luce, *Speculum of the Other Woman* (Ithaca: Cornell University Press, 1985).

Irwin, William (ed.), *The Death and Resurrection of the Author?* (Westport, CT: Greenwood, 2002).

Jackson, Leonard, *The Poverty of Structuralism: Literature and Structuralist Theory* (London: Longman, 1991).

Jakobson, Roman, 'Closing Statement: Linguistics and Poetics', in Thomas A. Sebeok, ed., *Style in Language* (Cambridge, MA: MIT Press, 1960).

Jameson, Fredric, *The Prison-House of Language: A Critical Account of Structuralism and Russian Formalism* (Princeton: Princeton University Press, 1972).

Jameson, Fredric, *The Political Unconscious: Narrative as a Socially Symbolic Act* (Ithaca: Cornell University Press, 1981), p. 20.

Jardine, Alice A., *Gynesis: Configurations of Woman and Modernity* (Ithaca: Cornell University Press, 1985).

Jaszi, Peter, and Martha Woodmansee, 'The Ethical Reaches of Authorship', *South Atlantic Quarterly* vol. 95, no. 4 (Fall 1996): pp. 947–77.

Jefferson, Ann and David Robey, *Modern Literary Theory: A Comparative Introduction* (London: Batsford, 1984).

Johnson, Barbara, *The Critical Difference* (Baltimore: Johns Hopkins University Press, 1980).

Josipovici, Gabriel, 'The Balzac of M. Barthes and the Balzac of M. de Guermantes', in Lawrence Lerner, ed., *Reconstructing Literature* (Oxford: Basil Blackwell, 1983), pp. 81–105.

Joyce, Michael, *Of Two Minds: Hypertext, Pedagogy and Poetics* (Ann Arbor: University of Michigan Press, 1995).

Kamuf, Peggy, *Signature Pieces: On the Institution of Authorship* (Ithaca: Cornell University Press, 1988).

Kant, Immanuel, *A Critique of Pure Reason*, trans. Norman Kemp Smith (London: Macmillan, 1933).

Kant, Immanuel, *The Critique of Judgement*, trans. James Creed Meredith (Oxford: Oxford University Press, 1952).

Kant, Immanuel, *Anthropology From a Pragmatic Point of View*, trans. Mary J. Gregor (Hague: Martinus Nijhoff, 1974).

Kewes, Paulina, *Authorship and Appropriation: Writing for the Stage in England, 1660–1710* (Oxford: Clarendon Press, 1998).

Kristeva, Julia, 'The System and the Speaking Subject', *The Times Literary Supplement*, 12 October 1973, pp. 1249–50.

Kristeva, Julia, *Desire in Language: A Semiotic Approach to Literature and Art,* ed. L. S. Roudiez (Oxford: Basil Blackwell, 1980).

Kristeva, Julia, *The Kristeva Reader,* ed. Toril Moi (Oxford: Basil Blackwell, 1986).

Kristeva, Julia, *Proust and the Sense of Time* (London: Faber, 1993).

Kurzweil, Edith, *The Age of Structuralism: Lévi-Strauss to Foucault* (New York: Columbia University Press, 1980).

Lacan, Jacques, *Écrits: A Selection* [1966], trans. Alan Sheridan (London: Tavistock, 1977).

Lacan, Jacques, 'Seminar on "The Purloined Letter"', trans. Jeffrey Mehlman, *Yale French Studies,* no. 48 (1972), pp. 38–72.

Lacan, Jacques, *The Four Fundamental Concepts of Psycho-analysis,* trans. Alan Sheridan (Harmondsworth: Penguin Books, 1977).

Laferte, Darril, 'Hypertext and Hypermedia: Toward a rhizorhetorical investigation of communication', *Readerly-Writerly-Text,* vol. 3, no. 1, Fall/Winter 1995, pp. 51–68.

Landow, George P., *Hypertext: The Convergence of Contemporary Critical Theory and Technology* (Baltimore and London: Johns Hopkins University Press, 1992).

Landow, George P., ed., *Hyper/Text/Theory* (Baltimore: Johns Hopkins University Press, 1994).

Landow, George P., *Hypertext 3.0: Critical Theory and New Media in an Era of Globalisation* (Baltimore: Johns Hopkins University Press, 2006).

Landow, George P., Julia Launhardt, and Paul D. Kahn, eds, *The Dickens Web,* Environment: Intermedia 3.5 (Providence, RI: Institute for Research in Information and Scholarship, 1988).

Lanham, R., *The Electronic Word: Democracy, Technology and the Arts* (Chicago: University of Chicago Press, 1994).

Lavers, Annette, *Roland Barthes: Structuralism and After* (London: Methuen, 1982).

Lecourt, Dominique, *Marxism and Epistemology: Bachelard, Canguilhem, Foucault,* trans. Ben Brewster (London: New Left Books, 1975).

Lehman, David, *Signs of the Times: Deconstruction and the Fall of Paul de Man* (London: André Deutsch, 1991).

Lemert, Charles C. and Garth Gillan, *Michel Foucault: Social Theory and Transgression* (New York: Columbia University Press, 1982).

Lentricchia, Frank, *After the New Criticism* (Chicago: University of Chicago Press, 1980).

Lévi-Strauss, Claude, *Tristes Tropiques,* trans. John Russell (London: Hutchinson, 1966).

Lévi-Strauss, Claude, *Structural Anthropology,* trans. Claire Jacobson and Brooke Grundfest Schoept (London: Allen Lane, 1967).

Lévi-Strauss, Claude, *The Elementary Structures of Kinship,* trans. James Harle Bell, John Richard von Sturmer and Rodney Needham (Boston: Beacon Press, 1969).

Levinson, Stephen C., *Pragmatics* (Cambridge: Cambridge University Press, 1983).

Lewis, Wyndam, *Time and Western Man* (London: Chatto and Windus, 1927).

Livingstone, Paisley, 'Intention in Art', in Jerome Levinson (ed.), *The Oxford Handbook of Aesthetics* (Oxford: Oxford University Press, 2003).

Llewelyn, John, *Derrida on the Threshold of Sense* (Basingstoke: Macmillan, 1986).

Lowenstein, Joseph, *The Author's Due: Printing and the Prehistory of Copyright* (Chicago: University of Chicago Press, 2002).

Lowry, Richard S., *'Littery Man': Mark Twain and Modern Authorship* (Oxford: Oxford University Press, 1996).

Luther, Arch C., *Authoring Interactive Multimedia* (Boston: AP Professional, 1994).

Lyotard, Jean-François, *The Postmodern Condition* (Manchester: Manchester University Press, 1985).

Macherey, Pierre, *A Theory of Literary Production,* trans. Geoffrey Wall (London: Routledge and Kegan Paul, 1978).

Mackie, J.L., *Ethics* (Harmondsworth: Penguin Books, 1977).

Macksey, Richard and Eugenio Donato, eds, *The Structuralist Controversy: The Languages of Criticism and the Sciences of Man* (Baltimore: Johns Hopkins University Press, 1972).

Major-Poetzl, Pamela, *Michel Foucault's Archaeology of Western Culture: Toward a New Science of History* (Brighton: Harvester Press, 1983).

Mallarmé, Stephane, 'Crisis in Verse', in T.G. West trans. and ed., *Symbolism: An Anthology* (London: Methuen, 1980), pp. 1–12.

Man, Paul de, *Blindness and Insight: Essays in the Rhetoric of Contemporary Criticism* [1971], second edition, revised and enlarged, ed. Wlad Godzich (London: Methuen, 1983).

Man, Paul de, *Allegories of Reading: Figural Language in Rousseau, Nietzsche, Rilke and Proust* (New Haven: Yale University Press, 1979)

Man, Paul de, *The Rhetoric of Romanticism* (New York: Columbia University Press, 1984).

Man, Paul de, *The Resistance to Theory* (Minneapolis: University of Minnesota Press, 1986).

Man, Paul de, *Wartime Journalism 1939–1943*, ed. Werner Hamacher, Neil Hertz and Thomas Keenan (Lincoln, NE: University of Nebraska Press, 1988).

Masten, Jeffrey, *Textual Intercourse: Collaboration, Authorship, and Sexualities in Renaissance Drama* (Cambridge: Cambridge University Press, 1997).

Matejka, Ladislav and Krystyna Pomorska, eds, *Readings in Russian Poetics: Formalist and Structuralist Views* (Cambridge, MA: MIT Press, 1971).

McGann, Jerome J., *The Beauty of Inflections: Literary Investigations in Historical Method and Theory* (Oxford: Clarendon Press, 1988).

McGann, Jerome J., *The Textual Condition* (Princeton: Princeton University Press, 1991).

McLuhan, Marshall, *The Gutenberg Galaxy: The Making of Typographic Man* (Toronto: University of Toronto Press, 1962).

Merleau-Ponty, Maurice, *The Phenomenology of Perception*, trans. Colin Smith (London: Routledge and Kegan Paul, 1962).

Merquior, J.S., *Foucault* (London: Fontana, 1985).

Michalak, Susan and Mary Coney, 'Hypertext and the author–reader dialogue', *Hypertext '93 Proceedings* (New York: ACM, 1993), pp. 174–82.

Miller, J. Hillis, 'The Literary Criticism of Georges Poulet', *Modern Language Notes,* 78 (1963), pp. 471–88.

Miller, J. Hillis, 'The Geneva School', in John K. Simon, ed., *Modern French Criticism from Proust to Valéry* (Chicago: University of Chicago Press, 1972).

Miller, J. Hillis, 'The Critic as Host', in Harold Bloom et al., eds, *Deconstruction and Criticism* (New York: Seabury Press, 1979), pp. 217–53.

Miller, J. Hillis, 'The Ethics of Hypertext', *Diacritics*, vol. 25, no. 3 (Fall 1995), pp. 27–39.

Miller, Nancy K., *Subject to Change: Reading Feminist Writing* (Ithaca: Cornell University Press, 1988).

Minnis, A.J., *Medieval Theory of Authorship: Scholastic Literary Attitudes in the Later Middle Ages* (London: Scolar Press, 1984).

Minnis, A.J., ed., *Medieval Literary Theory and Criticism c.1100–c.1375* (Oxford: Clarendon Press, 1988).

Mitchell, W.J.T., ed., *Against Theory: Literary Studies and the New Pragmatism* (Chicago: University of Chicago Press, 1985).

Moi, Toril, *Sexual/Textual Politics: Feminist Literary Theory* (London: Methuen, 1985).

Nesbit, Molly, 'What Was An Author?', *Yale French Studies*, 73 (1987), pp. 229–57.

Montrose, Louis, 'Professing the Renaissance: The Poetics and Politics of Culture', in *Literary Theory: An Anthology*, ed. Julie Rivkin and Michael Ryan (Oxford: Basil Blackwell, 1998), pp. 777–85.

Morse, David, 'Author–Reader–Language: Reflections on a Critical Closed Circuit' in Frank Gloversmith, ed., *The Theory of Reading* (Brighton: Harvester Press, 1984), pp. 53–92.

Moulthorp, Stuart, 'Travelling in the breakdown lane: a principle of resistance for hypertexts', *Mosaic*, vol. 28, no. 4, December 1995, pp. 55–77.

Nadel, Ira Bruce, *Biography: Fiction, Fact and Form* (London and Basingstoke: Macmillan, 1984).

Nagel, Thomas, *The View from Nowhere* (Oxford: Oxford University Press, 1986).

Nancy, Jean-Luc, *The Inoperative Community* (Minneapolis: University of Minnesota Press, 1991).

Nesbit, Molly, 'What Was An Author?', *Yale French Studies*, 73 (1987), pp. 229–57.

Nietzsche, Friedrich, *The Joyful Wisdom*, trans. Thomas Common (Edinburgh: Foulis, 1910).

Nietzsche, Friedrich, *The Birth of Tragedy and the Genealogy of Morals*, trans. Francis Golffing (New York: Doubleday, 1956).

Nietzsche, Friedrich, *Thus Spake Zarathustra: A Book for Everyone and No One*, trans. R.J. Hollingdale (Harmondsworth: Penguin Books, 1961).

Nietzsche, Friedrich, *The Will to Power*, trans. Walter Kaufmann and R.J. Hollingdale (New York: Vintage Books, 1968).

Nietzsche, Friedrich, *Beyond Good and Evil: Prelude to a Philosophy of the Future*, trans. R.J. Hollingdale (Harmondsworth: Penguin Books, 1973).

Nietzsche, Friedrich, *Ecce Homo: How One Becomes What One Is*, trans. R.J. Hollingdale (Harmondsworth: Penguin Books, 1979).

Nitzsche, Jane Chance, *The Genius Figure in Antiquity and the Middle Ages* (New York: Columbia University Press, 1975).

Norris, Christopher, *Deconstruction: Theory and Practice* (London and New York: Methuen, 1982).

Norris, Christopher, *The Contest of Faculties: Philosophy and Theory After Deconstruction* (London: Methuen, 1985).

Norris, Christopher, *Derrida* (London: Fontana, 1987).

Norris, Christopher, *Paul de Man: Deconstruction and the Critique of Aesthetic Ideology* (London: Routledge, 1988).

Norris, Christopher, *Spinoza and the Origins of Modern Critical Theory* (Oxford: Basil Blackwell, 1991).

Norris, Christopher, *Reclaiming Truth: Contribution to a Critique of Cultural Relativism* (London: Lawrence & Wishart, 1996).

Nunberg, Geoffrey, ed., *The Future of the Book* (Berkeley: University of California Press, 1996).

Nye, Andrea, *Feminist Theory and the Philosophies of Man* (New York: Croom Helm, 1988).

Olney, James, ed., *Autobiography: Essays Theoretical and Critical* (Princeton: Princeton University Press, 1980).

Olsen, Stein, *The End of Literary Theory* (Cambridge: Cambridge University Press, 1987).

Ong, Walter J., *Orality and Literacy: The Technologising of the Word* (London and New York: Methuen, 1982).

O'Toole, L.M. and Ann Shukman, eds, *Russian Poetics in Translation 4* (Colchester: University of Essex Press, 1977).

Parry, Milman, *The Making of Homeric Verse: The Collected Papers of Milman Parry*, ed. Adam Parry (Oxford: Oxford University Press, 1971).

Patterson, Annabel, 'Intention', in Frank Lentricchia and Thomas McLaughlin, eds, *Critical Terms for Literary Study* (Chicago and London: University of Chicago Press, 1990), pp. 135–46.

Paulson, William R., *The Noise of Culture: Literary Texts in a World of Information* (Ithaca: Cornell University Press, 1988).

Plant, Sadie, *Zeros and Ones: Digital Women and the New Technoculture* (London: Fourth Estate, 1997).

Plato, *The Collected Dialogues of Plato, Including the Letters*, ed. Edith Hamilton and

Huntington Cairns, Bollingen Series LXXI (Princeton: Princeton University Press, 1961).

Porter, Roy, ed., *Rewriting the Self: Histories from the Renaissance to the Present* (London and New York: Routledge, 1997).

Poulet, Georges, *Les Métamorphoses du Cercle* (Paris: Plon, 1961).

Poulet, Georges, 'Criticism and the Experience of Interiority', in Richard Macksey and Eugenio Donato, eds, *The Structuralist Controversy: The Languages of Criticism and the Sciences of Man* (Baltimore: Johns Hopkins University Press, 1972), pp. 56–72.

Powell, Jason, *Jacques Derrida: A Biography* (London and New York: Continuum, 2006).

Proust, Marcel, *Remembrance of Things Past*, 3 vols, trans. C.K. Scott Moncrieff and Terence Kilmartin (Harmondsworth: Penguin Books, 1983).

Quaint, David, *Origin and Originality in Renaissance Literature* (New Haven: Yale University Press, 1983).

Racevskis, Karlis, *Michel Foucault and the Subversion of Intellect* (Ithaca: Cornell University Press, 1983).

Ragland-Sullivan, Ellie and Mark Bracher, eds, *Lacan and the Subject of Language* (New York: Routledge and Kegan Paul, 1991).

Ratjchman, John, *Michel Foucault: The Freedom of Philosophy* (New York: Columbia University Press, 1985).

Ray, William, *Literary Meaning: From Phenomenology to Deconstruction* (Oxford: Basil Blackwell, 1984).

Riffaterre, Michael, 'Sade or Text as Fantasy', *Diacritics*, vol. 2, no. 3 (1971), pp. 2–9.

Robin, Léon, *Platon, Oeuvres Complètes IV. 3: Phèdre*, 2nd edition (Paris, 1950).

Rorty, Richard, *Philosophy and the Mirror of Nature* (Oxford: Basil Blackwell, 1980).

Rorty, Richard, *Consequences of Pragmatism: Essays 1972–1980* (Brighton: Harvester Press, 1982).

Rorty, Richard, *Objectivity, Relativism and Truth* (Cambridge: Cambridge University Press, 1991).

Rose, Mark, *Authors and Owners* (Cambridge, MA: Harvard University Press, 1993).

Rousseau, Jean-Jacques, *The Confessions of Jean-Jacques Rousseau*, trans. J.M. Cohen, (Harmondsworth: Penguin Books, 1953).

Rousseau, Jean-Jacques, *Essay on the Origin of Languages, which Treats of Melody and Musical Imitation*, trans. J.H. Moran and Alexander Gode (New York: Fredric Ungar, 1966).

Rousseau, Jean-Jacques, *The Social Contract and Discourses*, trans. G.D.H. Cole (London: Dent, 1973).

Rowe, C.J., *Plato: Phaedrus, with Translation and Commentary* (Warminster: Aris and Phillips, 1986).

Ryan, Kiernan, ed., *New Historicism and Cultural Materialism: A Reader* (London: Arnold, 1996).

Said, Edward, 'An Ethics of Language', *Diacritics*, vol. 4, no. 2 (Summer 1974), pp. 28–37.

Said, Edward, *Beginnings: Intention and Method* (Baltimore: Johns Hopkins University Press, 1975).

Sallis, John, ed., *Deconstruction and Philosophy: The Texts of Jacques Derrida* (Chicago and London: University of Chicago Press, 1987).

Salusinszsky, Irme, ed., *Criticism in Society: Interviews with Jacques Derrida, Northrop Frye, Harold Bloom, Geoffrey Hartman, Frank Kermode, Edward Said, Barbara Johnson, Frank Lentricchia and J.Hillis Miller* (London: Methuen, 1987).

Sartre, Jean-Paul, *Existentialism and Humanism*, trans. Philip Mairet (London: Methuen, 1948).

Sartre, Jean-Paul, *What is Literature?*, trans. Bernard Frechtman (London: Methuen, 1950).

Saussure, Ferdinand de, *A Course in General Linguistics*, trans. W. Baskin (London: Fontana, 1974).

Searle, John R., *Speech Acts: An Essay in the Philosophy of Language* (Cambridge: Cambridge University Press, 1969).

Searle, John R., 'Reiterating the Differences: A Reply to Derrida', *Glyph* I (1977), pp. 198–208.

Sell, Roger D., ed., *Literary Pragmatics* (London: Routledge and Kegan Paul, 1991).

Shattuck, Roger, *Proust* (London: Fontana, 1974).

Sheridan, Alan, *Michel Foucault: The Will to Truth* (London: Tavistock, 1980).

Showalter, Elaine, ed., *The New Feminist Criticism: Essays on Women, Literature and Theory* (New York: Pantheon Press, 1985).

Siebers, Tobin, *The Ethics of Criticism* (Ithaca: Cornell University Press, 1988).

Silverman, Hugh J., *Inscriptions: Between Phenomenology and Structuralism* (New York and London: Routledge and Kegan Paul, 1987).

Simion, Eugen, *The Return of the Author*, ed. James W. Newcomb, trans. James W. Newcomb and Lidia Vianu (Evanston, IL: Northwestern University Press, 1996).

Simms, Karl, ed., *Language and the Subject* (Amsterdam: Rodopi Press, 1997).

Simpson, David, *Irony and Authority in Romantic Poetry* (Totowa, NJ: Rowman and Littlefeld, 1979).

Smith, Barbara Herrnstein, *Contingencies of Value: Alternative Perspectives for Critical Theory* (Cambridge, Mass.: Harvard University Press, 1988).

Smith, Neil and Deirdre Wilson, *Modern Linguistics: The Results of Chomsky's Revolution* (Harmondsworth: Penguin, 1979).

Soper, Kate, *Humanism and Anti-Humanism* (London: Hutchinson, 1986).

Sperber, Dan and Deirdre Wilson, *Relevance: Communication and Cognition* (Oxford: Basil Blackwell, 1986).

Spivak, Gayatri Chakravorty, '*Glas* Piece: A *Compte Rendu*', *Diacritics*, vol. 7, no. 3 (1977), pp. 22–49.

Spivak, Gayatri Chakravorty, *The Post-Colonial Critic: Interviews, Strategies, Dialogues*, ed. Sarah Harasym (New York and London: Routledge, 1990).

Spivak, Gayatri Chakravorty, 'Can the Subaltern Speak?', in *Colonial Discourse and Post-Colonial Theory: A Reader*, ed. and introduced by Patrick Williams and Laura Chrisman (Hemel Hempstead: Harvester, 1993), pp. 66–111.

Spivak, Gayatri Chakravorty, 'Reading *The Satanic Verses*', in Maurice Biriotti and Nicole Miller, eds, *What is an Author?* (Manchester: Manchester University Press, 1993), pp. 103–34.

Sprinkler, Michael, 'Fictions of the Self: The End of Autobiography', in James Olney, ed., *Autobiography: Essays Theoretical and Critical* (Princeton: Princeton University Press, 1980), pp. 321–42.

Stillinger, Jack, *Multiple Authorship and the Myth of Solitary Genius* (New York and Oxford: Oxford University Press, 1991).

Strozier, Robert M., *Saussure, Derrida and the Metaphysics of Subjectivity* (Berlin: Mouton de Gruyter, 1988).

Sturrock, John, ed., *Structuralism and Since: From Lévi-Strauss to Derrida* (Oxford: Oxford University Press, 1979).

Taylor, Charles, *Sources of the Self: The Making of the Modern Identity* (Cambridge: Cambridge University Press, 1989).

Thody, Philip, *Roland Barthes: A Conservative Estimate* (London: Macmillan, 1977).

Todd, Jane Marie, *Autobiographics: Freud and Derrida* (New York: Garland, 1990).

Tomaschevsky, Boris, 'Literature and Biography', in Ladislav Matejka and Krystyna Pomorska, eds, *Readings in Russian Poetics: Formalist and Structuralist Views* (Cambridge, MA: MIT Press, 1971), pp. 47–55.

Troubetzkoy, Nikolai, *Principles of Phonology*, trans. Christiane A.M. Baltaxe (Berkeley and Los Angeles: University of California Press, 1969).

Ulmer, Gregory L., *Applied Grammatology: Post(e)-pedagogy from Jacques Derrida to Joseph Beuys* (Baltimore: Johns Hopkins University Press, 1985).

Ungar, Stephen, *Roland Barthes: The Professor of Desire* (Lincoln, NE: University of Nebraska Press, 1983).

Valéry, Paul, 'Remarks on Poetry', in T.G. West trans. and ed., *Symbolism: An Anthology* (London: Methuen, 1980), pp. 43–60.

Veeser, H. Aram, ed., *The New Historicism* (New York and London: Routledge and Kegan Paul, 1994).

Vickers, Brian, *'Counterfeiting' Shakespeare: Evidence, Authorship and John Ford's 'A Funerall Eleye'* (Cambridge: Cambridge University Press, 2002).

Vickers, Brian, *Shakespeare, Co-Author: A Historical Study of Five Collaborative Plays* (Oxford: Oxford University Press, 2002).

Waite, Geoff, *Nietzsche's Corps/e: Aesthetics, Politics, Prophecy, or, The Spectacular Technoculture of Everyday Life* (Durham and London: Duke University Press, 1996).

Wasserman, George R., *Roland Barthes* (Boston: Twayne Publishers, 1981).

Waters, Lindsay, and Wlad Godzich, eds, *Reading de Man Reading* (Minneapolis: University of Minnesota Press, 1989).

Waugh, Patricia, *Practising Postmodernism/Reading Modernism* (London: Edward Arnold, 1992).

Waugh, Patricia, ed., *Revolutions of the Word: Intellectual Contexts for the Study of Modern Literature* (London: Arnold, 1997).

Wexman, Virginia Wright (ed.), *Film and Authorship* (New Brunswick: Rutgers University Press, 2003).

Wilde, Oscar, 'The Critic as Artist', *Complete Works of Oscar Wilde* (London and Glasgow: Collins, 1948), pp. 1,009–59.

Wimsatt, W.K., Jr, *The Verbal Icon: Studies in the Meaning of Poetry* (Lexington: University of Kentucky Press, 1954).

Wimsatt, W.K., 'Genesis: A Fallacy Revisited', in Gregory T. Polletta, ed., *Issues in Contemporary Criticism* (Boston: Little Brown, 1973), pp. 255–76.

Wiseman, Mary Bittner, *The Ecstasies of Roland Barthes* (London and New York: Routledge, 1989).

Wittgenstein, Ludwig, *Tractatus Logico-Philosophicus*, trans. D.F. Pears and B.F. McGuinness (London: Routledge and Kegan Paul, 1962).

Wood, David and Robert Bernasconi, eds, *Derrida and Différance* (Warwick: Parousia Press, 1985).

Woodman, Tony and Jonathan Powell, eds, *Author and Audience in Latin Literature* (Cambridge: Cambridge University Press, 1992).

Woodmansee, Martha and Peter Jaszi (eds), *The Construction of Authorship: Textual Appropriation and Law in Literature* (Durham, NC: Duke University Press, 1994).

Wordsworth, William, *The Prelude*, ed. E. de Selincourt (Oxford: Clarendon Press, 1926).

Yeats, W.B., *Essays and Introductions* (London: Macmillan, 1969).

Young, Robert, *Untying the Text: A Post-Structuralist Reader* (London: Routledge and Kegan Paul, 1981).

Index